The Collected Oz

Volume Six

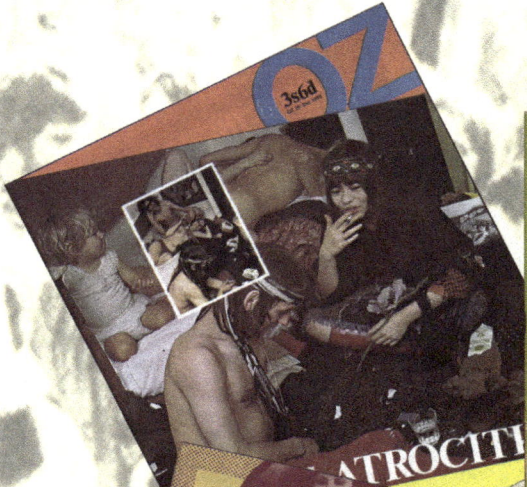

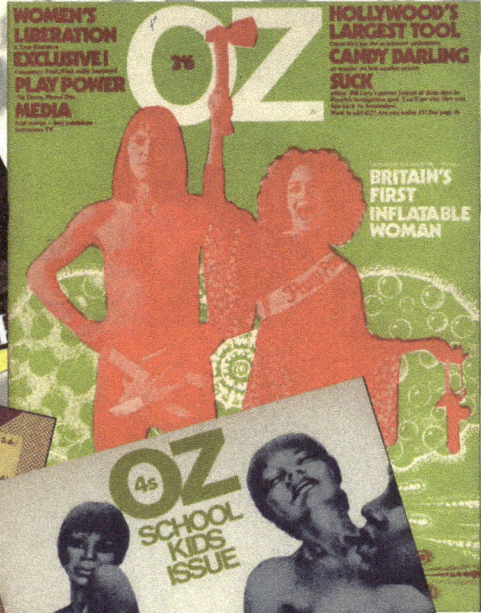

Richard Neville et al.

Edited by Wally the Comedy Rhinoceros
Typeset by Wally the Comedy Rhinoceros
Cover and Internal Layout by Spiderkat for Gonzo Multimedia
Using Microsoft Word 2000, Microsoft , Publisher 2000, Adobe Photoshop.

First edition published 2017 by Gonzo Multimedia

c/o Brooks City,
6th Floor New Baltic House
65 Fenchurch Street,
London EC3M 4BE
Fax: +44 (0)191 5121104
Tel: +44 (0) 191 5849144
International Numbers:
Germany: Freephone 08000 825 699
USA: Freephone 18666 747 289

ISBN: 978-1-908728-72-2

For Richard, Felix and Jim

Oz Obscenity Trial · Old Bailey London 1971

Trial begins 22 June
Any information contact Friends of Oz,
39a Pottery Lane, London W11. 01-229 5887.

Introduction

Back in the day, and this particular day was about twenty years ago, I was friendly with a notorious Irish Republican musical ensemble known as *Athenrye*, and particularly with their guitarist, a guy called Terry Manton. I was very angry about a lot of things at the time, and quite how drinking with various groups of slightly dodgy Hibernians actually made me feel any better I am not sure, but it seemed to have the desired effect.

On one of their albums there is a song about Éamon de Valera. For those of you not in the know, over to those jolly nice people at Wikipedia.

"Éamon de Valera first registered as George de Valero; changed some time before 1901 to Edward de Valera; 14 October 1882 – 29 August 1975) was a prominent politician and statesman in twentieth-century Ireland. His political career spanned over half a century, from 1917 to 1973; he served several terms as head of government and head of state. He also led the introduction of the Constitution of Ireland.

De Valera was a leader in the War of Independence and of the anti-Treaty opposition in the ensuing Irish Civil War (1922–1923). After leaving Sinn Féin in 1926 due to its policy of abstentionism, he founded Fianna Fáil, and was head of government (President of the Executive Council, later Taoiseach) from 1932 to 1948, 1951 to 1954, and 1957 to 1959, when he resigned after being elected as President of Ireland. His political creed evolved from militant republicanism to social and cultural conservatism.

Assessments of de Valera's career have varied; he has often been characterised as

Lucky man of our times

<u>Chorus</u>
He was loved he was hated he was cherished despised
There were rivers of tears when the chieftain he died
But love him or hate him I cannot decide
What to make of old Dev this man of our times."

And it ended up:

"Now Spain had it's Franco and France it's De Gaulle
We had our Dev and god rest his soul"

It has been many years since I bounced up and down in a weird Gaelic moshpit shouting "Tiocfaidh ár lá" and I strongly doubt whether I shall ever do so again. My foray into such things had more to do with my reaction to the way that I perceived that I had been treated by my family over my particularly scabrous divorce, than any genuine political fervour, although I thought then (and think now) that the British history in Ireland has not been our greatest or most honourable hour. However, today I have had that song going round and around my head, ever since I read an email from Tony Palmer telling me that Richard Neville had died at the age of 74, in Byron Bay, New South Wales, the Australian hippy enclave where Gilli Smyth breathed her last only a few days before.

Now I never met Neville. Our acquaintanceship was confined to two emails about five years ago when I was working on the new edition of Tony Palmer's *The Trials of Oz*. I exchanged a few more emails with Jim Anderson, and had no contact whatsoever with Felix Dennis, so I cannot really be called an insider of the *Oz* scene. But Neville came out with one of my favourite quotes from the counterculture: "There is some corner of a foreign field that is forever Woodstock", and was an undeniably major figure in that much maligned social movement.

He seemed to be someone who brought out strong reactions in people. Whilst I was working on *The Trials of Oz* I discovered that people were either terribly fond of the man or disliked him intensely. I never found anyone who was ambivalent towards him. Even after his death, as I sent emails around the usual suspects asking for their memories of him, most people refused to be drawn one way or the other, with those who had been friends with him at various periods of their lives being totally devastated that they had woken up this morning to a planet on which Richard Neville was no longer alive.

Me? I am no better than any of the others. I have no knowledge of him personally, and whereas I found large chunks of *Oz* unreadable, I was impressed by his book *Playpower* and in the passages about him in Tony Palmer's book he struck an undeniably heroic figure against the same sort of establishment malice which had (as alluded to above) turned me against my parents twenty years back.

His book *Hippy Hippy Shake* was entertaining, even though its hedonism left a slightly bitter taste in one's mouth, but I remember being told that the movie that was made from it was so bad that several of the major figures portrayed refused to let it come out. In July 2007, in a piece for *The Guardian*, feminist author Germaine Greer vehemently expressed her displeasure at being depicted, writing, "You used to have to die before assorted hacks started munching your remains and modelling a new version of you out of their own excreta." Greer refused to be involved with the film, just as she declined to read Neville's memoir before it was published (he had offered to change anything she found offensive). She did not want to meet with Emma Booth, who portrays her in the film, and concluded her article with her only advice for the actress: "Get an honest job."

So where is this taking me? I truly don't know, but if there had not been a Richard Neville, there might well not have been a *Gonzo Weekly* magazine. I first read *The Trials of Oz* whilst on holiday with my patients back when I was a Registered Nurse for the Mentally Subnormal [RNMS] nearly thirty years ago, and it was one of the sacred texts, together with *A Series of Shock Slogans and Mindless Token Tantrums* by Penny Rimbaud et al, that set me on the path that I am on now. But when I finally read the *Schoolkid's Oz*, I thought it was puerile bollocks, and was massively underwhelmed.

And I too find it hard to adjust to the fact that I have woken up this morning to a planet on which Richard Neville was no longer alive.

So, if I may:

"He was loved he was hated he was cherished despised
There were rivers of tears when the Oz editor died
But love him or hate him I cannot decide
What to make of old Nev this man of our times."

Hare Bol Mr Neville

GOD SAVE US
ELASTIC OZ BAND

OUTCRY AS OZ EDITORS ARE JAILED
Labour MPs attack 'act of revenge'
Daily Telegraph

FURY OVER OZ JAILINGS

Angry MPs join the wave of protest
The Sun

OZ: OBSCENE!
BUT WHY THE FEROCIOUS SENTENCES?

Fury as three editors are jailed
Daily Mirror

Oz sentences — Labour MPs sign protest

MPs condemn OZ gaolings as 'Establishment revenge' *The Guardian*

Demonstrations and protests against 'Oz' jail sentences

Daily Express
COMMENT

'Shocked MPs protest: It looks like revenge

Apple are donating royalties on this record to the Oz Obscenity Panel

STORM OVER OZ SENTENCES
Daily Mail

THE private company on whose edition of the magazine unleashed a storm of controversy has style

In Mitigation

So what was *Oz?* And why was it so important?

OZ was an underground alternative magazine. First published in Sydney, Australia, in 1963, a second version appeared in London, England from 1967 and is better known.

The original Australian *OZ* took the form of a satirical magazine published between 1963 and 1969, while the British incarnation was a "psychedelic hippy" magazine which appeared from 1967 to 1973. Strongly identified as part of the underground press, it was the subject of two celebrated obscenity trials, one in Australia in 1964 and the other in the United Kingdom in 1971. On both occasions the magazine's editors were acquitted on appeal after initially being found guilty and sentenced to harsh jail terms. An earlier, 1963 obscenity charge was dealt with expeditiously when, upon the advice of a solicitor, the three editors pleaded guilty.

The central editor throughout the magazine's life in both Australia and Britain was Richard Neville. Co-editors of the Sydney version were Richard Walsh and Martin Sharp. Co-editors of the London version were Jim Anderson and, later, Felix Dennis.

In early 1966 Neville and Sharp travelled to the UK and in early 1967, with fellow Australian Jim Anderson, they founded the London *OZ*. Contributors included Germaine Greer, artist and filmmaker Philippe Mora, illustrator Stewart Mackinnon, photographer Robert Whitaker, journalist Lillian Roxon, cartoonist Michael Leunig, Angelo Quattrocchi, Barney Bubbles and David Widgery.

With access to new print stocks, including metallic foils, new fluorescent inks and the freedom of layout offered by the offset printing system, Sharp's artistic skills came to the fore and *OZ* quickly won renown as one of the most visually exciting publications of its day. Several editions of *Oz* included dazzling psychedelic wrap-around or pull-out posters by Sharp, London design duo Hapshash and the Coloured Coat and others; these instantly became sought-after collectors' items and now command high prices. Another innovation was the cover of *Oz* No.11, which included a collection of detachable adhesive labels, printed in either red, yellow or green. The all-graphic "Magic Theatre" edition (*OZ* No.16, November 1968), overseen by Sharp and Mora, has been described by British author Jonathon Green as "arguably the greatest achievement of the entire British underground press". During this period Sharp also created the two famous psychedelic album covers for the group Cream, Disraeli Gears and Wheels Of Fire.

Sharp's involvement gradually decreased during 1968-69 and the "Magic Theatre" edition was one of his last major contributions to the magazine. In his place, young Londoner Felix Dennis, who had been selling issues on the street, was eventually brought in as Neville and Anderson's new partner. The magazine regularly enraged the British Establishment with a range of left-field stories including heavy critical coverage of the Vietnam War and the anti-war movement, discussions of drugs, sex and alternative lifestyles, and contentious political stories, such as the magazine's revelations about the torture of citizens under the rule of the military junta in Greece.

In 1970, reacting to criticism that *OZ* had lost touch with youth, the editors put a notice in the magazine inviting "school kids" to edit an issue. The opportunity was taken up by around 20 secondary school students (including Charles Shaar Murray and Deyan Sudjic), who were responsible for *OZ* No.28 (May 1970), generally known as "Schoolkids OZ". This term was widely misunderstood to mean that it was intended for schoolchildren, whereas it was an issue that had been created by them. As Richard Neville said in his opening statement, other issues had been assembled by gay people and members of the Female Liberation Movement. One of the resulting articles was a highly sexualised Rupert Bear parody. It was created by 15-year-old schoolboy Vivian Berger by pasting the head of Rupert onto the lead character of an X-rated satirical cartoon by Robert Crumb.

OZ was one of several 'underground' publications targeted by the Obscene Publications Squad, and their offices had already been raided on several occasions, but the conjunction of schoolchildren, and what some viewed as obscene material, set the scene for the *Oz* obscenity trial of 1971.

The trial was, at the time, the longest obscenity trial in British legal history, and it was the first time that an obscenity charge was combined with the charge of conspiring to corrupt public morals. Defence witnesses included artist Feliks Topolski, comedian Marty Feldman, artist and drugs activist Caroline Coon, DJ John Peel, musician and writer George Melly, legal philosopher Ronald Dworkin and academic Edward de Bono.

At the conclusion of the trial the "OZ Three" were found not guilty on the conspiracy charge, but they were convicted of two lesser offences and sentenced to imprisonment; although Dennis was given a lesser sentence because the judge, Justice Michael Argyle, considered that Dennis was "very much less intelligent" than the others. Shortly after the verdicts were handed down, they were taken to prison and their long hair forcibly cut, an act which caused an even greater stir on top of the already considerable outcry surrounding the trial and verdict.

The best known images of the trial come from the committal hearing, at which Neville, Dennis and Anderson all appeared, wearing rented schoolgirl costumes.

At the appeal trial (where the defendants appeared wearing long wigs) it was found that Justice Argyle had grossly misdirected the jury on numerous occasions and the defence also alleged that Berger, who was called as a prosecution witness, had been harassed and assaulted by police. The convictions were overturned. Years later, Felix Dennis told author Jonathon Green that on the night before the appeal was heard, the *OZ* editors were taken to a secret meeting with the Chief Justice, Lord Widgery, who reportedly said that Argyle had made a "fat mess" of the trial, and informed them that they would be acquitted, but insisted that they had to agree to give up work on *OZ*. Dennis also stated that, in his opinion, MPs Tony Benn and Michael Foot had interceded with Widgery on their behalf.

Despite their supposed undertaking to Lord Widgery, *OZ* continued after the trial, and thanks to the intense public interest the trial generated, its circulation briefly rose to 80,000. However its popularity faded over the next two years and by the time the last issue (*OZ* No.48) was published in November 1973 Oz Publications was £20,000 in debt and the magazine had "no readership worth the name".

We are publishing these magazines in these collected editions, partly as a tribute to the late Richard Neville (1943-2016) and partly because we believe that they constitute a valuable socio-political document reflecting the counterculture of 1967-74. This collection has been made available due to its historical and research importance. It contains explicit language and images that reflect attitudes of the era in which the material was originally published, and that some viewers may find confronting. However, we have taken the decision to blank out a very few images which would be seen as unacceptable in today's society.

Times have changed a lot in the past half century. The magazine's obsession with pornography, for example, has not stood the test of time very well, and some of the typography is so muddy as to be unreadable. Every effort has been made by the present publishers to clean up the typography, but in most cases it proved to be impossible, so we have left it as it was. The *Oz* readers of the late 1960s were unable to read it. Why should the present generation be any different?

Some of the pictures in the original magazine, especially artwork by Martin Sharp, was printed so it could fold out into a poster. We have therefore included these twice - as per the original pages so they can be read easily, and as extrapolations of the original artwork. Richard Neville stipulated in the extract from the notorious *Schoolkid's Oz* reproduced below that the material in these magazines could be used for any purpose, and we are taking him at his word.

Peace and Love

Ronnie Rooster
September 2016

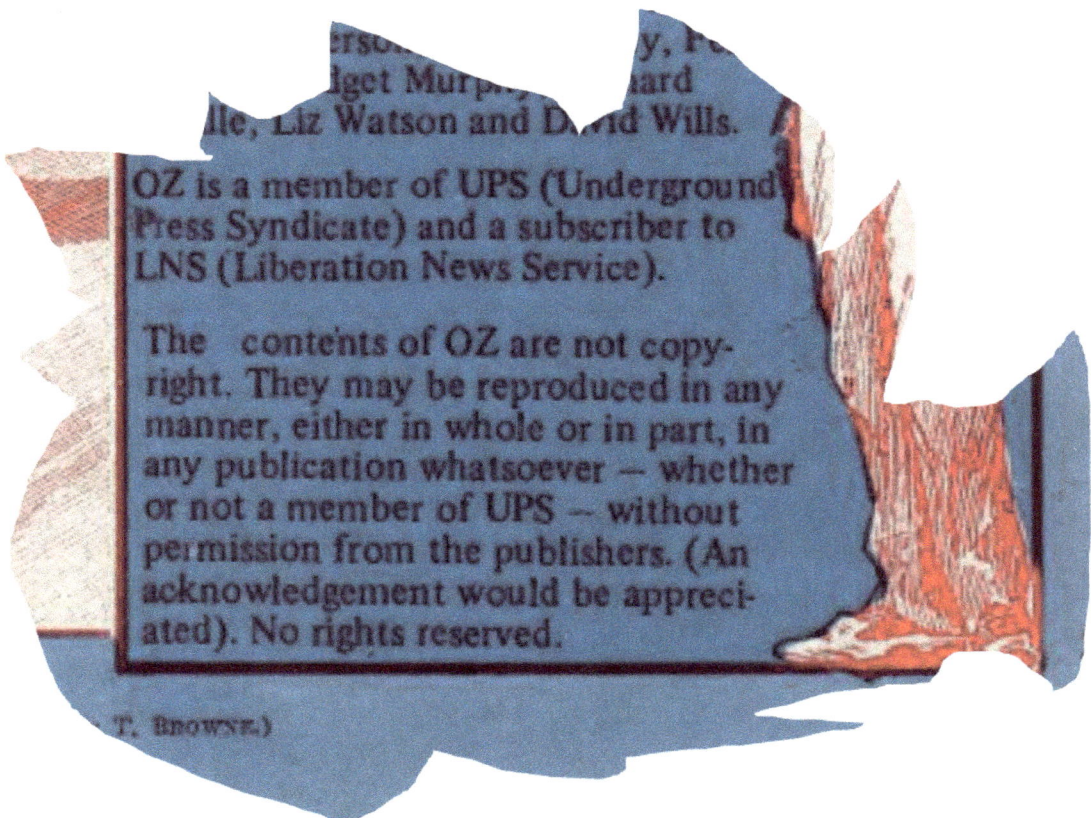

...rso... ...y, ...
...lget Murp..., ...ard
...lle, Liz Watson and D...id Wills.

OZ is a member of UPS (Underground Press Syndicate) and a subscriber to LNS (Liberation News Service).

The contents of OZ are not copyright. They may be reproduced in any manner, either in whole or in part, in any publication whatsoever — whether or not a member of UPS — without permission from the publishers. (An acknowledgement would be appreciated). No rights reserved.

T. Browne.)

OZ

3s6d

OZ 25 Dec 1969

HIPPIE ATROCITIES!

**MOTHERS —
WHERE IS YOUR
DAUGHTER TONIGHT?
THE FULL *SHOCK STORY*
FROM SIBERIA TO SCUNTHORPE**

Plus! Early Elvis, Jerry Lee Lewis, Carl Perkins,
Johnny Cash and - exclusive - complete
lyrics of Billy Lee Riley's 'Flying Saucers Rock'n Roll' -
The facts - LEPER RAPES VIRGIN

MOTT THE HOOPLE

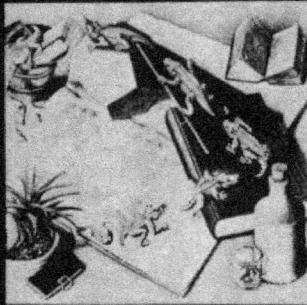

island records ltd basing street london w11

produced by Guy Stevens

Inside OZ

This OZ is about enslavement — of the body and of the spirit. 'We've lost the art of dreaming' writes Donald Reeves from his parish in that cellblock that is Morden, 'a community organised for death.' We sent two girls to that other hotbed of spiritual rigor mortis, Scunthorpe where they withstood for a whole weekend, seething distrust, rampant inertia and Special Chow Mein (with an egg).

Many of those who reject the lifestyle symbolised by these towns, end up in gaols and courtrooms. In this OZ there is a report from Chicago, where Yippie, New Left and black activists are on trial for conspiring to celebrate a Festival of Life. Also, Harvey Matusow, one of the first to focus attention on hippie prisoners in Turkey, now discovers more hash fiends languishing in Lebanon. Anthony Lorraine, gaoled for 15 months for a similar offence in various Russian prison camps, writes of his experiences. His internment was less stultifying than the three or four years of ingenious subjugation imposed by Oxford University. Two contributors remind us that tomorrow's 'leaders' are *still* being churned out with the same elitist set of prejudices, and the total inability to relate to or communicate with their fellow man, that has traditionally distinguished the Oxbridge product.

Unfreedom everywhere, but small breakthroughs: cultural renaissance via rock music, so a tribute to Sun records and its founder, Sam Phillips; and a tribute of another sort to the 'man without whom . . .' OZ probably wouldn't be here, Jack Kerouac, father of beat, founder of drop-out. His road now leads around the world, and from one lay-by, Ibiza, OZ reports on a personal liberation; learning to love idleness, fun, sun and life. Now read on.

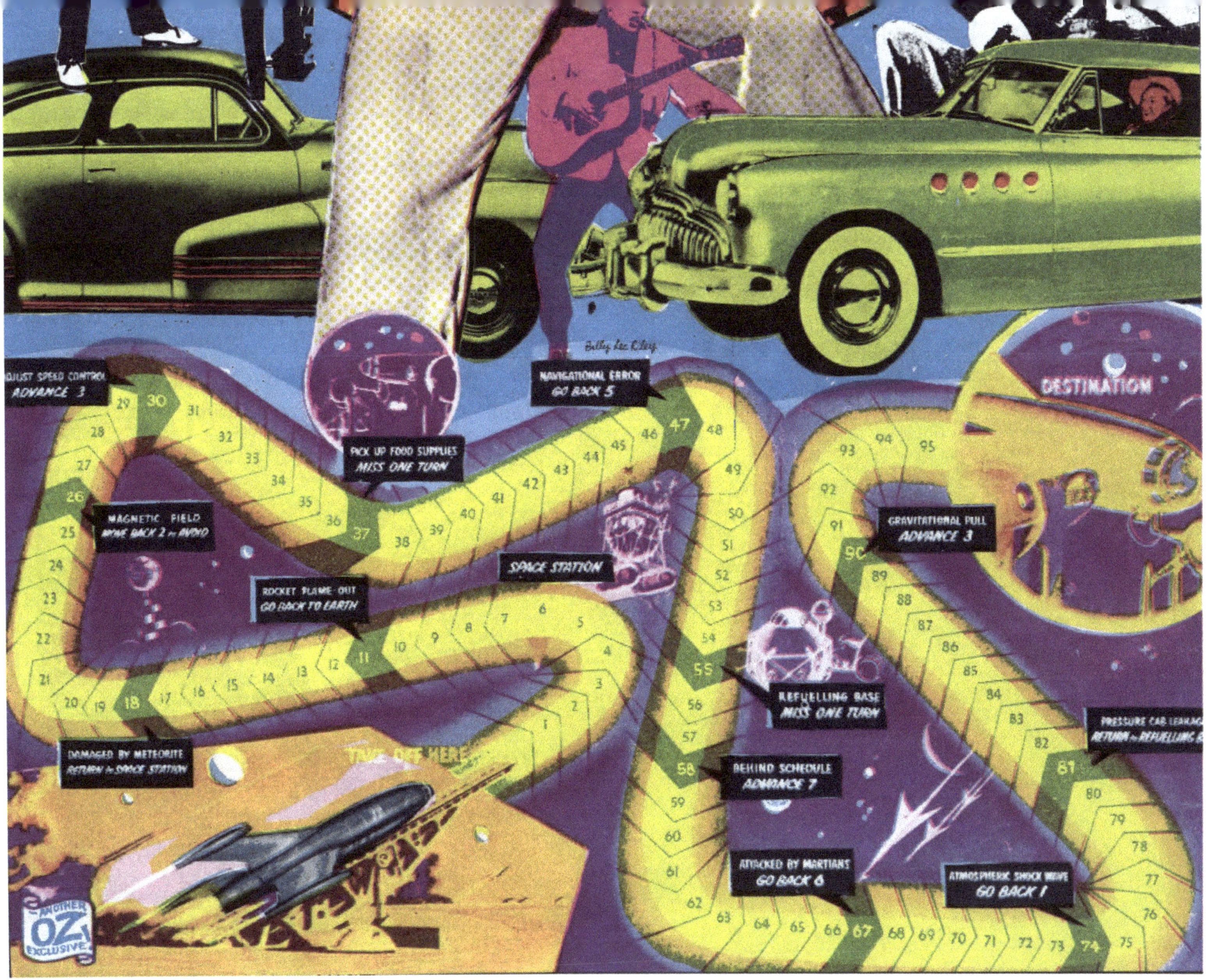

DESTINATION

PRESSURE CAB TEMPERATURE
RETURN to REFUELLING BASE

GRAVITATIONAL PULL
ADVANCE 3

ATMOSPHERIC SHOCK WAVE
GO BACK 1

REFUELLING BASE
MISS ONE TURN

BEHIND SCHEDULE
ADVANCE 7

ATTACKED BY MARTIANS
GO BACK 6

NAVIGATIONAL ERROR
GO BACK 5

SPACE STATION

PICK UP FOOD SUPPLIES
MISS ONE TURN

ROCKET FLAME OUT
GO BACK TO EARTH

MAGNETIC FIELD
MOVE BACK 2 to IMPRO

DAMAGED BY METEORITE
RETURN to SPACE STATION

ADJUST SPEED CONTROL
ADVANCE 3

ANOTHER OZ BROADSIDE

Here's Elvis (the Pelvis) Presley, as seen...

6

America's Real Uncle Sam

Robert Finnis Muzic Special

Everybody has heard of 'Blue Suede Shoes' or 'Great Balls of Fire'. They are stock phrases or classic statements in Pop. Even today's teenyboppers have faint notions of their presence. What have they both in common? Both were recorded in the middle-to-late 50's, both in the same Memphis Studio and by artists born within close proximity in the Southern States. Digging deeper, the two records belong to an impressive list of hits to emerge from one label in the fifties, which in three years was to grow from just another tiny label into a major force on the 50's rock n' roll scene and yet – this is significant – remain, by choice, a minor label; Sun Records. Tamla-Motown and Stax began in similar trappings (later in the time scale) but have by now, in the late 60's, become million dollar corporations. Only Spector's defunct Philles label can be compared with Sun in as much as they both made a readily identifiable sound which made a sizeable impression on record charts while remaining essentially, one man enterprise.

SUN RISE

Sam C. Phillips was born in Florence, Alabama in 1923. After forming a country group in his earlier days, he then became a D.J., and the early 50's found him cutting demos and masters of local blues singers, or 'race' records as they were still known in some parts. This was a minority market, but a steady one and Phillips did fairly well leasing suitable masters to labels such as Chess/Checker, R.P.M. and Modern, and coming up occasionally with his own, the 'Rocket 88', by Jackie Brenston on Chess (1951). At this stage his small studio had a few microphones (some say only 2 or 3!!!) but this was suitable for the blues sounds which didn't rely too much on perfection but general feel, soundwise. Others he recorded were Howlin' Wolf, B. B. King, Ike Turner, Rufus Thomas, Bobby Bland and Joe Hill Lewis. In 1953 he formed the Sun label and early releases included discs by Rufus Thomas, Willie Nix, Roscoe Gordon and a young Junior Parker, billed as Little Juniors Blue Flames. Soon they had a small hit, with a sad, melodic disc by the 'Prisonaires', inmates of the Tennessee State Penitentuary. The song, 'Just Walkin' in the Rain', was recorded 3 years later in 1956, by a then commercially popular white artist, Johnny Ray, who stole the honours.* Sun continued to put out discs by blues artists, but by 1954 a very few white singers appeared, some singing straight country boogie or C. & W. The label was now dealing with two ethnic groups, and releases were few and far between – a policy which was to remain.

ELVIS PRESLEY

The famous appearance of Elvis Presley on the label occurred in July, '54 with two simultaneous releases out of the blue, crammed in amongst a few blues/gospel discs and a country record:-

206 'Cotton Crop Blues'/'Hold Me In Your Arms' – James Cotton
207 'There Is Love In You'/'Wasn't You Do Next' – Prisonaires
208 'Right or Wrong'/'Why Do I Cry' – Buddy Cunningham
209 'That's Alright'/'Blue Moon of Kentucky' – Elvis Presley
210 'I Don't Care If The Sun Don't Shine'/'Good Rockin' Tonight' – Elvis Presley
211 'Just Rollin' Along'/'Drinking Wine' – Malcolm Yelvington
212 'The Boogie Disease'/'Juke Box Boogie' – Dr. Ross

Phillips was a shrewd man and the white kid was the first artist he had with a youthful image. The constant space of up-tempo blues and boogie tunes reveal that Phillip was intent on top of the scene and knew that something was about to break, although it's possible he didn't know what, otherwise he'd be the richest man in the world. He had Presley listen to the original 'That's Alright' by Arthur Crudup and told him to do it his way.

The biggest and most influential disc-jockey in Memphis, Dewey Phillips – no relation to Sam – played 'That's Alright' one night in July of '54. Presley hid in a cinema to avoid the embarrassment and tension (although he told his parents to listen in) of hearing himself.

Forty-seven listeners called in asking for the play and seven even found that it was available. This extended to playing the record seven times that night and it sold 7,000 in Memphis alone within a week. But then another D.J. signed Presley for a C. & W. show which came through the South.

A few releases later, Elvis followed up with 'Milk Cow Blues Boogie'/'You're a Heartbreaker' on Sun 215 and 'I'm Left, You're Right, She's gone'/'Baby Let's Play House' on 217. Other Sun releases still consisted mainly of blues names and in Autumn '55 Presley's last Sun release 'Mystery Train'/'I Forgot to Remember to Forget' (223) appeared. By this time he was the biggest celebrity in the South since Robert E. Lee. There was hunger for his kind of music, but the starving audiences at first didn't know what the hunger was for. When it came

*In 1953 five temporary residents of this Nashville Prison formed their own so called group – 'The Prisonaires' and wrote their own original material. 'Walking in the Rain' turned out to be a small hit, and then 20 per cent of the profits were turned over to a rehabilitation centre. Before Ray's version became a smash, four of the group had been released. Johnny Bragg, co-composer of the song, was still serving a sentence for an offence he committed in 1938 when he was 17. Johnny Ray's label Columbia held Bragg's royalties for him. The four others renamed themselves 'The Marigolds' and pursued a career in the South.

along in the form of a white boy moving in a field previously run by coloured guys, they recognised it. The late Steve Sholes of R.C.A. heard him and for the first time ever an executives fund was formed to raise the $35,000 Sam Phillips asked for Presley's contract and all Sun masters to date, including some unissued ones. They got Presley (who got $5,000 in the deal) and Phillips thought he'd got the best of the bargain.

The Sun masters had done next to nothing but while he knew Presley would be big, he 'never thought he'd be that big'.

The Sun recordings were all white kids singing the blues' – the first rockabilly sounds. The white kids emancipation of the blues.

As Rock n' Roll gradually came into it's own, Phillips began recording more and more white artists singing rock n' roll, while the minority-appeal blues artists were dropped. Even country artists were forced into rock n'roll because that's where the bread was, although at the grassroots level they were carrying on a tradition.

JOHNNY CASH

In the South there's been a long tradition of musical interaction between spiritual and gospel music. Suddenly blues merged with country. In this way the early pioneers of rock music presented what some call rock-a-billy music to the mass commercial market for the first time. It wasn't R & B, but it was a legitimate inheritor of the blues heritage and it served as a means of introducing some of the qualities of 'soul' to the mass American audience. It was an exciting and vital contrast to the northern tin-pan alley product of the day.

About the time Presley was hitting his peak with Sun, a country singer from Arkansas Johnny Cash (b. 1932) auditioned for Sam Phillips. Cash had been a farm boy who'd joined the airforce and in his spare time had learned the guitar and developed a style which came from the blood: he was a country singer. After he left the service he hit Memphis then the 'coolest' place and along with his Tennessee Two (Marshall Grant on string bass and the late Luther Perkins on lead) prepared for the audition. Phillips was impressed and 'Hey Porter'/'Cry, Cry, Cry' was issued on Sun 221 in late '55. It became a national hit, selling 100,000 in the South alone and a year later he was named as the most promising C. & W. artist of the year in 4 polls. The fact remains that Cash was the first young country singer to make it in the pop field on the scale of a pop artist with continued success, without ever veering from country, an extreme rarity in those days.

CARL PERKINS

On the rock n' roll front, Elvis had a contender with Carl Perkins. They say that Perkins could have given Presley a run for his money, if it wasn't for his

Sam C. Phillips in the original Sun studio.

Johnny Cash – before he met Bob Dylan.

Elvis's first recording: in '54 when Elvis was truck driving he used his first pay cheque to record 'Blue Moon' for his mother in the recording booth Sam Phillips let out for private recordings. A year later when Sam wanted a ballad recorded ('I Love you because') he called in Elvis, but he started to sing the blues, which led to his first release 'That's all right'.

One Sun recording was released approximately every three weeks.

7

crash, but this is doubtful. He wasn't as good looking as Presley, who had a kind of Valentino appeal. Perkins looked and was a pure country boy. But the ethnic value of his sound and contributions cannot be denied. His first appearance was on an obscure *Sun* subsidiary label, *Flip*. This was, according to Sam Phillips, a 'non-union label for testing out new talent'**

The disc was 'Movie Magg'/'Turn Around' (both C. & W.) on flip 501. It was withdrawn soon after and Perkins reappeared in Autumn '55 with a single on *Sun* 224 'Gone, Gone, Gone' (rockabilly)/'Let The Jukebox Keep on Playing' (C. & W.) Perkins was equally at home with country or rock n' roll and his raw, but fairly disciplined powerful voice, epitomised country-rock. The back-ups weren't very tight but more relaxed and rickety, a chug-a-long quality. Never any hard electric stuff. After 'Gone, Gone' did fairly well attracting D.J. interest in Perkins in the South, where he was playing successfully he wrote 'Blue Suede Shoes' reportedly after hearing a youngster at a dance date say another 'Uh uh don't step on my Blue Suede Shoes'. Phillips liked the song and it saw action on Boxing Day 1955, then on the flip side along with 'Honey Don't' it was issued on *Sun* 234 simultaneously with another Perkins disc, more in the country vein, 'Sure to Fall' ('Tennessee' (235). We know what happened to the first although Poor Old Carl had his shoes scuttled by the Elvis who later shamelessly covered it. Nevertheless it did become the very first *C. & W.* disc which topped all 3 charts (THE U.S. Musicand has a definite 'Record of Note' on quite highly rated energy, unfortunately a further subsection Respected On the way to the Publishers Show on March 22nd 1956, Perkins was seriously injured in a car smash at which his brother was killed. Perkins was in hospital for 6 months and Presley did the show instead, thus becoming the first rock n' roller onto a national T.V. Show probably the main factor in boosting rock n' roll against Perkins Payola. Perkins had made the most of the *Sun* label 'Boppin' the Blues' (1956) and 'Your True Love' (1957).

THE THREE SOUNDS OF SUN
1 – GRADE 'A' COOKING

The *Sun* sound can be split into 3 categories or sounds. The first includes all discs from 1953 to early '57 and was the best. It included a wide range of discs, both blues, and later '55-'57 rock n' roll or rockabilly. All these discs (as with most of the very best rock n' roll records) were recorded on comparatively primitive equipment and to compensate, voices, instruments, etc. were boosted or 'cooked' electronically with echo, compression, etc. so that the final sound consisted half of reality, half of 'dream distortion'.

What makes these records so good is that were they crystal clear, the crude reality of the sounds would be brought painfully out. However, with a cooked sound – what went into the mikes was very different from what came out in the booth – the reality was lost.

**It was discontinued after a man called Ed Wells, who ran another 'Flip' label (they had a 1956 hit with 'A Casual Look' by the 'Sixteens') sued Phillips over the name.

Of course the 'cooking' was beneficial. The most popular device flutter echo put a hard, extremely earthy edge to anybody's voice, a fierce back-alley echo. To begin with, this early sound had one important factor – bass. There was a lot of bass, especially bass drum, on some of the records. Most of the back-ups usually 3 piece, centred around the string bass, closely recorded and struck with a drum stick to produce that chugging, slapping sound. There was usually plenty of presence although the voice might be lifted into ghostly heights by the flutter echo. (A recent example of this contrast is 'Bad Moon Rising' by Creedence Clearwater, which is by their own admission an attempt at the Sun sound, and a very successful replica it is too.)

– JERRY LEE LEWIS

Jerry Lee Lewis was the kind of artist that had to happen. Wild, egotistical, extremely talented, he first appeared on *Sun* 259, 'Crazy Arms'/'End of the Road', in October '56. He was basically a country singer at this time although he had dabbled in boogie forms. 'Crazy Arms' didn't do much, but things went well and truly started up with his next release which climbed the way it charts 'Whole Lotta' Shakin' Goin' On'/'It'll be Me', on *Sun* 267. This song had been recorded early in March 1956, without success, by a coloured group called the 'Commodores' on *Dot* and theirs was more Haley like. (Also recorded by Dorothy later 'Dotty' Fredericks). Lewis went on to score more gold discs with *Sun* 281 'Great Balls of Fire'. *Sun* 288 'Breathless' and 'High School Confidential' on *Sun* 296. Then came the U.K. tour with the muck-raking nationals rooty-tooting about Jerry's under-age wife. (Presley could get away with it – Priscilla Beaulieu his wife, was only 12 or 13 when he began dating her in Germany in 1958, whilst in the army.) After a few gigs he returned home disillusioned and depressed and whether by coincidence or not the hits stopped coming. Soon as he got back home in U.K. (his, issued on *Sun* 301 it was called 'Clement Pittman' coupled with a later rendition by Lewis of the same number. The collage has been a sketch of George arriving back at the airport and being interviewed by the Memphis-worthy American Reporter, billed as 'George with Lewis' who began by asking how the latter was feeling after the appropriate airport noises. Suddenly the voice track was cut and a segment of Lewis' version of 'I'm Feeling Sorry' inserted. The collage with a play on words made up the whole track. Not surprisingly it didn't sell (wasn't issued here, natch!) but on the other hand it cost nothing to make and it must have made Jerry Lee feel a whole lot better. He was back on form two releases later with 'Break-Up' (*Sun* 301) but though this rocker sold well he couldn't match up to his previous success on disc, until 1961, when he had a surprise smash with 'What'd I Say' (*Sun* 356) after a period in the doldrums.

The early Lewis discs had represented the second style in development of the *Sun* sound. This was thinner with less bass than the earlier Presley, Perkins, Cash sound. The slapped bass had gone and the rhythm back-ups were more conventional with everybody following

Jerry's voice and piano, always in complete autistic control. One gets the feeling, as all the other instruments rumble on after him on his famous crescendos, that they were mindless pawns scuttling after the leader with cries of 'anything you say, Jerry Lee'. However, the weird recording technique and primitive acoustics of the sound were still in force up to mid '58. The way Sam Phillips recorded always produced a sound which can only be described as 'raw' and the simplest back-ups could be transformed into a wild, distorted, rave-up.

Sun wasn't the only label capable of this. All over the country exclusively between the years '55-'57 the smaller labels especially, because of lack of facilities, were turning out weirdies of studio gimmickry, some extremely exciting. Once they latched on, the bigger companies copied. *Capitol* with Gene Vincent & the Bluecaps on 'Be-Bop-a-Lula' and *Coral* with the Johnny Burnette Trio's utterly fantastic 'The Train Kept-a-Rollin' (both '56). Of course some were too primitive and laughable in comparison, on 'Red Headed Woman'/'Be Wanna' Boogie' by Sonny Burgess on *Sun* 247 (June '56) there's a lot amount going on, with a sax player and various people yelling in the background, but unfortunately it sounds as if it was all recorded through one microphone. A further example is someone like drummer having bass sounds as though he's frantically fondling with a pillow between him and the snare. On top of this the sax playing hell tills in the background sounds like a comb with lavatory paper, it adds up a an amusing sound.

3 – SETTING SUN

With the coming of better techniques and equipment by late '59 the studios had more or less tied down recording and could capture a singer's voice and instruments accurately. Of course, ironically, this was the dying day for rock n' roll. With the greater bonus went the earthy crude style forever. Compare the electronic chemistry of 'Great Balls of Fire', how Lewis's 'popping' effect (break-up) was fundamental to the nuke on his key instruments such as 'p' and 't', the breaks, to the faithfully captured 'Mabey' recorded in *Sun*'s newest studios in Nashville, 1960. In short by 1960 the *Sun* sound had been lost and entered the final phase whereby any of their discs could have been recorded by anyone, anywhere in America. The 60's brought a death blow to *Sun* (original rock n' roll had died by '59) but they had several more pop/rock hits like 'Lonely Weekends' by Charlie Rich (1960) 'Mountain of Love', Harold Dorman (1960) and 'Pretend' by Carl Mann (1960). Cash and Perkins had long left the label, but Lewis remained until 1963 when the label ceased to function except for a few sporadic releases. After 1960 Lewis was produced by Sam's elder brother Judd Phillips, in Nashville, who swamped Jerry Lee in brass and girly choruses in an attempt to modernise him ('Good Golly Miss Molly', 1962, 'What'd I Say', 1961) but succeeded only in recording Lewis, who was going through a bad period, into mediocrity.

Phillips never had any ambitions other than money and he never developed *Sun* into anything bigger. Everything was purely functional. He had several subsidiary labels Flip, Blackgold, and the

Well it's one for the money
And two for the show
Three to get ready now go cat go
Don't you step on my blue suede shoes
You can do anything that you want to do
But don't step on my blue suede shoes.
Burn my house
Drive my car
Steal my liquor from an old fruit jar
You can do anything
But lay off of my blue suede shoes
Blue Blue Blue, Blue Blue Blue,
You can do anything
But lay off of my blue suede shoes.

Blue Suede Shoes, according to a taped interview with Carl he woke up at 4 a.m. with the idea in his mind, wrote it down on a piece of brown paper and took over to Sam in the morning. They chewed it over for a few weeks before recording it. Story of overheard conversation was probably promotion material.

Carl Perkins missed the mainline – still down south.

'Return of Jerry Lee Lewis' never released in G.B. or London (although they had it) because part of lyrics went so:

Q. 'And What did you say to Queen Elizabeth?'
A. 'Goodness gracious, great Balls of Fire!'

Jerry Lee Lewis

THE RETURN OF JERRY LEE
GEORGE AND LEWIS
MEMPHIS TENNESSEE

U.314
2.30

largest 'Phillips Int.' which featured Charlie Rich and Bill Justis, the Sun house-arranger who hit with the instr. 'Raunchy' (1957) and Jack Clement a house writer/Producer.

There was a philanthropic workshop atmosphere at the label, with everybody playing on everybody else's records anonymously and besides it was a good way to make a few bucks. In the mists of time, however, nobody knows who played where and even Elvis is supposed to have played on a record by Billy 'The Kid' Emerson, called 'Red Hot'/'No Greater Love' (Sun 219), circa early '55. 'Play guitar, Elvis,' yells Emerson on the latter title, just before the break.

On a sadder note, were the guys on Sun who never made the big time. Names like Sonny Burgess, Warren Smith, Roy Orbison, Hayden Thompson. They were all talented but only a few could make it 'National' and most fell by the wayside doomed to regional success, usually in the South, where some were bit stars after only a few discs on an unprolific label, released free.

Roy Orbison developed a new romantic singing and writing style on joining Nashville's Monument label in 1959 and consequently became one of the classic names of pop with many hits on that label. Prior to this success, in 1956, Orbison had been a High School student in Texas and impressed by Buddy Holly's progress he formed a group called the 'Teenkings' which performed locally. Holly introduced Orbison to Norman Petty the former 'Svengali' and Roy cut four sides in Petty's tiny studio in Clovis, N. Mexico, two of which were released on the local Jewel label, 'Ooby Dooby'/'Trying to Get to You'. These didn't happen, but on Johnny Cash's recommendation Orbison sent them to Sam Phillips who liked them and had him re-cut 'Ooby' and put it out on Sun 242. The record sold 350,000 just scraping the national charts. He had several more Sun releases billed as 'Roy Orbison and the Teenkings' and Orbison moved to Memphis where he lived for a while. The subsequent releases didn't sell but he appeared on all the rockabilly tours.

'On our early tours, we had two Cadillacs. One for me and one for my group. We couldn't really afford them. On one tour, Johnny Cash, Jerry Lee Lewis, Warren Smith and myself and band all had our own Caddies — about seven or eight. We formed a caravan and followed each other into town. I'd put in as much as 5,000 miles in that car in one week, driving myself.'

Elvis had a Cadillac, too. It wasn't his, but we didn't know that. He's appeared in the Southern States in a pink Cadillac and in his lace pink and black outfit. The outfit came from a man's shop in Memphis, on Beale Street. It was called 'Lansky Brothers'. They had all this wild gear. The coloured guys were the first to wear those clothes. That was a big thing, to get those clothes, a diamond ring and a Cadillac. All the rockabillies got their clothes there.'

Phillips is quoted as saying (of Orbison) 'I knew his voice was pure gold, but I'd felt he'd be dead inside a month if people saw him'.

Others like Ray Smith and Hayden Thompson were losers because they were derivatives of the more successful Sun artists. Although they cut some good sides, they sound either identical to a more successful stablemate or a conglomerate of two or three. Smith

sounds like Jerry Lee/Carl Perkins, while Thompson is more like Presley. He even went around in a truck with 'You Ain't Nothin' But A Hound Dog' on the side, dressing and behaving like Elvis. Sonny Burgess could easily be mistaken for Perkins, while others like Warren Smith became pawns. Smith was a pure C. & W. singer but rock n' roll was where the gold was and Phillips had him record this style.

His first 'Rock n' Roll Ruby' on Sun 239 (penned by Johnny Cash) sold well but didn't go national and he cut others in the rock n' roll vein like 'Ubangi Stomp' and 'Miss Froggie' (both '56).

These were all early Sun classics with plenty of 'bottom' 'Ubangi Stomp' in particular, popping, as pleasing as it allowing Smith's dislike of singing rock n' roll, his flair always being country.

The humourous lyrics are sung in an utterly indifferent, dry, unhappy sounding voice:

'Well I've rocked over Italy and I've rocked over Spain
I rocked in Memphis, it was all the same,
I've rocked through Africa and rolled off the ship,
Saw them natives doin' an odd lookin' trip,
Well I looked up the chief, he invited me in,
Heap big jam session 'bout to begin.'

He was glad to leave Sun to record his real love, country, but has long since been lost in the morass.

BILLY LEE RILEY

Sam was perceptive but overlooked this singer who had the looks and style to have made it in a very big way but as pop history has it, he remained popular only regionally.

His name was Billy (Lee) Riley. Unlike all the others, Riley didn't have the typical 'Southern Boy' looks of Perkins, Lee Lewis, Ray Smith, etc. but more mysterious in the Presley register, and this was partly due to his Red Indian blood. He had very high cheek bones, a very hard face and was a little younger than the rest, being 20 and whereas the others looked like grown men Riley retained a boyish quality like Presley whom he vaguely resembled. In 1956 after a long stint in the army, he recorded a master in Memphis with Jack Clement (who was soon after to join Sun), which Phillips purchased and issued in June '56; 'Trouble Bound' 'Rock With Me Baby' the disc, a la Presley, didn't do a thing, but Sam Phillips saw something in the boy although as with Elvis overlooked his total potential. Riley's next release recorded at Sun was 'Flying Saucers Rock n' Roll' (Sun 266, Oct. '56). The record wasn't as cumbersome as its title but a great sound, well recommended. A typical rock tune (or anti-tune) it was primitive, echo-laden and a typical Sun smasher. His voice was literally all grits n' gravel and after a session like this his vocal chords must have looked like rhubarb. He made Cochran sound like a honey-voiced choir-boy. Too early to be derivative Riley was singing what was in the blood, like all those early singers circa 1956. It sold about 30,000 and Riley with the enthusiasm of a young guy on the make, thought he was in for the big time. But he wasn't. He began to tour on the Rockabilly shows and his next release sold 50,000, became very big in the South and nearly broke out in the rest of the country. This was 'Red Hot', similar to 'Saucers' but not as

good, being bogged down by a back-up vocal chorus. After bordering on the brink this disc with Carl Perkins on guitar, didn't live up to its initial promise but Riley found himself popular especially on tours.

'Talent will out' didn't seem to work for Riley though, and his subsequent releases bombed. He sessioneered for Johnny Cash and Jerry Lee, but left the label in 1960 and has since been lost in the mists of time, making discs for other labels, some of which made use of his harmonica prowess. Until his very recent release on U.K. Stax 'Gon' Back to Memphis' he had never had an English release in 13 years

London Decca, an excellent, diverse label in its heyday, never saw fit to issue many Sun discs over here.

THE GREATS

Pop has never been acknowledged as a music of the people like Jazz, blues, folk, etc., but as a worthless money-raking media. Sam Phillips had ulterior motives beyond the only paid artist to the music so, but what he was putting down was basically a valid music form, young identified Americana expressing itself in a new found way. He claims to have to believe in a record before he put it out and the comparatively few releases bears out this claim.

If you take a 20-25 year old singer from a group today and get him to sing even the simplest songs like 'Good Golly Miss Molly' he'll sound ill at ease and in control; subservient to the song. On those early Sun records the vocalists had it all naturally, they were men before their time and this applies, of course, to others like Little Richard, early Gene Vincent and to a certain extent Johnny Burnette.

SAM PHILLIPS

Today, Sam Phillips, now 46, looks exactly the same. He is immensely rich and has various broadcasting and recording interests, but the Sun rights have been taken over by Shelby Singleton, the writer/producer/publisher, although Phillips still has some controlling interest.

Recently Singleton activated a 'new' Sun label and several albums of the original Sun hits by Cash and Lewis, re-mixed in Stereo, have been issued, also others by Charlie Rich and Roy Orbison.

There is a large stockpile of unissued material, especially of blues artists from the pre-1955 days. The original studio, where all the million sellers were recorded, has been pulled down and the Sam Phillips complex is now located close to the heart of Downtown Memphis, where the studio is hired out to all labels/producers.

There are many more companies today than in the old days of Sun and the later Stax. More studios, more companies, many of them operated by producers and engineers who originally cut their teeth in the '50's with artists from the Sun stable, like Roland Janes, lead guitar on 'Whole Lotta' Shakin', who owns the 'Sonic Sound Studios'.

Sam Phillips turned down Conway Twitty, Buddy Holly ('too much like Elvis') Sam Cooke, sadly neglected Billy Riley and sold Elvis for £10,000. But all in all the list of names Phillips introduced to records is staggering, so total, that it will probably remain unbeatable. Unbeatable till eternity

Well the little green men were real hep cats
Rockin' and a rollin' to the crazy flats,
I couldn't understand a word they said,
But the crazy beat real stopped me dead
Well I come out of hiding and I started to rock
And the little green men taught me how to bop
They was three foot high Hit a few bars
Brought rock and roll all the way from Mars.

Billy Lee Riley – his Red Indian heritage very apparent.

Sam Phillips started out in 1950 as D.J. and Band Promoter at the Peabody Hotel, Memphis. He set up Sun Studios in 1952. He is now a Millionaire, owning the three studios in Memphis where most of Memphis Soul is recorded.

Not the original studios, but its all we could find

JOHN & YOKO
KLAUS VOORMANN
ALAN WHITE

ERIC CLAPTON
courtesy of Polydor
Records

With fab pics and poetry
in 1970 calendar!

PLASTIC ONO BAND—LIVE PEACE IN TORONTO APPLE RECORDS CORE 2001 OUT NOW

The Great White Wonder

Felix Dennis

The Great White Wonder (Bob Dylan with his pants down)
Bob Dylan (& Guests) No labelling number.

November the 24th 1969. 'The Great White Wonder' hit London in bulk today as Jeff The Fireman handed round copies from a cardboard box tucked nervously under his arm. 'Fair bit o' art, man . . . take it or leave it . . . sorry, cash, no cheques . . . take it or leave it . . .' Mostly they were taking. Five pounds and ten shillings might seem a lot to pay for two records, even a bootlegged double Dylan L.P., especially as only last September Rolling Stone reported it retailing in Los Angeles stores at under half that price.

It's being marketed like dope. There's the same tarnished air of paranoia, the absurd metaphorical telephone calls . . . 'You know, man . . . THE album . . . look, man, this is an open line . . . Whaddaya mean which album?? . . . stupid motherfucks . . . THE album . . .', the hushed street corner conversations in the 'Gate, a flash of blue notes and everybody wanting just who is buying who.

Jeff is hustling, but handing over each copy sadly as his stock dwindles. His contact tells him this will be the only shipment to London for three months and he wishes he had more. He refuses to tell just how many have been sent . . . 'Don't want no aggro' from C.B.S. do I? . . .', but it's obvious that buyers are not hard to find. Although we've been hearing whispers about 'those tapes' for months now, they've been hard to locate. I can remember a freak at the original Arts Lab excitedly playing me half a side on a battered cassette recorder as long ago as November '68, but generally they've only been available at an unbelievable price from under the counter of one very hip London record store, which specialises in the 'import-friendship' game, or from friends of friends of friends who have friends in the States . . .

And where, exactly, did they come from anyway, these treasured great white elephants? The mysterious promoters of what must be the biggest pop music find/fraud since Mrs. Holly so 'luckily' stumbled over the forgotten facings of

her dear, departed Buddy whilst clearing out the attic, seem to have availed themselves of two major sources of material. The first is from a tape allegedly taken in a Minneapolis hotel room back in December 1961, featuring Dylan singing obscurely on four tracks and singing on twelve others, accompanying himself with guitar and harmonica. If the date is correct this would mean Dylan had not at that time signed his recording deal with Columbia Records, and indeed, two of the songs included, 'Man Of Constant Sorrow' and 'See That My Grave Is Kept Clean', are merely earlier versions of numbers included on 'Bob Dylan', his first Columbia L.P. Apart from one other song on the package, 'Only A Hobo', (which had previously been released on the Broadside label as 'Broadside Ballads Volume One: A Handful Of Songs About Our Time', with Dylan masquerading as a certain Blind Boy Grunt), none of the other twenty odd cuts have seen the light of day before, except as material for artistes like Manfred Mann, The Byrds, Brian Auger & Julie Driscoll and The Band. It's The Band, too, who provide the musical accompaniment for Dylan on the second tape source, the by now infamous 'basement tapes' recorded in the cellar of Dylan's upstate New York home, just prior to his journey to Nashville early in '67 to cut 'John Wesley Harding'. Titles from this session include, 'Mighty Quinn', 'If You Gotta Go – Go Now', 'Tears of Rage', 'Wheels On Fire' and 'Nothing Was Delivered'.

The last, and most recent track in the whole collection, 'Livin' The Blues', was taped directly from Dylan's appearance on the 'Johnny Cash Show', televised in the U.S. earlier this summer. It features Bob mechanically C & W'ing his way through a composition suspiciously reminiscent in both title and chord structure to the old Tommy Steele hit, 'Singing The Blues'. This is pure Skyline Dylan. The Isle of Wight soiled hype who smiled condescendingly through his beard at us for an hour in September. Here, as then, he sounds vaguely bored with his own performance. The audience is a mark.

Sound quality throughout the twenty six tracks might at best be described as muddy. At worst, it's absolutely

dreadful. Generally speaking, the Minneapolis tape seems to have suffered most in the transition to flat plastic. Many of the cuts on the 'basement tape' sound at times as if they were recorded by an enterprising neighbour from a room adjacent to the cellar, or as if at some point they had been subjected to re-recording over a long distance telephone hookup. It would hardly be fair to suggest that this represents The Band at their best. Often bass and high treble frequencies are lost altogether, songs fade abruptly in mid chorus and words are buried in hum and feedback. Poor Richard Manuel (of The Band), who, if I'm not mistaken, is harmonising with Dylan on these songs, either had a really bum mike or a sore throat . . . listen carefully in 'Mighty Quinn' and you'll hear what I mean.

Remember that none of this material was ever intended for release. And, in a way of course, there lies half the appeal of The Great White Wonder. Here's Mr. Dylan with his pants down. Dylan **exposed**. Dylan **vulnerable**. Dylan without the stifling protection of Albert Grossman, CBS Studios, Bob Johnson, handpicked Nashville session musicians and the best engineers that money can buy. Proof that behind the publicity 'week of Bob Dylan' there lies . . . what? A happy family man who digs jamming with friends in his own cellar? It would be nice to think so.

Technical hangups aside, it's still fascinating to hear America's answer to Donovan prove that when it comes down to it, nobody, but nobody sings Dylan, like Dylan. 'Tears Of Rage', for example, is so far removed from The Band's own version that I had difficulty in placing the song at first. His phrasing, timing and delivery are, as always, superb and completely unique. With Dylan singing it, this song takes on a whole new meaning; the story of a man confused and utterly bewildered at the miserable condition of his own country. A man outraged by his treatment and the treatment of his friends and fellow citizens from the 'authorities'. This is 'Desolation Row' Dylan . . . 'Tears Of Rage, Tears of Grief/**Why** must I always be the thief?' Why? Why? Why? He may well ask.

Of the new material on the 'basement

tape', 'Open The Door Richard', is probably the most outstanding. Now, wait a minute. Don't I remember that chorus from an old, warped 78 by, er . . . yeah . . . Roy Fox and His All Star Band? Wasn't 'Open The Door Richard' a kneels up rung out of the pre-war madness of my mother's childhood? I ran her. Yes, of course she knew 'Open The Door Richard'. She sang it to me and I listened in embarrassment . . . It was the same. Another Dylan put-on. O.K. I know he's mumbling, 'I've heard that song before . . . right after the chorus . . . irony with a capital 'I' . . . but is that why such an amazing song (and it is an amazing song), was never released? How long does copyright last on a song anyway; not that plagiarism ever bothered Dylan before.

For those who like their Dylan straight, undiluted and non-electric, the hotel tapes contain a wealth of nostalgia and 'honest Bob'. That bitter, angry young man, passionately denouncing the Klu Klux Klan for beatin' up them niggers because they git uppity if they ain't kept down, boy . . . on the farm . . . cotton sacks/on their backs/railway tracks/peepin' thro' the cracks/of the wooden shanks . . . the white man's preacher screams at a black man who's had the impudence to learn to read . . . 'What you don't un'erstan' boy is that there is lots o' **good** ways f'r a man to be wicked!' Oh, really!

Or try this, from 'Abner Till', its story of the beating of an innocent negro . . . . And I'm just singing you this song/& remind you that this sort of thing is still goin' on/ . . . an' so that we can make this great land of ours even greater f' live in . . . . How far from Woodstock Nation, Abbie Hoffman or the analogies and metaphors of 'Highway 61' could you get? Why, even Dylan might permit himself an indulgent smile at these tapes. Still, it's good to listen to him singing in that nasal voice and picking his guitar and blowing his harmonica and coughing and rapping and pretending he's (the new) Woody Guthrie. He was young and poor in those days, and like he said later on in 'Just Like A Rolling Stone', . . . 'when you ain't got nothin', you ain't got nothin' to lose . . .'. That's exactly how he handles these sixteen cuts; easy, relaxed and like he ain't got nothin' to lose. Which he hasn't.

The Byrds—
always
beyond today

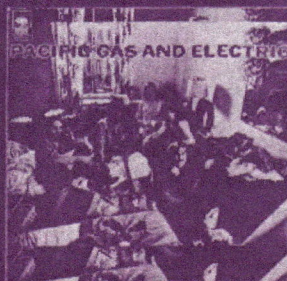

Do you ever get the feeling that you want to disengage yourself from life?
To withdraw into some kind of solitary contemplation just to think about
everything for a while? Everything. You. Her. It. Them.

Well that's how a poet feels, because he's no different from everyone
else. What makes a poet different is that he takes time to put it all
down on paper. Beautifully. And what makes Leonard Cohen
very different poet is that he turns his poetry into songs.

He did it for SONGS OF LEONARD COHEN, his first
album. And it achieved a rare kind of success.

The first time we sprang him on you cold, and people
had to get warmed up to this very unusual artist. But now
there's actually a demand up front for Leonard Cohen.

Then there came SONGS FROM A ROOM, the
second Leonard Cohen album for the growing number
of people who have identified with him. And what he
feels. But don't have that rare poetic vision.

There could be millions of Leonard Cohens in the
world. You may even be him yourself.

THE SOUND OF
THE SEVENTIES

SONGS FROM A ROOM

SONGS OF LEONARD COHEN

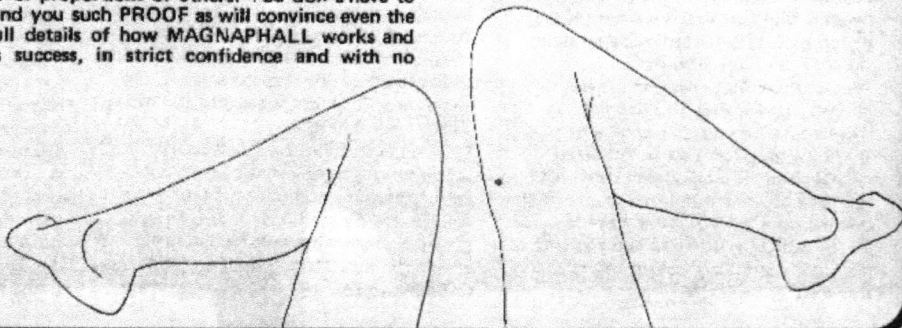

"I'm a looser, a clumsy clown
So why does she come around
acting so sweet... Is she just
laughing at me ?????"

EVERYONE COME TO THE BALL
I AM IN LOVE WITH YOU ALL

"The True Love Of A Good
Woman Is The Only Thing
Missing From My Life."

"I See Her Face
Each Time I Sing."

Tiny has seen this vision, this inspiration,
for as long as he has been singing. "She
has never deserted me," he declares. "She
is between 15 and 25, and is always with
me. I guess I always needed an audience,
and back in those very hard times when I
was first starting to sing, I had to invent
one. Anyway, this is my dream girl, and I
think one of the reasons that I must go on
singing is the strong hope I carry that she
will someday really appear, in the flesh."

Secret love, where are you?

"When I met my future wife
I knew I had seen her before....
she had come to me in a dream as
a fairy princess. I fell in love with
her. I shed a little tear and put it
in an envelope to keep."

"He held out his hand
and she had to comply,
he spoke with his eyes and
a beautiful lady became Mrs. Brady"

AND NOW THE MOST
PROFOUND DUET IN THE LONG
HISTORY OF SONG!

"COME COME
MY LIFE IS LONELY
LONG FOR YOU"

"COME COME
LOVE YOU ONLY
MY HEART IS TRUE"

"GOT YOU
BABE
GOT YOU"

MISS VICKI

"I heard a linnet courting
his lady in the spring.
His mates were wild
shortly,
Nor stayed to hear him
sing,
his song
of love.

I fear my
speech distorting
his tender
love."

& MONEY

WHAT HAS BECOME OF THE HANDICAPPED CHILDREN I USED TO —

"You can know it all
if you choose
Remember lovers never
loose
They are free
Free FREEEEE"

Loveliness is EVERYWHERE
fear's just in your head
Forget your head
and you'll be free
FREE FREEEEEEE

THE WORLD IS WIDE
WITH MANY TIN
BUT FEW SO RARE AS
TINY TIM.

THE ARTICULATE AUDIBLE VOICE OF THE PAST,
WHEN THE BODY AND MATERIAL SUBSTANCE OF
IT HAS ALTOGETHER VANISHED LIKE A DREAM.

"God bless us every one !" said Tiny Tim, the last of all.
He sat very close to his father's side, upon his little stool. Bob
held his withered little hand in his, as if he loved the child, and
wished to keep him by his side, and dreaded that he might be
taken from him.

"Spirit," said Scrooge, with an interest he had never felt before,
"tell me if Tiny Tim will live."

"I see a vacant seat," replied the Ghost, "in the poor chimney-
corner, and a crutch without an owner, carefully preserved.
If these shadows remain unaltered by the Future, the child will
die."

"No, no," said Scrooge. "Oh, no, kind Spirit! say he will be
spared."

"If these shadows remain unaltered by the Future, none other
of my race," returned the Ghost, "will find him here. What then?"

TINY TIM
WANDERING THE STREETS OF NEW YORK,
SINGING TO ALL WHO WOULD LISTEN, IS A TRUE MINSTREL OF THE
AGE. HE IS THE WISEMAN PLAYING THE FOOL, AMBIGUOUS, MULTI VOICED
EMERGING AS A GREAT STAR AT A LATE AGE AFTER YEARS OF DEVELOPING HIS ART IN OBSCURITY.
HIS 1968 CONCERT AT THE ALBERTHALL, BACKED BY THE LONDON PHILHARMONIC, CONDUCTED BY MISS
ARDMBER, RICHARD PERRY WAS A TRULY VIRTUOSO PERFORMANCE. ON FIRST HEARING AND SIGHT
TO THESE EARS AND EYES IT WAS.. DARE I SAY MIND BLOWING!......
HE GAVE AND GAVE AND GAVE... MUTATING BEFORE ONES EYES FROM
THE IMMORTAL INNOCENT TINY TIM.. TO AL JOLSON...TO WILL ROGERS
TO RUDY VALLEE.. TO BOB DYLAN DISSOLVING AND RE FORMING
SPLITTING IN HALF, MALE AND FEMALE, EACH SINGING A LOVE SONG
TO THE OTHER... MERGING AGAIN
TO ELVIS PRESLEY... RUSS
COLOMBO... BING CROSBY...
THE ONE SINGER WHO IS
ALL SINGERS. A PROFOUND
CLOWN. A GREAT
ROMANTIC. THE
SPIRIT OF POPULAR
MUSIC MADE
FLESH. THE
MOST
INCREDIBLE
VOICE IN CAPTIVITY

"The ICE CAPS ARE MELTING
THE TIDE IS RUSHING IN
ALL THE WORLD IS DROWNING
TO WASH AWAY THE SIN"

WHAT THE WORLD NEEDS NOW IS LOVE SWEET LOVE
NO NOT JUST FOR SOME - BUT FOR EVERYONE

'... round and round; and by-and-bye they had a song, about a
lost child travelling in the snow, from Tiny Tim, who had a
plaintive little voice, and sang it very well indeed.'

Piping down the valleys wild
Piping songs of pleasant glee
On a cloud I saw a child
And he laughing said to me

Pipe a song about a Lamb
So I piped with merry cheer,
Piper pipe that song again —
So I piped, he wept to hear.

Drop thy pipe thy happy pipe
Sing thy songs of happy cheer,
So I sung the same again
While he wept with joy to hear.

there are three main rea-
sons why I sing. The first is to give thanks
to God for the gift he gave me. Number
two is to cheer people whether they are
young or old, with a song of the past or
present. And number three, and perhaps
above all, is because of all the lovely women
who with their beauty cause my heart to
overflow with joy.

So PURE, SO SURREAL... WHAT MORE CAN BE SAID,
IF YOU HAVE EARS TO HEAR LEND THEM TO
DERRY DOVER, LARRY LOVE, TEXICALI TEX, JUDAS
FOXGLOVE, TINY TIM HE WILL THEM TO
OVERFLOWING.
"GOD BLESS US EVERYONE!" said Tiny
Tim... the last of all..........

IF I MADE A MOVIE I SHOULD LIKE TO PLAY "SCROOGE" IN "A CHRISTMAS CAROL"

Hip Pocrates

QUESTION: I am a very early riser, strictly a morning man, and my mate is a late sleeper. Therein lies my dilemma.

There is nothing I like better than having intercourse with her as she awakes, or more precisely, waking her up with the actual coital act. When first awakened, she sometimes is a bit irritable but quickly gets over this.

Since there is little or no foreplay involved, I cannot sustain myself long enough for her to achieve complete sexual gratification. I'm beginning to be concerned about the wisdom of this practice but I don't want to give it up because it really does turn me on.

We are not up-tight about this thing but I do feel the need to improve the situation for more mutual satisfaction. What can we do to help my mate achieve sexual gratification on short notice? P.S. This letter is on the level.

ANSWER: You could spend months or years of psychotherapy trying to determine why you wish to take your wife unawares — or adjust to the situation. If this is a frequent practice your wife isn't really surprised. But if she can't get any satisfaction, neither will you, fully.

Sounds as if you two should discuss very openly with each other your mutual needs and wants. Incidentally, my laboratory assistant says she can think of no better way to start the day.

QUESTION: I have a story I would like to relate to you. Here it is. Herb visited Linda in December and again in July. He did not see her in the six months inbetween and therefore did not ball her during that time.

Linda stopped taking her birth control pills early in April and became pregnant later that month. She claims that Herb is the father. That she carried around the sperm for the fertilized egg from December until April and when she stopped taking birth control pills became pregnant. She is now four months pregnant.

A psychiatrist told Herb that this is possible. The Free Clinic said it was impossible. I personally don't believe it.

Have you ever heard of this? Do you think it could happen?

ANSWER: Linda will have to accept some other explanation. Pregnancy could occur, for example, without intercourse if the sperm were deposited at or near the vaginal entrance. Perhaps Herb misinterpreted the psychiatrist's words. He might have said something like "Well . . . anything is possible, but . . ."

Spermatozoa can remain alive in the vagina no more than 2 or 3 days, whether or not a woman is taking birth control pills. Deep-freezing can maintain sperm cells in a state of suspended animation for long periods of time. But your friend would have had to be quite literally frigid for this phenomenon to occur.

QUESTION: If you have been circumcised, can you become uncircumcised through a skin graft? One of my friends has been to Japan, and he says there it is quite common for men who have been circumcised to get skin grafts.

ANSWER: Medical opinion remains divided regarding the merits of routine circumcision.

Urologists, mohels, and other proponents cite the lack of penile cancer in Jewish men and the low incidence of cancer of the cervix in their wives. Circumcision prevents an accumulation of smegma, the cheesy substance beneath the foreskin thought to be a cancer-producing irritant. Routine circumcision also prevents tightening of the foreskin and certain penile irritations of infancy. Opponents of routine circumcision point out that psychological effects on the infant are unknown. How does he perceive this attack on his privates? No anesthetics are used and the baby almost always cries, though many physicians say the baby feels no pain (they mean it doesn't hurt the physician). Freud neglected this area, perhaps because

he was a victim of the ritual. Claims have been made that uncircumcised males are more sensitive, but the few objective tests made of this question have shown no difference in sensitivity.

My own opinion is that routine circumcision is unnecessary if mothers learn how to care for their infant sons. The foreskin should be regularly (and gently) pulled back from the head of the penis and accumulated smegma cleansed with soap and water. Boys should be taught this as a matter of personal hygiene. But even with scrupulous cleansing, some males will have persistent irritations and tightened foreskins requiring circumcision later in life. And circumcision in adult males requires hospitalization for several days (several months ago I printed a letter from a fellow who broke some stitches while kissing his girl goodnight).

Skin grafts to replace severed foreskins are possible. But so is the graft of an entire penis (non-functional, except for the elimination of urine).

A physician proponent of routine circumcision said of his opposition. 'They are wrong to the amount of difference.' Or maybe it's much ado about little.

QUESTION: For almost as long as I can remember I have had small pimples on the lower underside of my penis. They are about the size of goose pimples.

At first I thought that this was normal but then I began to wonder. Please tell me if my condition is abnormal and, if so, what to do about it.

ANSWER: The 'goosebumps' you describe are oil glands, many of which contain hairs. They are a perfectly normal part of the adult male anatomy. If you still have doubts, why not ask your physician next time you have an annual examination.

Dear Dr Hip Pocrates is a collection of letters and answers published by Grove Press $5.
Send your questions c/o OZ.

ARE ON
VERTIGO

A PHILIPS RECORDS PRODUCT

This interview with Peter Fonda is extracted from the Georgia Straight, an Underground newspaper published in Vancouver, British Columbia.

These dudes on their bikes   I dig 'em   far out stuff...

terrible to do that now you're a big hero and everybody's going to think it's alright — I'm not a hero, I think nobody's going to score cocaine, I don't think it's going to happen. But people have said it will, and How come you don't have more about that, it just was so easy, you just simply went in and tasted it and it was all friendly, the guy hugs you like he's your father, and his name's Jesus, and so forth . . . and everything's so easy and just get to the airport, everybody is smiling and planes are landing already and you give it to Phil Spector and he gives you the money and everything's cool and you split.

GS: *But he's really uptight; that's nice.*
FONDA: He was *terrified* of those planes. He really didn't know . . . we didn't know whether they'd hit us or not, they were really right over the top of our heads. The gig is if we'd had some big *dramatic* scene of scoring the cocaine, where there was a lot of danger in what we were doing, and people chasing us or something, it would have lifted it off what we had done. All we did was a sample, illegal, immoral *federal* act. We could have been selling newspapers like William Randolph Hearst, it's the same act. He's pushing, he *was* in his time pushing false hope, false, you know, lies and shit like that, no matter who went down . . . he built San Simeon . . . no matter what it cost, and it cost several lives. So we score cocaine no matter who goes down, but we make it as if we just went to the supermarket . . . because that's the American attitude.
We were sure that what we were doing was right, we felt honest about it. We took dramatic license in being non-dramatic. By being underplaying, by never giving a speech to the audience really, by never indicating what we were doing before, why we were doing what we were doing or even where we were going, really, other than just a few small lines here and there — never making a point to the trip other than the trip itself.

GS: *How did you come to develop the relationship between yourselves and Dennis? I really liked the way he kind of functioned as a foil to you, in the sense that he didn't present himself as just being a nice guy, but like he was kind of uptight and angry.*
FONDA: Well I insisted 'I don't want to say anything in the movie. I want to carry an existentialist point throughout the film, without really getting involved but seeing everything so that the audience, who is with *me* — whatever part of the audience is with me — can also make their own mind up about what they see. But we *need* somebody in there with the reality — hard-nosed, paranoiac attitude . . . we call him the angry speed freak in the film — who's got to be the other side of my personality. Actually we're just one person — but we get away with it; he's my sidestick, he's my foil, he's Sancho Panza and I'm Don Quixote, you know, in our own way. It was developed in the idea that he had that ability, he's that kind of guy, he's aggressive, he's a Taurus you know, and he's really bull-headed and stubborn, that's how he can direct the bloody thing anyway, and act in it — it was a tough job.
He drinks, he gets uptight and he's up on uppers — that's his character, Dennis. So Dennis brought *his* character to the film and made it work as my foil — goes out and does my battles . . . because I won't fight . . . and somebody has to fight otherwise we're going to get done. So he goes out and *does* my battles, and he *gets* uptight. You know, although I know I'm not going to stay at the hippie commune, for example, he's really the catalyst — 'come we're going, come let's go, come on'. You know, he could not take it . . . it was nowhere for him even though he's long-haired with beads, it meant nothing to him — he was into the money . . . he was a hard-nosed street guy . . .
The hippie commune is the weakest part of the film as far as I'm concerned. It was the one we had the most trouble with. Whether it was conceptual or not I'm not sure . . . well, I have my ideas about it, I've seen it 116 times now but . . . We were sure that we didn't want to go in and do a hippie commune sequence that everbody was going to say Ah well look it they're all saying pro-hippie, isn't hippie wonderful. Well hippie ain't wonderful, and it's a bummer life out there, and they're eating dead horses, and they're getting shot at by the Indians, the Chicanos and the townspeople, and they don't know what they're doing, and they're diseased. I mean, these are cats who we went and lived with, and talked with . . . we can't show it like a paradise either. And we don't want to promote it, we just want to show it as an alternative, which Captain America chooses not to get involved with. He says, Yeah, yeah I know about time but I just got to go . . . which is the thing with *everybody.*

GS: *At the end you say 'We blew it Billy'. Is that what you were saying earlier, that it was all reacting against you and you weren't like making it? . . .*
FONDA: We simply went out and acted, the whole time we just did a thing . . . At the top, the *first* sign, after we get kicked out of the motel during the title sequence . . . the first thing is that I'd gotten like totally uninvolved with him going to New Orleans . . . and I'm really withdrawn about the act . . . but I never

cop out to saying Man, I wonder if we did something wrong. I just don't say anything about it at all, and I keep on removing further and further, I get a little bit involved with Jack Nicholson George Hansen, the guy who comes in but I keep getting further removed until he gets killed, and that really snaps me. And then in the trip in the graveyard we do a holy communion with the acid, and the wine you know, breaking it out and passing it around and drinking it . . . and I cop out to my mother – which is like the thing that's going down with everybody, that whole generation; Momism, you know.

The thing is there and Momism is the gig that did it . . . to us, to the French, the Russians, to everybody, man – maybe the Chinese are not because they're so psyched out anyway – but Momism is the thing that really cooked us all up. So copping out to it, coming on as an existentialist hero, and then suddenly copping out to Mom . . .

It was a bit scary for me, you know. Dennis says Get up there on that statue and ask your mother why she copped out on you. And I said Oh man, wow! I said Gee, you know, is that relevant to the picture? I said Listen, man, I want to be an existentialist hero in this film, I don't want to say anything until it's all over and then say We blew it, you understand? And that's my whole gig in this picture, and he says No man, no, go up there and cop out and ask your mother why she left you. And he's *crying* as he's telling me. This's our one chance, d'you understand, and I started crying and I said You're right. And I climbed up on that statue and I was waiting for two hours, as they kept reloading on us – I was really into it. Unfortunately, he got so taken away with what I was doing up there that he kept talking through the whole thing, so we can only use snatches of it, you keep hearing him saying Oh, yeah man, oh yeah! We had two live mikes – one with the chick who's reading I believe in God the Father, and me up on the statue, which was all simultaneous. That was

our little technical mistake, but it was *our* mistake . . . After it was over I came up and I said I think we ought to take it out of the film . . . He said Why? and I said You Know, like, if I'm up holding onto the statue . . . of liberty there, saying Why did you leave me, Mom, the whole audience is going to think I've left Captain America and now I'm Peter Fonda. I really had this thing going in my head, and he kept saying No, no, no, not at all, leave it in, it's got to be in, it's the one thing that brings you down there . . .

GS: I was curious to know what kind of crew you had, how large.
FONDA: Including what I call gofers –

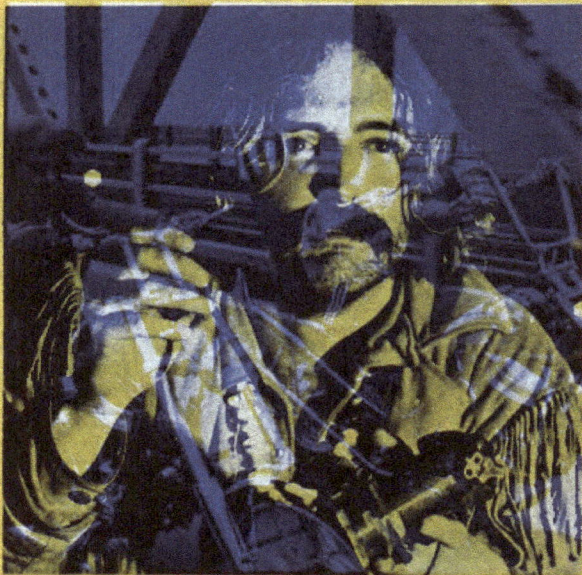

the kids who do everything, right? – 23 people . . . at the most. Not including all the actors in the hippie scene. On the road we had one lighting truck, a generator, a camera truck . . . well, it wasn't a big truck . . . We shot out of the back of a Chevy convertible, all those travelling shots . ,. We used an Arriflex and blimped it for the sound sequences and kept back . . . you get the camera away. you see, which gives the idea like the camera's not there . . . cause the camera's removed . . . Angenieux zoom . . . which is a beautiful lens, man. I've never been photographed that beautifully . . . and it also gives you great mobility . . . because although I hate zoom – cause it's always overdone –

this guy's such a good cameraman . . . he shoots with both eyes open, so he can seen everything that's happening, and he'll slightly adjust . . . and you could hardly see it, he'll just open a little more, to cover something, close down and make it in focus. And we do rack-focuses, which can always be overdone, but we do them just right to direct attention . . . but it's always when you least expect it to happen . . . and I like that.

GS: Where did you pick up your cameraman? I agree, he's really good.
FONDA: We saw this guy's work on two other motorcycle films: 'Hell's Angels on Wheels' and 'The Savage Seven', and then a film called 'Psych-Out' . . . all of them low-budget, Joe Soloman type films and we said Far out, man, this cat really knows how to work a long lens. Well Antonioni came down to see a rough-cut, flipped out, just literally flipped out, tried to get him right away . . . the cameraman was off in Hawaii shooting an ad or something like that, but Antonioni says, You know, I've gotta have that *man* – He's fantastic . . . Antonioni really, he's got this tic, man, it's incredible. During our movie though you know, his tic started and then it began to stop and then at the end like he was just like that, watching it. Then he came out and said It's the most honest film that's come out of America that I've ever seen.

GS: That's wonderful.
FONDA: Yeah . . . and he went around telling everybody else about it too, and I feel good, you know.
You see, we're into communications, man, not entertainment. I mean I want to entertain people too . . . and we do have great musical numbers and those bikes look beautiful, and we have some great jokes . . .

GS: But in a way we're all beyond entertainment these days.
FONDA: We have to be . . . we have no time left.

man, that ride.

HALL BATHS

SCUNTHORPE

WEDNESDAY NOV. 26

COMMENCE 7-0

Presented by
RELWYSKOW & GREEN
PROMOTIONS LTD

WRESTLING

TAG TEAM CONTEST

WE MEET A HEAD

Next the Worthing Hotel, scene of Scunthorpe's second discotheque. This involved walking some distance through the town (town being mainly brown). On the bridge some cats stopped us to drop the word 'Are your knuckles brown?' Everybody seemed to have long hair, mainly early Beatles cut and everybody came over straight, straight, straight. Up dark streets, nobody, pressure of a dropping town, heavy and getting creepy, then from nowhere five or six cats, one streaming blood from a gashed face, finally lobotomy-type haircuts, mad eyes focused on us, gang rhythm, Terror Flick with wet change to lonely menacing nowhere. Brief fumbled contact, the hippie hatred and wet wisps floating after us.

PUB CRAWL

We fled into The Worthing. They didn't like us, though we were beans trying to con drinks after hours, dinner impossible. In the dining room last lunch at the Beaumont, a restaurant café with a faintly exotic flavour and largely by its non-British nationality of its owners. Supposed to be a bit posh. Decor appropriate, including two be-called girl Miss Brief Figurehead lounging from the wall. Not a variety anyone. Kids drinking coffee, mixture of white collars and the odd young executives eating steaks. The omelette came with at least 2¼ each worth of chips, reckoning by the chip portion. That's a lot of chips. In the doorway we talked to a kid waiting. He wanted to score. What if two were free? The questions died unanswered. We weren't and he knew it. At last. In this town one real live head. He worked as a moulder in the steel factory, was 17, grooved on soul and blues, went to Riddings, a housing estate one mile out of town to Soul Scene discotheque. Saturday night only, closing time 10.30. Spent Sunday nights at Riddings Youth Centre that is until the witching hour of 10.30, dancing and

"Do you like it?"

"No."

"Why don't you leave?"

"Don't want to."

He was 18, and also lived with his parents. Dropped out of Doncaster College of Art, coming home, but disliked Scunthorpe, also London, doesn't want to be part of any scene, would move eventually to Scandinavia, somewhere colder (!) prefers always to be alone, grooves on painting and sounds — like Cream, has chicks but no one special, most people are, like his sisters, marry young, he won't. Doesn't read any underground stuff although he could get anything if he was interested, knows of about 15 people who smoke, most of then blacks, has had just, but not really good stuff, pulling suckle, gets on well with straight people but has no special friends, is hip to the narrowness of Scunthorpe, feels safe in his private world, detached, is amused by

'Look out Scunthorpe here we come.'

Scunthorpe's the only town I've ever eased thoroughly in 4½ hours. It took a lot longer to get there. We made Kings Cross Saturday 2.45p m, bought cigarettes, Trebor mints, found a 2nd class booth, sat opposite a man with a pipe and the Pocket Book of Logarithms and at 3 p.m. lurched off backwards to the dark satanic mills. British Rail afforded tea, change, last trip of cellophane wrapped goodies served on silver plate, out of the window marshland movie getting murkier. Then Doncaster, graveless, grimy precise image of the North set in all our skulls, slow shuffle from Ladies to Buffet. A few yards to the railway bridge (setting, predictably, for the Bridge Hotel, Scunthorpe's jewel) then right and straight down, Oswald Road turned into Frodingham was crossed by Doncaster turning into High. A perfect square. Town centre.

THE SCUNTHORPE HUSTLE

We roamed a little. The set was international English-speaking, shopping suburbia. Windmill Palace, Co-ops, Congregational Church, High School, non-residential Britannia pub. Two ancient fixtures outside the Britannia signalled our alarm at our being unescorted. It was 6.30 or so, and Saturday-night-on-the-town was in full swing. Rockers on the corner, kids in pairs, in bunches, stilt-heeled 20's attached at the elbow to grey suits. Monument, we were set off down a side street to The Parkinson Arms. 'We regret that your canine friends cannot accompany you into the lounge'. The plaque on the door should have made us hip to what followed. For one neon second we stood, tufty-pile carpet and blinked at Laminex luxury when a tweedy person flung open the door booming 'Sorry!' This was intoned three times. Nothing moved, orange gins fixed midflight to gaping mouths. A message began to seep through. He hustled us outside, when pressed he said he had no rooms, that if he did have any he wouldn't rent them to us, to anyone, in fact, in trousers, long jackets or denims. To my females it all sounded, I was so calm me, put in that I had a certain clientele which did not and I ever would induce riff-raff (no tap room, no bar, lounge only).

'Anyway, you're clearly from The People coming here and asking all these questions.'

In our long jackets we trudged back to the Britannia. The chicks, frozen legs mottled in nylon, a tribute to British stayin power, all wore mains, obviously compulsory Saturday night gear. Two cops waited us off the Britannia, indicated we were out of our heads to be in Scunthorpe at all and sent us up Doncaster Road to the Royal. The reception fucked, the proprietoress was cool, we had a room.

The Freddie Mark Extravaganza were playing at the Public Baths Hall to eighteen and over, 6s. 6d., 11.30 finish. Campbell's Tcen-Beat Discotheque, rockers, hangout housed in a side entrance to the Inter Affiliated Conservative Club founded in 1937, played host to fifteens and over till 10.30 (Friday nights 13+). Playland was full of old ladies playing a variation of bingo, the Britannia was packed with all male boozers, Curry's on Something was showing at the Majestic, Yangtse River at the A.B.C., and right opposite The Straight Arrow Bingo Club (formerly Straight Arrow Bowling Alley) crammed them in.

TEDDY BOY SUIT

Under the circumstances we lit up and growed a little on the roses and central heading. Much later it was pouring. Playland had closed, the kids were spilling out of Campbell's down to the corner, couldn't place Freddie Mark (Mecca of the straights' teens) so we had a drink at the Britannia (street sherry) were offered a fuck by long-haired alkies knocking 17 and coming spit, stood on the corner like everyone else. There seemed nowhere to eat, the cafes were shut, the rockers, bored out of their heads slumbered across the road the pub waiting to drop dead on by the eight apple-faced cops who obviously went through this ritual every weekend. Two were hustled into the van, a dignified few felt each other up in shop doorways, most of them started walking home, felt vaguely hopeful seeing a rocker with Hells Angel emblazoned on his leather jacket but he spun home too, a double decker turned the corner, flashes of lacquered bouffants and fake fur collars pointing at far out the rockers, big busted queen conductor Tony Curtis curt pressed into place.

discotheque, Saturday night only, had closed at 10.30. The rule said we wouldn't have qualified anyway. Paranoid and hungry and eager to avoid further day street encounters till we had eaten, at least, we took a cab to the Chinese restaurant which stretched closing time, Saturdays, till 11.30. That was a mistake, Moderne neon, everybody out shoulder to shoulder, everything came with chips. Except the Special Chow Mein. That came with egg, also gravy and meat soy sauce. A couple, maybe 18 and 19, took a booth, T.vn wedding rings, sausages and chips, hamburger and chips.

'He didn't come to Freddie Mark'.
'No.'
'What's his name?'
'Stuart.'
'What's he like?'
'Nice.'

That was it till they grin, which they did after the last mouthful. So did everybody. Average time for food consumption roughly 25 minutes. We left, spurred on by the arrival of the lobotomy loonies, bloodless but not freaky still.

Outside it was pouring and deserted. The choice lay between late night swedish sex at the Majestic or bed. We walked back to the Royal, scoring Tszi and kit-kats from the closing fish shop on the way. A police car pulled up. 'What are you two doing out so late?' It was 11.15. We rang the night bell, woke the proprietress, went to bed and got smashed.

Sunday, grey black, still raining. In my direction rows of liver brick semis, woodwork painted hardware red and yellow. A few more prosperous detached houses conforming more to much the same aesthetic liver turning orange. Plastic shops. In the nothofar distance on their sides sombre smokestacks; the steel industry on which the town is based. Gazed at the newsagent's Fabulous, Teddy Bear, Princess, Bingo Special, Fefix, Love Comix etc. All the ads are for hamsters. No underground papers. No demands. Some would order if requested. Biggest local paper the Scunthorpe Evening Telegraph. Its full window display of photos features a new A.A. sign on a highway out of town and a scene from the damn club's production of The Rotters — lot of knickers showing there.

'How about the groups?' to the girl in the fish shop.
'Well, we had the Seekers, or is the Searchers? And someone very famous last week but I can't remember any.'

Freddie Mark's Extravaganza ad, still fluttered next to the Skipper Baths sign

cared — so it was cool. He found music (never live) just about every night except Tuesdays and Thursdays. Didn't have his own pad. Hardly anyone did — everybody lived with their parents. Difficult not to in town like this. Knew about ten cats who smoked shit, twice as many who's tried because it was a thing, then reverted to the beer. Never turned on birds — they blabbed to their mothers. Nor did they improve. Lost his last girl because of that. Went part time to one college in town, technical college. Any activities there? Not that sort of college, you just walk in, do your course and split.

He was keen to leave Scunthorpe and live in London so he dealt a little. Would bring it up North, knows a cat who started with two quid's worth and now has a good thing going. Still costs a lot more up North, always a corner for London, good field for dealer. Police? He'd been up for the times for possession, three each time. Was little to be searched at night. Not exactly drug squad though. Do they even read any local papers, magazines, etc, interested in turning people on? No. Where's he want it can get it at most people don't want it. Hadn't dropped acid, unsurious, none around. Hard stuff? No junkies in town. Pointless for them to stay, but has a friend working at the hospital who can score morphe. Said kids like him were called mods — still — but couldn't see any point in categorizing. Kept away from the rockers' disco, although they all listened to Soul, drug soccer and followed the local team. The rockers and schoolkids were on pills, mainly speed, if anything. There was very little friction, between groups. Spades? He didn't know any, didn't want to either. They lived in their own section of town and their own territory. Pakistanis. No reason. Just didn't like them to stay. He questioned them.

Dark again, raining still. Rail to the Royal, pausing to buy 25b pangaric cough drops. Also a few thousand smarties and chocolate peanuts. Ritzzy evening meal scene in the dining room of the pub. Dover sole and camel coloured lurex. Gave that a miss and got into the wallpaper of Room 3, with a little help.

SUNDAY PAINTER

Late, again in the Bucaneer pub with no beer set, examining its straight faces, greys, browns, gabardine, woollens, boy meets girl, coffee, last bus home, we saw another Rend, spaced very beautiful, with a chick, not so beautiful.
'Where do you live?' (to her)
'At home, with my parents'.

in here' surveying the Bucaneer 'is on £30 a week'. Thinks Scunthorpe is pretty like all other small English northern towns he's been in. Score weekly if he gets the bread from a London contact, doesn't go to clubs, digs spades, has a spade friend, seems unperturbed by the few of instant suggestion policy, seems unperturbed by anything.

On the way back along to nilly deserted streets, no clubs open on Sundays, no lights in any houses, a Chinese approaches, orders in the rain doubletake, says Bonjour and disappears. We keep paragan after that.

MONDAY MONDAY

The sun came out on Monday. That changed the colour if not the temperature.
'Where's the park?'
'The What?'
'The Park.'
'The Park?'

We found one (there are three) at the end of Frodingham Street, terrifying in its symmetry, a mangam of tennis court, bowling green, asphalt paths, locked huts, a few trees and an aviary. No one there at all — just us and the birds. One cold parrot, some pigeons, a canary and two lovebirds. We smoked in the only sheltered spot, entrance to the gents, not understanding the principle of the automatic flush and hallucinating ghosts. End of park romp. Impossible to find a taxi to take us to the station. Then we met George. George is very old. He was going the same way and didn't want to walk either. He said he'd find a cab and he said we'd take him to the station. That meant a lengthy stop at Arnold's house but Arnold wasn't in. A grey non-too pulled carefully into the drive and Arnold got out with two dozen fresh eggs and another old man. We all got in. On the way George and Arnold spotted an enormous lady. She got in. She was off to Mrs Wingates and assumed we were too. 'It is Sharon, isn't it?' It wasn't but it didn't matter. All very Scunthorpian but different. This was the life we hadn't seen. One hundred years ago the town was fifty houses. Then the steel industry and now 18,000 people. But obviously wedges of the village life remained here and there, people looked after each other, the old weren't necessarily redundant — it seemed a new simplicity to set against insularity and lack of imagination. But this all fell by go out at Mr Wingates. George went to the insurance office and Arnold dropped us at the station.
'How much?'
'That's up to you.'

Morden

'Nothing ever happens in Morden' said a local journalist. Those words look right; most people don't even know where Morden is. It's the last station at the Southern end of the Northern line. At the station entrance you stand near the edge of a housing estate of some ten thousand houses. 'Nothing ever happens in Morden' - yes, those words look right. One street looks just like another. You go down one, and you've been down the list. It was built before the days of planning. It's a ghetto. You live on the estate, you say. It's a ghetto because families were put here in the early 'thirties from inner London. They weren't asked what they thought about this. But the L.C.C. had to do something about the London slums. They had the bright idea of building vast housing estates in outer London, so people were uprooted from Rotherhithe, Wapping, Islington and Walworth and housed in tiny 2-bedroomed or 3-bedroomed houses with no adequate heating facilities, and three thousand of them without bathrooms. But it was a bit like the country, the L.C.C., and now the G.L.C., call the houses "cottages". They each have a strip of garden, and in the old days the Horticultural Society was really thriving.

But not now. All the organisations complain of apathy - the Churches, the Tenants' Associations, the Labour Party Group, Parent/Teacher Associations don't get off the ground; the local Councillors complain about apathy.

In fact, the estate is a community organised for non-participation, for non-consultation - yes, even to death. There are hordes of social workers around patching up the crises. But they are not concerned with the family or with the community. They can't do any preventive work. There are lots of volunteers from the flourishing bourgeois communities of Wallington, Carshalton, Sutton and Croydon doing good everywhere.

But somewhere I want to say to all this good work (and it is) - STOP - you are killing the people. They have had so much done for them that they no longer realise they have resources in themselves to look after one another. I do not know of one organisation - voluntary or statutory - which has representatives from the estate on their Committees. It's all decided for them.

All this is made worse because we have more than our share of the old people's explosion. The G.L.C., still the landlord, says to young people who want to live where they've been brought up, that when they get married they've got to move out so there are about 15,000 people in a few square miles.

'Nothing ever happens in Morden', these words may seem right, but in fact they are nonsensical. There are thirty thousand PEOPLE living on the estate, and these people are affected by institutions like the G.L.C., and the two real Tory Councils whose goals need questioning severely. And everything is not well. There is grumbling, complaining, anger and just occasionally violence - which is in Morden at least exploding apathy.

Apathy is all over the place. A few months ago Mary Smith of Roche Walk, Carshalton was found dead on the kitchen floor. She had put her head in the gas oven. It had all been carefully prepared. In a note she said, 'I'm so lonely. I've no friends' - friends belong to the past." Three days later there was by chance a public meeting on the problems of the elderly. Mary's death should have been a catalyst, for people to DO something. Instead, there was a sense of frustration and helplessness. Why aren't *they* doing more?

Then we have bathroom problems. The G.L.C. is a tired, inefficient and incompetent organisation as far as its modernisation of old houses goes. Enormous delays occur between various stages of the installation of these suites; people complain about the way the builders behave. And after they have all left - perhaps after a period of six months instead of two weeks as Horace Cutler, the G.L.C. Housing Chairman, proudly said - they leave a lot of rubbish all over the place. But no-one feels strong enough to turn their complaints into action. They just hope that someone will do something for them.

Just Bloody Tenants

Rev. Donald Reeves

Then there are all the questions about Housing. 'You're just a bloody tenant' said an official at the local G.L.C. office in Middleton Road to a tenant making an enquiry. The G.L.C. have been benevolent despots as landlords on this estate; they regularly cut hedges, do a limited amount of interior decorating, and normally take trouble with requests for transfers. But, and it's the biggest bit, they have no understanding at all of the need for tenants to take a share in the running of the estate - in, for instance, the making of local by-laws.

The situation is going to get much worse. In April next year, the G.L.C. begins to shed its responsibilities as a landlord. One-third of the estate will be transferred to the High Tory Council of Sutton. Up will go the rents, and then shortly after down will come the houses. The land will be sold to private developing companies. The Council will make a packet, and have removed some Council houses. The tenants will be rehoused elsewhere. It is likely that that is what is going to happen - a Councillor said you can't consult people about their homes; tenants feel too strongly about them. So it will be demolition without consultation because after all the Council know best, and know the wider picture - so they say.

As I write all the posh papers are moralising about the atrocities in Vietnam. That's predictable. But the tone of their moralising turns me off; it's much the same as some so-called revolutionary underground Press who go on and on about Biafra, Bolivia, or the Jews or the Blacks in the ghetto in Harlem. It all sounds the same - a lot of well-heeled liberals pontificating about these big issues and ignoring their own turf.

Revolution has got to come. It's got to come in such unlikely places as these barrack-like, transit camp, anonymous housing estates where people feel like children (because they are treated like children and so feel unable to stand up and say stop - we are not going to be pushed around any more.

One of the things I believe is that this can happen - provided you are able to discover a point of indignation (through an action survey done by the tenants based on the old Socratic maxim 'An unexamined life is not worth living'), and so generate curiosity and hope. Out of this will come new leaders who will bring the people together and put right whatever is wrong. It's a long, slow haul. But it can and does work. It falls the stifling paternalism of so many of the caring professions. The revolution will come when local pressure groups insist on being a real part of the decision making process. This cuts right across the old political arguments - political parties are then just irrelevant.

But there are no blue prints. The revolution in Morden may take the form of an old people's charter written by them for them, or 'No demolition without consultation', but the revolution will come on specific issues. Even in Morden some of us are, as McLuhan would say, part of the cool generation, who want direct, intense involvement on matters which want putting right rather than fighting for some worked out Utopian style community.

To that extent our vision is blurred and barren. We've lost the art of dreaming in a post-metaphysical world we've got no language to talk about God, or at another level about the Black/White thing, or our gut level responses to space travel, or to what communities are about. Our language has run out.

I've said nothing about the Church in Morden. We are a tiny group of people, about 150 to 200 representative of the estate. The Church of England has had a love affair with the working classes ever since the Industrial Revolution, but it has never been consummated. But if the Church has any relevance at all it's got to lead the Morden Revolution, and it's beginning to do so. And when the Revolution's over, then we have a wealth of symbol and theme to help the world *celebrate*, to look for new idols, to keep open the future, and even to have something to offer in shaping it. Morden like so many places has forgotten how to celebrate, because there is apparently nothing to celebrate. But Morden is wrong. We have something to celebrate - and we do in a big way from time to time. But that's another story.

Chicago

The most important courtroom confrontation in the history of the Underground is now taking place. The US Government has indicted eight people on charges of conspiracy arising out of incidents and demonstrations during the Democratic Convention in Chicago, August 1968. The 'Academy Award of Protest' went to Rennie Davis, Abbie Hoffman, Lee Weiner, Dave Dellinger, John Froines, Jerry Rubin, Bobby Seale and Tom Hayden.

THE FIRST DAY 26 SEPT '69

It has taken Judge Julius Hoffman one day to accomplish what most observers here had speculated would take one week to a month to complete. But almost singlehandedly, Judge Hoffman has accumulated a jury, a 12-member Panel which appears to illustrate *Newsweeks* "Troubled Americans" rather than any clear-headed application of jurisprudent impartiality. This morning they are ushered into the courtroom; 10 women (2 black) and 2 men, plus 4 alternates (all female, one black). A couple of them are retired, some have adult children, all are straight working class people, and only one, a 23-year-old girl, could in any way be considered a "peer" of the eight defendants on trial.

At first glance, the jury en masse has the vaguely formidable appearance of 12 people who are not here to goose around. They sit erect, hands folded in their laps, eyes riveted on the defendants' table which they face. As the hours and days pass, postures are noticed to have undergone imperceptible shifts; N.Y. appears in the courtroom. Lefcourt is also in custody of the U.S. Marshal, having been arrested upstairs in the Court of Appeals while filing an appeal on the warrant issued by Judge Hoffman for *his* arrest.

It is learned that authorities in San Francisco have refused to issue arrest warrants for Michael Kennedy and Dennis Roberts, the two other lawyers who had been hired by the defense only for pre-trial work.

Judge Hoffman refuses to drop contempt charges against Tigar and Lefcourt, stating that he will release them from custody on the condition that they sit as counsel at the defendants' tables, a rather clumsily calculated move intended to show that the defendants have adequate legal counsel for the trial to proceed without Garry. A 10-minute recess is called to allow Tigar and Lefcourt to meet with the 8 defendants, Kunstler and Weinglass and decide whether or not they should withdraw from the case.

As the courtroom is clearing, there is a mild scuffle as U.S. Marshalls attempt to handcuff Tigar in the courtroom and place him in custody.

Defendant Abbie Hoffman shouts; "We object to the treatment of our lawyers – they are needed in trials like this one going on all over the

34

country. They're not just our lawyers, they're our brothers." The court reconvenes and Judge Hoffman is still not satisfied with the defenses decision to consent to the withdrawal of Tigar and Lefcourt, provided the defendants do not have to waive their 6th Amendment right that would allow for a Postponement until the return of Chief Counsel Garry. Hoffman denies the motion and orders the two attorneys – still in custody – to sit at the defense table. At the end of the day, Hoffman orders them jailed over the weekend, denies them bail and sets no sentence.

Following another motion by Kunstler, Hoffman also refuses to allow for the withdrawal of attorneys Irving Birnbaum and Stanley Bass – local attorneys who by law are required to represent the defendants *in the event that out-of-state Counsel is not present*. Hoffman orders these two men to appear in court every day, even though their participation is unnecessary.

FIST WAVING

Refusing to hear further objections from the defense, Hoffman calls in the jury, and Ass. U.S. Attorney Shultz opens the government's case. He begins with a carefully enunciated run-down of the defendants, and as their names are mentioned, each stands and faces the jury. It goes along well enough until Tom Hayden stands and gives a friendly sort of fist salute, nothing intended as a threat, just a sort of convivial fist salute that freaks out the judge. The jury is dismissed. Hoffman goes through a terribly long, elaborate riff about "fist waving" in his courtroom. "It's my customary salute, Your Honor," explains Hayden. Hoffman wheezes something about fist waving and finally calls the jurors back.

Shultz picks up where he left off in his opening address, the next name being Abbie Hoffman.

Abbie stands up obediently and tosses a kiss to the jurors just before sitting down.

Caught off-guard again, Judge Hoffman quavers out an order that the jury "disregard the kiss just thrown by Defendant Hoffman." Shultz continues without further interruption from either side, and having "dropped" all the defendants' names, proceeds with some pretty heavy accusations, which he says the government intends to prove. In essence, the prosecution holds the position that Defendants Rubin, Hoffman and Davis made non-negotiable demands on the city of Chicago so that they would be turned down, and the allegedly pre-planned riots could then break out. David Dellinger was claimed to be the "architect of the revolution," and the Yippies were accused of demanding $100,000 from city of Chicago to prevent the riots. The rest of it seemed to have come out of *For Whom the Bell Tolls*.

William Kunstler opens the case for

the defense. His address emphasizes the right to dissent, the right to protest an illegal, unjust and immoral war. The defense will prove that they came to the '68 Democratic Convention with thousands of other Americans who wanted to protest continuation of the war in South Vietnam, a war which had been within the jurisdiction of the political party that was in power. Well aware of their Constitutional rights, these thousands of Americans came to protest the involvement of their country in that war, and they came to the most obvious place, the Chicago convention, to show that dissent. The real conspiracy, declares Kunstler, was not on the part of these 8 defendants, but on the part of national political figures and the local police to suppress the demonstrations.

"As individuals, these men (the defendants) are unimportant – what is important is the threat to everyone's freedom to dissent, the threat. The threat to our freedom of speech. Ladies and gentlemen of the jury, these defendants will stand before you as classic examples of The People against the government."

LUNCH RECESS PRESS CONFERENCE

Davis: It's a stacked trial, loaded against us. It will be impossible to get a fair trial here, because the way Judge Hoffman is conducting the trial shows him to be completely in the arms of the government." An attorney representing the ACLU: "We are deeply concerned with the treatment of the attorneys in this case and with Judge Hoffman's issuance of arrest warrants on 4 of them. This is unheard of and shocking."

AFTERNOON SESSION

Leonard Weinglass' opening statement for the defense emphasizes the new life style, youth culture and the Yippies, these young people came to Chicago to show that there was an emergent new culture in the country and in the world. Throughout Weinglass' address, Judge Hoffman and assistant flunky Shultz have played the "objection-sustained" game, a game that will continue to be played between the Hoffman-Shultz-Foran team of pawns for the prosecution in an attempt to humiliate the defense attorneys in front of the jury. As the trial plods on exposing the hideous entrails of the Nixon administration with every desperate motion and ploy, it will become necessary only for Foran to stand up, and Hoffman will ask on call, "Do you object? – I'll sustain the objection." The travesty is apparently being allowed to continue until one of his grim reapers advises the President what to do. Or until things become so hopelessly convoluted that, having no alternative, the federal government flies up its own asshole. At the completion of the Weinglass address, Judge Hoffman asks, "Are there any other defense attorneys

who wish to speak?" Defendant Bobby Seale stands and walks to the lectern. Hoffman: "Who's your lawyer?" Seale: "Charles R. Garry."

NO VISIBLE JUSTICE

Hoffman dismisses the jury. He then demands to know which of the attorneys at the defendants' table represents Defendant Seale. Citing the statement addressed to the bench this morning by Seale, Kunstler states that since he has "fired" the attorneys present and petitioned for representation by Garry, neither he nor Weinglass have the authority to speak for Seale. Hoffman denies Bobby Seale the right to give an opening statement in his own defense. Bobby Seale, defendant in a government trial, sits in a courtroom in Chicago, and, for all technical reasons, he is without legal counsel.

The first witness for the prosecution is put on the stand: Raymond Simon, Corporate Counsel for the City of Chicago, legal representative of Mayor Daley and the city aldermen, and of the City of Chicago as a corporate entity. He speaks at length of meetings with Abbie Hoffman, Jerry Rubin and Rennie Davis in the months prior to the convention their applications for park and matching permits and their "non-negotiable" demands. Things lurch along until finally the court is recessed, followed by word that the U.S. Court of Appeals has denied the defense's Mandamus action for postponement until Charles R. Garry can appear. It has also denied the defense's motion to release its 4 attorneys from the threat of arrest. When this announcement was made to the court by Hoffman, he followed up by stating that attorneys Lefcourt and Tigar would be held in custody over the weekend without bail. *About*

racy Trial

CONSPIRACY V. KANGAROOS

On October 14, the defense moved to have the trial adjourned for one day in observance of the October 15th Moratorium. The judge denied the motion, so next day, Abbie Hoffman and Rennie Davis unfurled a Viet Cong flag in the courtroom and had a tug of war with a Federal Marshall before it was taken away. The defendants wore black armbands (as they had on October 8 — anniversary of the death of Che Guevara) and Dave Dellinger read names of Americans killed in Vietnam until the judge entered the chamber and ordered him to stop.

The Yippies have published an 'official souvenir program' for the trial, which they parodied as a baseball match between The Chicago Conspiracy (the defense) and The Washington Kangaroos (the prosecution).

Abbie Hoffman and Jerry Rubin made an after hours trip to Washington where they posed in boxing gloves and offered to fight the US Attorney General, but Tom Hayden, writing for the *Guardian* (a New York radical weekly) on November 1 noted that the trial had ceased to have its initial carnival atmosphere.

'We no longer humorously refer to federal judge Julius Hoffman as "Magoo" (a reference to a comic character the judge is said to resemble) but as "Adolph Hitler Hoffman."

The first 21 government witnesses have been from the Chicago police department and the FBI. Their testimony has unfolded as an attack on the movement, political ideas, language and style rather than on concrete crimes. The most concrete action charged any of the defendants so far was letting the air out of police car tires, throwing sweaters at undercover agents and other trivia which defense attorney William Kunstler asserts belong in a municipal police court, not before the federal bench.

NO SHINS KICKED

Occasionally there is a fantastic claim such as the one that Rennie Davis arranged for live television coverage in front of the Conrad Hilton hotel August 27 and then ordered Mobilization marshalls to kick the line of policemen in the shins so demonstrators would be clubbed before the TV audience. On this particular charge as on many others, cross-examination revealed no shins were kicked. The heavy emphasis in the police testimony has been on the provocative language and identity of the defendants. With a pretense at embarrassment officer after officer tells the jury that the defendants shouted, "Fuck LBJ," "Ho, Ho, Ho Chi Minh" and other chants.

When defense attorneys ask police if any obscenities were used by them while clubbing demonstrators, they are given pious denials. The most any police witness has acknowledged is that he heard one officer say to another, "These little sons of bitches are really tough . . ."

The Conspiracy is attempting to pinpoint the blame for the Chicago malee on authorities at the highest level and show that the trial is an integral part of a national policy to institute a legalized fascism. The Nixon administration, according to the defendants, is rigging the Supreme Court and Justice Department with reactionary political figures prepared to go beyond present Constitutional standards towards a new policy of reaction.

As examples of a move toward fascism, there are the proceedings of the Conspiracy trial itself. For example, the government has admitted illegal wiretapping of defendants but asks the court to uphold wiretapping in the overriding interest of national security. Furthermore, the prosecution case cites as "evidence" of crime speeches given before and during the convention to public meetings where there was no evidence whatsoever of a 'clear and present danger to the peace.'

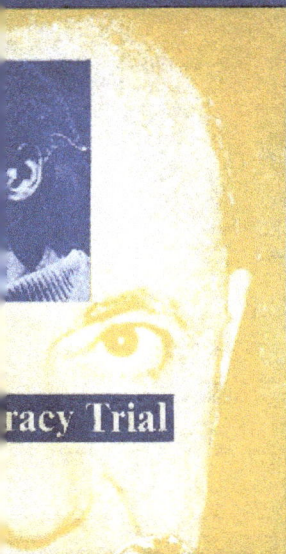

The Conspiracy is waging a struggle co-ordinating the defense inside the courtroom with a political campaign on the outside to stop the trial. The defense case will try to re-enact what happened in Chicago and bring political figures such as Lyndon Johnson and Mayor Richard Daley to explain their policies. Leaders of the civil rights, academic and liberal communities are expected to testify about what happened in Chicago as well as ordinary people who were beaten or gassed in the streets.

SHOWDOWN AT CHICAGO

The Conspiracy hopes to make part of its defense a "people's case" and encourages all witnesses to return to testify.

Since the trial has sparked widespread international concern, the Conspiracy hopes to turn it into a political showdown.

Dave Dellinger, at the request of the Black Panther party, announced the possibility of releasing U.S. military prisoners in Vietnam if and when the U.S. unconditionally released Bobby Seale and Panther leader Huey Newton. Panther Eldridge Cleaver has been in consultation with the Vietnamese about this. The political import is that Seale and Newton are not simply political prisoners but prisoners of war because it's a military policy the government utilizes against the Panthers. Dellinger and Davis asked to be allowed to go to Paris to discuss release of American prisoners with the North Vietnamese delegation to the peace talks. Hoffman denied permission, but lawyer Kunstler went instead.

CAKE NAPPING

One of the most tumultuous scenes in the court last week was when seven Panthers were not permitted to bring a cake into the courtroom to celebrate defendant Seale's 34th birthday. Hoffman denied a request from Kunstler to celebrate the birthday. After a recess, as the defendants emerged from the conference room in ceremonial procession with the cake inscribed "Free Huey and Bobby" across it, a line of marshals wrested the cake from Jerry Rubin.

"That's a cake-napping!" shouted Abbie Hoffman and Rennie Davis turned to Seale and said "Hey Bobby, they've arrested your cake."

"They've arrested a cake," said Seale loudly, "but they can't arrest a revolution."

The Panthers seated in the second row shouted "Right on!" and raised their fists.

When Hoffman ordered the spectators to be silent Seale turned to his supporters and said, "Okay, brothers, just sit in the courtroom and listen and don't say anything."

"I give the orders here, sir," said Hoffman.

"They don't take orders from a racist judge," Seale replied.

Seale was soon to have more troubles than the loss of a birthday cake.

Seale as slave: the word from Chicago is "Stop the trial" headlined *Liberation News Service:* "Bobby Seale the national leader of a militant political group dedicated to the liberation of black people, has been gagged and strapped to his chair . . . If it weren't Bobby Seale, if presiding Judge Julius J. Hoffman didn't have the power of the state on his side, one might see it all as a tableau from the Theatre of Cruelty. But Bobby Seale's situation is more than symbolic. It is real, and there is only one way to describe it — slavery. Seale is a black man in chains whose fate is now determined by the masters in their mansions . . . Seale's ordeal is a reasoned if cruel response to his position as leader of the Black Panther Party.

SEALE AS SLAVE

Some time before he and his chair are carried into the wood-panelled courtroom, a team of marshals go to work on him. His boots are loosened and his legs are bound with heavy leather straps to the legs of a folding chair. His wrists, wound several times with leather, are buckled to its arms. Several layers of gauze, adhesive tape, and cloth are wound around his mouth and tied at the back of his head. A similar gag is wound vertically around his jaw and tied at the top of his head. The type of gauze used resembles that used by football players to hold a trick knee in place . . . The press, the judge and the prosecution have attempted to portray Seale as a wildman engaging in 'disruption' and 'outbursts'. It is clear, however, that there would be no shouting if the judge would allow Seale to defend himself, or postpone the trial until Seale's lawyer, Charles R. Garry, recovers from an operation.

. . . On Seale's second day in the rig, prosecuting attorney Richard Schultz provoked Seale by falsely accusing him of inciting violence (Seale had told Panthers in the courtroom to cool it but to act in self defense if attacked) Seale shouted through the gag in protest and tipped over his chair. The marshals attacked him, punching him in the face and groin. Jerry Rubin rose to protest, but a marshal elbowed him in the mouth . . . Tom Hayden's plea that Seale should not be put 'in a position of slavery' fell on deaf ears. Rennie Davis tried to tell the jury about Seale's mistreatment, but was silenced and threatened with contempt charges . . . Abbie Hoffman put the courtroom blowups in context: "The disruption started when 'these marshals' got into overkill. Referring to the heated atmosphere and gridded ceiling of ghostly white fluorescent lighting, Abbie remarked, "This ain't a courtroom. It's a neon oven."

BARREL SCRAPINGS

The prosecution case is baking slowly. Observers both friendly and hostile to the Justice Department have expressed surprise at the legal weakness of the government's case. So far, almost all testimony has come from hack politicians loyal to Mayor Daley, policemen, and paid informers. "We're scraping the bottom of the barrel," prosecutor Schultz was overheard saying. Meanwhile, Movement forces around the country are beginning to mobilise around the necessity of stopping the trial. No one knows how or if it can be stopped, but the trial is making it absolutely clear that the courts are an integral part of America's repressive machinery. Demanding an end to this trial and freedom for all political prisoners is a logical extension of the struggles for black liberation and against imperialistic war . . . because this repression is a blatant attempt to destroy those movements as well as to wipe out the insurgent youth politics and culture which threaten the sick and dying regime." L.N.S.

Anthony Lorraine has returned home to Oxford after spending fifteen months in a Russian prison. He was arrested in Tashkent on a charge of smuggling cannabis and given a three year sentence. He was released in October — along with fellow hash-head Michael Parsons and 'spy' Gerald Brook — in exchange for the Krogers. Judging from an account of the latter's thuggish incarceration in Parkhurst and Holloway (see Private Eye No. 198), the Russians enjoyed a relatively civilised treatment notwithstanding the chilling indifference of the British consul in Moscow. Lorraine was surprised by his arrest, as the Russians generally overlook petty smugglers, preferring instead to extract the dollars from the tourists. Five months were spent in solitary confinement, awaiting trial, then 11 months in a forced labour camp and the rest in a Moscow prison. This is Anthony Lorraine's own story.

Tashkent

For those of us who came out of Hindustan going west into Germanic Europe it was against the water. Bombay was another white bread and quick cutting Hollywood satellite, but India still gave: colour and silks and a gentle hospitality in passage. In Goa we emerged from the sea, naked-salted, to bathe in sweet landwater and fruit juices. From Katmandu the mountain Tibetans offered goat's milk and vengeance.

A day's waiting on the steps of the Afghani consul in Peshawar got us visas. As cholera mounted to close the Iran land border the Soviets were quite willing to offer their side-route. Come please pay in dollars.

BUSTED
The Central Asian Soviet republics illegalised cannabis in 1942. But generally the cops show the cool, not in the streets. This was a bad month in Tashkent. I was caught holding in pockets and shoulder bag ... on the customs declaration you signed on entering the country ...

Oxford

1. The Great Alienator

After his fifteen months in a Russian prison Anthony Lorraine returns home to Oxford – where, according to our student contributors, another prison system is in full swing – the University. Its effect is more subtly and extensively pernicious, because, as these students point out, the inmates are unaware of their own oppression.

In 1209, there was widespread rioting after the lynching of two undergraduates; as a result the University nearly collapsed.

In 1355, on St. Scholastica's day, every member of the University was killed, wounded, or driven out; for this massacre, the townsfolk had to say a penitentiary Mass annually until 1825. In 1969, what? On the surface, little – the old student-skinhead clash, the yearly injunction to Gentlemen not to venture out on Bonfire Night, a drunken brawl when an undergraduate ventures into a Town pub. To most people – many students included – the old Town-Gown split has disappeared; but a tragic rift still exists and the machinery of the University – by accident or design – creates this rift.

On coming up, the student is met firstly with servility. He is cast in the role of Young Gentlemen; the town is here to serve him, and when he doesn't exploit

it, he can just ignore it. His meals are served to him, his shoes are polished, his cups are washed, his bed is made. Old Bert and Mrs Baggins scurry round his mausoleum, tidying him up.

Scouts and bedders (they make beds, not sleep in them) earn £8-£12 a week, and often live in tied houses. They can start work as early as 6 a.m., cleaning lavatories and scrubbing floors before they call their young gentlemen for breakfast. To supplement their income, they also serve meals in Hall and work in the kitchens.

After his college servants, the only other townie a student will be in regular contact with is his landlady. Moral watchdog, warder extraordinary, she will (s)mother him ruthlessly. Their conversation, far from being restricted to discussions on the weather and one's health, soars to such philosophical heights as to encompass the morality of leaving a dirty ring around the bath.

Undergraduates have to live in registered lodgings on pain of losing their degree. Digs cannot be registered unless they have a resident landlady whose duty it is to enforce the same fascist rules imposed on a student living in college – no loud music, no guests after midnight, no cooking in rooms, no radical alterations to be made to the sterile decor, &c, &c. As of October 1970 – nearly a year after 18-year-olds become adults in law – undergraduates will be able to live in unregistered digs, if approval is given by the College Dean; this could mean even more restrictive rules.

When he isn't met with servility, the Oxford student finds hostility. He is taught only one way of relating to people – via the father-son relationship. He shows filial loyalty and obedience to his college and a paternal interest in, and difference from, his scout and bedder. Having been told how wonderful he is to have got to Oxford (crap!), the only attitude he can have towards townies is one of patronage; after all, the only townies he meets are college servants. He

is a little put out when this pose is resented by his contemporaries who are natives of Oxford. The great Youth Culture which transcends all barriers of class, race and wealth just hasn't been heard of in Oxford. Students dress as they please, and can usually afford more and better clothes anyway; there are society meetings/plays/happenings every night – but open only to 'members of the University and their guests'; the best groups come to play at exclusively student functions, such as Summer balls (one recent exception was Jethro Tull at the Town Hall).

The young adults in the town – mostly assembly-line workers from Cowley – feel justifiably bitter about their underprivileged status. It's the working class/middle class conflict all over again, here accentuated by the fact that the middle class element is also immigrant. In theory, 10% of Oxford students are working class, but there is no class-consciousness, no attempt to identify with the working-class youths of Oxford; the only calls for student-worker solidarity come from ex-public schoolboys having a last (and first) fling before going into Daddy's firm. The fact is that working class students are here because they want to be middle class, and therefore hold to bourgeois values more fervently than the actual scions of the bourgeoisie.

The antagonism between undergraduates and citizen, usually transmuted into apathy and mutual contempt and ignorance, is carried on into the student's later life. At Oxford he is imbued with the elitist ideal and convinced of his own superiority; he is destined to become a manager, a manipulator of men. Yet there is no one more singularly ill-fitted for this task than the Oxford graduate. A greater awareness among people that they are people, not objects, necessitates not just a change in management techniques, but the complete abolition of the manager/worker dichotomy. But Oxford still churns out reactionary anachronisms, committed to the perpetuation of the System. Yet it is not enough to change the University; society itself is still class-structured, still demands an aristocracy. To think a change in the academic world will precipitate revolution on a wider front (a common delusion among 'Revolutionary socialist students') is like believing a change of condom will bring about a fresh erection; the underlying structure needs to be revitalised and reoriented. So what can we do who faintly perceive and incoherently outline the rottenness that is the University, not just the rottenness that is in it? The apathetic revolutionary is just as much a product of the system as the grey man; and he stands just as much chance of breaking out. We are all prisoners, we are all dead, we are all unborn.

Roj Jarman (St. Peters)

2. The Great Masturbatorium

Oxford University is a prison, if an open one, and the colleges are its cells; only their inmates stay there of their own accord, and the locks and bars that kill the freedom in them are only partly physical. As a rule, the serfdom of students in Oxford is accepted by them without reflection or regret. It is an integral part of the voluntary servitude and abnegation of human possibilities that is the typical form of contemporary bureaucratic capitalist society. Moreover, in Oxford as elsewhere, a glittering spectacle has evolved as a compensation for the real poverty of everyday life. Each person finds consolation for his lack of genuine identity or satisfaction in life by discovering, almost as if by accident, a ready-made role in the ongoing spectacle – fearless free thinker, sexy young bluestocking, youthful protester ... Though most students are none of these things, except in front of cameras or the eyes of admiring spectators, the pretence that they are enables the spectacle to be perpetuated endlessly – a rehearsal for a drama that is never actually performed, but which receives the enthusiastic acclaim or indignant criticism of reviewers.

The first emotion of virtually every undergraduate on arrival in Oxford is astonished disappointment that there are so few women (one to every five men). The second feeling, experienced by a significant minority of men after having met a few of these women, is grateful relief that there aren't any more about than there are already. For the Oxford undergraduate is, as a rule, stupid, sexless and ugly. She spends almost all of her time working, and whatever leisure she permits herself she consumes in ostentatious public appearances with domesticated, easily manageable, and altogether innocent males.

It cannot be denied, on the other hand, that this is a state of affairs about which few Oxford men experience any great anxiety. For most undergraduates, sex is like toothache, a nuisance of not much importance, and certainly nowhere near as absorbing as work, sport or drink. Vestigial physical needs can always be purged by pornography or masturbatory phantasy (Oxford must surely be the world's wet dream capital). Like castrated tomcats, undergraduates have better things to do than to screw. Oxford students have, it is true, no lack of plausible excuses for putting up with this situation. Most colleges lock up their inmates at or around midnight, and special permission of a passkey is needed to be absent overnight. Being discovered with a girl in your room after visiting hours (which vary from college to college) still entails disciplinary sanctions – loss of one's rooms in college, or even rustication. All undergraduates have servants who are obliged to enter one's bedroom every morning, and wake one Why do so few students at Oxford try to erode the system of supervision and inspection or even actively resent it? It must be confessed that students at

Oxford are only conforming to the University's expectations in regard to them. The system of selection, relying heavily as it does on special scholarship examinations and personal interviews in the college to which one has applied, predetermines the character-types of those who are admitted about as effectively as it domesticates them even further once they are inmates. The ideal Oxford applicant is highly uninventive, wholly apolitical, sexually neutered, and, on the whole, not very bright.

In all justice, however, the internal social system of Oxford University cannot be arbitrarily separated for purposes of analysis from the social system of Britain as a whole. The ancient universities perform an indispensable function in securing the social totality against the threat of qualitative change posed by its own contradictions. A new breed of servile specialist must be developed to harry the workers into their scientifically managed factories and rationalised offices. Oxford succeeds in doing this with its placid traditions of urbanity and moral agnosticism; Oxford soon assimilates, moreover, all but an intransigent minority of its working-class intake. Finally, Oxford provides for the rest of society an indispensable spectacle of contemporary student life – permissive and fearlessly critical, free loving and free thinking – which is objectively necessary to a system that provides as much for liberal reformists (who applaud student life) as for conservative Jeremiahs (who deplore it), and, in both cases, supplies them with the appropriate mirage of the student's predicament.

To those not caught up in the situation, it is almost inconceivable, but to those who are in it, it is almost intolerable. What can be done? Nothing will be achieved if we await the eventual awakening of the sleeping majority of the students in Oxford. They are happy slaves, and they do not find their fate at all objectionable. Nor can any effective organisation of dissidence be achieved if it relies on the discredited strategies of passive political mobilisation and rentacrowd militancy favoured by the Left in Oxford. Rather what is required of the critical minority in Oxford is a determined attempt to construct an alternative mode of everyday life, freed of the banality and emptiness of its established opponent. And at the same time, by a non-stop cultural harrassment, to ridicule and scorn both the pieties of the system and the pretences of our fellow undergraduates. A resolute refusal to invent any role for oneself in the obscene spectacle of Oxford life; a rigorous struggle to contest, deflate and demolish its decadent carnival; and a patient effort to construct an authentic alternative to the spectacle (rather than an alternative spectacle); a mode of everyday life that isn't any longer a variation of the death-game – nothing less can possibly be enough.

John N Gray (Exeter)

'The Lebanon:'

The Hole of the Lebanese Black

by Harvey Matusow

The Lebanese caught the bug, and in March started to crack down on westerners on the hash scene. Since the crackdown started upwards of fifty British, American and other Europeans have been busted. The majority of these arrested are in their twenties or early thirties, but one British women age 64 was also gaoled.

The Lebanese law provides for no extenuating circumstances — no consideration of the individual's background or the fact that the offense may have been the individual's first — In addition to this, there is no remission for good behavior, and no parole.

The law there calls for sentences of between three and fifteen years if you are convicted of trafficking, and a one year sentence if you're found in possession of hash for your own use.

CONNED BY DEALERS

If you get the one year sentence it's possible to serve it in the Asfourieh mental hospital, and you can get a reduction to six months if the doctor there certifies that you've given up using the stuff.

One of the dangers in Lebanon is that the kids are being conned by Lebanese hash dealers into believing that the stuff is legal, and that they can make a connection with someone at customs. There are a few documented cases where the Lebanese pusher sold a cat some hash, and a double bottom suit case, then informed to the customs so as to collect a reward of 50 Lebanese pounds for every pound of stuff you're caught with.

One British chick was caught recently with 25 pounds of hashish strapped around her waist, claimed that she was forced by her boy friend to carry it. She was convicted, then suffered a nervous breakdown — had to be moved to a mental hospital — and is now back in prison.

While most of those busted plead guilty at least two Americans recently busted claimed that they were innocent victims of others who tried to smuggle the stuff out by planting it in their cars. It's not infrequent to hear the assertion that smugglers pick a patsy who has a car, and then conceal the hashish in the car — inside the petrol tank or the tyres or elsewhere, where a confederate can recover it when the cat reaches its destination.

SLEEPING LIKE SPOONS

One American who just finished a three year sentence, Elliot Fayad claimed this happened to him. He told about the prison conditions in the Sands Prison where people await trial with others already convicted.

He said it was built in Ottoman times to house 600 people and now has over 1,200.

'Seventy to eighty persons occupy rooms 20 by 30 feet' he said, 'and at night they have to sleep on their sides, fitted together like spoons, and in the daytime they roll up their blankets to form passageways among them. There are no beds.'

'Only one hour a day is allowed for exercise, walking in the courtyard, while others, usually the poor ones who'd been paid with cigarettes clean the place up.'

'Food is brought in once a day. It's cooked, but cold on arrival, and is a real problem for non-Lebanese to get used to.'

He also said that once a week they had a meal of rice and beans which was considered a treat.

The toilet is a hole in the floor that tended to fill up after 9 PM when the water was turned off.

Foreigners had a double problem in not understanding the language. The noise he claimed was unbelievable. There are at least two fights a day, and if the guard sees it, both men are beaten.

HEADS FOR SCAPE-GOATS

Fayad said he saw shortly before his release, two Americans severely beaten by the guards and thrown into a dungeon for four days, after they were caught smoking some hash which had been smuggled in.

All in all, the scene in Lebanon today is acutely anti-Western, mainly due to the political tensions in the Middle-East, and any western kid caught is liable to get an extra pounding. Putting an 'imperialist pot smoker' in prison, is a good diversion in a country split down the middle politically and needing scape-goats.

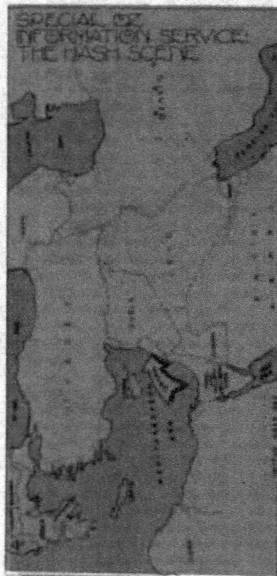

SPECIAL OZ INFORMATION SERVICE: THE HASH SCENE

I.T. 27, ENDELL ST. LONDON W.C.2 3 QUID A YEAR

November 15th is the threshold of our dream

THRESHOLD

The Moody Blues
To Our Childrens Childrens Children
THM–THS 1 (album)

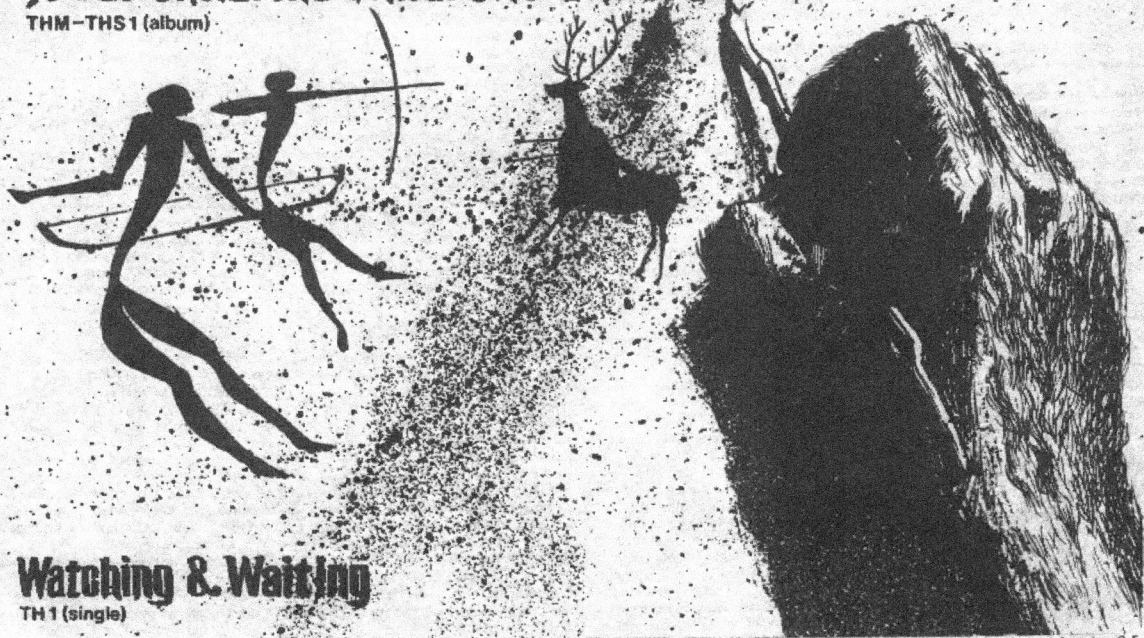

Watching & Waiting
TH 1 (single)

THRESHOLD RECORDS, THE DECCA RECORD COMPANY LIMITED, Decca House, 9 Albert Embankment, London S E 1

Goodbye Jack Kerouac

David Widgery

VILLAGE FRUIT MARKET

'KIND KING MIND/Allen Ginsberg called me' *Mexico City Blues, 5th Chorus*, 'a girl once told me I had a steel trap brain, meaning I'd catch her out with a statement she'd made an hour ago even though our talk had rambled a million light years from that point' *Jack Kerouac*. 'Poets are God's spies' *F8 Shelley*.

Ti Jean, Vanity Duluoz, Sal Kerouac, you're gone now. You died age 46 in your house in Lowell, Mass. where you lived with your crippled mother and suspicious wife of one year, Stella, and they decided to do to you the American death thing and have you mummified, thread your veins with formaldehyde, tie a bow tie in position and clad your face in certain deathly cosmetics. And though Ginsberg, Orlovsky and Holmes stayed by you gently at night, dawn was soon and a Massachusetts funeral.

MARMITE AND BOP

To read Kerouac when you were 15, scrabbling through the Ks of Slough Public Library, was a social message of discontent; the sudden realisation of an utter subversiveness and licence. He legitimised all the papery efforts of a child writer, dream books, pretend novellas, invented games, planned and described walkouts. He expressed a solution to the pentupness, restlessness of youth that feeling of wanking off inside all the time.[1] Everyone I know remembers where they were when they read 'On The Road' whether newly expelled from school, public librarians (trainee) in Hammersmith, car park attendants in Dorking, knowledgeable Eisenhower drunks or hospital porters because of the sudden sense of infinite possibility. You could, just like that, get off out of it into infinite hitchhiking futures. Armed only with a duffle coat you could be listening to wild jazz on the banks of the Tyne or travelling east-west, across the Pennines. Mostly we never actually went, or the beer wore off by Baldock High Street and you were sober and so cold. But we were able to recognise each other by that fine, wild, windy prose and the running away motif that made so much sense. I, like ten

thousand other fifth formers, wrote series of letters in imitation of Kerouac, spiralling indiscriminate word patterns and being able, in his shadow, to write thewordstogether if I so wanted to. A Canadian friend who thought he was Dean Moriarty sent me a notebook bound in smelly red cellophane about his runaway with an autocycle and packet of marmite sandwiches which he was forced to abandon in a snow drift after two miles. The notebook was about 80 pages yet seemed proper and as it ought to happen and all accountable within the terms of spontaneous bop prosody. Jazz was the other part of our underground because it meant beer and beards and arguing about the 4th trumpet in Kenton's reconstructed front line like stamp collectors. We would get three-quarters drunk and listen to Charlie Parker who seemed to be trying to sound like Kerouac too if you listened to the breath sounds and the oral punctuation. 'Yes, jazz and bop, in the sense of a, say, tenor man drawing a breath and blowing a phrase on his saxophone, till he runs out of breath, and when he does, his sentence, his statement has been made . . . that's how I therefore separate my sentences as breath separations of the mind . . . there's the raciness and freedom and humour of jazz instead of all that dreary analysis and things like 'James entered the room and lit a cigarette. He thought Jane might have thought this but made a gesture.'[1] When Honey Carmichael heard Bix Biederbeck, he fell off his chair. When Tom Pione was in hiding, he found shelter at the house of William Blake. Now I'd been getting bored with the stereotyped changes that were being used all the time, and I kept thinking there's bound to be something else, I could hear it sometimes but I couldn't play it. I was doing alright until I tried double tempo on Body and Soul. Everyone fell out laughing, I went home and cried and didn't play again for three months.[2]

RED SHIFT, BIG BANG

Kerouac's writing started with home drawn comic strips, home made comix, whole childhood exercise book novels, long systems for horse-racing and basketball games in the comfort of your front room played with symbols and pieces of paper money. At 18 I read Hemingway and Saroyan and began writing terse little stories in that general style. Then I read Tom Wolfe and began to write in the rolling style. Then I read Joyce and wrote a juvenile novel like Ulysses called "Vanity of Duluoz". Then

came Dostoevsky. Finally, I entered a romantic phase with Rimbaud and Blake which I called my "self-ultimacy period", blurring what I wrote in order to be self-ultimate. At the age of 24, I was groomed for the Western idealistic concept of letters from reading Goethe's Dichtung und Wahreit. The discovery of a style of my own based on a spontaneous get-with-it, came after reading the marvellous free narrative letters of Neal Cassady, a great writer who happens to be the Dean Moriarty of "On The Road".[3] Cassady might, reluctantly, be compared to Trotsky in his historical span. Just as Trotsky is the sole link between Bolshevism and the post-war revolutionary movement so it was Cassady who was the only human link between the West Coast beats and the post-Leary hippies, acting as the driver of Ken Kesey's acidic bus Further. He stayed magnificently the same. In Kerouac he's this incredible talker, lost into a blue streak that's going to last all his life, pulsating even when silent where once Dean would have talked his way out, he now feels silent himself, but standing in front of everyone, ragged and broken and idiotic, right in front of the light bulbs, his mind face covered with sweat and throbbing veins, saying "Yes, yes," just as though tremendous revelations were pouring into him the whole time now, and I am convinced they were, and the others suspected as much and were frightened. He was BEAT-the root, the soul of beatific.[4] And 16 years later when drug-casseroled ex-novelist Kesey makes his American migration, there Cassady sat driving the bus Cassady had been a rock on the trip the 'totally dependable person, when everyone else was stroked out with fatigue or the various pressures, Cassady could be still depended on to move. It was as if he never slept and didn't need to.

For all his wild driving, he always made it through the last oiled nap in the maze, like he knew it would be there all the time, which it always was. When the bus broke down, Cassady drove into its innards and fixed it. He changed tyres, tugging and heaving and jolting and bolting with his fantastic muscles popping out striation by striation and his basilic veins gorged with blood and speed.[5] Now Cassady's dead too. His body was found beside a railroad track outside the town of San Miguel de Allende in Mexico. It was said that he had been despondent and felt that he was growing old and had been on a long downer and had made the mistake of drinking alcohol or top of barbiturates. His body was cremated. (Marshall Bloom founding figure of the American Underground Press killed himself six weeks ago by connecting the exhaust pipe of a running car to the closed car interior but this he's not in this story.)

BULLET BEAT

Cassady's writing had started, like Kerouac's, in the slow painstaking, creative-writing-course-by-post way. Then he wrote The First Third a novel about his childhood with his alcoholic father in the Denver alley wineshops and Greyhound station johns and the way they talked to each other (like Kesey's acid soaked Pranksters) with 'minds weakened by liquor and an obsequious manner of existence, seeming continually preoccupied with bringing up short observations of obvious trash, said in such a way as to be instantly recognisable to the listener, who has heard it all before and whose own prime concern was to nod at everything said, then continue the conversation with a remark of his own, equally transparent and loaded with generalities.[6] Cassady sent Kerouac a 40,000 word letter (now called the Joan Anderson letter) which Kerouac describes as 'the greatest piece of writing I ever saw, better'n anyone in America, or at least enough to make Melville, Twain, Dreiser, Wolfe I dunno who, spin in their graves' and which disappeared overboard into the sea. Kerouac and Cassady could talk each other into a state of semi-trance where their unrepressed word-slinging boiled up into a big shootout, bulletwords

40

wizzing backwards and forwards with words that were slippery without being gelatinous and made you tremble when you read them. We did much fast talking, on tape recorders, way back in '52 and listened to them so much we both got the secret of LINGO in telling a tale and figure that was the only way to express the speed and tension and the extatic torn foolery of the age. Kerouac/Cassady learned from this to cerve and move their acoustic prose in the air, sustaining the long line by breath, rubbish image, riff, dazzling phrasing making an awkward tightrope walk like Chaplin about to fall but never quite doing so since able to 'add alluvials to the end of your line when all is exhausted but something has to be said for some specified irrational reason'. It's from Kerouac's sound not the coterie poetics of Creely/Olson that is behind Ginsberg's rush on language. And from all three Americans the florid young British poets of the 50s fed, watching bootlegged copies from Ferlinghetti's City Lights Press and the other artistic contraband which made possible the dense undergrowth of the British small poetry magazines (especially Poetmeat, early Underdog, and the shortbreathed and 'substantial' New Departures). Mike Horovitz, whose

mattress prose, tour is interior spring describes the impact of the American orals on or off the page. British poetry wonderfully well in his afterword to Penguins Poetry of the 'Underground' in Britain.

Ferlinghetti had always been social and political 'all this droopy corn about the beat generation and its being "existentialist" is as phoney as a tick dollar piece of lettuce . . . only the dead are disengaged. And the wage earners of the beat hipster, if carried to the logical consequences actually means the death of the creative artist himself.' Ginsberg increasingly became political after his decision to 'expose self and accuse America'. But not Kerouac 'I agree with Joyce, as Joyce said to Ezra Pound in the 1920s, "Don't bother me with politics, the only thing that interests me is style".' Nowadays he seems to dismiss the holy goofing grey cats and wine lips of the San Francisco poetry gang 'Ferlinghetti and Ginsberg, they are very socialistically minded and wanted everyone to live in some sort of frantic kibbutz, solidarity and all that. I'm a loner'. Kerouac was the lonesome traveller jumping out of cars, into freight waggons, merchant holds, going and going as if by his movement alone he could become a molecule in a marvellous unity. He deeply wanted to believe in a total unification of the Golden Buddhist eternity; his religion was his ultimate resource and he saw it mostly in nature; the misty swelling and blooming of the seasons, sea and red wood trees he watched over for a spell. This was the wonderful still centre within all his energy; the baby Ti Jean with kitten and candy bar on pillow while the absolutely evil Dr Sax caused the swelling city dust to rise sucking and slapping in the streets of Lowell.

It is said that as a child Kerouac discovered trying to fuck the world found with his prick buried in snow.

WHAT HAPPENED

This handsome traveling man who drove and wrote across the bigness of the States as a great figure of the real vagrant American. To the fake America of the fifties of Ike and Perry Mason's fight against freedom, in the symbol worshipping, silent, bad sociology writing, thick fifties, his very existence was a protest. Against that world's addiction to the reasonable, Kerouac's response was not political or critical — he just damned them with his energy.

Against the moral ruin of their world he replied in every second of his time with his creative act. He insulted them, almost without knowing it himself, with his exuberance, his wonder, his emotions, almost crazed by the torrent of experience and finally devoured by his own appetite. Compared with him the alleged novelists of dissent on the side of Atlantic look and were mean, conservative and trivial.

But he seemed imprisoned within his wonder and his age, the Fifties. He doesn't so much develop as a writer as accumulate reworking the themes of his witness of the beats, of his brother Gerald and finally, of Mexico City and Paris with a steadily growing intensity. The compulsive nature of his writing could turn pathological; drugs and writing were the organising principles of his life, and death. Notoriety and public confession in literary form is a frontier of the heart you were born with, believe me'. He was unable to alter the pace set by his mind which was as out of breath at 45 as it was at his birth around 15. He wrote, like Victor Serge, single spacing on a continuous typewriter roll at a punishing rate (in Tangier he typed Naked Lunch for Burroughs). The Subterraneans was written in three days a physical feat much harder than the athletic struggles of the windy field leaving him as white as a sheet and having lost 15 pounds and looking strange in the mirror. His bubble brook book Sartori in Paris was written on cognac and malt whiskey. Tristessa the fine mystic novel about a Mexican girl faint for morphine and the remarkable Mexico City poems were direct from his life in Mexico where his life and writing intersected dangerously. The vain records of the pagerity of the West Coast Beats 'Desolation Angels' 'Big Sur' and 'The Subs' indicate the pace at which he lived, the tension level at which the books are charged. Book of Dreams used even his sleeping life for material 'in a style of a person half awake from sleep

and ripping it out in pencil by the bed . . . yes, pencil . . . what a job, bleary eyes, insaned mind teaming and mystified by sleep, details that pop out even as you write them you don't know what they mean, till you wake up have coffee, look at it and see the logic of the dream from the language itself.' He was the last American to write quite like this, the great Romantic a naked sheet wound round experience and registering it in wonder 'the true story of what I saw and how I saw it'.

As he grew unrelentingly older, he grew, logically patriotic and sentimental. A rare public meeting he spoke to in Southern Italy was broken up by dumbfounded Italian kids when he defended the American war in Vietnam. His drunkenness, made adventuring, lumberjack clothes (now looking uncannily like the handsome Ronald Reagan) were of a different world now. He must have sensed it was impossible to keep hold of his old human universe when he retreated to his bungalow in Lowell. Like Dylan his quietism is only objectionable if you interpret politically which, of course you have to. When people started fighting back against the monster America the nitrose radicals, Trotskyists, Black Panthers they do so in a way that excludes him . . . even disgusts him. For now protest is nowhere near enough. It's too conventional and we need to fight America with all the science it is using to destroy us. And we must win.

We have to blaspheme against Kerouac's religiosity and be wary of his colossal nervous system. He is a precious voice but from the past. When we win we can name streets and stars after him.

1. Paris Review 43, Kerouac Interview.
2. 'Hear Me Talking to You' P. 342 Charlie Parker.
3. The New American Poetry, Don Allen P. 43.
4. 'On the Road'.
5. 'The Electric Cool Aid Acid Test' Tom Wolfe P. 101.
6. 'The First Third' City Lights Journal Number 2.
7. The New American Poetry' Don Allen P. 414.
8. The New American Poetry' Don Allen P. 412.
9. Eric Mottram Introduction 'Flight From America' All other Kerouac quotations Paris Review.

A Sad Letter

Dear Sir!
Some weeks ago I saw an invitation in your paper asking all foreigners in Turkish prisons to report about their cases, sentences and about general circumstances.

I was arrested in spring of '66 being in possession of 1 Kg. of hash. It happened at the frontier station 'Uzunkopru' on the occasion of custom control on my way back to Germany. After five months I was sentenced to 'lifetime' only the fact being a seriously disabled man (Brain injured and now again right sides paralysed) cut down this sentence to '30 years'. During the hearings 'without lawyer' and in unknowledge of the law in this country but the Turkish court didn't bother about that.

My consulate wrote a request to the court asking for a lawyer, but no result and I was punished without possibility of defence. At least finally I tried to make a speech for the defence myself, but the Judge didn't like it and cut off my speech.

I mentioned several times I smoke hash myself and the stuff is for my own use, because I am seriously war disabled and suffering very much from pain, but no reaction at all.

After getting my sentence still in court, the translator told me I had got to serve my time but 'only 20 years' because 10 years of my sentence is a free part if I am a good prisoner, isn't that broad-minded? On the whole and by and large they really improve their barbarism.

My next thought was to appeal, of course it is possible, but the question was how to do it? During the whole trial without a bill of indictment, that means, without number of files, and after the condemnation without argument of trial, last nothing at all. The same day after condemnation I informed my consulate by an urgent letter and they tried to get the number of the files. If you don't mind I am telling you, after the consulate got this damn number, it was too late to do something, because the 'appointed time' was up. No chance to appeal any more. Up till today, not a single sheet of paper, like, bill of indictment, or bill of trial, nothing, but insist on their law.

If it would be useful for your paper here are some facts how they treat me in prison. I told already about my invalidity, before I got arrested I could walk normally without stick, now I am forced to use a stick for every step and almost not more than 5 minutes. I spent a lot of time in Turkish hospitals but without success. Here isn't much knowledge about medical treatment in cases like mine. Other things happened, but I get tired at mentioning them all again. I got medical expert evidence several times, but the last one, it seems, is the importance of all, said: S (that's me) needs help and nursing all the time, he can't take care of himself. That's the correct translation. Now my consulate is trying something but in this fatalist country maybe they are successful after my funeral because they kicked me right down and now it doesn't really matter anyway. All in all, to be amongst murderers, thieves and slave sellers, is the biggest misfortune I ever took part. What a nuisance, to be a smoker of hash, is a bigger crime 'than a simple murder case' which would be punished 24 years. But otherwise they are eager-joining every modern European institution that means every time a step nearer to the money but without carrying out obligations of humanity in their own country. For instance they joined the European Court in Strasburg too and now they take a look to the convention of this high European Court about humanity. I don't have the intention to give my thoughts about humanity for discussion only so much, I got a lot of compassion for this world.

My regards to you and I am hoping my letter will help somewhat to beat the drum about the prisoners in an awful and backward country.
H. Schonwalder

OTHER SCENES

IS THE MOST INTERESTING PAPER IN AMERICA

John Wilcock's *Other Scenes* digs Cleaver, Crumb, Christo, Hoffman, Krassner, Kupferberg, Lester, Leary, Oldenburg, Rubin, Warhol & Michael X.....and runs all of them as often as possible.

OTHER SCENES *IS HIP TO THE WHOLE WORLD*

Wilcock writes $5-a-day books (*Greece, India, Japan, Mexico, Yugoslavia & California*) and his paper tells what the international freaks are up to everywhere.

Other Scenes costs $7 a year but for a single dollar we'll mail you three recent issues, plus fascinating Lifestory of Our Founder. Send $1 (or $7) in any valid currency to Other Scenes, 204 W. 10th Street, New York 10014, N.Y., U.S.A.

Name...
....
....
....

Dynamite the BBC

Dear Oz,
It is not surprising that Tony Palmer felt it was necessary to disassociate himself from the remarks he was reported to have made about the B.B.C. Anyone who has anything good to say about B.B.C. Radio and Television has got to be speaking out of the top of his head.

The most indicative example of the B.B.C.'s attitude towards its audiences is the Radio One. DJs, in choosing that have taken place in the Rock music scene during the past twelve years, they are still trying to make us believe that things haven't changed since 1958. We still hear teeny groups each day on wonderful Radio One when every available pointer tells us that the teeny scene is dead. We still hear nothing but singles when albums, for the first time ever, are selling in greater numbers.

The power is there and by using the B.B.C. as its whipping boy, the Government is showing, as it did with the sacking of the pirates, that it is becoming increasingly aware that the recording industry is the only one over which it has no control.

Censorship mutilates television, radio and the daily and 'popular' magazines are controlled so much the same way, and the cinema and the theatre rely almost entirely on lucrative outlets. Of the 'underground press', 'Time Out' appears to possess the greatest potential for change (on every page) but is misusing it. IT has gone into music for the wrong reasons and OZ needs to be taken more seriously. Our music, however, is completely our own. It is the only medium which does not have to rely on a lowest-common denominator appeal to get itself across. It is rooted in the community and the community accepts and understands it.

Rock music in 1969 is not the Radio One Fun Thirty (nor are the composers competing with Schubert or Bach). It is a point of contact for thousands of otherwise isolated people, providing them with the only solid form of communication.
In 15 years we will rule the world. The revolution is in our heads and that's the most important place of all. Meanwhile, the Beatles say what is on our minds.
R. Harris

50

All Fence Down!

Michael Gross

On Memorial Day, May 30, the Park Committee Asks All to Rally in Berkeley

Together

We Will March to Peoples' Park!

James Rector is dead in Berkeley of a police bullet in his heart. A sadistic Alameda County Sheriff's deputy killed him as Rector, from a rooftop, watched the massive assault on hundreds of brothers, some of whom he had met in a park built on vacant land. He was shot by a single policeman, but Sheriff Madigan distributed the shotguns, and the University of California pulled the trigger. The University fired the police guns which shot a hundred others on the bloody day of May 15th. It swung the clubs which have wounded, even crippled, dozens of others since that day, in methodical, conscious and indiscriminate violence.

Berkeley has undergone ten days of siege by 2700 National Guardsmen and thousands of police. All political and constitutional rights have been suspended by Reagan's fiat. A reign of terror, with heavily armed police teargassing and breaking into homes and dormitories has hit the university community.

All this because the University of California expropriated Peoples
Park from the Berkeley community

Kill for Love

The Police and the Law:
It will not be long before you can recognise the police. The ordinary "constable" is familiarly known as a "Bobby", though he likes to be addressed as "officer" unless he has three stripes, in which case call him "sergeant". He patrols his beat on foot, or is seen on traffic control duty.

Buses:
You may smoke "upstairs" or "on top", but not "downstairs" or "inside".

Underground Railways:
Stations are marked UNDERGROUND in white letters on a blue ground.

Dear Richard,

Having been presented as an asthmatic impotent, tone deaf, sadist wierd, I am now about to fall into the trap of writing a letter in reply to Germaine's piece 'Mozic and the Revolution' OZ 24 and will probably confirm all of her suspicions.

It would appear that the main problem in contemporary revolution, with the exception of the Guerilla wars in S. America is that all action takes place within territory held by the enemy. This fact destroys the idealistic approach to revolution, because in order to survive, the Revolutionary has to connive, cheat, lie and above all, develop a mental attitude which often is cynical and occasionally sadistic. This problem of expediency and passive idealism was exposed two years ago at UFO with Germaine Greer forcibly learning that it is not sufficient to embrace marauding skinheads and murmur 'Peace and Love' to them. A number of people, including myself found we were in the enviable position of having to face gangs of skinheads on their own terms in order to save genuinely peaceful people from getting their heads broken. In this way we were forced, on one hand, into compromising our own ideals (To kill a man is simply murder; it is revolution to turn him on), while on the other we earned the distrust of the flower people following these displays of violence.

If the Rock revolution is going to succeed in this society, it is painful, but necessary for some of us to sacrifice our own chances of the promised land, so that

those like Dr. G. who are already into peacefully doing their own thing, will not have to compromise themselves in order to survive. In some ways the Revolutionary is the least suited to live in the Utopia supposedly created out of revolution. This is sad, but there it is.

We have been hearing Rock solidly for the last ten years and despite what Germaine says, we have gone (even me in my condition), 'pretty far into our bodies'. The very fact that a white southern kid like Elvis Presley can go so far against his culture as to strut, and stomp like a nigger is a far greater part of revolution than all the feedback imaginable. Sure, we have got down into our bodies, the problem now is to find a way for rock to begin to make us rediscover our brains. Dylan begin to move in that direction, and maybe John Sinclair was helping it along the way, but my great fear is that the process will not be fast enough to be completed before the red necks shoot us as well.

Mick Farren

First Meeting:
When British people are introduced to each other, they give a faint smile and say: "How do you do?" There is no answer to this question. They occasionally shake hands, especially if formally introduced, but they do not shake hands with men and women they see often.

How to Make an insurrection:
People do not make revolution eagerly.
C. Wright Mills

EVERYBODY who is interested in giving recitations should have a book of monologues at his or her elbow. The usual repertoire of pieces in sober verse is well enough in its way, but when a few monologues are added, the repertoire becomes much more popular and acceptable.

It usually helps a great deal if suitable clothing is worn. A scarf or a hat may easily make all the difference to the effect, and a few pieces of furniture, such as a table and a chair, help in suggesting the proper atmosphere.

Though there is usually more to learn in a monologue than in a set of rhymed verses, the monologue is often mastered more quickly, and there is not the need to memorise the passages with the same word-accuracy.

My young nephew knows everything. You know the type — went to school until he was seventeen — seventeen mind you! — then went to a university and came away thinking the old folks couldn't teach him anything. All I said was wrong, and everything he did was right. Well, anyway, he got married last Easter. Married a bit of a thing as bad as he was — and the ideas the pair of them had! Everything was going to be done the modern way and they wouldn't take any advice — no, not even at the wedding reception. It really upset his mother, who believed in the old fashioned way of doing everything. I knew it was no good talking so I just said nothing — I even gave them the wedding present they wanted. Not what you'd expect — a case of cutlery, a carpet sweeper, or something useful but a Chinese vase! Fancy, a Chinese vase to put in the hall! A Chinese vase! Well, that just shows you.

We all went to their house after the reception to look at the presents and you never saw such a house in all your born days. Everything had to be modern — whether it worked or not. The kitchen was modern, the dining room was modern, the hall was modern, the bathroom was modern, the bedrooms were modern. They even had modern twin beds.

"Twin beds," I said, "I've never heard of such a thing. What's the matter with a good old-fashioned brass bedstead?"

They both just looked at me and I was sorry I'd spoken. I didn't say anything, but I thought quite a bit.

Well, after we'd seen the presents we all came away and left them to themselves, and it wasn't until three or four weeks later that I heard anything more of them. I got a letter saying this and that, but at the end was the bit I'd been waiting for.

"We can't understand," said my newphew, "where the Chinese vase is that you gave us." I thought it was worth a telegram. I went down to the Post Office and sent it off straight away — I only wish I could have seen their faces when they opened it.

"Look in the other bed," I said.

46

Caroline does a nasty

19th Nov.
Catford College,
Goudhurst Road,
Downham.

Dear Oz,
This is yet another in the series of all you-hear-about-Caroline-Coon-may-be-boring-but-it's-fucking-true.
OK so Release is a great service and a lot of the credit must go to Caroline, fine. Of late the fuzz have been super-active and so it isn't surprising that friends get busted, and Release are good to us. Someone thinks it would be nice to raise some money which no doubt Release could use. How about a benefit.

Well Release how do you feel about a benefit? 'Groovy, come up and chat about it', So we do. Everyone seems to feel good about the whole thing. Carry on. So we carry on. It seems that with an effort most people will help. We move next door to OZ and the girl says that we should be able to get some free advertising.

With some fixing we persuade another college with a larger hall to let us have it for the evening. With some fixing they get the local council to let them have it for nothing. Back at the college strings are franticly being pulled, by the end of the week we've got more than enough groups plus the aid of those concert vetdrans in the Rookery. Things are really working. We've even got a press willing to print cheap.

Get a call from Des Banks, 'Would we come up and see Caroline and tell all.' Sure. So we arrive and Caroline is wondering where the best sights in Germany are to be seen. Then someone tells us to sit down. We wait around for a bit, Someone has nicked the coffee. They have a long discussion on padlocks and signs. Then someone notices us in the corner. Can they help us 'Benefit? Oh yeah. Well, like it's difficult. You know, I mean like we've had hundreds of benefits and er just not benefited.' Oh. So they go back to the coffee. By now we're shit tired of the whole thing. So get up to go. Caroline spots us. 'Like you know I'm sorry but you know how it is.'

So we stand at the door and she tells us how. If the benefit flops people will still go around thinking Release have benefited. Caroline could'nt you have said so on the phone? It would have saved us god knows how much money and a fuck of a lot of time and trouble.

Sorry but you know how it is. Oh yeah do you want to stay and watch the moonshot? I suppose the fact that if you look there are hundreds of people willing to help a good cause, is good enough in itself, but I wish Caroline would sometimes stop and think.
Anyway, thanks to the Soft Machine, Al Stewart, Blackhill, OZ, N.U.S., the Rookery, The Notting Hill Press, Des and all others who were naive enough to think it might have worked.
Richard, Martin, Jon, Carol, and 1000's more.

Please...

Dear Sir,
I am 24 years of age and having read an account of your works as published in the People, Sunday September 7th, 1969, I would love to learn more about your magazine as you say love is beautiful, it is and all of us women know it. But like me, few of us are getting any Intimate Personal attention. Like my man for instance. From mounting me and getting it up into me, to rolling off me, four minutes and then deep snores. That is called love. But it only leaves me with an insatiable gash under my belly that is thrust forward elongated and gaping immensely, greedily yearning to be explored and used and served, as well as skilfully and dexterously operarated into me by hand. No there is none of this for me only a very deep frustration. Day by day I come on heat as I go about my work in the home or on the street, there is nothing I can do about it, as I am not getting the tool shoved up into me that would take this feeling away from me, and do me the most good. I have to just carry on. I thought your book would teach him what and how to do to me the things that would get him the most pleasure it is possible to get out of me. Lasting pleasure that is. What a God's Gift of Love to a woman in my present position to be held forcibly down unable to move, until by his ego and over indulgence all of me has been exposed and exhibited for his vision and the enormous vast channel of pleasure that he could obtain from working up into me dilegently. Well I will close now. I cannot see any of this happening, but it gives me comfort and happiness to talk about it all. It is a pity we cannot swap open discussion by correspondence with men. But discretion would have to be used, so that neither party could be traced if letters got lost. Only anonymously could this be possible. Will close now.
Name supplied but witheld.

Learning the virgins

Dear Sir,
Does your magazine learn people? Such as myself? I am a VIRGIN. Perhaps it would be better if you and your friends would do something of good nature to the country. I don't know why OZ causes such storms. I have just been reading in the paper that a so-called woman [dog in my eyes] can sleep with two so-called men [dogs]. Why? How? I don't understand it. Will your mag learn me? I'll just have one copy for now. To see if I can find out things. My parents and family were VIRGINS and abhor anything outside marriage, I am the same, I enclose the 3/-. Would you put it in a plain envelope? No we don't have anything like it in the house. I am curious, I suddenly want to know, at 24 years old!!! But VIRGIN I STAY
Name and address witheld.

Letter from a hospital

Dear OZ,
I watched the Stone's concert on the T.V. the other day amid a frantic putting down of the people there by the nurses and the patients (who are alcoholics) and saw a lot of people I knew, good to see they are still around. But where.
One good piece of news anyway, I am getting out in a few weeks or so, but I will remain a day patient, which is not to bad as I have only to attend here about three days a week. So maybe I can get my head sorted out and come up to London, and even back to Oxford for a week or so, I have had an invite from bro. Simon Tugwell (whom you may know) to go and stay at Blackfriars for a weekend. I may just do that.
(hope you don't mind me writing to you like this but as I said in my last letter, things are a drag, and I maybe in need to talk about things I and the other person know about.)
It is obvious that there are things that I cannot talk about in a letter, like, why I am here, and why I dig the East.
Funny things happen here at the hospital like;
(a) I had been here a week and was going up to occupational therapy one day, it was cold so I wore my poncho, the next thing I knew was the doctor wanted to see me, the conversation went like this:
Me I hear you want to see me Mr . . .
Him. Yes Barry, it's about your, er, er, blankat thing.
Me O. yes, it's very beautiful isn't it.
Him. Why did you wear it around the hospital this morning.
Me. Cos it was cold and I don't have a jacket.
Him. Er, well if you have a problem like that you know you must come to us and we will give you one.
Me. But I don't consider it a problem. (long silence)
Him. Well, we can't have you walking around the hospital like that I forbid you to wear it (pause) if you think like that you are not normal.
(b). Last night I went into the grounds and sat under a weeping willow tree listening to the John Peel show, and then to a concert for about two hours until a nurse came along and asked me what I was doing, so I told him. With the result he told me to go inside because it wasn't normal for people to sit under trees at night listening to a radio, and looking at the stars and field mice that lived in the tree I sat next to.
(c) They tell me speed is harmless and you can't get hooked on it
(d) They get angry at me for messing up their experiment that they were doing with me by putting me with 15 alcoholics, you see they told me they would bring in a 23 year old alcoholic so that I could identify myself with him, when he came I found that he was a drag and all he could talk about was booze, how he beat up freaks for fun when he was drunk, and the winner of the last race the day before. Well, what do you think happened.
(maybe I am intolerant).
love and flowers
Barry Fitton.

A. Stephanson 69.

THE Sun

FORWARD WITH THE PEOPLE 6d. Tuesday, November 25, 1969. No. 1

THE SUN SAYS

Making monsters of people

GENETIC engineering is one of those scientific phrases invented not to convey a meaning, but to obscure it.

We do not want to breed slaves. And there is a master race already. It is the human race. All of it. White and coloured. Aryan and non-Aryan. Let's leave it at that, says The Sun.

A NEW sexual revolution is being waged in the United States.

LEPER RAPES GIRL —SHE GIVES BIRTH TO A MONSTER BABY

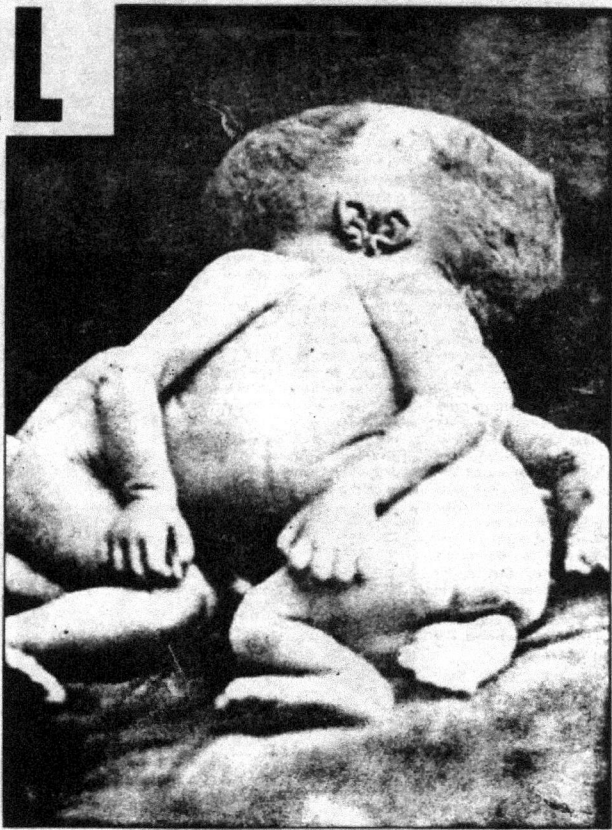

LEPER RAPES GIRL

She Gives Birth To Monster Baby

by CLINTON THAMES

There have been many despicable crimes committed against minors in this country, but none more revolting than the one inflicted on Caroline Riley, 17, of Houston, Texas.

Caroline, a virgin, was walking home from school 7 months ago when she was suddenly attacked by an escaped leper!

The shock of the hideous rape was too much for the ravaged child to bear and she spent six months in a mental institution recovering from the strain.

But just as Caroline regained her sanity another shock hit her — she was pregnant.

Three weeks later it happened — Caroline gave birth to a hideously deformed monster baby!

"Now the doctors say she'll never recover, that she'll be a vegetable for the rest of her life!" sobbed Emily Riley, 41, Caroline's mom.

"Giving birth to that thing snapped any saneness my poor child had left in her."

The horrible rape happened in a suburban park that Caroline always walked through to get home. Mom Emily still remembers the hysterical shrieking of her daughter after her disheveled body was found behind a clump of bushes.

"I rushed right to the park when the neighbors notified me something had happened," she told SUN "The sight I saw made me want to tear the hair out of my head and die.

"My poor baby was lying there with her clothes torn off and the most horrible expression in her eyes.

"It wasn't until I looked closer that I saw the decrepit looking scab that was smeared across her flesh."

"It was so sickening that I puked all over my daughter's body."

Police arrived moments later and immediately got on the case.

The results showed within an hour when a leper, his decaying flesh practically oozing from his body, was found hiding behind a trash can in an alley.

"The child was too hysterical to give us any help," Police Lt. Chuck Hamson told SUN "but the doctors looking after the victim said the loose scab on her body was human scab.

"It didn't click that the rapist was a leper until the pervert was discovered in the lane.

"The clincher came when we searched him. The girl's nylons and her torn panties were found stuffed into his pockets."

The leper, Manuel Rodriguez, an escapee from a Mexican leper colony, was deported to Mexico City where he was tried and committed to a high security section of the colony.

But that didn't help young Caroline — the shock of being molested by a slimy pervert was so great that she went berserk.

"It took three months before she could speak and another three months until she was healthy enough to be released from the institute," Dr. Wilson Richards, her psychiatrist, revealed.

"We had told her by then that she was pregnant and she took it as well as could be expected. She said she was ready for it.

"She probably was ready for childbirth, but not for the monstrous event that did happen."

The monstrous event that Dr. Richards was referring to was the birth to Caroline of a 9-lb. faceless freak.

"It was the most revolting creature I'd ever come across," the doctor, who was at Caroline's bedside to give her confidence, stated.

"The monster had two heads hideously welded together at the face. There were no eyes, mouths, no noses, nothing except four ears.

"It died moments after it was pulled from Caroline's womb but it was too late by then — the poor, hypersensitive girl saw her freak baby and screamed convulsively.

"By the time we calmed her down with drugs she was a whimpering mass of tissue, oblivious to the life going on around her.

"She's stayed that way ever since and I'm afraid nothing is going to pull her out of it.

"No human could go through as much torment as this child and stay sane."

This diagnosis has been corroborated by other experts but that isn't stopping the Riley parents from hoping.

"We pray every day that a miracle will cure our Caroline," Emily admitted. "With God's help she will one day be healthy and living with us again."

SUN then asked

gynecologist Dr. James Waterman, 48, who assisted in the birth of the freak, whether deformity and leprosy will always go hand in hand.

"Yes, I'm afraid so," he replied. Usually, a leper's hormone structure is so imbalanced by the slow rot of leprosy that a normal offspring is out of the question.

"But no one could expect a freak with two bodies and one head!"

Leper Manuel had escaped from Mexican colony. He's now back

Caroline today is insane. She was unable to cope with double disaster

Hideous double-headed freak was result of foul mating between leper & teen virgin Caroline

Gal's mom, Mrs. Riley, prays every day that Caroline will recover

49

I have never had much time for the in depth interpretation, the 'what we're trying to say is', or the supposedly hidden meaning, in music. The Dylanologist and the intellectualiser are to-day's rock Philistines. And so with Quintessence' first LP, In Blissful Company, I was very happy to accept it as one of the most joyous and spontaneous records I had heard since the balmy days of Traffic, and Who Knows What Tomorrow May Bring.

Notting Hill Gate, for example, transcends a tendency towards total banality in the lyrics and achieves the status of a minor classic. Having missed Quintessence on the battlefields of Implosion, All Saints Hall and the Speakeasy, I was surprised to find the group is still very much your 'typical' English blues rock outfit. The eastern influence is there, of course (there's more than a touch of Asian exoticism in **Ganga Mai**) but having heard of the Quintessence life style and seen from afar members of the group swanning around the Grove in their robes and sandals, I had expected an oriental trip at least as heavy as George Harrison's. Partly to find out why In Blissful Company succeeds so brilliantly, partly because I happened to meet Shiva the group's vocalist in Portobello Road one afternoon, I found myself cross legged on a cushion in his incense laden pad, sipping peppermint tea, slightly distracted by the Indian petit-point of the carpets and wall hangings, mesmerised by the caste mark on his forehead, listening to his serious, gentle talk.

"Behind the music is a very close family life in which basically, we are all following the same philosophy which is the quickest way to realisation of God for us. We are fairly organised, with meetings outside group practices, at which the families get together in one of our pads and sing mantras, especially Hare Krishna. This brings about a much closer communication among the families, and in particular among members of the group when playing."

I wonder how much family harmony there was behind Blind (virtuosity for its own boring sake) Faith.

"The inner circle of the Quintessence amounts to six individual families, about twenty people. Occasionally we have kirtan which is devotional singing, used to invoke Krishna Consciousness. It produces a state of complete relaxation and happiness. Getting audiences to join in, which we always try to do, frees their minds from fetters, makes them forget earthly problems."

In Blissful Company is in fact, a devotional record. Religious music, closely identified with Quintessence's faith and way of life. None of your gloomy hymn-singing, Wesleyan moral fog, but akin to Italian Renaissance church music, which, produced at a time when Christianity still had something going for it, was rich, passionate and inspired.

"The best way I can express my feelings about God is through my music and I want all my physical actions directed towards this."

The group's Swami, and study of the Bhagavad Gita and the Upanishads have left indelible marks, and Shiva is now an orthodox Hindu, a long way from his days as Phil Jones, singing with The Unknown Blues, a still unknown pop group in Australia.

"To transcend their egos, all members of the band take part in the kirtan, but some are more involved in occultism, a western path towards realisation. This is why we still have as much an English as an Indian sound — the music necessarily reflects both philosophies. At the moment our sound is simple, our eastern influence is likely to grow, and we may have an album devoted entirely to chanting, which may be more difficult to understand."

My musical appreciation capabilities being, by an unfortunate quirk of birth, permanently stunted (I am tone deaf), I will no doubt be left behind as the group makes their journey to Bombay and all points east. When I departed, Shiva was playing an electric organ and Vidya, his wife, was making another peppermint tea.

"The message that we are trying to put across in our music is that it is within the grasp of everyone to attain infinite knowledge, love and peace. Every track on the record reflects upon the infinite consciousness which pervades everything."

Which brings me back to where I started. The music comes first, the message comes second. Even when it's a beautiful message like that. For Quintessence, the two are inextricably intertwined. But the direction they are going is not that of the majority of those who will buy and love the record. The music of Quintessence says a thousand things, and you can pluck from it what you will.

Jim Anderson.

There are many groups that seem to go on for years at what you might call the Klooks Kleek level. In other words, they achieve a mild sort of reputation but never manage to break out of the endless round of one nighters up and down the country.

If the music business was all fair and honest — credit where credit was due and so forth — one could say that this kind of group didn't succeed because it didn't deserve to; because it just didn't have what it takes to turn a Klooks Kleek group into a Royal Command performance act. As it is, of course, success depends less on how well you can play than who you know (how else do you explain the Ryan twins?)

Maybe this is the reason why Mighty Baby (nee the Action) have been around for so long without ever really making it. Perhaps they haven't got engaging smiles, or they aren't evil-looking enough, or they're not as under-privileged as they ought to be — I don't know.

The important thing about Mighty Baby (right — enough soft-soaking) is that their first album is very good indeed.

Obviously their music slightly resembles the hard rock blues that the Action used to play. I don't think it's too whimsical to say that it's pure electric music throughout. Mighty Baby seem content to explore the possibilities inherent in a drums/bass/lead/organ/sax line-up — they're not into the we're-as-versatile-as-any-symphony-orchestra thing. They make a kind of Buffalo Springfield sound at times too, but they're never merely imitative — you get the feeling that they write all their own material because they want to express themselves in their own way, not because somebody told them that to progress in the business you have to do your own numbers. Every track is, to a greater or lesser degree, satisfying, there are no space-fillers.

The best numbers on the album are those, like 'House Without Windows' and 'A Friend You Know But Never See', where they lay down and develop a solid rock and roll riff. Here you can see the advantage of playing for years: each musician instinctively maintains and enhances the balance of the song. Unlike those bands which are merely showcases for one soloist Mighty Baby are a group in the fullest sense.

The sleeve is good too, dig the frantic Martin Sharp front cover.

John Leaver

John Mayall The Turning Point Polydor 583571 Push as you pull Led Zeppelin Two Atlantic 588198

Pump and Jump. Pick and Bash are at it again. The Undercurrent of Led Zeppelin has become a reality. Varoom!!! Are we big enough to accept their brute force? Shugshug bokbok. Go away you pox, let me hear it. Baby baby baby.

Robert Plant is screaming songs in tune. Bonham and Jones are stomping, and Flash Harry Page is showing his class. They define heavy.

Plant is no longer just a member, he's out front leading Led Zeppelin. He's singing duets with the Jones' bass continually, the Flash is happy filling the gaps. You can't describe the pieces as songs, you can't whistle them in your mausoleum. I mean the Fifth Dimension did 'Sunshine of Your Love'. 'Squeeze me til the juice runs down my legs' has got to remain pure Plant. I promise you after one hearing you will not return Page, Bonham, Plant and Jones. You could win a bird for the night with Led Zeppelin Two.

I think Page was trying too hard on the first album, the sweat was honest but overpowering. But as much as you attack this one you can't dent 'What is and what should Never Be', 'Ramble On', and the middle section of 'The Lemon Song'. At first hearing there are some unnecessary things: Bonham's drum solo, the electric clapping on track one, the Burbon intonation on 'Thank You'. But they serve some purpose in providing contrast for the brilliant bits. Notwithstanding the heavy blues business, there are musical chuckles woven into the album. This is a must when you're smashing ears with a million watts. Sadly, there are a lot of musicians who lack humour.

A huge bonus is the joyous physicality not present on any other record since Bayou Country. The simmering melancholia in many of the records released over the last three months is a sore even if it's a description of the way things are. A bit of 'wham bam thankyou mam' from the leading guitrippers may exercise the split scene.

John Mayall and Led Zeppelin have the same audience. They've got to difference between them that counts. Mayall's voice is scratchy but Plant's hair is curly. In fact Mayall tries to look after my head, and Led pulls at my heart.

That John Mayall, there's a man who's stuck to his guns. The British have been searching for him for 20 years, a homegrown jazzman, recognisably British in mode and music. Clap clap clap. He's been round and he's found himself. Hear it all on 'Turning Point'. If you add Reggae we have equality with U.S.A. on all musical fronts. Clap clap clap. Jesus what a relief, we can provide a complete alternative music for the free world. Applause.

If Miles Davis dropped dead tomorrow, there would be somebody to take his place. Not so with Mayall. He's a one man band, literally and metaphorically. Silence. And he's not dead yet. Rousing cheers, cheers. I'd love to stay, but my wife's warming up the headphones, we've got the Gary Burton import on the Dual. That's what you're up against Mister Mayall.

Turning Point has some great harmonica, the drumless-rhythm section is not too strained. The new boys are learning fast. Hear it at least twice.

T. R. Zelenka

A teeny bopper reviews King Crimson — In the Court of the Crimson King. Island ILPS-9111

I have the record — a present from last month's beautiful 'freak', Lee, for having looked after his cats and goldfish while he struggled with arch enemy F.C. Pulley — and it sits in rather isolated pink and purple glory as far as possible from the previous crown of my record collection: The Troggs Greatest Hits. I didn't really hear much of King Crimson at their free Hyde Park concert — I was fully three hundred yards away, much distracted by a long-haired 13 year old boy who pissed on me from the branch of a tree, chanting skin heads, and a couple of wandering fuzz who caused the girl I was with to accidentally stub her joint out on her dress. Paranoia. I certainly wasn't at the Speakeasy for the gig that (according to usually unreliable sources) for some obscure sociological, rather than musical reason, King Crimson has forever after been trying to live down. I read somewhere that the group has been over-exposed, over-acclaimed, over-promoted, over-rated and the victim of what is known as The Group Hype. Anyway, it must be obvious by now that until I got the record I had not heard King Crimson play a single note. I felt nervous. Read quickly through the lyrics inside the cover. Very poetic I suppose. 'Call her moonchild/Dancing in the shallows of a river/Lonely moonchild/Dreaming in the shadow of the willow.' What was this? Not another Gandalf's Garden group! Admired the hideous cover. Those nostrils! Accidentally played the second side first and wondered if I was going to get value for money. Sounded like Donovan. Tyrannosaurus Rex? — drawing two names out of my limited repertoire. Mood music. Very pretty. Very cool. Then bam! A full blooded heavily orchestrated classical theme — **In the Hall of the Mountain King**. I mean, **In the Court of the Crimson King**. No connection really, but brought up on Grieg and Buddy Holly I got confused. I turned up the treble to enjoy the harsh screams of **21st century Schizoid Man**, thought it was Paul McCartney singing **I Talk to the Wind**, found **Epitaph** the most original and beautiful track on the record. I sat very still on the floor throughout. No dancing.

Pop music has travelled a long and increasingly sophisticated way to arrive at something as finely chiselled as King Crimson. But the end of this particular road is near and King Crimson (or Blind Faith, or Quintessence, or Mighty Baby or Soft Machine or whatever) at the Purcell Room, the Wigmore Hall or even Ronnie Scotts is a probability in the near future. Look what happened to that thing called jazz. 15 year olds now are never going to grow into King Crimson. They will instead be starting the long process of doing the same thing to reggae or whatever new thing their musical imagination gets into. As for me, I'll never make it to the Purcell Room, but there's always those nostalgic journeys into the past — Conway Twitty at The Talk of the Town, Bill Haley at the Speakeasy, things like that.

Jim Anderson

After all, tomorrow is another day.   SCARLETT O'HARA

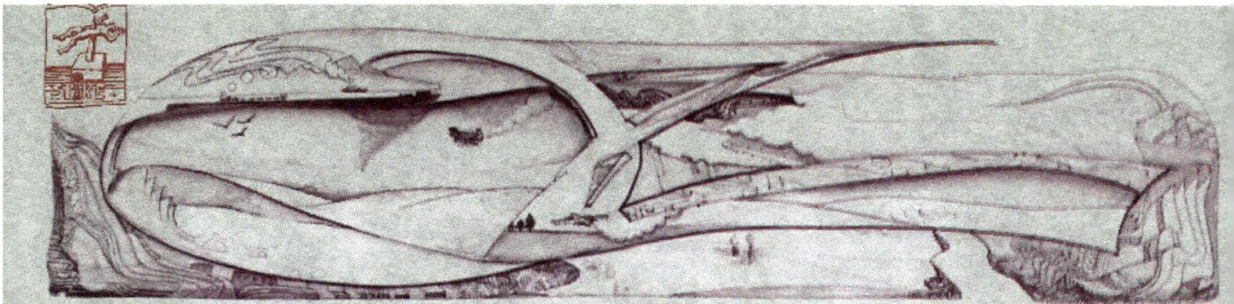

OZ 25
December 1969
OZ is published by OZ Publications Ink Ltd. 52 Princedale Road, London, W.11.
Telephone: 229 7541
Advertising: Contact Felix Dennis at 727 8456
Subscriptions: Send 42/- or 6 dollars for 12 issues to above address.
Printed by OZ Publications Ink Ltd.

This issue appears with the help of Richard Neville, Felix Dennis, Jim Anderson, David Wills, Gary Brayley, Louise Ferrier, Martin Sharp and Bridget Murphy.

Cover photograph by Keith Morris.

Distribution:
UK: Moore Harness Ltd. 11 Lever St. London, EC1. CLE 4882
Transmutation, Guildford 65694
California: Rattner Distributors 2428 McGee St. Berkeley, California, 94703.
Holland: Thomas Rap, Regulieswarstraat 91, Amsterdam, Tel: 020-227065
Denmark: George Streeton, The Underground, Larsbjorn Straede 13, Copenhagen K.
Morocco: Lee Heater.

Thanks to David Nutter for the photograph on p.30 and drawings by David Powell p.42/44, David Goard p.36, Chris Rogers p.22, Alan Stephenson on p.37/46 and Steve Morris (who did more than we could use) p.52

SEIZE THE TIME!

The musical 'Hair' is not exactly to [illegible] but even at its most corrupted, Hair generally reflects the Underground's belief that one's politics and lifestyle should be identical. Its authors would no doubt be amused by the irony of Gloria Stewart being fired from the cast for exercising her fundamental democratic right to protest — she disrupted the auditions for another musical, the Black and White Minstrel Show. "I have yet to speak to a black person who did not fail to express anger and disgust at the mere mention of the Minstrel Show," she told OZ. "The traditional show was conceived in an era of the Ku-Klux-Klan and economic slavery of our people. It was born when lynching, rape, castration and miscegenation were commonplace in the so-called United States of America. Let us not forget that the "Americans" in this case were newly arrived English immigrants who started the whole damned thing. Is such a tradition worth preserving in the name of good entertainment fit for Grandmothers and elderly ladies in such a great country [illegible] becoming restless, angry and tired of the laughing game?"

OZ presents below a selection from the many letters Gloria received as a result of her protest (original spellings).

Gloria Stewart
Why don't you get wise to yourself? Why do you imagen English people put up with negros?
Its because the vast magoritie of them are stupid enough to imagen that negros are all singing and dancing people., like in the Black and white Minstrel Show. Instead of mean vioucos evil minded bigots who hate everything white, and are out too destroy and defile and smirch it. And I hope that you are not under the misaprenshion, that all your white friends are completely integratet and do not notice your colour or your monkey type features. Because I can tell you now that when all the bars are down, and they are looking for a word to describe you and your kind, you will always be a black bastard. And your white boy friends will climb into your bed, will not be be able to get out of it fast enough., till they tell there pals about the bit of Black ham they had away last night. So lets face it you are black, you will always be black, your descendents will be black.
You dont belong to this country, but we have to put up with you. If you and your ilk and any real pride and self respect, you would not try to force yourselfe upon, people who dont like or need you. So leave the black and White Minstrel show alone, and let the idols have there fairy tales.
Signed A. White
p.s. After working with niggers I cant even stand nat king cole ella fitzgerall? dina washington Share Mayhan Brook Benton Sactahome, you name them I hate them. Why dont yougohome, back to your family tree? please by bye black bird!!?

Can you not even leave we ordinary people of Great Britain just **one** show that is not polluted by this filthy generation, white or coloured? We are sick of your style of show?? The Black and White Minstrels are beloved of **decent** people who do not care if the artistes are white or coloured. Just a happy band of **ladies & gentlemen** who give us entertainment even fit for elderly ladies. But your generation would not understand that and, no doubt, would like to take over the whole show and pollute it by your filth. Because Margaret Snowdon and the Establishment applaud your sort of thing do not think decent people do so too. Go back to your own country from whence all this pollution came, "Can any good things come from America?" You have racialism on the brain. I am an ex-Lillis girl, have travelled all over the world and still remaind friends of all races, creeds and colours. The only thing that matters is to be a good artiste and that is why the Black & White Minstrels will be remembered affectionately long after such degrading shows as yours will be forgotten, thank the God whom your generation rejects.
unsigned

Why not keep your big mouth shut about the Black & White Minstrels show. We are sick of your type, expressing your views about what **you** think of our people in our own country — so shut your big fat lips — We don't like what we have been forced to have in a white country. By the way why do you call yourselves by English or Scottish names — We prefer the Minstrel singing to your filthy type of show. Go home. Tell the others to get their hair cut.
unsigned

THIS IS ENGLAND: If you, and the coloured community that have invaded **MY COUNTRY** object to white people blacking their faces then clear out to your own jungle and hovels that the vast majority have come from.
To approach a princess re the subject was colossal cheek and ignorance and proves how **jealous** you are of the white man who cannot be held responsible for black or coloured **skins!**
As for dignity!!! How many blacks try to whiten their skins, straighten their hair. Wear european clothes and wigs and eat our food, etc. etc. etc. Now you come here lower our standards abuse, cause mischief, filth everywhere, morals nil, except to invade our best clubs, hotels, whilst we sit meekly by!
Had it not been for the courageous leader and our own brave **white** man in the British isles during the last war **YOU AND YOUR LIKE** would not be living in luxury, demonstrating, causing mischief, bringing drugs & jungle behaviour to this once clean honest country. **YOU WOULD ALL** be slaves. I predict **SLAVERY WILL RETURN.**
You would like the white man exterminated. Your own to be rulers. Should that ever happen my prediction will come true. We pour the ratepayers money into your country's more so since home rule, where does it go. Why do you and your like flock to this overcrowded island?
YOU AND YOUR LIKE CANNOT DO WITHOUT THE WHITE MAN.
We are not fools. We know what is going on the black power, etc. If this lot succeed god help you and your lot eventually. You will be slaves to your own kind.
We whites have had enough.
unsigned

Miss
Why don't you mind your own business, and go back to the States we can do without any foreigners over here, especially the bloody wogs. Fuck the white man's burden.
P.A. Dawes.

Written on two pieces of toilet tissue:
You been making to much noise and protest — about what nigro woman? If you don't like it nor do we like you and we don't like the noisy you make. Soon wer going to teach you a leson you won't like either you and some other filth like you. We know were to get you and we will soon then we'll see what your black face looks like with some razor stripes. So remember shut it — your noise and your black monky face — we'll get you for sure.
signed. The nigger knife
(drawing of a dripping dagger)

It is against such a background of British bigotry that Michael Abdul Malik has embarked on what seems like his most constructive attempt to [illegible] race relations so far — the newly formed RAAS (Racial Adjustment Action Society) a supermarket size communal complex at 95-101 Holloway Road, N.7. Basically, it is an educational project involving discussion groups, [illegible] library and a school. In return for any donations (minimum 27/6) RAAS offers an autographed first edition of the book 'From Michael de Freitas to Michael X' which will be sent post free.

On October 27, Sergeants Tilley and Kent of Scotland Yard entered the OZ office with a warrant issued under the Obscene Publications Act. They confiscated one copy of OZ 23 (The Homosexual issue and the only one left in the office) and various files relating to printing, distributions and binding. Minutes before their arrival we had been tipped off by a phonecall from IT — police had also searched their office for "obscene literature" — ie the homosexual OZ. Nothing more has been heard from them yet, but we soon will, judging from a subsequent charge against the directors of IT: "conspiring with persons inserting advertisements and with other persons to induce readers to resort to the said advertisements for the purpose of homosexual practice, thereby to debauch and corrupt public morals contrary to common law".
Another charge brought against the three directors, Peter Stansill, Graham Keen and Dave Hall, alleges that public decency was outruged by "lewd,

isgusting and offensive matter — ontrary to common law". These come at Wells Street Magistrates Court on anuary 16 and are then likely to roceed to the Old Bailey. The 'common w' charge means that, unlike a rosecution brought under the Obscene ublications Act, the usual defences rtistic, literary merit etc) are not vailable. Yet another example of Britain's swinging new permissiveness occurred last month when one of the eople said to be connected with urope's first English Language Sex aper, Suck, was imprisoned at Harwich or three days. He was returning to ngland from Amsterdam with copies of he first issue. They were confiscated, he as summarily incarcerated and later eported. Anyone wishing to obtain rther information about Suck should write to: Joy Publishing, Alexander oerstraat 20, Amsterdam, Holland.

Revolution In Our Lifetime

During the death throes of English Rolling Stone, a hottest copies of a letter sent by ann Wenner, (founder and editor of US Rolling Stone) to Jane Nicholson, the K editor, initially hired by Wenner w source of the photostat copies is not now. The letter in part, reads:

Your business practices are appalling and the level of expenditure is not justifiable ther by the quantity or the quality of hat you have been doing. It cannot be called a "sense of loss" when, but when expensing accounting your business, because all the basic costs have already been met. How did you leave what is apparently unchecked, without proper ss ick's money squandered to be bankrupt ith all kinds of money breaking even. You are spending his money with expensive accountants and when no his financial advisors and accountant remains it...

Clearly every director, instruction and policy I agreed upon has not been followed. You have done very little that I have asked and this has led Trans-Oceanic to the edge of financial disaster and made it an editorial laughing stock.

I have no objection whatsoever to a separate edition in London, one with its own distinct and unique character. But you have assembled, paid and put in print a group of people — all of whom I can only be honestly described as rank amateurs. I am sorry to say it, but the English edition of Rolling Stone is not even as good as I.T. or OZ. What you have done in altering our material and in adding your own has been appalling.

If I felt any assurance at all that you would follow my directions, I think the situation might be salvageable, but you have consistently disregarded them on down the line. The more British material you add, the more advertising declines. June, I have not heard from anyone — whether in the underground or in the music business or publishing, whether English or American — I have not heard su much as just one favourable comment about the English edition. Every time I get your new issue I ask myself: What are we doing being involved with these people? It's embarrassing to me and it is a travesty on what Rolling Stone has ever done or meant. Is this some kind of joke?

What has happened to Rolling Stone in London bears no resemblance to what Mick and I originally discussed and planned for us to do in England or Europe. It has become farce, and I can no longer be a part of it . . . You are a bunch of amateurs and kids playing at the game of publishing, taking a ride on the established reputation and material of Rolling Stone and on Mick's bank account.

Mick arrives in Los Angeles in

mid-October and I hope that we will agree on what has to be done. In the meantime, I would suggest that you suspend operations and payroll for the next month and ask Rupert to have a chartered accountant audit the books. I hope that Mick and I have will have a solution soon and put this mess into workable shape, but it means turning the entire operation around and restructuring it from top to bottom. Sincerely, Jann Wenner Editor

Since that letter was sent, English Rolling Stone has changed its title to 'Friends' and the staff have received various warnings from US Rolling Stone's solicitors that injunctions will be served if Friends resembles its former self in any way. Meanwhile, the printer, Woodrow Wyatt, never a man to rely on when the chips are down, has demanded from them an impossible £10,000 indemnity.

Another paper crippled by administrative disputes is **Play**, a breezy, intelligent tabloid 'concerned with young people and the creative arts'. On November 18, Inter Action, the trustees of **Play**, suspended publication indefinitely. The editors intend to continue with their own paper, **Generation**. 'People pretend to bend over backwards in their concern for young people,' says Mike Segal, one of the ousted Players, 'and wonder why they get nothing back but hatred and distrust'. **Generation** wants its readers to 'think about kids' and to involve themselves with young people in a constructive and creative way. More information: 01-836 9329.

Grass Eye 163-67 Market Street, Manchester is a crisply and originally presented Underground paper produced by a 'loose bunch of radicals who support people's struggles to find a way out of the mess we're living in' and well worth sending a shilling for. Other Mancunians feel 'it is time for another OZ to emerge' and will soon be launching **Growth**, a monthly mag of fun and revolution. The comparison with OZ is already bringing them bad luck with printers . . . anyone with suggestion or manuscripts write to Dave Robinson, 56 Crow Hill North, Alkrington, Middleton, Manchester.

No doubt encouraged by their acceptance for distribution by W. H. Smith's, **Time Out** too are joining in the Manchester Underground Press explosion. Those interested in co-operating with Time Out,

£40,000 and ordered ¾ million copies before it was published, expected a children's book — to be marketed through the national Children's Book League. Originally Dell objected to 13 pieces of artwork, but finally accepted four alterations. However, they insisted that several Beatle quotes concerning drugs be dropped from the book. Aldridge himself is slightly disappointed with the standard of his own work because he had to rush it through in nine weeks. Several artists failed to deliver their commissions, leaving even more work for Aldridge's studios. He thinks the British publishers, BPC did a "fantastically good job" but says also that the "Americans dominated the whole fucking issue and BPC were beholden to them". He is also somewhat bemused by the lack of response from the Beatles who received most of the £25,000 advance paid by BPC. BPC themselves are delighted with Aldridge, "The book's a bloody good product", smiled their man as he navigated his face with a flexless Phillshave, "we've sold the rights to 36 countries and it's still selling". The Portugal edition will contain no illustrations, no songs and a 'revised' cover.

. . . at Twickenham. Although not with the mass of demonstrators, who they began chanting immediately he was bundled off with extravagant force to the nearest police station where he joined a queue of 150 demonstrators and policemen. Suddenly the Detective Sergeant who had arrested him clutched his stomach and fell to the ground screaming 'Why did you hit me?' Horrified at this behaviour, our friend raised both his hands and shouted to the crowd: 'I want you here to see that I am being accused of striking this man and that I have not so assulted him . . . I have assaulted nobody. Our friend is accused of assault and will be immediately . . .

John Lennon has joined the Digger Action Movement the 25 acre island of Dornish, off Ireland. Anyone interested in joining the community envisaged there or any other Digger projects (free stalls in Portobello Road, head schools and urban communes) contact Sid Rawle, 116, Lower Cippenham Lane, Slough, Bucks.

From The People, 30/11/69
A LOVE LIFE has been given by the National Health Service to a wife whose husband is a paraplegic — paralysed from the waist downwards.
He has been supplied with an artificial sex organ (price £15) after his application, supported by several doctors, was approved at high level at the Health Ministry's headquarters.
Said his 38-year-old wife: 'The psychological effect was fantastic. It has made a new man of him.'
Said her husband, a 40-year-old war disabled ex-army sergeant: 'I feel like a real human being again.'

The cock was supplied by OZ's most persistent advertiser, Pellon Personal Products. 'Yes (disabled) men . . . it can be done!

The Love Germ by Jill Neville. Weidenfeld and Nicholson 25/-. This book is about VD and the Paris Revolution 1968. It is a fantastic, earth shattering, dynamic, brilliant, beautiful, touching, sensitive, unbelievable, out of sight, deeply moving book written by my sister. RN

THE LAST OF THE WINOS
They're playing mock rock at Buckingham Palace. Originally went out with Alice and the bathwater. To complement American Ambassador Annenberg's penchant for reproduction Chippendale furniture and reproduction language (remember 'elementary processes of refurnishing and rehabilitation'?) goes a current royal craze for reproduction pop, played by this season's favoured group, the DARK BLUES; one quartet, three former Oxford boys, one music salesman. If the GPO mislaid your invitation, you will have missed hearing them play at Prince Charles' 21st.
They are dedicated to playing most of the current hit parade 'so that when you walk into the room you think it's the record'. Nigel Tully, computer man at IBM, group leader, slim, English blond sideboards, neat short back and white lacy stretch shirt, tight shiny yellow trousers. 'For gigs we wear see-through red lacy shirts, usually black trousers. It's not a uniform, just a bloody good marketing idea.' Sober suits during the day. 'We don't have an identity to sell. We're there to give audiences what they want. Audiences are a phenomenon. Whether they're hairy, dinner-suited or dukes, they all want a good time.' Charles came up and said thank you very much. His 21st at the palace: 'We accepted before we want that it wasn't going to be a "yeah" night and we didn't play rave-up numbers. The Queen didn't drop her wig; they were just nice ordinary people having a nice ordinary party.' The DARK

BLUES have played together for 8 years, 'good crap rock and roll. My three great gods are Little Richard, Jerry Lee Lewis, Gene Vincent. There's no-one who can arouse that old chair-slashing excitement any more... I don't particularly want to break out of the capitalist wages scene! I doubt if we could satisfy an Underground audience; we haven't tried to get that kind of work.'
Politics?
'I refuse to have positive views about anything that doesn't affect me directly... Athenian democracy is probably the right way to run a country — a democracy of the elite, you only get to have a vote if you're bright, good at something.'
Drugs?
'I've never tried any, never been offered. No-one has ever said, "Here, try some hash", But I think I'd probably try it. Are the DARK BLUES a sexy act?
'Nah.'
Pushed is anything important?
'I think that drinking good wine is terribly important and drinking bad wine is a bad thing. My philosophy is to go along with good thinking — I'm not particularly convinced there was any good thinking about Haight Ashbury.'

If the way to the royal psyche is through the DARK BLUES, then Plan your Party now. Inquiries to agents: Party Planners, run by Lady Elizabeth Anson, 229 9666. As a result of publicity about the royal gigs their fees are going up, though I couldn't find out how much the palace paid. The DARK BLUES are turning royal blue fast. MV

53

Blow your minds this yuletide with happy Blackhill Enterprises

Live Freaky, Die Freaky   32 Alexander Street London W2   01-229 5718

Al Stewart
Barefoot
Battered Ornaments
Bridget St John
The Deviants and Mick Farren
Dr Strangely Strange
The Dubliners
Edgar Broughton Band
Forest
Formerly Fat Harry

Judy Grind
John Martyn
The Johnstons
Martin Karthy
Ralph McTell
Stefan Grossman
Shirley and Dolly Collins
Sweeney's Men
Third Ear Band

WEDDING ALBUM

JOHN & YOKO

SAPCOR 11 OUT NOW

Books received:

Twenty Love Poems and a Song of Despair by Pablo Neruda.
Poems 1956-1968 by Leonard Cohen.
Poems by Adrian Mitchell.
Published by Jonathan Cape at 8/- each.

Lush, overblown, romantic poetry of love, in the grand old operatic manner from Chilean Mr. Neruda, who is, as Jerry Lee Lewis would put it 'one of the best poets in the business.' Consider a verse from **Drunk with Turpentine**:
Drunk with turpentine and long kisses,
Like summer I steer the fast sail of the roses,
bent towards the death of the thin day,
stuck into my solid marine madness.

Love, life, passion and a lot of the pain, without the music from Canadian Mr. Cohen, including **Suzanne takes you down**. Take a look at the index of first lines in the back of the book (A kite is a victim you are sure of, Claim me, blood, if you have a story. I am locked in a very expensive suit. My lady was found mutilated, Towering black nuns frighten us, etc.) and you will learn a lot about Leonard Cohen and probably read the poems as well.

If you liked Aldermaston you'll love English Mr. Mitchell, although he himself tends to be a little circumspect: Most people ignore most poetry/because/most poetry ignores most people/ Not as many pages as Cohen, but you get instead a highly developed social conscience, four children's poems (Lovers lie around in it./Broken glass is found in it/Grass/I like that stuff. Tuna fish get trapped in it/Legs come wrapped in it/Nylon/I like that stuff — Eskimos and tramps chew it/Madam Tussaud gave status to it/Wax/I like that stuff — Cigarettes are lit by it/Pensioners get happy when they sit by it/Fire/I like that stuff and so on for several more quite delightful verses) and poems like this:

Fascist Speaker
Armoured like a rhinoceros
He hurls his tons into the crowd.
From half a dozen minds he rips
Triangles of flesh and blood.
Six shouts, six cardboard banners rise
Daubed with slogans saying Pain,
But wilt and tear in the hundredfold
Applause of men as mild as rain.

Embers by Peter Cadle, Fopp, 18 Honeygate, Luton, Beds. 1/3.
Watershed
Between
Happiness and sorrow
Tears and laughter,
Rapture and agony,
Life and death,
One millionth of an inch.
Jim Anderson

The Confessions of Aleister Crowley ed by Kenneth Grant and John Symonds Cape 5gns
Poet, mystic, painter, publisher, mountain climber, heroin addict (on and off), gourmet (food and women) — Aleister Crowley had a sort of poetic life hunger peculiar to the early 19th Century. He inherited £40,000 from his father, a Plymouth Brethren fanatic, which enabled him to finance his climbing expeditions to Mexico and the Himalayas and publish his books at his own expense.

Crowley was an expert on the use of drugs (not a crime in the early days of the century — Freud turned his friends on to cocaine, telling them he had discovered the 'wonder drug'). Crowley introduced anhalonium (another name for mescalin) to Europe, and wrote the best study of heroin addiction up to that time in 'John St John'.

On the publication of these deliberately literary (and therefore much censored) autobiographical confessions last month, his reputation as 'the wickedest man in the world' did not fail, and reviewers made heyday of his perversions and the bizarre events of his life. Whatever personal experience these reviews contained, most of it was of the 'I once saw Crowley . . . etc.' variety, and by and large they put Crowley down as a charlatan, or at best, misguided.

The main problem with Crowley, and the reason for the widespread fear of him, is that he was completely self-motivated. His biographer, and tenacious holder of the Crowley copyrights – John Symonds – denounced Crowley on TV for his 'lack of discipline' basing this on Crowley's dictum 'Do what Thou Wilt, shall be the Whole of the Law' and conveniently forgetting the complementary rider — 'Love is the Law, Love under Will.' Mr. Symonds, filled with pious Christian bigotry, is frightened by 'Do What thou Wilt' which in fact, simply means that Crowley recognized no greater authority than himself on earth. Symond's slightly hysterical attitude has been given some edge by the fact that the Underground has picked up Crowley – Symonds cited the picture of Crowley on Sgt. Pepper, but neglected to mention his own fury when Kenneth Anger announced he was going to do a film on Crowley. (Anger owns the Abbey of Thelema in Sicily and has cleaned the whitewash off Crowley's paintings there) Magic is undefinable and mysterious. What magicians are really trying to do is tap the hidden wellsprings in their bodies and minds.

With his expert knowledge of logics and mathematics to support him Crowley blew the minds of those pussyfooting around with magic which at the time was little more than Sunday afternoon entertainment. He introduced Egyptian and Vedantic traditions and to rid his neophytes at the Abbey of the ego, he issued them with razors to cut themselves with whenever they said 'I'. Sex was an open part of the rituals, and many dilettantes went crazy or committed suicide. Crowley still horrifies people by saying that he wanted to sacrifice someone in a sex-magick rite. He would be hated less if he had actually done so (as the Nazis did as a matter of course). Writing about

it is apparently a greater crime. Other justifications for Crowley's 'wickedest man in the world' title? — he practised black magic (Crowley would deny this. He thought Christ was a student of the left hand path because he tried to control the body); he fucked a few women and left them; enjoyed anal sex; used heroin and was mean to his friends (especially Victor Neuberg); was arrogant and contemptuous of the Establishment ('You're all a pack of cards') and didn't mind owing money to people. In short Crowley was the epitome of that mythical Wicked Person you are told about at Sunday School.

Crowley remains a scapegoat and whatever merit or interest his ideas have are still shrouded in a mist of misleading publicity. 'Wickedest man in the world' is puritanical bullshit. Crowley is straight, unlike the people who handle him and overprice his work (he wanted his Equinox to sell for 1/- a volume). The leader of the Druids 'was a man — he lived', as Maugham once said, and that's all you need to remember about Crowley.
Ian Stocks

Bernadette Devlin The Price of my Soul (Andre Deutsch, 25s also in paperback) Witty, committed, breathless; as Irish a yarn as an Englishman could wish, this is Bernadette's and People's Democracy's story from the beginning. The familiar tale loses nothing in her telling: best of all, it emphasizes precisely those shortcomings in the movement that need exposing if committed radicals are to do more than stagger from barricade to barricade. From the splits with the Old Left to the 'dealings' with the 'sympathetic' members of the government, whose every promise was as false as our own Prime Minister, Bernadette lays bare the limitations of protest action. Nothing can be done in Westminster: 'What we have now is a kind of Animal Farm, all-pigs-are-equal system, whereby the pigs with MP after their name are entitled to sit in the farmhouse, and the rest of us are just common four-footed animals'. Nothing can be done without some organization that can provide new recruits when the old ones are tired. Nothing can be done if everyone emphasises their own purity of doctrine and refuses to recognize anyone else's: in Ireland this is a simple matter between Catholics and Protestants.

Bernadette wants people to realise what can be achieved by organized action which not only embraces all kinds of beliefs amongst young people, but also the real suffering of the Irish working class, of whatever religion. She believes that action and organizing in the streets is one of the most important tasks facing radicals. But, as the French students found after the May events, you can only build after the barricades if you've formed an organization that works, however loosely, at the bottom: the famous grass roots. Bernadette's upbringing taught her to take on personal responsibility for her actions — this is what she has tried to do in the fight for civil rights. If the movement gets anywhere, people will have learnt to take that kind of responsibility. This is a good book for those who believe 'it can never happen here'.
Peter Buckman

Mighty Baby: 'Mighty Baby' (Head HDLS 6002)

There are many groups that seem to go on for years at what you might call the Klooks Kleek level. In other words, they achieve a mild sort of reputation but never manage to break out of the endless round of one-nighters up and down the country.

If the music business was all fair and honest — credit where credit was due and so forth — one could say that this kind of group didn't succeed because it didn't deserve to: because it just didn't have what it takes to turn a Klooks Kleek group into a Royal Command performance act. As it is, of course, success depends less on how well you can play than who you know (how else do you explain the Ryan twins?)

Maybe this is the reason why Mighty Baby (nee the Action) have been around for so long without ever really making it. Perhaps they haven't got engaging accents, or they aren't evil-looking enough, or they're not as under-privileged as they ought to be — I don't know.
The important thing about Mighty Baby (fright — enough soft-selling) is that their first album is very good indeed.

Obviously their music slightly resembles the hard rock-blues that the Action used to play. It's pure electric music throughout: Mighty Baby seems content to explore the possibilities inherent in a drums/bass/lead/organ/sax line-up — they're not into the we're as versatile-as-any-symphony-orchestra thing. They make a kind of Buffalo Springfield sound at times too, but they're never merely imitative — you get the feeling that they write all their own material because they want to express themselves in their own way, not because somebody told them that no progress in the business you have to do your own numbers. Every track is, to a greater or lesser degree, satisfying, there are no space-fillers.

The best numbers on the album are those, like 'House Without Windows' and 'A Friend You Know But Never See', where they lay down and develop a solid rock and roll riff. Here you can see the advantage of playing for years: each musician instinctively maintains and enhances the balance of the song. Unlike those bands which are merely showcases for one soloist Mighty Baby are a group in the fullest sense.
The sleeve is good too, dig the frantic Martin Sharp front cover.
John Leaver.

Byrds Preflyte Together Records ST-T-1001 (Available on Import only)

During the past five years few groups have captured our imagination like the Byrds. In a sense, the West Coast movement began with them. They were the first rock group to be signed by Columbia in the States, forerunning Moby Grape, Spirit, Blood Sweat and Tears and United States of America, etc. They were one of the first bands to understand the importance of Dylan's songs and they were the first group to produce music from a communal environment. At one point fifteen or twenty people were directly involved in the creation of their music.

Now a new American record company has dug up a master of old Byrd recordings and released it in the States under the title 'Preflyte'. All of the material was recorded in 1964, before the Byrds signed with Columbia, and the album contains the original recording of 'Mr Tamborine Man'. It is a beautiful L.P. The music is naieve and in places imprecise, yet is has an incredible vitality and charm. Through it we can clearly see the Byrds early influences — the Everly Brothers, the Beatles, Chuck Berry and Dylan. It helps us put their later music into perspective and, more important, shows clearly why, despite never having produced a really world class album, the Byrds have become a legend.

We identified with the Byrds. The Beatles hair was growing — but the Byrds had grown theirs longer. British groups were still wearing uniform on stage — the Byrds played in jeans and T-shirts. They were untogether, moody and unpredictable and, when everyone about them was hustling into the Liverpool scene, the Byrds produced a new sound. Their teeny tour in 1965 was a disaster. We weren't ready for them. When they came back two years later they got a twenty minute ovation after a two hour set at Middle Earth.

But the album isn't just a point of reference. Some of the music compares with any they subsequently recorded. 'Here Without You' is gentle, melodic and emotional. 'You Don't Have To Cry' has a strong Beatles influence but all the Byrds trademarks are there — Jim McGuinn's voice, the vocal harmonies and the unmistakeable guitar sound. And, of course, there is 'Mr Tamborine Man'.
The original Byrds have long since parted but their influence is as strong as ever. Through Crosby Stills and Nash, the Flying Burrito Brothers and Dillard they are producing music of the highest quality.
We didn't realise it at the time but the Byrds were the first American super group.
Bob Harris.

ROLLING STONES / LET IT BLEED

THIS RECORD SHOULD BE PLAYED LOUD

LET IT BLEED ☐ LOVE IN VAIN ☐ MIDNIGHT RAMBLER ☐ GIMMIE SHELTER ☐ YOU GOT THE SILVER
YOU CAN'T ALWAYS GET WHAT YOU WANT ☐ LIVE WITH ME ☐ MONKEY MAN ☐ COUNTRY HONK

DECCA

(S) SKL 5025 (M) LK 5025

12″ Stereo or Mono LP   The Decca Record Company Limited   Decca House   Albert Embankment   London SE1

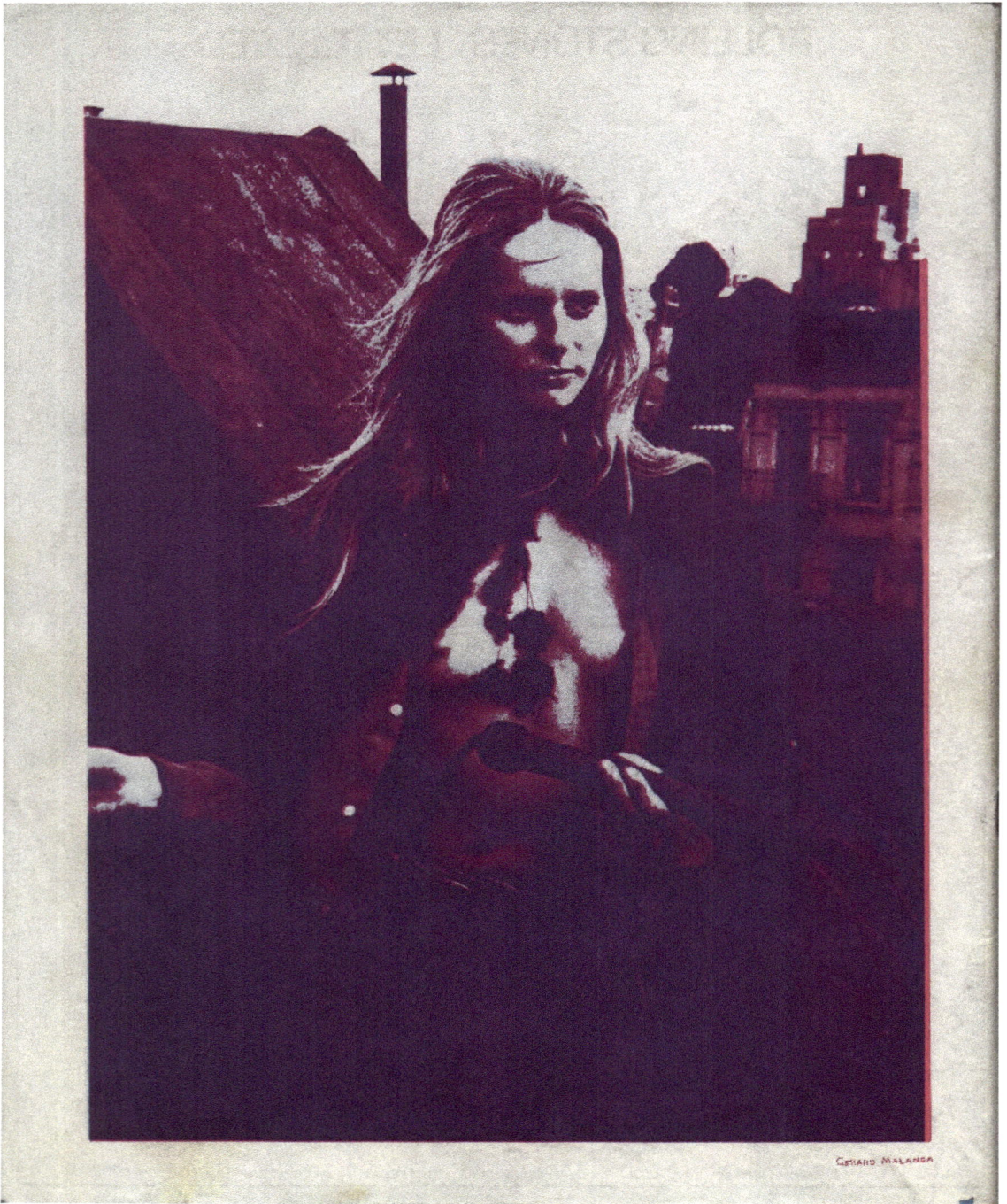

GERARD MALANGA

OZ

3/6

WOMEN'S LIBERATION
A True Romance
EXCLUSIVE!
Conspiracy Trial. What really happened
PLAY POWER
Put Down, Played Out.
MEDIA
Acid movies – lazy publishers –
tomorrows TV

HOLLYWOOD'S LARGEST TOOL
Guess who has the reinforced underpants.
CANDY DARLING
no wonder we lost another printer
SUCK
editor Bill Levy's private journal of three days in
Harwich immigration gaol. You'll see why they sent
him back to Amsterdam.
Want to edit OZ? Are you under 18? See page 46

Undryable but holdable ... ... only

BRITAIN'S FIRST INFLATABLE WOMAN

A SANE REVOLUTION

IF you make a revolution, make it for fun,
don't make it in ghastly seriousness,
don't do it in deadly earnest,
do it for fun.

Don't do it because you hate people,
do it just to spit in their eye.

Don't do it for the money,
do it and be damned to the money.

Don't do it for equality,
do it because we've got too much equality
and it would be fun to upset the apple-cart
and see which way the apples would go a-rolling.

Don't do it for the working classes.
Do it so that we can all of us be little aristocracies on
    our own
and kick our heels like jolly escaped asses.

Don't do it, anyhow, for international Labour.
Labour is the one thing a man has had too much of.

Let's abolish labour, let's have done with labouring!
Work can be fun, and men can enjoy it; then it's not
    labour.
Let's have it so! Let's make a revolution for fun!

D. H. Lawrence

OZ 26
February/March 1970
OZ is published by OZ Publications Ink
Ltd, 52 Princedale Road, London, W.11
Telephone: 229 7541
Advertising: Contact Felix Dennis at 727
8456
Subscriptions: Send 42/- or 6 dollars for
12 issues to above address
Printed by OZ Publications Ink Ltd

This issue appears with the help of
Richard Neville, Felix Dennis, Jim
Anderson, David Wills, Gary Brayley
Martin Sharp and Bridget Murphy
Cover photograph by David Nutter
FOR CANDY DARLING AND several
of the overlays used in this issue we
thank
NEWSPAPER WITHOUT WORDS
188 SECOND AVENUE
NY CITY 10002
SUBSCRIPTIONS $6 PER YEAR

Distribution:
UK: Moore Harness Ltd. 11 Lever St
London E C 1 CLE 4882
Transmutation Guildford 65694
California: Rattner Distributors 2428
McGee St Berkley California 94703
Holland: Van Gelderen Amsterdam
Denmark: George Streeton, The
Underground, Larsbjorn Straede 13,

TAKE THE PLUNGE!
COMMIT A
REVOLUTIONARY
ACT

Subscribe
to OZ

To: OZ 52 Princedale Road London W11   42s or $6 for 12 issues

NAME:

ADDRESS:

portrait of a bolshevist

YOU MEET IN SECRET PLACES AND IN YOUR SLIMY MINDS YOU CONCOCT FOUL SCHEMES WHICH, INCREDIBLE THOUGH IT MAY SEEM HAVE SO FAR HAD MORE THAN A FAIR MEASURE OF SUCCESS IN THIS COUNTRY

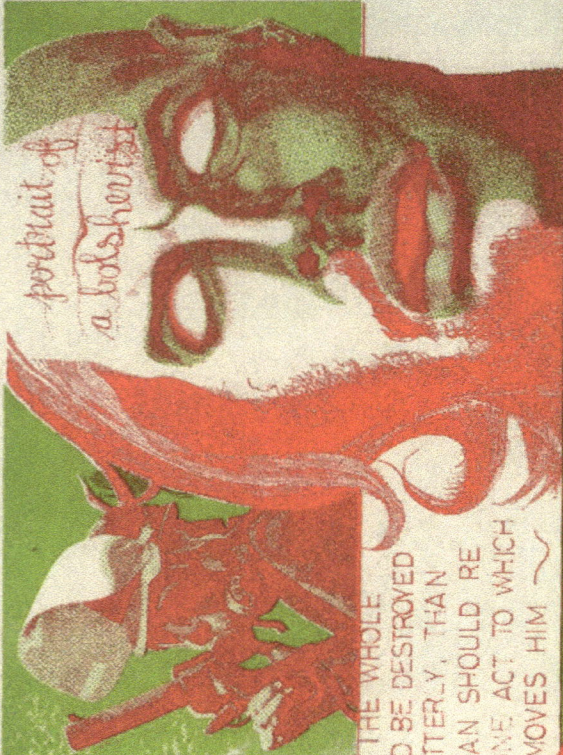

BETTER THAT THE WHOLE WORLD SHOULD BE DESTROYED AND PERISH UTTERLY, THAN THAT A FREEMAN SHOULD RE FRAIN FROM ONE ACT TO WHICH HIS NATURE MOVES HIM

AND WHAT OF THOSE WHO ARE MOVED TO PHANTASISE, MUST THEY THEN ACT?

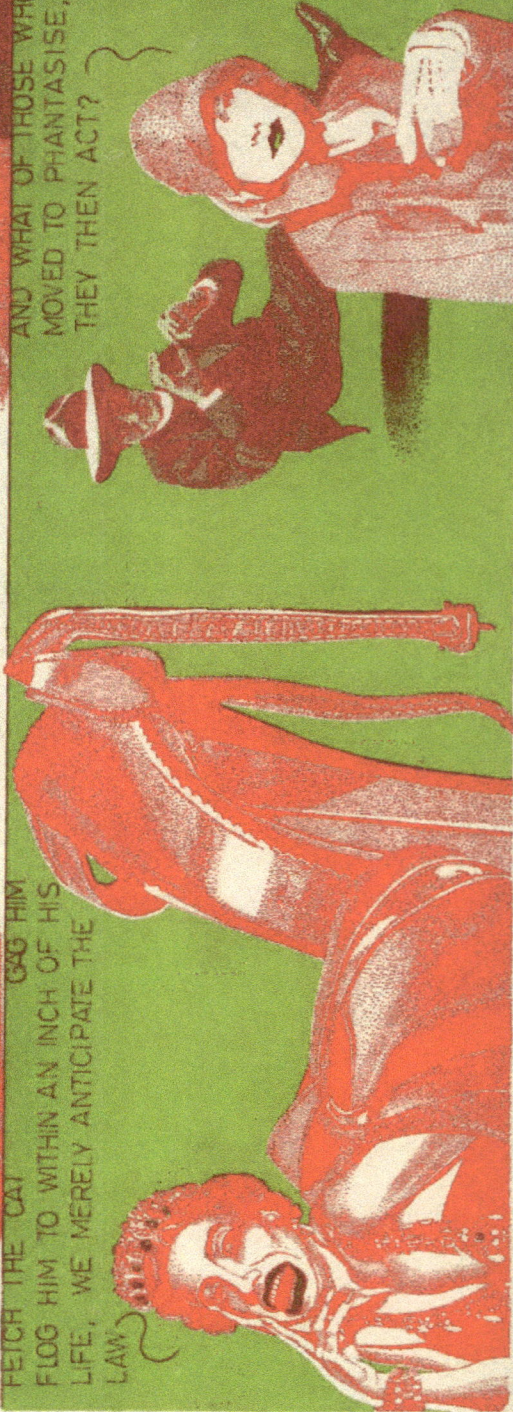

FETCH THE CAT GAG HIM FLOG HIM TO WITHIN AN INCH OF HIS LIFE. WE MERELY ANTICIPATE THE LAW

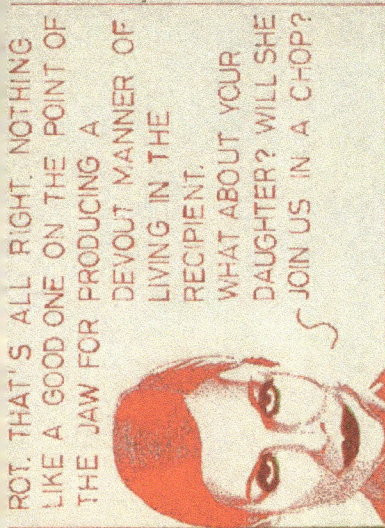

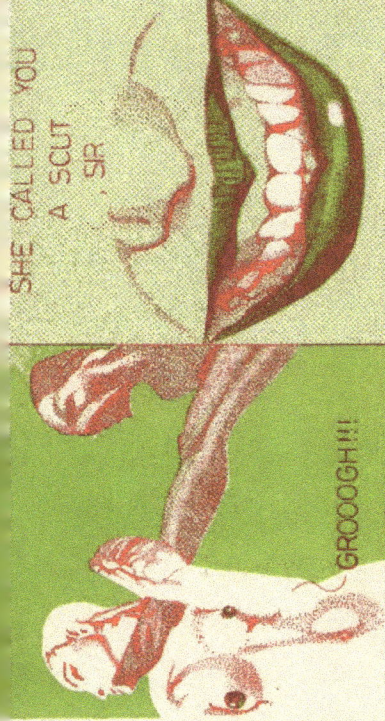

To Love
Blackhill
Enterprises
Is To
Love Life

Al Stewart
Barefoot
Battered Ornaments
Bridget St John
The Deviants and Mick Farren
Dr Strangely Strange
The Dubliners
Edgar Broughton Band
Forest
Formerly Fat Harry
Jody Grind
John Martyn
The Johnstons
Martin Carthy
Ralph McTell
Stefan Grossman
Shirley and Dolly Collins
Sweeney's Men
Third Ear Band

32 Alexander Street
London W2
01 229 6718

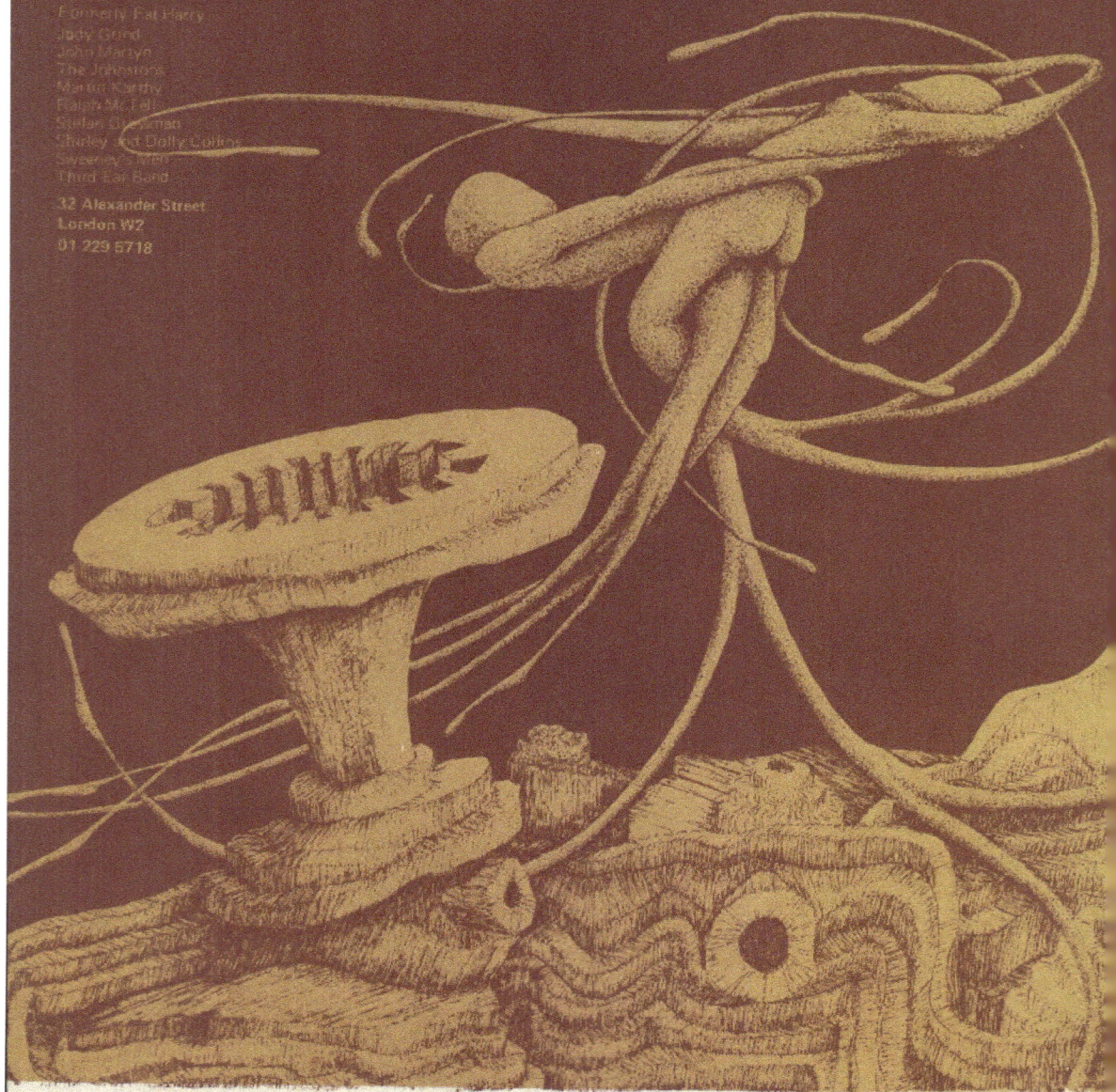

Bill Levy cont. from P23

until further representation can be made on my behalf. Also says Home Office had a report filed by doctor that I'm a "Drug addict". We have a long talk — an hour and a half — we admit each of us made mistakes have become armoured with each other. Abby says she sees Susan from her letters as feminine, vivacious, probably a colourful dresser, all the things she (Abby) is not.

"Susan is supportive", I say, "we are supportive with each other".

Religion is sexy
& so is Susan.

Abby and I talk about past present future. Both agree there are still elements we love in each. She has been telling herself without belief she doesn't love me any longer. I'm told Peter Jackson M.P. (Lab) for High Peak, Derb. is coming to see me. What will he see?

See Chief Inspector to find out names of doctor. The one who examined me first is called Dr. Doupe. He is Port Medical Officer attached to Essex County Council and ultimately to the Minister of Health. Tell Chief Inspector I plan to break that man; sue him for criminal libel; have him removed from Medical List. Chief Inspector concerned I'll make a complaint about police. Says Dr. Doupe is with Immigration people.

Being a drug addict is not a question of opinion but one of fact. Besides the man never examined me.

Fucking bureaucrats. When they saw I might not be what they claimed they falsified evidence to justify the decision.

Force myself to smile when I return to detention cell.

"We can't change the world. We can only change ourselves", Bill Sands.

Rain today. Sky dark, blue silver, pink along horizon. Thunder and lightning.

No longer thinking of cunt.

All in all, I've found friends people willing to help when in need in unexpected places. Heathcote and Abby have responded like family. Guess its my fathers teaching to think of those closest as family.

Must remember to ask to see Aleister Crowley sex diary juss Tom Driberg alluded to in his "News of the World" article, late October.

Find out Baroness Wootton won't do anything for me because she says in my testimony before her committee I admitted breaking the law; should have expected that. So much for politicians of all stripe.

Left Amsterdam after two days of lightning and thunder, elemental skies. Now I'm leaving England perhaps forever, after another similar cosmic storm.

If one jumps over the edge one is bound to land somewhere.

But isn't it very risky?

Five hours until I leave. No feeling in cock and balls. I don't even have bladder filled morning erections. Now I know what Hoppy meant when he said he was impotent for two months after getting out of Wormwood Scrubs Prison. Did prison make Michael impotent as well? I must ask him when we meet next.

The total absurdity of it all; seven or eight able bodied policemen keeping 24 hour watch on this horney endomorphic jewish intellectual.

Stale smell of nervous sweat in armpits.

Beginning to hallucinate. Thought I heard someone call my name from train platform outside window.

Rain stopped. Still unsure whether I'll be turned back from Holand.

Abby is a dear. Her first thought upon hearing I'm to be deported was how to get me my winter coat.

6 o'clock train arrives from London. Is Peter Jackson on this one or was report of his visit a false alarm?

Feel as if I'm treading in the air, quite unstable.

Dinner at British Rail Canteen, as usual.

Heathcote phones. Both solemn about parting. He says Jean left London today at noon for Chicago to judge a Bunny contest with Bill Crosby. Jean   is special. The only person I know capable of the sustained passion of a W. H. Hudson heroine. A Scorpio, with Venus in Scorpio. Heathcote says if he goes to New York to contact him through Grove Press.

Notice on Police Bulletin board next to telephone: Harwi Police, Traffic Division, Stag Night; "We expect to have tw strippers, a drag act and a comedian".

Abby phones. Asks if I would like her to come see me o and go with me as far as the Hoof. First sexual feeling I've h in a week. Abby has chosen to put up a fight! Good. It's t only chance we have of winning.

Jackson, M.P., never posts. DEPORTED. When a count closes its borders, an election can't be far behind!

It can only get crazier.

When Abby and I get to cabin on board the ferry, I vom then wretch, sweat and tremble. Get over this after an hou For Abby, release in tears.

Abby and I stay up all night. We lie in bed nude — havi friendly, gentle sex without cosmic quality. Talk talk.

Mixed Feelings about Abby and Les fucking while I was Amsterdam.

1. Les and I have been good friends for 16 years. We ha never shared a girl. This brings us closer together. Silent compose a letter to Les:

Dear Fluke,

I've been deported from England as a gangster of love.

If you asked again, I think China might come to Turkey.

She needs the support that you, more than I, can give.

2   Reminds me of a Susan Janssen story. When she w temporarily blinded after an accident, her boyfriend broug another girl to the flat — a girl with one leg — and fucked t new girl while Susan was in the room, bed-ridden and blin She could hear what was going on but that perception w denied by boyfriend.

3   Abby says now Les is her boyfriend as well as mine.

A cock and ball polaroid photo of Les on the cover of t journal. When I draw Abby's attention she replies descriptive "Yes, he has a bigger cock than you. It felt different fro yours, but you know it's not the size that counts . . . Sti then yours is more attractive"

We discuss our sexual preferences. It's a subject I ha always avoided. Abby says she likes to be fucked at least twi in a session. She likes all positions.   I tell Abby I enjo sucking her cunt. She thought I did it only to please her: "It the only thing that melts me", she says.

Abby expresses concern about never having had a vagir orgasm. In her group sex scene with Chris and Darryl Brey she noticed that Darryl had a powerful orgiastic release enou though Chris came rather quickly.

I tell Abby how much I enjoy the muscular dance of h cunt!!!

Ferry arrives at Hook of Holland . . .

"You had tomatoes for dinner", Abby notices as she loo from mirror to sink while getting dressed in the morning.

Letting go takes courage . . .

And if you ask how I regret this parting

It is like the flowers at Spring's end Confused, whorled, in tangle.

What is the use of talking

And there is no end of talking,

There is no end to things in the heart . . .

Ezra Pound, *Exile's Lett*

Postscripts:
1. See also, Edgar Allen Poe's story, *The System of Dr. To and Professor Feather*. Here the lunatics take over an asylum and entertain an unwary guest.
2. If we limit ourselves to what is understandable we have n increased the scope of what might be understood. Offic contacts with the unknown always finish in some commer ialized undertaking like Lourdes, or a police raid, like Gilles Reis

William Levy for peace 1970

The new word

Po

The new word PO upsets many people. It would not have been worth inventing if it did not have this effect — at least to begin with.

The Mechanism of Mind (published by Jonathan Cape) is about the way the mind works as a pattern-making system.

A pattern-making system requires a 'discontinuity function' in order to change the patterns and bring them up to date.

We have never developed any discontinuity tool in language because we have been obsessed by the need for the continuity of sequential logic.

The new word PO is a discontinuity tool for language and thought. Just as NO is the basis of logical thinking so PO is the basis of lateral thinking. NO is the negative of language. PO is the laxative of language.

PO can be used in a variety of ways but underlying them all is the single function of making easier the creative jump.

1 *Provocation*: PO allows one to use information in ways which cannot be justified on any other grounds.

Sex PO paper-clips. . . capitalism PO ketchup. . . are not meant to describe anything but to set off ideas.

PO cars should have square wheels. . . allows one to use an 'intermediate impossible' as a step to a new idea.

2 *Challenge*: Applied to a whole argument or to a single concept PO is never a judgement but working outside the YES/NO judgement system PO challenges the rigidity and dogmatic absolutism of concepts. PO implies, "That is a convenient cliché concept — try changing it."

PO is a refusal to accept assumptions.

3 *As reaction*: Faced with a situation one reacts immediately with whatever standard reaction pattern slips into place. PO breaks the continuity and by providing a pause reaction allows one to proceed to a new reaction.

4 *As attitude*: Even if one never actually uses PO it serves as a symbol of the arbitrariness of fixed patterns that have arisen for historical reasons. This should temper arrogance and rigidity.

(Those who want more details of the use of PO should consult *The Mechanism of Mind*).

PO is but an information tool to break the continuity of fixed patterns and so allow available information to come together to give new ideas.

Being a tool PO is only as useful as one acquires skill in using it. Since all training should at least be enjoyable below is an opportunity to practise ONE ASPECT of the use of PO. With PO one sets up an impossible situation — and then one resolves it.

You can play this game by yourself or with other people. You select a name in the first list and then you (or someone else) selects a word in the second list. You put them together: as PO Marshall McLuhan is Brighton pier.

Then you resolve the situation.

Po

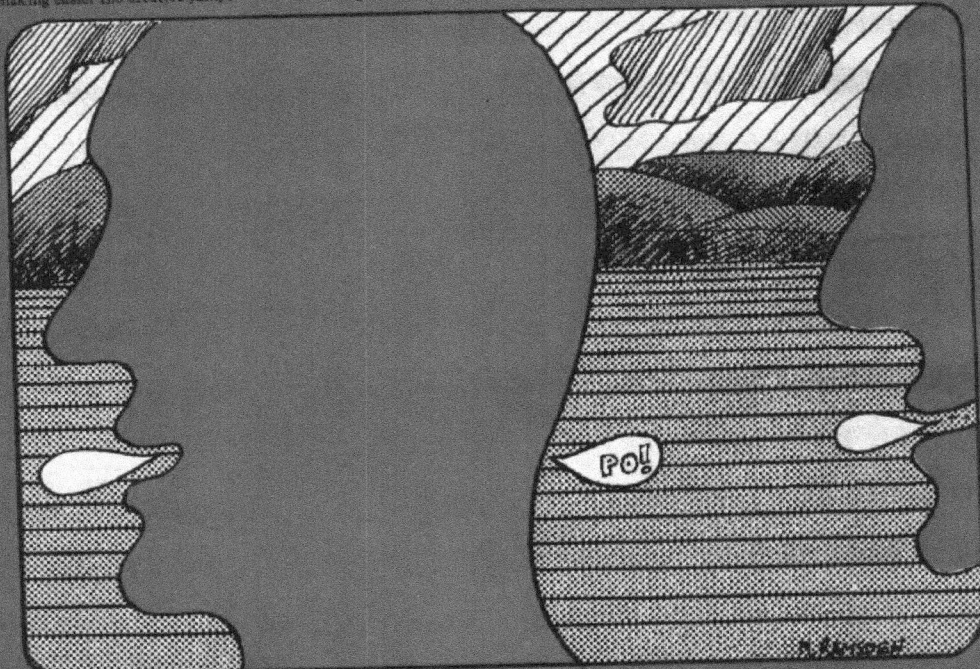

Harold Wilson	spaghetti
Malcolm Muggeridge	Brighton pier
David Frost	tce-mail clippings
John Lennon	The New Statesman
Marshall McLuhan	a beer mat
Richard Nixon	BBC-2
Raquel Welch	a pair of braces
Ted Heath	lipstick
Spiro Agnew	a flash of lightning
Enoch Powell	mushroom
Tiny Tim	fish-fingers

PO Marshall McLuhan is Brighton pier . . .

. . . a bridge that only has one end

. . . heavily advertised but disappointing when you get there
. . . more known than used
. . . the seeing butler of modern society

PO Harold Wilson is a packet of cornflakes . . .

. . . promises on the outside, half-empty inside

. . . fireworks that dazzle without illuminating

I shall be inclined to give some copies of the book mentioned above to any splendid examples that may come up (send them to me via OZ).

Edward De Bono
author of *The Mechanism of Mind, The Five Day Course in Thinking, The Use of Lateral Thinking.*

HEAVY SHIT...

Felix Dennis

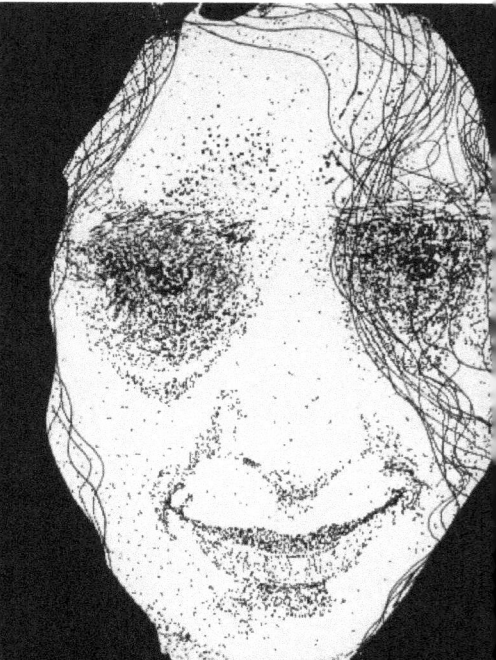

VICAR CHARGED WITH KIDNAP OF BABY
Daily Express
Fri Sept 27th 1946

Blackhill Bullshit, that seedy but amusing house journal from *Blackhill Enterprises* (of Free Concerts fame), has seen fit to bestow its Annual Award for the 'most obscene advertisement of the year' on *OZ*. Regular readers of *OZ* might remember the ad (issue 24), designed by us for Blackhill's band, the new defunct Buttered Ornaments, it showed a photograph (stolen from *Evergreen*) of a beautiful and naked chick abusing herself; in addition it carried the EMI logo on her right thigh. According to the *Bullshit* it has caused apoplexy among countless EMI executives, whose permission to run the advertisement was unfortunately not obtained prior to publication.

Farewell Aldebaran, a new LP, slows down around its own... A X Ahead the Remble. The Battle of North-West Six. Spends... have been actually neglect... I record to everything in... First album Halfbreed... composed in bliss and instant integration of old and new... later studio, fixing and... instrumental efficiency in... music alone. Mon of Harlech, Picture Harley, buccaneered and Bronzed lighting fires in the setting sun of Laurel Canyon ... something of an acquired taste.

Hopefully, Key will soon get the breaks forewhich Mayall worked so long. Though I can hardly lay the blame on them when the blues-based compositions...

LONDON BALLOON BARRAGE TEST TODAY
News Chronicle
Sat Oct 18th 1938

It's no news that Radio One(derful) is even more boring now than in its pre-Pirate days, when we all called it the Light Programme, so it was unusual to hear somebody other than the Peel/Drummond syndrome getting into a little head music on 247 metres last month. *Seen & Heard*, no less, featuring *Laura Nyro's* latest LP, **New York Tendaberry**, on *CBS*. And to be strictly fair, their summary of Nyro's talents was crystal clear, if a little clinical.

They remarked that it 'remained to be seen' if Laura ever 'made it', (nasty phrase), as a singer/performer, although 'no-one could dispute her talents as a song-writer', (she has already given several hits to *Three Dog Night*, *Fifth Dimension* and *Blood Sweat & Tears* in the U.S.A.). Would this new album sell in its own right or remain 'merely a showcase for her unique compositions?' *Seen & Heard* sounded doubtful that New York Tendaberry would sell, and so am I, but they missed the point; commercial potential is hardly a fair yardstick to measure musical ability ... or as Zappa

has noted of the mass record-buying public ... 'these kids wouldn't know music if it came up and bit them on the arse.' Exactly.

Laura sings and plays the piano in an absorbed meticulous style, each note plucked like a ripe plum. Discords are her speciality ... jarring the senses, breaking up what might otherwise remain too barren a landscape, too monotonous a view ... dischordant phrasing and timing. Stilted, even ponderous in places, her songs often break unpredictably in mid-verse, melody torn to tattered shreds, calculated solecism. Although her consultant/conductor (strange title?) has added brass and a little orchestration on a few tracks they have been used sparingly and are all the more effective for it. And always it's that startling jazzy fingerwork, that high strangled voice up front dominating the mood and tempo completely.

Her compositions are as melancholy, for the most part, as Leonard Cohen's but there's a peculiar high-strung, paranoid quality about them, the jittery speed of a meths freak, that stamps them unmistakably as her own. Laura Nyro is exhausting but rewarding listening. Brilliant music to fuck to.

BREAD TO BE RATIONED IN GREAT BRITAIN?
Sir Ben Smith Gives Warning.
The New Yorker
Apr 20 1946

When are British record companies going to stop packaging their products in soft, toilet roll cardboard? Double sleeves in the U.K. are actually thinner than single American covers. Even for giving the generally God awful standard of graphics, records like *Let It Bleed* and *Abbey Road*, guaranteed to sell, and make, millions, surely deserve better treatment than a slap-a-bit-of-shiny-on-both-sides of flabby board attitude. Of all the companies, only *Island* seem to give a fuck about the production of their sleeves.

And talking about fuck and sleeves, why has that very word been omitted from the lyrics supplied with Volunteers, the latest *Jefferson Airplane* album? It's quite audible on the record, but the word 'Fred' has been substituted rather lamely in its place in print. A member of R.C.A.'s publicity office explained to *OZ* that... 'This is a decision made from our New York office ...but you have to remember we have a responsibility to the public ... it's possible that old people or kiddies might pick up this record and be offended by it ...or something.' He didn't know what the *Jefferson Airplane* thought about it, and didn't seem to care, in fact he hadn't known anything about it until we called him. It's interesting to remember that RCA are the company who recently booked a double page splash in Zig Zag imploring kiddies (and old people), to 'take a short trip' (to their record dealers), to really, 'turn you on' (to their miserable selection of 'progressive' sounds), which are really young high ...care to join them? No

10

"IT'S ALLRIGHT!"
HITLER POSTPONES
MOBILISATION
There Is Hope — Real Hope —
For Peace
Daily Express
Thurs Sept 29th 1938

Heartening news for those of you who may already have heard via *Rolling Stone* of the new bootleg albums available in the States. Two long haired entrepreneurs, who preferred us to forget their names and faces, called at the *OZ* offices last week to divulge their plans for the production, distribution and marketing of LIVER *Than You'll Ever Be*, the reportedly fantastic, stereo recording of the *Stones* playing live on their U.S. tour, together with Stealin' and Gww John Birch Society Blues, the two new Dylan L.P.s following up **The Great White Wonder** (see OZ 25); these two albums contain between them a total of twenty seven songs, only eight or nine of which have ever been issued before, in different versions, on previously released *Dylan/CBS* records.

"The sound quality on the Dylan albums, especially Stealin' is fine," promised the taller hustler, "much, much better than 'Wonder. And the *Stones*, oh man, you gotta hear it to believe it. Unbelievably good."

His friend continued, "When the 'Wonder hit here last December we didn't do too well. Only one batch was actually produced here: the rest were imported from Canada. That meant high prices, too many questions and too many other cats crowdin' the market with shittily produced goods. Some of the home-grown albums, well.. people who bought from some of our ... er ... competitors are probably pretty pissed off. The plastic should be worn through just about now! This time, man, we've got it all sussed ... all the albums gonna be made here, first class jobs."

Did they envisage any problems persuading stores to sell illegal goods? "Who says it's fuckin' illegal? Who says it is? Anyway, if it's the *Stones* and *Dylan* it'll sell. Plenty of the big record stores carried 'Wonder – under the counter like. We'll have those fuckin' albums out here in wholesale quantities by the beginning of March. And I mean fuckin' *wholesale!*"

Did they have any moral qualms about releasing an artist's material without his knowledge or consent?

"Fuck all that! Music belongs to the people ..."

He was keeping a straight face but his partner blew it with a sly grin; "Don't listen to him man. In '67 he was wearing a kaftan floggin' beads 'n' bells to the tourists. We're only in this for the money ..." How true to the spirit of the British underground.

...a basket of musical bubbles

Ever since *Rolling Stone*, in their review of the underground press, so graciously labelled *OZ* as .. the happiest under-ground magazine any-where ... so hip they're insult-ing about it ... (oh really?) certain American record companies have taken to mailing us albums direct from the States, presumably for review and at a phenomenal cost in air-freight to boot. Fair enough, except that for every *B. B. King* that arrives, (thank you *ABC Records*), we have been deluged in other crap, bearing liner notes like the following:

". . . The *Billy Mitchell Group* is a 'Madonna And Child'. The Group is basic, beautiful and funky. The group makes the listener a viewer – makes him see with his ears. Listen and you will see the masterful splashes and strokes of da Vinci, the gentle but obvious shadings to comple-ment the whole. Listen to *The Billy Mitchell Group* and see their musical sketches. It's magic ..."

It's not. Try to imagine *The Happy Wanderers* up Oxford Street on a foggy day, featur-ing a selection of numbers from last year's entries in the Eurovision Song Contest ... well, it's worse. So thank you *Calla Records*, but no. And could *Calla Records* be a sub-sidiary of *Roulette Records*, who, last month, were also responsible for sending *OZ*, among other goodies The Best of Tommy James and The Shondells, proudly bellowing on *their* liner notes that they sold more single hit records than *any other artist* last year. Over six million in fact

As our editor, Richard Neville, admits in his illuminating, and more important, just published, book, *Play Power*, he is nearly thirty; born in a mid-way generation ... "already pubertal by the time Carl Perkins ... happened". This perhaps explains his incessant obsession, (often denied, but painfully obvious), with early Rock - And - Roll. The voluminous article on early *Sun Records* in the last *OZ*, certainly the longest single article on any subject in this magazine, at least to my memory, is clear proof of this insatiable thirst for the reliving of days filled with Australian sunshine, bopping with Sweet Little Sixteen at the High School Confidental ... etc. etc. Even Zappa, (I must stop quoting him), refers to this music as 'greasy love songs of cretin simplicity', but as anyone who has heard *Ruben And the Jets* will know, he too is an addict and his sneer is patently tinged with loving reverence.

Imagine then, if you can, Richard's unbounded fury on discovering an almost criminal fraud committed in the name of Rock-And-Roll by a certain *Ember Records*. It seems that they have released an album, Mr. Rock And Roll, which by its graphic design, (or rather by the lack of it), and detailed sleeve notes, purports to be a collection of early and original material by the living kiss curl himself, William Haley. Numbers like See You Later Alligator, ("In A While Crocodile", retorted Her Royal Highness wittily after a Royal Command Performance), Rock Around the Clock and Shake Rattle and Roll are all listed, alongside notes mentioning 'this vintage Haley platter' .. 'relive the excitement of...". .. still sounds as fresh today as when it was recorded in 1954 ... etc.

In fact the tracks contain nothing but contemporary Haley, and it must be sadly recorded here that he has not improved as a musician in any of those fifteen years. To be honest he sounds a great deal worse; the arrangements and instrumentalists who accompany him have been hurriedly assembled and recorded in what must surely have been a series of disasterous and lightning 'first takes', probably on one of their recent tours of Europe. *OZ* telephoned *Ember* in a self-righteous frame of mind, to demand on explanation.

The publicity man was embarrassed. Our interpretation of the liner notes was only 'our opinion'. He could not agree that they were deliberately misleading to the public. They were 'our business'. Not his business. He had, in any case, never read the notes. What did we want him to say? Any thing he said 'would sound trite'. We agreed, and rung off to the whine of, 'please don't slate us'. He rang back, flustered. He repeated his arguments. Did we realise the notes were written by no less an authority than THE PRESIDENT OF THE *BILL HALEY FAN CLUB?* We had not realised. But did that alter the contents? 'Not really' he signed. We hung up.

Be warned *Ember Records*, and any other record company foolish enough to invite the wrath of ageing romantics, memories are not to be tampered with. If you must hype business, stick to Reggae, teenyboppers who read the *New Statesman* are not so easily deceived.

VICE-PROTEST
TO HOME OFFICE
Residents say: Stop
this vicious trade. £20 a night:
That's what prostitutes earn on Clapham Common
Clapham Observer
Fri Nov 14th 1958

Putdown of the month prize to Robbie Robertson from *Time Magazine's* in-depth article on The Band, (we'll show *Newsweek* who's really heavy), quoted as sneering ... "The new *Rolling Stones* album sounds like a bunch of blues orientated cowboys."

11

BLUE AFTERNOON *Tim Buckley*

Tim Buckley's first album hailed from that period when the West Coast had just discovered *Bob Dylan* and had given birth to the *Byrds* and folk-rock. The album bore the hall-marks of inexperience; it had some beautiful songs but also a certain amount of make-weight material. Overall, the music was divided between quiet, folksy type numbers with a minimum of accompaniment, and hard, crisp, percussive rock. This division was in itself a weakness – it was as if *Buckley* couldn't decide where he wanted to go, as if he was trying to assimilate too much of what was happening on the West Coast at the time. The record was promising, but no one could have been really prepared for the album which followed: *Goodbye and Hello*. In my view this is one of the essential pop albums, ranking alongside *Sergeant Pepper* in its beauty and inventiveness. True, the achievement was as much producer *Jerry Yester's* as *Buckley's*. *Yester* took *Buckley's* basic music, added a line up of top, West Coast session musicians, and produced a schizophrenic album, playing off *Buckley's* amazing voice, thin and taut, like a mellow scream, against some really staggering arrangements. The final effect in music which says so much on so many different levels that, like *Pepper*, it will stand any amount of replaying.

Perhaps *Buckley* found the arrangements *too* overpowering, for on *Happy Sad*, his third album, he was down to a basic 'group' of four musicians: *Lee Underwood, Carter C. Collins, John Miller* and *David Freedman*, and a minimum of production tricks. The group took the songs as they came, using *Buckley's* incisive guitar rhythms as a basis for improvisation. It produced some nice sounds but the total effect, (especially after the colour and flare of *Goodbye and hello)*, was a little samey.

It was obviously the style and format, however, that *Buckley* had been after all the time, for it remains, virtually unchanged, on **Blue Afternoon**, his first album for *Frank Zappa's Straight* label and the first to be produced by *Buckley* himself.

Despite the apparent lack of progression, Blue Afternoon is, in fact, a valid development of *Buckley's* music. It's an exploration, in greater depth than ever before, of the sad side of Tim's *Happy sad* coin. The music is poignant and introverted, dealing with themes of loneliness, loss and parting. It's white mind-blues rather than black gut-blues, and even a coming home song like *Happy Time*, with superficially joyful lyrics, is given a melancholy treatment that etches in an unspoken background of loneliness. The album is emotionally, rather than musically, 'heavy', but the songs avoid self-pity and the final effect is uplifting rather than depressing. Whatever else it may be, this album is pure *Buckley*, purer than ever before. That can't be bad.
Graham Charnock

Taj Mahal **Giant Step/De Ole Folks At Home**. Not really knowing much about Taj Mahal (except that he couldn't possibly be a building in India, and probably was not the son of a Mr. and Mrs. Mahal) I looked him up in Lillian Roxon's Rock Encyclopaedia (published in New York by Grosset & Dunlap $9.95c) She hadn't forgotten him, and there he was dutifully listed under M between Mad River and Mamas and the Papas. Found none of those intimate personal details which would have satisfied my teeny bopper, fan magazine heart, but I did read this:

"The irony with the traditional country blues is that black singers, whose people originated them, have outgrown them emotionally and feel the need to move into something more sophisticated. So young white singers have taken them on, caring for them with the love of a true archivist. For Taj Mahal, who is black, to do these blues is an even further turn of the screw. One of the very few sophisticated young black singers, he brought back the sound of authentic blues, flatly refusing to gloss over or stylise."

So, Taj is not an Uncle Tom, but an archivist. On De Ole Folks At Home he has dug up an incredible collection of negro folk songs, which, to the accompaniment of himself on banjo – a beautiful rich funky sound – he sings in the friendliest manner possible; in pure rustic blues style, but without the stretches of anguish or the blue corners. A University background, simple living, vegetarianism and California weather have made him as mellow as yellow. Trouble is, he otherwise sounds as ancient and the same as the men who originally sang these songs – Howling wolf, Lightning Hopkins, Muddy Waters, Sleepy John Estes, Son House and others of that band of reincarnated black tortoises – which is very strange for someone who is only about twenty seven. Somehow it seem a waste. Is it a guilty search for his lost black heritage, or a lack of true imagination which has caused him, like a classicist, to look to interpretation of historic texts for inspiration? I am glad he hasn't turned the screw even further and gotten into German beer hall songs or something.

The tracks themselves are fine. Some of them, like *Lining Track*, have always been crude, undeveloped and not particularly likeable, while others, such as *Fishing Blues*, and *Annie's Lover* are so pretty that it is a delight to have them sung as well as Taj does it. Compare his singing of *Candy Man* with Blind Boy Grunt's version on Great White Wonder.

The other record, **Giant Step** is much more the Taj Mahal we all know and love. *Take a Giant Step, Give Your Woman What She Wants* and *Farther on Down the Road* were the tracks I liked best. The whole feeling of the record is easygoing, reflective, totally relaxed and in accordance with the atmosphere and image that Taj Mahal projects – that of the courtly gentleman-farmer musician, sitting in the shade on his wooden porch, big hat firmly on his head, happy stoned grin on his face, friends always around, chickens scratching in the sun, bucolic peace and good will radiating to all. His version of *Good Morning Little Schoolgirl* is a handholding affair. When Alvin Lee does it for Ten Years on Shhh it's more like child molesting or rape.

This is not a sensational record. No new ground is covered, and **Giant Step** is probably a misleading title. Taj is sitting still (probably in a rocking chair) and resting on his laurels. Which is a lovely thing to do. Everyone should do it a little more. He's just a big kindly man who loves to sing and talk about the blues. There's a lot of the homespun philosopher teacher in Taj as you will realise as you happily listen to these two records. He's not heading in any particular direction, but "he's looking fine and feeling good, man, how about you?"
Jim Anderson.

In a silent way *Miles Davis*

There are listeners who don't hear the jazz genius of the sixties, they don't care for his lyrical stuff, they demand not-front dynamics, the self-imposed silence of the Davis personality, regardless of the Rolling Stone interview, offends many, but not me baby. All I need is a pair of Koss headphones, and the soothing transmudulations, wow, of the Miles magic, and you could cut my leg off and I wouldn't know. But I'm like that, a martyr to music. Others still keep demanding dynamism, they want the artist to cut his leg off in front of them.

The aforementioned would look at the line-up and see *Davis*, *Wayne Shorter* on soprano sax, and ostensibly a six-piece rhythm section of three electric pianos, bass, guitar, and drums. They'd say that Davis fancies himself, or he must be a gutless wonder to need all those people shugging behind him. Both views are right because they're necessary to make his music. He wants individual expression, and at the same time he wants them to play his way. This is an apparent contradiction unless put in terms of he's the boss, but they're free to get on with their work. Or maybe here's the whole, let's *see* if the parts fit. If you've got talent, they will.

The trouble with *Davis* records is that often you don't have the job of waiting for solos, and when they arrive there's that special kick and you say to your friend listen to that *Dulcie*. From the beginning it seems to be the whole *Miles Davis* band, and the bits and parts are not particularly noticeable. This record is like that all the way. The whole is greater than the sum of the parts could have been. The music has an atmosphere of an Abbey Road side two, a Nashville Skyline, . . . is slow down, look around, start again.

For the English there's some local colour with the presence of *John McLaughlin* on guitar and *Dave Holland* on bass. *McLaughlin's* strength on Marmalade shows why he's in the Davis band, and there are a lot of heavies there to complement or compete with.

If you want a lead into In a silent way listen to the *Mademoiselle Mabry* track on 'Filles de Kilimanjaro". The new album is a multi-coloured, three-dimensional extension of that single line.
Hire some headphones.
T. R. Zelinka

RENAISSANCE

You've got to accept that *Island* have a special sound. They've been up north of Oxford Street, pouring nitrates on the transplanted heads, cultivating the pink crop, and not quite putting them in the Safeways' stands as exotic vegetables. And if you do your record shopping in the usual way, you can't miss them, the packaging stands out, good or bad. And so it should, I mean, there's the sound, enthusiastic, fresh, and idealistically apropos. The problem that *Island* is fast approaching is that when a label sound becomes identifiable, the individual artists must be suffering. Motown Memories, etc. The December bunch of *Renaissance* are suffering There's too much *Island* in them. Shades of the pink label surround the sounds. I want to get into them, but I'm too quickly reminded of the commandments established by *Traffic, Jethro Tull* and the oldies.

Thou shalt be original, Thou shalt be English, and latterly Thou shalt be commercial, the latter attributable to producers, engineers, and the label, less often the artists. Commerciality is a nasty word only when it's obvious and superfluous, and in the long run *Renaissance* are the losers, not *Island*.

After wading knee-deep through your toccatas, fugues and fantasies, nocturnas and impromptus, Slow-finger *Hawken* humps the harpsichord behind the icy, crystal, cool, menthol voice of *Jane Relf*, and slopes into muddy mangrove stomping supporting the strangled vowels of the lead boy singer.

You can't help but like *RENAISSANCE* if you like me you fancy the piano, and they're real strong on keyboards. The *Bach* and *Beethoven, Mozart* and *Schubert, Chopin* and *Dr. John* snatches amongst the variable '69 rock are vigorous and amusing and perfectly compatible with the whole set. But not enough concrete to sustain life-long listening. *Keith Relf* as an old quality name, mutter, mutter, Yardbirds, mutter, has an attraction, but there's that piano man doing all the work. Maybe *Relf* and *RENAISSANCE* are like *Pappalardi* and *Cream, Glyn Johns* and the *Steve Miller Band* in relationship, except that they don't put all the musical responsibility on one man's back. The album could have been called *Island* Graduation Concert featuring *John Hawken*.

In spite of the weight, *RENAISSANCE* finish the course, and you mark them in your form book as highly promising.

Some of my lay friends would think the record was a delightful send-up.
T.R. Zelinka

don't compromise, because the music doesn't.

lock
antana
pirit
acific gas & electric
hicago
anis joplin
aura nyro
ohnny winter
aj mahal

LAN
MON & GARFUNKEL
RDS
OOD SWEAT & TEARS
KE BLOOMFIELD
KOOPER

LEONARD COHEN
MOBY GRAPE
TIM HARDIN
SLY & THE FAMILY STONE
CHAMBERS BROTHERS
FILLMORE

THE SOUND OF THE SEVENTIES

CBS

CBS Records 28/30 Theobalds Road, London W.C.1

The Flock (S) 63733

Their name is The Flock.
Run with them.

The Flock is unique. A pace-setting new group.
John Mayall (a musician's musician) called them the best band
he'd heard in America. Listen to their album. See if you agree.
Then run with The Flock. And watch them spread.

THE SOUND OF THE SEVENTIES

BLOOD SWEAT & TEARS IS NOT AFRAID

TO BE DIFFERENT.

The great contemporary themes played with pure rock power.
Blood Sweat & Tears is not afraid to be different. On CBS Records.

BLOOD SWEAT & TEARS
(S) 63504

CHILD IS FATHER TO THE MAN
(S) 63296

Reprinted from November 1969 VICE-ROI

THE BIGGEST TOOL IN SHOW-BIZ

Do You Feel INFERIOR?

JED TANNER

Roddy McDowell never gets the super star billing that close pals of his like Richard Burton and Liz Taylor do — but Roddy McDowell doesn't really need them

And that's mainly because McDowell, at 37 years of age, has the biggest hidden asset in show business — and that isn't his camera or his acting ability, either.

The talent that Roddy packs into 10 powerful inches is the kind that makes gals flock to him for a torrid night between the sheets.

It also causes famous show biz couples to hire him as a sort of informal marriage counsellor — he puts the punch back into their soured weddings, just by unleashing his hidden asset and springing it indiscriminately on everybody in sight.

Invited to every orgy going for the same Reason, Roddy somehow manages to stay out of all the headlines and the scandals that periodically rock Hollywood's image.

"I enjoy life," he grinned happily when VICE ROI interviewed him.

"I don't push myself down people's throats, if you know what I mean.

"I just sort of lie back and let it all come to me."

Roddy got his first big show business break when he starred in "How Green Was My Valley".

Roddy was also making it big, between takes on the set of "National Velvet," when he had a constant stream of female companion lining up for a session with his massive hidden asset.

A tall lanky man, with a face that belies his astonishing sexuality — he's so young looking that he could pass for a teenage virgin in a Sunday school class — McDowell gets better in every way as he gets older.

"Age mellows a man," he grinned.

It seems that most of the Hollywood he-men secretly pride themselves on being supermen when it comes to doing what counts.

So Frank Sinatra had all the great studs of Beverly Hills gathered in his mansion for an unofficial heavy weight contest.

Peter O'Toole, Dean Martin, Rock Hudson, Paul Newman, Robert Mitchum, Big John Wayne, Sammy Davis — they were all there. And so was Roddy.

One by one they dropped their pants and displayed their armaments. McDowell, who was at the end of the line, didn't even blink when he spied the formidable equipment that everybody from O'Toole to Caine were in the process of displaying.

When it was his turn, he quietly unzipped his trousers, folded back the double folds on his custom made undies (the only kind he can wear for support, they cost him $20 a pair, and last a long time) and exposed an organ that could have served as an ICBM if the Defense Department fought its wars in bed.

"Amazing!" stammered Sinatra, who up till then thought he was the heftiest man around.

"Incredible"! gasped Peter O'Toole, whose reputation in Dublin had him pegged as a real winner when it came to doing what counts.

"Wow!" freaked Rock Hudson, who couldn't get his eyes back into their sockets.

But that's the story of easy going Roddy McDowell's action packed life.

On top of all that, he's one of the best actors Hollywood has ever seen, a formidable photographer, and an all around likeable chap.

Having a hidden talent as big as Roddy's is bound to bring a guy all the success that life can offer.

And nobody could blame Roddy for taking as much advantage of it as he can.

The slag heap erupts

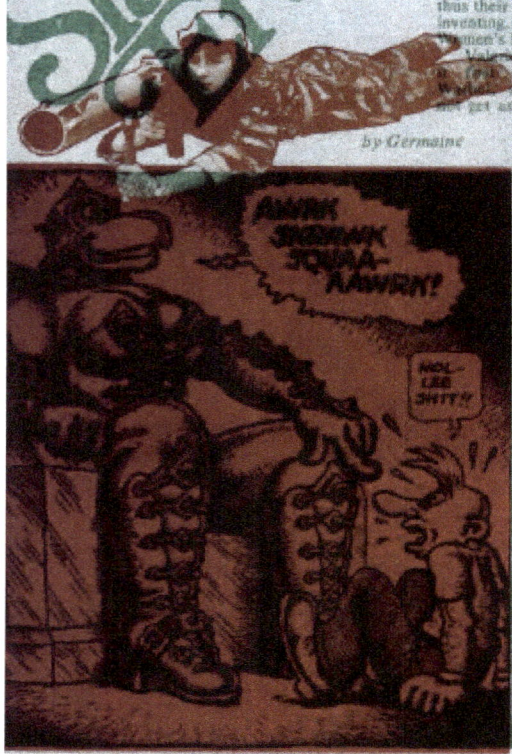

by Germaine

The 1969 'second wave' of women's liberation movement, were very much a manifestation of those sinister forces in our society which we call the media. While pulling in millions of pounds, dollars, lire and what-have-you by brainwashing women into demanding the emulsified fats, perfumed deodorants and disinfectants, liver-corroding analgesics and other consumer 'products' which are as necessary to keep our economies on an even keel as the threat of war or anarchist insurrection, the newspapers kept up their circulation, and thus their sale of advertising by inventing a new sensation — Women's Liberation.

Valerie Solanas got them at it, by shooting Andy Warhol, which they could not get as much out of that as they might have liked because the matter was sub judice for quite a while. Still that tactic meant that Girodias got round to publishing the Manifesto, which is still most of what most people know about women's liberation. It did not take long for other women to grasp the principle of Solanas' shock tactics, especially when they saw young blacks exciting WASP paranoia by similar means on every campus and university subway.

When the House Commission for Unamerican Activities was officially called a witch-hunt, one group of radical women suddenly realised that was what they wanted to be, so WITCH, Women's International Terrorist Conspiracy from Hell, was formed. Ballyhoo was their business and from the beginning they were good at it. Dressed in black and riding broomsticks, they hexed the Chase Manhattan Bank, distorting the familiar slogan in a fashion fatuous enough for J. Walter Thomson himself, to 'You have a Fiend in the Chase Manhattan'. When they bewitched Wall St. the market obligingly suffered a frisson of five points and then pulled itself together again. Bra-burning and invading the annual Bride Fair in Madison Square Garden were good fun and good copy too. Nowadays

Illegal Practices. Bar Flic

WITCH is a little leery of the Tactical Police Force and has gone underground and anonymous, a heavy fate for ballyhoo.

Whorey

Betty Friedan's National Organisation of Women takes itself much more seriously than WITCH, although after Valerie Solanas showed them how, they ran around with slogans like 'A Chicken in Every Pot and a Whore in Every Home', until they managed to weed such vulgarity out of their ranks and into extremist movements like the Feminists and the October 17th Group where they belong. Mrs Friedan did not want to endanger her beautiful relationship with congress: after all a girl in a congressional committee is worth a thousand in the bush. Nevertheless she capitulated to the media by 'forcing' (you recognise the journalese as in 'Frost hits railways', 'forcing' here means 'persuading') the New York Times to demonstrate its freedom from male chauvinism by desegregation of the Want Ads. Of course she could not 'force' anybody to desegregate the jobs. The immediate result of her action was that more women wasted more time reading about, applying for and getting rejected from jobs they had no chance of getting in the first place.

The problem is at least partly a problem of image and self image. Men don't really like women, and that is really why they don't employ them: women don't really like women,

and they can usually be relied upon to employ men in preference to women as well. Playing grotesque pranks in Wall Street was at least an attempt to increase the possibilities and break down the stereotype of the female image. However, such a strategy relies upon an inhuman freedom from paranoia. Valerie Solanas had to shoot her man to get him to take more than patronising notice of her. So Abbey Rockefeller and Roxanne Dunbar teach karate to the Boston Women's Liberation Movement. When nobody likes you, and you really don't much like yourself, the most common reaction is to turn nasty and attack first. Unfortunately any skinhead could tell Miss Rockefeller that cowardice and steel tipped boots, broken bottles and safety in numbers, is better technique than any bloody karate which you can learn in debutante schools. But women don't even like each other enough to want to travel in packs like the Chelsea supporters.

Bitch

The real reason why Female Liberation is a hot number in the Sunday mags and the glossies is because it smacks of lesbianism, female depravity, freakishness, perversion and solemn absurdity. The tone of the reportage is most commonly derisive. The karate experts try to censor their meetings, regarding all the female journalists who imply that they are ugly, frustrated poor things like Irma Kurtz did in England nd Julie Baumgold in New York, as Aunt Tomasinas who apitulate to the enemy. The only perceptible result of such a on-tactic is that the journalists re not even restrained by courtesy and the meetings read more like witches' covens than ver.

And yet, militant women owe a great deal to the media hat guy them. The average housewife is dulled and confused by her day-to-day diet f pulp journalism and crap elevision. She does not catch he nuances of contempt that ding around the images of abbey Rockefeller splitting a oard with her head. Threading er way through clouds of lever-clever verbiage she etains the overwhelming mpression that 'something is appening here', even if 'what is ain't exactly lear'. Most of er life she has erved fashion without demur, nd now the media have reated the ashion of female iberation. At last he fucking media ook like they are hoist with heir own petard. The trend is ased upon a iny reality. etty Friedan tarted NOW n 1966, and its membership is even now not nove than 000 odd. The ucleus of he Boston novement is welve, and the ational convention called out 00. The average local group ounts twenty-five as a bumper urnout. The groups divide and ubdivide every month, the ames proliferate, New York Radical Women, the Feminists, he Redstockings, the October 7th Movement, New Women, ell 55 and so on. As far as the apers are concerned, new ames mean new stories, and he phenomenon grows. Most f the groups are more or less cademic, workshops with eading lists, research projects, iscussion groups. The basic exts are confused and epetitive. The membership is ostly educated middle class women who have revolted gainst male chauvinism in the ew left, with especially omplex problems of priorities nd strategies. On the one hand t is argued that oppression of women is the first example of lass oppression, and that they annot be emancipated until rivate property has been bolished and the state has withered away, and on the ther hand, as most of them earned when fighting for the ights and opportunities of the

blacks, that you cannot be liberated fighting other people's battles. Russia, China and Cuba all used women's bodies to fight their battles, and once the new regime was established put them right back in their place again. Of course, most women are not radical leftists, or unmarried university students, and the luxury of such theorising is not accessible to them in any way at all. Mrs. Smith who tends a bottling machine by day and husband and kids morning and night has no use for a reading list however exhaustive.

In England the situation is a paler and more confused reflection of the American scene. Middle class suburbs boast their Women's Liberation Workshops but finding out about them is virtually impossible. Agitprop import the publications of the New England Free Press, but when I rang up it took two hours before anyone realised that most of the advertised titles hadn't arrived yet, and nobody knew how I could get back copies of Shrew. Calling the Tufnell Park Women's Liberation Workshop proved even more fruitless. When an energetic bunch of women from Warwick University joined the Miss World demo, chanting and dancing rings around the police, the Tufnell Park ladies clung quietly to their banners (which said 'We are not sexual objects' - a proposition which nobody seemed inclined to dispute) and begged them to desist. Shrew officially lamented the demeanour of the interlopers, but reminded itself in seigneurial fashion that they were probably working class housewives who knew no better, the people, in fact, they meant to 'help'. In fact the Coventry group of privileged girls is one of the very few that are actually attended by working class women who tell them how it is.

Many militant women show too plainly by their inefficiency, their obesity and their belligerence that they have not succeeded in finding any measure of liberation in their own company. They are still beset with middle class sexual scruples, so that they cannot find any alternative to the phony concept of female sexuality as monogamy and child-bearing, except, as some extremists have advocated,

masturbation, lesbianism or celibacy. These alternatives are more compulsive and repressive than the despised heterosexual confrontation, and the result must be to debilitate the movement, because repression consumes energy which might be used creatively. Masters and Johnson's discovery of the clitoris is assumed to be the elimination of the vagina, and the sexual response of the middle class American of the 1960's, hung about with electronic equipment, is assumed to be a physiological absolute. Rather than increasing the possibilities in a revolutionary fashion, militant feminism is reducing them, imprisoning the new women in a wilderness of theory which grew itself out of a hopelessly distorted situation in which clear sight was impossibility. Rebellious women have always been able to find liberty, independence and culture in convents, but that never changed a thing, even when a much larger proportion of women did it. 'Confrontation is political awareness'. A woman who cannot organise her sex life in her own best interest is hardly likely to transform society.

Bites

Men are the enemy. They know it; at least they all know that there is a sex war on, an especially cold one. They have no perverse desire to remain enemies, but sexual assemblies vote overwhelmingly in favour of a new definition of women's role, for if women liberate themselves, they will also free men of their neurotic dependence and the fearful inauthenticity of sexual relationships. A hidden factor in the situation is the desirability of the tearaway girl, the bitch, the unpredictable. Many men hate brassieres and vaginal douches as much and more than women do. They are as tired of guilt as women are of shame. The bourgeois perversion of motherhood has been assailed by male psychologists and obstetricians: ought we not to listen to them? SDS and IS men may be chauvinistic, and may reap female adulation as a reward for conspicuousness in the movement. We have all seen Tariq marching with his classy blonde chicks. If women had the guts and the imagination to look beyond their epicene middle class environment, and start fucking for sex instead of ego and prestige, they might discover that in working-class homes mum was the brains of the family. Working-class men don't regard educated women as intellectual rivals: they have no respect for most of their irrelevant learning in any case. Women automatically take on

the class of their husbands, so it's good Marxist strategy to mate down instead of up. Some of your academic expertise might actually end up at the service of the class it is supposed to serve. It's a more attractive prospect than typing, distributing leaflets, making tea, and bed and love, for some arrogant IS male.

Dog Man

So far the self-appointed leaders of female revolution have remained the dupes of their phony middle-class 'education', and their demands are circumscribed by cautious notions of 'equality of opportunity'. Their organisations are built upon political structures derived from the patterns of male grouping, and at the very worst they fall for the colossal perversion of male sexuality, which is where it all began, the perversion called violence. The only genetic 'superiority' that men have to women is their capacity for violence, which in an age of total weaponry is now not limited to man alone. We all need to be rescued from the computer-aimed nuclear phallus: what women have to do is invent a genuine alternative. The cunt must take the steel out of the cock; female masochism must be eradicated if male sadism is to become ineffectual. There are signs that it is happening, but slowly, and so far without prophetesses, but not in the workshops and chapters of the spasm misnamed the 'Movement'.

In May we will attempt a positive statement of Cuntpower - female tactics for survival in a world destined for the typically masculine end of suicide. This article has been a goad to stimulate energetic women to some new thinking. We want to expose that new thinking in Cunt-power OZ. If it comes out with blank pages you can draw the obvious conclusion.

**Gangster
of love
deported.**

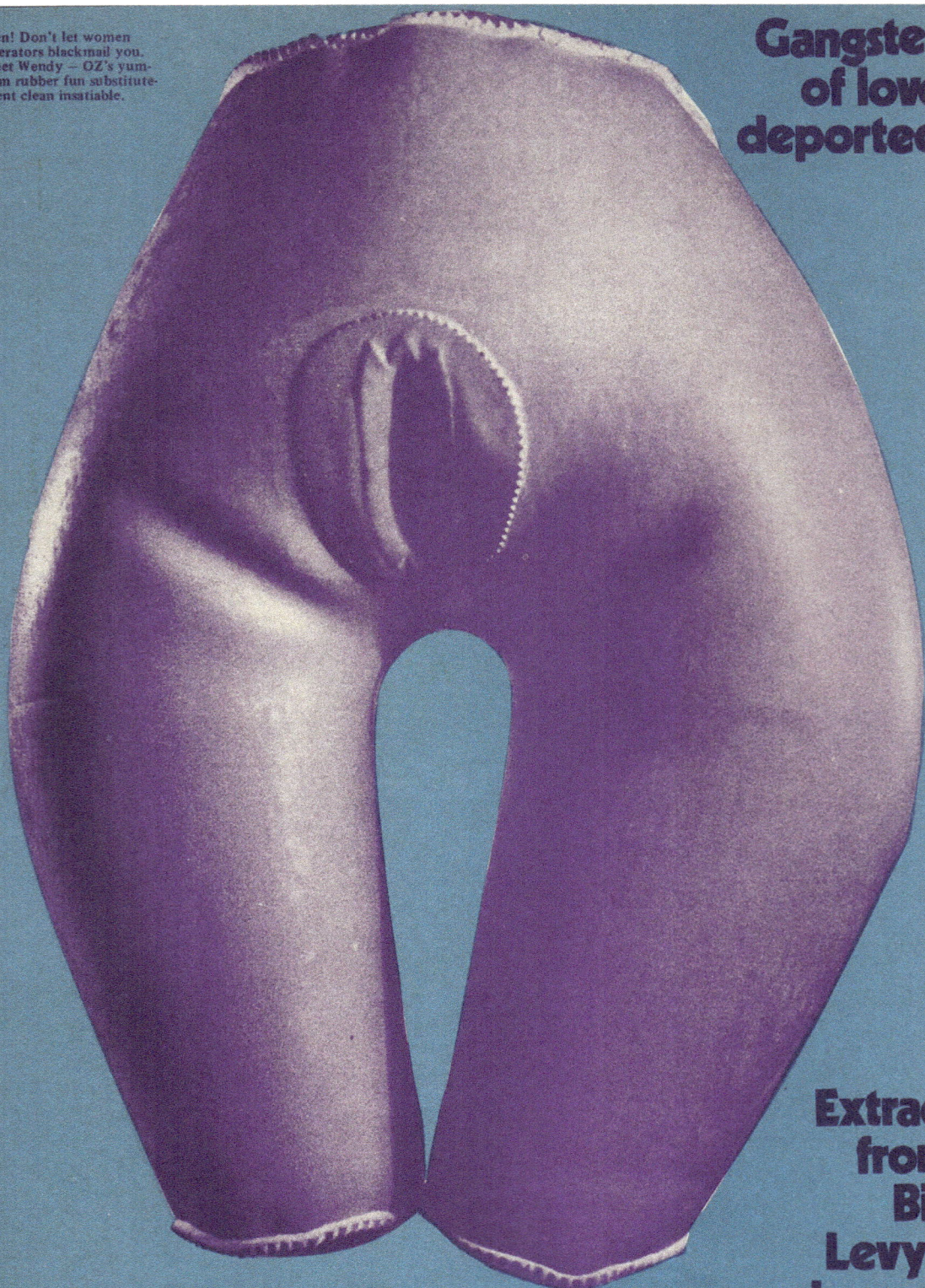

**Extract
from
Bill
Levy's
journal**

10 Nov 69 First Day.

Went to cabin immediately upon arriving on boat — took a shower, shaved, went to bed. The boat flopped around. Every once in a while I heard a crash. When it really got rough there was a sudden drop in air pressure. As a result I floated/levitated a fraction of an inch off my mattress five different times during the night. In the morning we were told the disturbance had been a force eleven gale, or one less than hurricane.

Arrived in Harwich feeling ill, swollen glands on my neck, a heavy head and congested chest. Immigration Officer suspicious. My answers are vague and indefinite. Takes me to Customs where bag is searched. Customs men find and seize 6 copies of SUCK, American sex papers *Kiss*, *Pleasure*, and *Screw*, one each, catalogue from Copenhagen Sex Fair and other sex items. They are not interested in my two speed vibrator. My person is searched presumably for drugs. None are found, of course. What interests them (Special Branch) most is a letter I wrote to George Streeton in Copenhagen, mss copies of press releases written by Lynn, Katherine, Jim, Susan Coxshead, myself and this journal.

Sitting alone in search room I hear myself described as a "thoroughly undesirable character". The sound travels easily through the wall. I hear also the letters mss and my notebook are to be photocopied as evidence. With the help of a phone call (to Scotland Yard) police identify me as one of *those* in nude group photo on page 15 of SUCK.

An immigration officer arrives. Tells me I have been refused permission to land in the U.K. because, he says with indignation, I'm a dealer in pornography and possibly a dealer in drugs.

Phone Abby in London at 3 p.m. to explain what has happened. Ask her to phone Nick Cowan, a solicitor and school friend of Heathcote who gets Home Office to delay deportation for 24 hours. Nick says he will speak with Home Office in the morning to give reasons why I should be allowed entry. *Let's hope it works.*

Also in detention with me a Kenyan who was refused entry because he didn't have a proper visa. His wife and child live in Liverpool. He has never seen his child. He has been studying sociology at University of Warsaw, Poland. The guard told him instead of being returned to Holland he would be driven to Heathrow and from there flown to Nairobi. Home Office could at least allow him into England for a week for humanitarian, if not legal reasons.

Abby phones again says it was she who got Nick Cowan to phone Home Office. While speaking with Abby a Mr. What phones on another line. It turns out to be Heathcote who says he would try to get some friends of his moving on my behalf. While speaking with Heathcote an old man wearing a uniform insists I terminate phone call immediately. "I have a committee meeting", he says.

I'm led into a room where short fag doctor and big bull-dyke nurse are waiting for me. He asks me to fill out a form with questions like: "Have you suffered from Epilepsy, Venereal Desease or Mental Illness?" Answer: Yes or No! (Why, I've been crazy all my life, doctor). After I fill out form, doctor says: "You told immigration officer you took marihuana".

"No, I did not tell them any such thing, they read it in my journal"

"How often do you take marihuana?"

"Every chance I get".

"How often is that?"

"I'M lucky enough to get a chance almost every day"

"Do you take heroine?" he asks

"NO!!"

He asks me to take off my sweater so he might examine my arms. I comply. He finds nothing of course! When I tell the doctor I'm ill with a case of flu and I'm glad he came, he refuses to examine me. Police later arrive with aspirin.

Interrogation by two Immigration Officials, they want to know about porno/drugs. I tell them pornography is a generic term of an art form and there is no such thing according to law. I admit to being editorially involved with SUCK, but deny having broken any laws of the U.K. Admit smoking hashish, but say that is a matter of public record in my testimony to Wootton Committee on Drugs.

Another phone call from Heathcote. He says Peregrine

(Lord) Eliot will guarantee my financial security and testify to my good character. Things are looking up. I'm encouraged.

When I return to detention centre there is a third person: a Pakistani who gives a completely unintelligible account of a money complication resulting in his being refused permission to enter England.

Pakistanis are bats.

The woman in the British Rail Canteen objects to the contents of this journal. She asked that I not bring the notebook to breakfast.

11 Nov 69 Second Day

Uneventful morning. Taken by police to post office in Harwich to cash money order sent by Abby. Mail a letter to Susan Janssen in Amsterdam. Return to detention center and read Newsweek and two Marvel Comics "Spiderman" and "X MEN" bought at W. H. Smith kiosk on platform of Parkston Quay Rail Station.

Still no word either way from Home Office. If I'm not allowed entry now, with the forces I've brought to bear, it will be even more difficult to gain entry from Holland. In Amsterdam, Susan and I could be together. But whether that would be beneficial to either of us under forced conditions, is at best, unproven.

Terrible lunch of Beef Curry and Rice. The Kenyan and I have been living on British Rail Canteen food for over 24 hours. That's enough to depress anyone.

The police say detention center is not a prison. It looks like one to me. Although there are no bars we are locked in. The windows are reinforced with steel mesh and smaller ventilation windows open only a few inches.

Look in mirror. Look as bad as I feel. I thought prison would give me a heightened sexual awareness. I was wrong. Haven't had an erection since interned. Maybe due to flu, or anxiety about future, or being totally wasted sexually after two weeks with Susan.

Sex with Susan is cosmic. In many ways Abby performs better, but our sex life has been a disaster except for brief encounters. My fault mostly — a pseudo-mystical stance that sex was irrelevant. With Susan sex is a trip. Feelings of being born again, of time travel, floating, cell explosion, involuntary rhythmic pelvic movements after orgasm, transformation: earth to water.

2.30 p.m. More questioning. This time the police want to know my wife's name the address of her place of employment and whether or not I have keys to our flat on Regents Park Road.

Today I'm nervous when questioned. Last night I was relaxed and confident. My horoscope today: "You can relax and expect important developments". There is nothing else I can do.

Thinking about cunt: Abby's and Susan's.

Sleepy afternoon. Dream of Susan in two, possibly three, separate sequences.

Kenyan and I for word waiting.

Another terrible meal: tomato soup, welsh rarebit, beef and kidney pie and a pepsi. Before dinner I'm told if no other orders come from Home Office I will be on a boat leaving noon tomorrow.

After dinner I phone Abby. She says a man from Customs and Detective Sergeant Clark from C.I.D., Scotland Yard, were waiting at the door when she returned home. They had a search warrant under Obscene Publications Act. Both of them looked in all the drawers, under the bed, through my papers and a thorough check of my bookcase. Det. Sergeant Clark insisted upon taking away all the Insect Trust Gazettes (about 125) a literary mag I edit, he said to protect us from having anything that might be pornographic. What!

Visit by Brain Police.

Abby says both officials were kind and polite., i.e. impersonal. They asked whether she knew Willem de Ridder or Jim Haynes. They also thought it odd that Jim and I had some lawyer.

Can't keep my mind off cunt. Abby can use her cunt muscles like a firm handshake pumping out the last drop of sperm. Susan's cunt is warm and moist.

We are joined by an oriental about 25 years old of unknown nationality. The Kenyan, told before dinner he was to be deported on 10 p.m. ferry gets another reprieve. The cop

says "Your case is with the High Commissioner now".

Can't get to sleep. Treating myself to physic *mea culpa* an working myself into an orgy of rage. Thinking if I had looke Immigration Officer in the eye, mentioned that my wife Abby, was in London teaching school and I had been t Amsterdam on business not pleasure, that would have bee enough. Also think I must have wanted this to happen. "Ther are no accidents": Bill Burroughs. About 3 a.m. — moo changes. I remember all the others before me who had been i jail. Jail is an honour. Fall asleep near dawn.

12 Nov '69 Third day:

When I don't get up for breakfast three cops enquire "Why?" say I'm not feeling well, besides I find the food at British Ra Canteen disgusting. The Chief Inspector visits to ask if we hav been treated properly. I tell him everyone has been considerat save the doctor who refused to examine me due to his urgen committee meeting.

New doctor arrives. The kind of man who is embarrasse about being alive. Takes him five minutes to ask whether bein deprived of marihuana has made me sick. I laugh. Tell him as doctor he should know that could not be the case. Doctor replies he is familiar with drugs. "I have a talk on drugs" h says. Examines me takes notes. I find out later he is unable to prescribe anything for my cold, and has instructed the polic that I buy aspirin.

On one side of the detention center — 15 yards from th window — railroad tracks. Fifty yards on other side is water Avalon sitting in the channel, a few lightboats and on the qua two huge machines that lift trucks and load them o freighters. Noise night and day. Pile driver for new quay eche across channel.

Canteen prepares special lunch, a salad and dish of plai white rice. Earlier when I had been asked what I wanted to ea I was told "We only eat rice here as a pudding. What you wan is a continental meal." I had asked for brown rice and fresl vegetables. The English don't know anything but meat, chees and potatoes. That is why their persons and politics ar constipated.

Before lunch Nick Cowan phoned. He said it doesn't loo very good, for me. The Home Office is awaiting the report o Harwich Immigration Officials.

There is no question now of financial security. Th question is whether I'm a distributor of obscene literature i Britain.

The Immigration Office has a letter in my own hand sayin 4000 copies of SUCK were smuggled into U.K. *This is untrue* More wishful thinking on my part. At any rate, Scotland Yar have raided two places in London looking for SUCK. In bot cases not a single copy was found. The Yard has sent two me to Amsterdam to investigate SUCK. Nothing there either They can't be very serious about this matter if the case ha been trusted to someone as stupid as Det. Sergeant Clark. H can't find anything.

Can't keep my mind off cunt!!

Beginning to get feeling back in genitals. Heathcote phone Speaking with him always lifts me up. Perhaps we shoul sleep together — I mean *suck* and fuck each other. I has been in the air. A powerful and represse friendship. Heathcote mentions a new projec called SUNDAY HEAD PAPER starting wit reprints from Ramparts, Evergreen plus loca stuff. A sunday paper that does the job o keeping one occupied on Sunday. I' rather fuck on Sundays. He asks, I'm writing my "Pisan Cantos" There is not much poetry with cun Here comes the sun! Bright day. Silve clouds.

Horoscope today — Wednesday November twelfth: "Lif gets more and mor interesting"

Justifiable Homicide: See
MANSLAUGHTER

Yet, life gets more interesting.

Alexander Chege's wife and daughter arrive. He is to be deported this evening. The Kenyan High Commission could do nothing. It's the first time he has seen his daughter. "I feel like a father now."

While having tea with Alexander, his wife Keyiah and daughter Julia, I receive a phone call from Peter Jackson, Member of Parliament. Long time pause. He says Civil Liberties Union has voted him to look into my case. Tell him a bit about myself. Jackson says to this day and me being held for pornography is ridiculous. I ask his phone either. Heathcote or Abby for further information and for a copy of SUCK.

Alexander's wife and daughter leave. He is very dejected, I am sleepy. Alexander and wife make Swahili together. First time I've heard it spoken. Makes Greer or hair pounds feeding. Wants to get to Stockholm to see about getting a scholarship for post-graduate work in Sweden.

I fall asleep. When I awake Alexander says goodbye and leaves. Deported to gloom of Holland, to face the unknown. After he leaves I find a scrap of paper on the floor with a note to his wife.

My dearest wife Keyiah. We can ascend from potential unknown to an actual unknown. If used dispensing to the administration in Nairobi, you should not bother within ourselves. It is not the government but the initiative of people acting on their own that makes a better world and in so doing makes a better person. Thank you darling. I love you and our daughter Julia.

Another terrible B.R. dinner beef and kidney pie cellophane wrapped, charged and told me to which another pie and dishwater tea. All without taste.

Try to phone Jim in Paris. Instruct him to speak with Debbie Friedman. Wonder what her cunt is like. Ask her to have Jim phone me as soon as possible. Ask him about the Keeler book. Will he get the message?

Make my bed. Top bunk left as you enter and settle down reading a book given to me by Alexander Chege called "My shadow ran first" by Bill Sands. An autobiography of a judge's son who wound up in San Quentin, meets a kindly warden, goes straight and has a lot of adventures.

Mr. What phones with Heathcote. Abby had a meeting this evening with Peter Jackson M.P. who described himself as a 19th century liberal. Heathcote says Jackson ignored him and directed attention to Abby. I think there's a bit of jealousy on my part here. He would like to depose them. England. Find out he was Harvey Matusow who got Civil Liberties Union to act on my behalf. Good old Harvey!

Jim phones from Paris. He hasn't started the lecture because of a teachers' strike. Maybe he'll he scored money for next issue of SUCK. SUCK more.

Abby phones. Says last three days have been very exciting for her, e.g. this evening she was at House of Commons, has another appointment with Jackson M.P. tomorrow. Maybe they will have a romance. I think I'd like that. Abby asks if I have a girlfriend in Amsterdam, I don't answer. Still very much in love with Abigail, with what we could be together and haven't been for a long time. A fortnight phone conversation for both of us. Long silence, there are a lot of women out there, but Abby is something special, I'm sure of that and sure I've treated her badly.

Looking at Susan's photo. She seems remote, somehow outside myself, or so much inside as to be indistinguishable from self. Do I love Susan? Or am I in love with equalities of self I see in her. Or did I fall into her a kind of boredom, or love?

Abbey asks me to prepare a dossier on my activities once I came to London. Hate to account for myself and relate to other people in that way.

Whenever I go for a walk, to eat, phone I am accompanied by a policeman.

Masturbated last night for first time in about three weeks. Wasn't satisfying. Not as good as mouth, cunt, anybody.

Reading Mordecai Richler's book, COCKSURE. Made me laugh out loud twice. Recommend as a film.

Alone in detention center. Sleep.

Nov '69 Fourth Day

Morning cup is good natured. Woke me at 8:30 a.m. saying I've been joined by countrymen. Two more men and a Hannah

detention center. One American. One German. It is dispiriting after being alone. Also joined by oriental who was deported day before last. Holland wouldn't take him either. Tomorrow he will be brought to Heathrow and flown back to Hong Kong.

 Phone call to Abby. She is working very hard on my behalf. Phoning people and making contacts. Overcoming her shyness. After I hang-up friendly morning cup tells me if nothing further happens with my case I'm to be deported at 10 p.m. The American and German return to Holland at noon today.

Horoscope for today: "Good prospects, provided you are helpful and elastic in your decisions. Progress at work."

Man from Hong Kong farts loudly.

Policeman with Scottish accent takes me for a refreshing walk to Paddington Town. On the way back, we meet Chief Inspector who jokes he is going to put a bobbie's helmet on me and put me to work. Return to detention center. Take a long shower on forthside docked 10 yards from front door.

 A message: "Michael phoned" when I return from dinner. Hope if phones again. Young comrade tries to lead me into giving him Michael's surname. Momentarily tempted by cheap police trick.

 Get radio to show me what they are writing down in their books about me. Policeman lets me keep two buns; one at the door in detention with calm disposition with letters of support from Lords, Ladies, M.P., literary people and journalists. Tell them I'm to be deported at 10 p.m.

Jay Landesman phones. Tells me the copies of SUCK were seized by customs when he returned from Denmark. A desperate anything he can do. The police ask me to identify the caller for their dog book. I refuse. The matter is dropped. Immigration Officer arrives to tell me I've been given another stay until tomorrow. Will this go on forever? A small place of my own private hell. Trapped sexless world between two women.

 Peter Jackson, M.P. phones. He says my request for a visa has been denied due to distribution activities involved with SUCK unusually going to Sex Fair in Copenhagen and having 7000 copies of SUCK seized at German border. Jackson says he has appointment tomorrow with Mr. Merlyn Rees Deputy Home Secretary. He hopes to get me a month to clear up affairs. Says I shouldn't hope for anything more.

Most depressing news I've heard. Feel worse now than I've felt in a year. As if a judgement point had been reached that I'm doomed I'm unprepared to make. All the signs this could happen were there: last time I threw I-CHING it told of financial when Martin read cards in Adam after we put together last issue of SUCK, they told of temporary success followed by disaster; and that dream last week, caught in the branches of a tree in a grassy area outside a huge Babylonian temple that was "London" while headless clowns danced around me laughing, the unnatural disaster and lightning and that evil cat weekend.

 Entropy is winning.

 Home Office describes my case as "unsavoury"

 Jackson M.P. is an O.K. dude.

14 Nov '69 Fifth Day

Wake up with Kenyan Alexander Chege's deep bush voice in room. He was deported from England in the end, because of his political activities in Kenya. Secretary General of Farm Laborers Union, in Watson, President of Foreign Students Association. Dutch authorities told him once he was kept by England more than two days the Dutch are not obliged to accept him. Dutch kept Chege in a small cell than sent him back to Harwich.

 Horoscope: "A very urgent matter turns out successfully"

 Chege is taken out to be deported again to Holland on noon ferry crossing. A commonwealth passport in U.K. approaches nearing zero.

 Abby phones. She tells me I'm to be deported at 10 p.m. for certain. My only chance is Continued on page 8

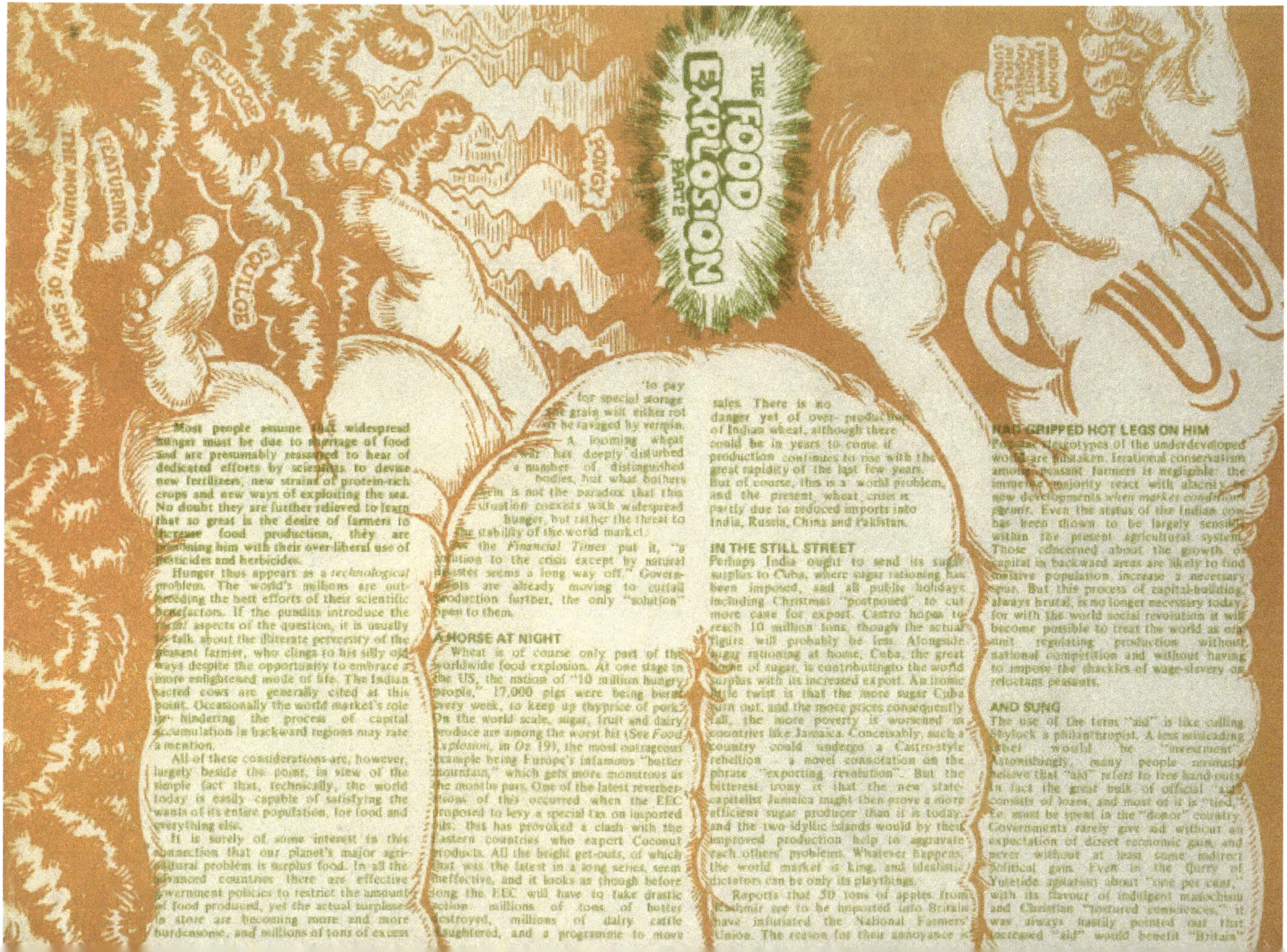

AND NOW I WANNA PEANUT RASPBERRY RIPPLE SUNDAE!

THE **FOOD EXPLOSION** PART 2

PONGY

SPLUDGE

SQUILGE

FEATURING THE MOUNTAIN OF SHIT

HE STRIPPED HOT LEGS ON HIM

AND SUNG

IN THE STILL STREET

A HORSE AT NIGHT

New light on Sun sound Stars

Dear Sir,

I would like to correct some errors which were made in the article "America's Real Uncle Sam" by Robert Finnis (OZ, December 1969), but first may I express my opinion that Rock 'n' Roll — by this I mean 1950's Rock 'n' Roll, not Rock, Acid Rock or the new Rock Groups — should not be dealt with as a subject by the so-called "underground" publications such as yours. I do not mean by this that I object to the existence of OZ, etc., merely that I was under the impression that you stood for "Now", whereas Rock 'n' Roll is an integral part of a past age and is dead except for certain rare instances.

Now, before I offer my corrections, I must say that Robert's article was better than many I have seen on this subject. Had this not been the case I would not have bothered to reply, my "letters to the editor" career has been almost non-existent.

Without taxing my memory or checking through papers I shall now endeavour to correct some of the main errors in Robert's article.

First, Elvis. Sam Phillips did not have Elvis listen to Crudup's "That's alright" before recording it. Elvis, Bill Black and Scotty Moore had failed to make a successful take of any of the set session numbers and "That's alright" was a number that the trio were fooling around with during a break in recording. Sam liked this version and cut it. An interesting fact is that Carl Perkins was featuring this number on stage before Elvis recorded it. Although the late Dewey Phillips was, by legend, the first D.J. to give "That's alright" air time there is serious doubt that he was the VERY first to play it on the air. Another note of interest is that although R.C.A. — Victor bought the masters of the Sun cuts the actual tapes were remixed by R.C.A. — Victor, therefore some of the "Sun" sound was lost on these re-releases. Sun records had more than one master of each track, one was found recently in Memphis — an Elvis master — which is now somewhere in the U.K. Also the main side which Elvis recorded for his mother was "My happiness", not "Blue Moon."

I cannot fault much with the section on Johnny Cash, as few hard facts are given. However, I am unable to agree with the statement that John was successful in the pop field without every veering from country material. The various use of chorus, both male and female, the piano style of Jack Clement — who also produced the majority of John's "pop" sessions on Sun — and sundry other gimmicks, were not at that time accepted as pure country. John himself was said at the time to be not happy with Clement's production techniques as applied to his particular sound.

Now on to Carl Perkins. It is ridiculous to state that it is doubtful whether Carl could have given Elvis a "run for his money". Carl not only gave Elvis a run, he left him standing! It was Carl's "Blue Suede Shoes" that received a gold disc for U.S. sales and topped the charts in all three categories, not Elvis'. Here in the U.K. Carl was only one place behind Elvis in the charts, in spite of the far superior promotion and publicity the Presley version received. An even more conclusive argument is that when Carl, Elvis and Johnny Cash had the same manager, Bob Neal, they all toured together. John would open the show, Carl next, with Elvis closing. During the tour Elvis got booed off the stage on three successive nights as the audience wanted — and got — Carl back. Elvis left the tour and has never appeared with Carl since. Carl had the advantages of being an accomplished guitarist, unlike Elvis, and an excellent dancer, bopping all over the stage, unlike the pelvic gyrations of Elvis. The record said to have been issued at the same time as "Blue Suede Shoes", "Sure to fall"/ "Tennessee" on Sun 235, was never released. No record was issued on this catalogue number.

A brief word on the cooking of the sounds — quote: "what went into the mikes was very different to what came out in the booth". Have mercy, the current son-of-a-bitch sounds have more electronic aids used on one album than nearly all the Sun catalogue put together. Take a REAL listen to the earlier Sun cuts and you will hear bum notes, background noises and voices, even the odd guitar string breaking! Hear any of that on todays "reality" records? NEVER! Today so much attention is paid to editing, splicing and general patching-up.

Before going on to the Jerry Lee section I would like to thank Robert for the suprisingly nice opening words on Jerry, and congratulate him on being only the second person to point out the age of Priscilla Beaulieu when Elvis began dating her as a comparison to the 1959 Jerry Lee "scandal"! Only two real mistakes here, the only others are ones of omission. "Crazy arms"/"End of the road" was not the flop that Robert made it appear. It sold very well in the South. Although this was Jerry's first commercial record he had made demos before and been for auditions, but had always been turned down as the record companies were afraid to take a chance with his new wild sound which was, like Presley's, too near a so-called coloured sound for white Southern audiences. Anyone who knows Jerry will realise that any resemblance between his sound and the coloured sound was a complete accident and totally unintentional! Anyway, it wasn't until he heard Elvis on Sun that he thought here was the one man, Sam Philips, who might listen. Jerry went up to Memphis and sat outside 706 Union Avenue proclaiming that he would not move until he got an audition. The rest is well-known history. When he joined Sun he was, unlike the rest of Sam's roster of talent, already a seasoned performer, this being the probable reason why he sounds more "in control" on his records than the rest. The disc "The Return of Jerry Lee" was not issued for the main reason stated, but was released with the INTENTION of attracting small sales returns, as one of Jerry's ex-wives was claiming more alimony because of Jerry's great popularity and earnings, so he wanted a disc to flop so he could say his latest record brought small royalties. The flip, "Louis Boogie", is not an instrumental as stated, but a vocal and piano work-out that is now recognised as a Jerry Lee classic. The only instrumental disc by Jerry Lee ever issued was "In the mood"/"I get the blues when it rains" on Sun's sister company Phillips' International, catalogue number P.I. 3559, under the name of "The Hawk".

The reference to "Red headed woman"/"We wanna boogie" by Sonny Burgess being laughable, amusing and too primitive is a sad insult to this record and leads me to the assumption that Robert does not truly know and understand the Sun magic. True, if you are basing your opinion on the technical merits of this disc, it is a bad record, but the beat, overall sound and sheer exuberance that comes from these two tracks make it a double-sider no fan of true Rock 'n' Roll should be without. When Carl Perkins was asked who backed Sonny on these two tracks he said "Oh he (Sam Phillips) probably dragged them in off the street. He did things like that you know". Despite Robert finding it an amusing disc it sold very well in the South, without making the national charts.

Apart from the two quoted stories on how "Blue Suede Shoes" was composed there is a third one that says Carl wrote it on a sack while he was still a baker in Jackson, Tennessee. It is doubtful whether Carl himself remembers how he wrote it, as before it became a hit the song was just one of many. For instance, "Movie Magg", the flip of his first record, was written by Carl at the age of twelve. The story of Elvis backing Billy Riley is a growth of something heard by someone who wasn't listening closely enough. Billy calls out the name "Alvin", NOT "Elvis".

The original Sun studios at 706 Union Avenue have not been pulled down, at least not as late as August, 1969, as I have photographs of them taken during that month. The building is, however, now deserted. When Sun left 706 Union the building was used by other small record companies, among these being the "Memphis" label, who recorded Eddie Bond in these studios. By coincidence Eddie had an album of religious numbers issued on the Phillips' International label!

In closing I would like to say that I hope this has helped shed a little more light on the history of the Sun label and has been of interest to some of you.

Stay cool,
The Mad Skulker

OZ-bog paper of the mind

Dear OZ,

My friend and myself are baffled with regard to your article about the 'Rape of a Virgin by a Leper' in OZ 25.

Now, if this is a true and correct testimonial, we feel that you have added yet another 'Gem' to your sick, sadistic publication; if this is untrue and dug up from the past and similied as a newspaper article (The Sun??) then we feel that a trip to the local psychiatrist for sadistic tendencied people is called for; if this is untrue and The Sun don't know you have printed this under such a guise, then I hope, and I know my friend and many others would agree undoubtedly, that they sue you until this 'underground' shit is no more.

Please don't get the idea that I am an aging fuddy duddy spinster with hang-ups about the Underground Press — nor my friend — I am a 19 year old, perfectly healthy reader of IT, Rolling Stone etc., and enjoy most of the current progressive bands. I am, and I speak for my friend, thoroughly and utterly disgusted that fuckers like you lot can be allowed to wallow in someone's tit (it's true and not a figment of your imaginations or the print room's equipment) agony and misfortune (for want of better words).

Your record reviews were good; Hippocrates was interesting; Smalls was informative, but we now will stop reading your toilet paper which would be an insult to our arses and wish you every downfall in the New Year.

yours A. Dean
(no address supplied)

I have deleted my address from the head of this letter as I am not quite sure if you can take action for such insulting behaviour via me and my pal, so please excuse blockouts — it'll remind you of your own minds.

Fuckers,

I agree entirely with my friend. You lot are sick, just sick. It was just filthy, barbarism, shit and I hope you wallow in your own sick. Sadists!
Irene.

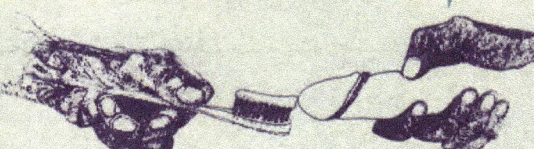

Pen Pals Corner

Dear Oz,

Reading about Ibiza (Dec.) inspires me to write and tell of a similar scene further East. This year two chicks and I got enough bread together (parents *can be useful sometimes!*) and flew to Eilat (Israel) to see what was happening out there.

I'll never regret going. The people there have really got a beautiful scene going — and no fuzz hang round there — only soldiers, who score themselves, anyway.

The people there feed you if you are hungry — and hash is smoked Oh so publicly. Tourists keep away I think they're afraid of us. The sky blends with the mountains colours, and everything is peaceful. Met a guy and many others there who turned me on for the first time — and my eyes were opened.

But now, back in my own secure suberbia (how d'you spell it anyway?) I have become confused. The change has been too quick. I am only 15, I don't know what I'm doing and I have no one to show me the way anymore. If anybody recognises this as the same scene they have been through, I would be grateful if they'd write to me (genuine people). If I don't talk to someone soon I'll just flip.

respond please

C. Boyde

P.S. I cannot get any shit either, my friends have split to other lands, they are free, by some law which makes them independant to their parents (over 18 etc, etc).
P.P.S. I sold my record player to make part of my fare — and I'm lonely now.
1, Lovatt Close,
Edgware,
Middlesex.

Caroline is nice

Dear Oz,

In reply to the letter from Richard, Martin, John, Carol and "1000's more", with the caption "Caroline does a nasty" I would like to correct them on a few very important points.

When they came to see us it was I who spoke to them and Caroline only joined the conversation when she saw that they were leaving our office unhappily. I am not even mentioned in their letter, let alone attacked, and the whole tone of it seems to be weighted against Caroline.

What I said to them is what we have to tell everybody when they come in with an offer of this kind. We only have to do this because in the past our experiences have been so unfortunate. Organizers, the groups, and their audiences are our friends, and we like to make sure that everybody gets a fair deal, but in the past big name groups have helped with Release benefits, travelling to some remote place to do a gig, often for nothing or only for expenses. They are left with the impression that they have done all in their power to help us, but we have never seen any of the proceeds. I can only remember two occasions on which we have received anything from a benefit. One amount was only a quarter of what we had been led to expect, and the other was a £10 cheque which initially bounced. Sometimes we only hear of an impending Release benefit when we read the publicity in the press.

I remember saying to Richard that because we would rather not have the name of Release used in the publicity, it did not mean that they would have to call the event off, and not put on a groovy show. They should make the niceness of the show their priority and use the profits, if any, for whatever cause they wanted.

What I also did not like was the implication that they were treated in an off hand way. If there was a fuck up it would have been because when they first contacted us, both Caroline and myself were away, and it was the right thing to refer them to us on our return. I did not know till I saw them that they had already been to see us once and only when they came again were we able to apologise for any inconvenience caused by their second visit. The message that had reached both of us was that there were some people who wanted to come up and talk about a benefit, neither of us had any idea that there might be any distance and inconvenience involved, or that any energy and goodwill had already been spent. In their letter they ask whether Caroline could not have said all this on the phone, and that they wish she would stop and think. If either Caroline or myself had been available at the time of their initial enquiry we would still have invited them to come and talk to us as it is not always easy for people to understand our point of view and we would rather explain it to them personally than on the telephone.

Release does need bread and we really appreciate offers for help from anybody. Our concern is not to dampen any good will but to really make the most of it. There are many ways of raising money and one of these should certainly be through the underground pop scene, but the outlay involved in making a worthwhile profit is substantial. It is really hard to look at some of the vast profits that are made by the pop industry and to understand why it can't be done by everybody, but there is a world of difference between setting up a groovy scene which pays for itself and announcing it as a benefit without knowing whether it's going to make a profit or not.

We are running Release on a shoestring with no regular source of income and it is an uphill struggle. Sometimes it is very difficult when people offer to help to know exactly how they can best do so. This is why we have made a widespread appeal for cigarette coupons and trading stamps, so that a person, whatever his means, may contribute and help keep us going, as it is always great to hear from sympathizers.

One thing which hinders the underground getting together community services or good entertainments is the writing of paranoid letters as appeared in the last Oz. I feel it is unfair to attack Caroline for something admittedly unfortunate, but unavoidable. Isn't it better to get together to discuss complaints with the people against whom they are made?

love Rufus Harris.

29

LENNON/ONO
with The Plastic Ono Band

INSTANT KARMA!
B/w Who has seen the wind?
Produced by Phil Spector
Ritten, Recorded, Remixed 27th Jan 1970

APPLE RECORDS   APPLES1003

Dear Doctor Hippocrates

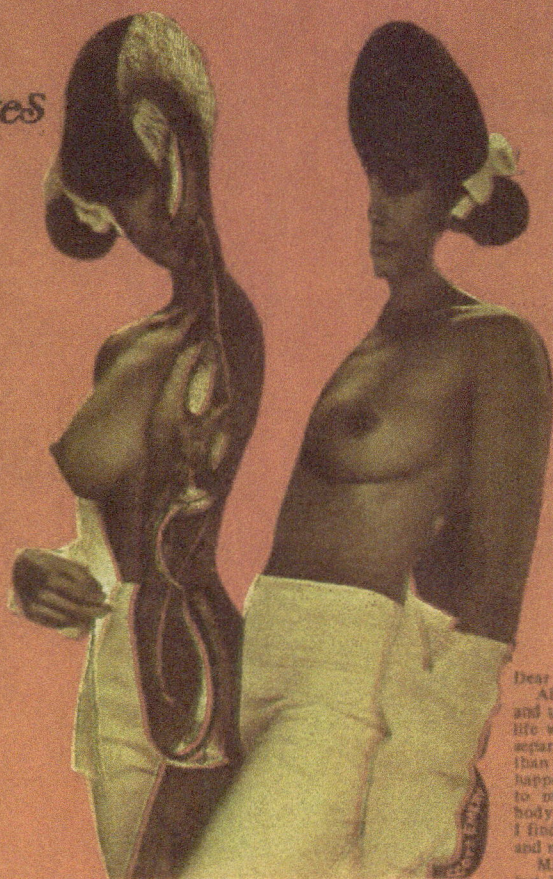

Question: Because I work full time, am a part-time student and at the same time try to carry on a decent social life, something's got to give timewise.

I find myself whittling away hours from sleep, hoping to "train" myself to manage on 5 or 6 hours of sleep per night. I'd love to continue to burn my candle at both ends but wonder whether this can go on indefinately.

Although I'm already in my mid-thirties I've never attained a particulary stable life pattern. And I don't seem to have the kind of body awareness that a lot of the younger crowd have. Half of the time I don't know whether I really feel well. I know when I feel very very good or very bad.

P.S. My father carried on an enormously busy and stressful medical practice, slept 4 hours a night and lived to be 71.

Answer: Body awareness techniques have been developed for several years at the Esalen Institute. Some of these methods are described in Bernard Günther's *Sensory Awareness* and William Schutz's *Joy*.

Sensitivity to one's body and feelings may be achieved in many ways. You could change your surroundings at periodic intervals, for example. The original trip is a trip. A vacation, alters the things your eyes see, the sounds heard, the smells, the feel of air against your body.

The average person sleeps 7 to 8 hours a night. Some people seem to do well with a little less sleep. Older individuals commonly sleep less than younger people.

But candles burned at both ends don't last very long.

Question: Whenever my boyfriend and I have intercourse, during each stroke his balls slap against my body.

In addition to this being painful to him, the slapping sound is so amusing that we have to momentarily stop because we start laughing.

We have thought of taping his balls to his torso. Is there any other solution to our problem?
Slap Happy

Answer: There is certainly a place for humour in sex but if breaking up threatens to break you up I'm sure you'll find a way to handle the problem.

Question: Why does my left testicle persist in upsetting the symmetry of my body by hanging lower than my right?

Answer: Medical research has uncovered the fact that "lefties" predominate in this part of the male anatomy. The reason is unknown.

My blood communications coordinator believes that psychological balance is more important.

Question: My roommates and I were wondering whether you answer non-sexual questions. So here is mine.

I have insomnia for weeks at a time, several times throughout the year (maybe this is a sexual question after all). The rest of the time I sleep well.

I've tried mild sleeping pills, counting sheep, etc., but nothing short of drinking a six pack of beer every night gets me to sleep before 3 AM.

Any suggestions?

Answer: Since you have insomnia only at certain times during the year, you might try to examine your activities during these periods. Are you facing pressures from schoolwork or a job? Personal social problems perhaps?

Most people find that exercise followed by a warm bath gives relief from insomnia. Relying on drugs like alcohol or barbiturates for treating insomnia may lead to serious problems.

Dear Dr. Hip Pocrates:

Although I have a normal and usually most successful sex life with my lover, when I am separated from him for more than a week, as occasionally happens, I find I have to resort to masturbation to keep my body quiet. If I do not do this, I find myself getting very tense and nervous.

Masturbation relieves this, but it never gives me anything like the pleasure that I find in real love-making, even on those occasions when I cannot achieve orgasm and my chief pleasure is pleasing my lover and satisfying him.

I would like to know whether there is any physiological basis for this, or whether, in your opinion, it is all in my head.

Answer: Masturbation is a normal means of sexual release. In HUMAN SEXUAL RESPONSE, Masters and Johnson report that, physiologically, an "orgasm is an orgasm", however it is achieved. But most people find greater satisfaction when sex is shared with another person.

"I don't care what Masters & Johnson found in their research, it's up here that counts", my secretary wisely pointed out, tapping her head.

DEAR DR. HIPPOCRATES is a collection of letters and answers published by Grove Press. 5/.

Dr. Schoenfeld welcomes your letters. Write to him c/o OZ.

acid flix

When Tony Conrad's THE FLICKER was first shown to New York audiences in 1966 they were warned that the film might cause them to have epileptic seizures or mild symptoms of shock treatment. When projected, this purely black & white imageless film caused audiences to see colors & lacey patterns, and to have an expanded perception of light in the room.

In San Francisco Bruce Connor incorporated the same effect into the narrative structure of his film REPORT (1964-65) on the death of Jack Kennedy. At the instant Kennedy is shot his film breaks into a frequency of black & white frames creating a breakdown of normal mental processes & the illusion of fleeting colours — an uncanny simulation of death far more telling than a photographic simulation of the event. *

These films are striking examples of New Cinema, abandoning the literary encumberances of novels & plays that have restricted the aesthetics of Hollywood films for so long. They are aimed directly at the senses, bypassing intellectual preconceptions, & are the result of a renewed interest in the essential nature of film, upon the fact that movies are in fact a series of still pictures projected sequentially in a linear time scale.

These days the established "speed" of film thru projectors is 24 frames per second (or often 25 frames per second to allow more accurate scanning by television systems). But the 24 frames that pass thru the projector do so at an intermittent rate — each is stopped in the aperture or "gate" of the projector for approximately a fiftieth of a second before moving on, and while the next frame is being pulled into position there is approximately a fiftieth of a second of darkness while the "gate" is shut.

In normal states of perception the eye does not see these periods of darkness, nor does it perceive the picture on the screen as a still frame. In fact, after the gate is shut & the next frame is being pulled into position, the image is still retained on the retina, and when the next frame appears, it is superimposed in the eye, giving the illusion of continuous movement. This is the essential illusion of the movies, long taken for granted by film-makers, but now being re-explored in order to create new states of consciousness.

Antonin Artaud saw the peyote rituals of the Mexican Indians, and the mystical theatre of the orient, and demanded a western theatre that created 'a delirium that is communicative'. Such a theatre did not appear until very recently when American artists, inspired by LSD experiences, created multi-media lightshow environments that expanded the senses, and created the very communicative delirium that Artaud hungered for.

The ancient Hindus discovered the power of mantras, words which when repeated constantly set up a brain rhythm which leads to expanded consciousness. In organising the rhythmic patterns of the frames of their films, film-makers of the New Cinema are achieiving the same results. Californian film-maker Jordan Belson, a yogi deeply immersed in Eastern mysticism creates his films "not to be seen, but to be experienced", and this could be said of a whole range of current West Coast work, as often as not emanating from acid experiences as from yogic contemplation.

Scott Bartlett's MOON 69, recently shown in London, utilises multiple printing & controlled frame frequencies to simulate the Apollo splashdown, in a way far more telling than any of the "live" tv coverages.

This film makes extensive use of the optical printing machine, which has become more characteristic of recent film-making than any camera technique. Basically a camera connected to a projector for rephotographing filmed material, the optical printer has in the past been relegated to such rudimentary functions as titling, or montage sequences, the only Hollywood concession to experimentation. The demands of television commercials, with the need for compression of information & maximum stimulation within a short period of time, have led to extensive use of the optical printer, and a new film grammer which abandons established notions of continuity & time structures.

Recent use of home-made optical printers, such as in Los Angles film-maker David Laurie's PROJECT ONE, give film-makers freedom to photograph single frames over & over again, altering image-perception rates in a way totally different from the slow motion achieved by speeding the rate at which objects are photographed by the "live" camera, or by slowing the rate at which they pass thru the projector. The most frequent application of this technique is the freeze frame, by which an action is frozen and held stationary on the screen for some time to drive home its significance. Truffaut used it to end 400 BLOWS and Hollywood quickly integrated it into its vocabulary. But film-makers such as Laurie are not merely freezing single frames, but repeating sequences of frames, elongating movements in time, playing on retinal superimpositions, forcing attention beyond the action into the whole texture of the film.

Most of the experiments of the American underground have been largely visual, partly because of the expense of sound recording, & partly in reaction to the literary monopolisation of Hollywood since the advent of sound. Stan Brakhage has been most influential in leading film-makers to abandon sound altogether from their films. Most of hs films are silent, & his current work in progress, SCENES FROM UNDER CHILDHOOD, has sound 'for study purposes only' to be removed from the complete version of the film.

However, sound experimentation, developed so extensively thru the imagination of engineers & composers of affluent electric rock groups, is becoming an increasing concern ofunderground film-makers. Oakland film-maker Barry Spinello is working in the almost-forgotten area of 'visual sound' — sound created by printing shapes directly onto film.

Most film soundtracks are optically printed, with the sound waves being converted into light modulations & printed in a thin strip alongside the image on the film. A light in the projector shines thru this printed strip & reconverts the light modulations into sound modulations. Spinello dispenses with the first process, creating light modulations directly onto the film. He did this initially by drawing them onto the film, meticulous work which had strict limitations. Many years ago Norman McLaren did this by photographing drawn sound and printing it on the film in the usual way. But Spinello wanted a direct relationship with the image, & since he had drawn his image directly onto the film he wanted the sound to be an extension for the same creative process. The desire for control of sound & image frequency led him to use pre-printed stick-on mesh patterns manufactured for graphic artists (the fetraset variety). This gives him controlled image patterns which can be duplicated exactly on the soundtrack to give an image-sound correlation as in his recent SOUNDTRACK (1969). More recently he has been working on some film loops which have been used in John Cage music concerts in California.

These days, when television has become the most available means of seeing films, audiences have virtually abandoned cinemas. When they do go, the commercialisation of distribution ensures that they are fully prepared for what they are going to see, & since this cinema tends to share a common aethetic with novels and plays, they tend to get cinema which gives mild exercise to their minds.

Film-makers in California and elsewhere are no longer content to fill this function of dull aperitifs to life, and are aiming at films which change peoples' lives. They are resorting to methods which are closely allied to experiments with consciousness-expanding drugs, and are affecting peoples' consciousness in similar ways. At the moment most of their experiments are being restricted from audiences in the same way that LSD and other drugs are, but because of the slightly different attitude taken to cinema by the protectors of our morality, we have a greater chance of breaking thru. Young people are making the effort to go to Arts Labs and underground cinemas where these films are being shown, and young people are having their consciousness expanded. Their image-perception rate is further developed than their parents, and they see images on screen that are just blurs to their parents. They are creating a demand which will stimulate production & lead to far-reaching discoveries.

Film has developed little since the early experiments at the end of the last century. Equipment used today differs very little from that used to create the films of Griffith & Chaplin. But things are changing rapidly, with film assuming a greater importance then ever before. The Apollo men found film indispensible, and the demands of interstellar flight will lead to advances in equipment until now stultified by the limitations of Hollywood. With new equipment new perceptions will be possible, & new discoveries will lead to a universal expansion of consciousness beyond present dreams.

Albie Thoms

FLOGGING CRITICS

Bitching about the way one's book was published, sold, received by the critics, etc, is no way to pass the time. Those letters you see from authors, written in immense sorrow that scarcely hides the anger, make the writer look more pathetic than the critic. "Mr X is, of course, entitled to his opinion, but I would like to point out that when he quotes from my book he distorts my whole meaning." Overground readers couldn't care less. But the underground is getting very good at understanding how things work, and the more knowledge there is the better. I'm writing this, then, not as an apology in any sense, but as a report on how things went.

My book THE LIMITS OF PROTEST was published by Victor Gollancz on January the 8th. It was originally going to be published last autumn, but my editor said it would never get reviews then, with all the Xmas rush, and that January was a great month because then critics had nothing good to read. I didn't object to that – not that it would have made any difference – but I was violently critical of the price they charged: fifty bob. For a book of 288 pages, that's too much, but my editor said they would earn back the money they'd paid me, jacker, and that it was the right price for the people who'd want it. He wasn't particularly happy about the style of the book – he said it was turgid – but he couldn't suggest any way in which I could improve it. We had a few arguments about content, all of which I referred to his satisfaction. He wouldn't commit himself when I asked him what he thought of the book, but said it would get big reviews.

It did, I got two raves – Michael Foot in the STANDARD and Dennis Potter in THE TIMES – and acres and yards of space elsewhere: all the weeklies except THE SPECTATOR, the Sundays, and lovely stuff in non-London papers like THE SCOTSMAN, THE IRISH TIMES and the like. THE DAILY TELEGRAPH attacked it over three columns on its leader-page; the MORNING STAR attacked it over four. At least I wasn't discriminated against.

Even if this was a complaining piece, so far there hasn't been a thing to complain about. Yet when I went to my editor with a new idea for a book – without any attention he'd been keen to commission me – he told me how BADLY the book was doing. I said I hadn't seen it in some shops that it ought to have been in, like in the Charing Cross Road, and he said he'd see to that (nothing's happened). But, said he, it wasn't selling because I just hadn't been able to write clearly enough. The reviews, he maintained, bore him out.

Now I'm not going to start quoting reviews that prove him utterly wrong, because that's boring. But critics did NOT agree with him. I took nearly two years to write the book, he took two weeks to go over it with a toothcomb, and couldn't suggest any radical changes. Could it possibly be that the price charged and the way in which his firm distributed the book had something to do with it not selling?

Well, all publishers have too much to do, and do the best job they can, and defend every move they make. And all authors complain – it's the most usual topic of conversation amongst publishers. I know because I was one. But publishers cover themselves by saying they give each book INDIVIDUAL ATTENTION, which is what makes publishing a "profession", not a "trade". And that's crap. They don't have time, or courage, or knowledge, or professionalism enough to see that each book is properly taken care of. While no other viable way of getting what you write to the public exists, publishing ought to live up to its promises. Or we ought to find a better way of doing things, such as a direct-mail book-club of original writing, or as suggested by B S Johnson – a sort of writers' co-operative where the members control the means of production, distribution, and exchange.

But if publishing is bad, reviewing is worse. I was warned to expect good and bad notices, especially as the book is critical both of "the system" and those who protest against it – subjects on which every thinking person might be expected to have an opinion. I was told that it was a favourite trick of a critic to take a sentence out of context and hold it up to ridicule. They did. And here I am beginning to sound like the author who writes letters to the editor. But what is most strange is that those people on the Left who should have understood what I was trying to say distorted my views just as badly as those on the Right or Centre. You would expect the TELEGRAPH to ridicule the idea that "all Western communities are in the grip of what he calls 'the system' or 'the straight society', which has command of all instruments of control and communication. Ordinary people are stifled in the system's massive grip." You might even expect the anonymous reviewer in the TLS to criticize my style, albeit in a style I for one consider worse than my own. The TLS man called me "totally plain wrong" but then brings his opinions, not facts. Chris Myant in the MORNING STAR said "the book suffers from one great fault – a lack of historical understanding of the types and possibilities of revolutionary activity." Anyone who reads the last two chapters, on radicals and revolutionaries and on revolution as a way of life, not to mention the opening chapter on perspectives, should emerge with a greater knowledge about the immediate history of current protest than before.) emphasise that the mood and tone of contemporary protest is new because there is a new consciousness around, one impatient of talk and dogma, and bureaucracy. Maybe the MORNING STAR, the paper of the British Communist Party, is upset because I dismiss the role of the Communist Parties in fostering the revolution. Anyone who was in France in May '68 knows what a fuck up the PCF made. Is the British CP's historical understanding making revolutionaries of us all?

Peter Cadogan, one of the founders of the Committee of 100, also went on about my ignorance of history. He claimed that "it was the Direct Action Committee, the Committee of 100 and Zengakuren that gave birth to the mood and practice of do-it-yourself politics in the years 1958 ff. This is quite beyond Peter Buckman who, wearing neo-Marxist blinkers and looking at the LATER developments in the USA writes 'Only in America did a movement of dissent grow that was a radical departure from the past.' None so blind . . ." Well, Mr Cadogan sir, if you see the same mood amongst the squatters, the VSC, the Irish students, and above all amongst the underground that you saw ten years ago, then your perspective is very peculiar. The Committee of 100 was fine, but both it and CND (and I'm sorry, I'm now going to quote myself) "were tightly disciplined, with elected officers and a reasonably efficient bureaucracy. Both emphasised planning, co-ordination, 'thinking ahead', getting the 'right sort of publicity', and the responsibility of adherents for abiding by decisions taken centrally." There are still groups, especially on the sectarian Left, who go by those sort of ideas. But they've been no more successful than those of ten years ago. Today's protest initiatives are MAKING history, not abiding by its precedents.

Perhaps most interesting of all were the two long reviews in the NEW STATESMAN and THE LISTENER: Paul Foot in the first and D A N Jones in the second both took me to task for for asking "class analysis". Both maintained that when I talk about the French events of May, I only discuss the students. Mr Jones said that I displayed "no interest in social ownership, no interest in capital's struggle with labour". Paul, talking about France, said that "Nowhere does he discuss the interaction or, more important, the lack of interaction, of such movements with the continuing struggle of workers to better their standard of living. There is nothing, or almost nothing, about unofficial strikes, productivity deals, tenants' organisations." Now I'm not going to bore you by quoting the number of pages I devote to working-class struggles, union sell-outs, and the difficulties students have had in getting to the workers and vice versa – take it from me there's lots. As far as I know I'm the only English writer to talk at length about the setting-up of the self-governing community in the town of Nantes, where workers, students, and farmers combined to run an entire town for a few days in May 1968. I go on and on about the dangers of underground communes not being able to combine with neighbourhood workers or avoid living off them and being attacked by them. All that's in the book. What's saddest is that my Left critics have used my book as an excuse to parade their own ideas without being affected by mine.

All that may be my fault. But considering the length I devote to analysing the workings of "the system" – which Paul Foot gives me backhanded credit for – it's a pity none of my Left-wing critics seemed to have grasped the simple point that the old Marxist analysis of the class struggle no longer has the relevance it did. Sure, capital is still exploiting labour like crazy – and incidentally it's madness for women's liberation fighters to forget this. But what is going on in protest that is slowly but surely changing the climate bears less and less resemblance to a class struggle: it's a struggle for CONSCIOUSNESS. It's the kids, and the blacks, and the underground who are making all the running. They're up against "the system" and out to destroy it – but not because of their status as an economic class. Those who are most exploited in those terms are the most reactionary – look at factory workers, not all of them, to be sure, but AS A CLASS.

I wrote a book that criticized much protest strategy, so it's hardly surprising that I get attacked by those I criticized. I emphasise again that I'm not complaining. But the whole treatment that my book has got, and the way in which it was published, should make you think twice before wanting to be published in this manner. In a way it's a demonstration of one of the themes in the book the TELEGRAPH ridiculed, that "the system" kills new ideas stone dead by its consensual attitude. Let some of those Lefties review this, they say – and the sad thing is the result is just the same as if they'd been Right. Well, you must buy the book – but wait till it comes out in paperback in a few months time. And meanwhile let's try and work out a better way of getting our writing to the public. After all, I want to write another book.

Peter Buckman

Small Ads

Synthesis

Underground Pop, Cinema, Theatre and Poetry Magazine. Special offer: three seperate issues covering Art and homosexuality, Art and Destruction and modern Surrealism + a free print of a grotesque African Head on fine art paper all for 5s. + 1s. P & P.
Synthesis Publications, 17, Colebrooke Row London N.1.

Midnight cowboy wants Chelsea stallion for rodeo weekend. Send oilpainting (Photo will do). Box No. 26/

Leslie you came into our life pasting up where are you now? ring 969 8229

Fun car 2CV Citroen one year M.O.T. 4 months tax right & left hand drive 80 MPG convertible & estate versions £150 approx. Try 01.878.2622. It may be just what you want.

Actors and actresses for new work shop production, Brighton Combination, singing essential, musical instruments an advantage. Write details to: Noel Greig, 9 Clifton Road, Brighton.

Free! Adverts

in 'HAPPINESS', Britain's big new social-introduction mag. Girl and boy friends galore! Sections for twosomes, threesomes and foursomes. Heterosexuals, homosexuals, bisexuals. Also jobs, accommodation, articles and services.
Up to 1000 ads. And NO forwarding fees!
Send s.a.e. for details.
OZ 26, Arcade Recording Circuit, 23 Arcadian Gardens, London N.22.

LEATHER UNDERWEAR: SHEATHED POSING POUCHES, BRIEFS ETC. ALL CUSTOM HAND-MADE: NEIL YOUNG, 46 HAWTHORN RD., EDMONTON, LONDON, N.18.

PORNO SWEDEN Yes, you still have to send to Sweden for your Porno. For £1 we will send you Glossy samples. Richly colour catalogues on Films, Colour-S Photos, Magazines and Books accept I.R.C.s International coupons which you can buy Post Office. Cash Postal Or cheques are also acceptabl leave all payee columns bla EUROPA DESIGN 2000, 33068, 126 11 Stockholm 32 Sweden.

UNRETOUCHED NUDIST BOOKS AND MAGAZINES — Wide range of Books from £2 upwards; Magazines galore from 7/- upwards — Why pay more? Latest title: "Naturism & Sexual Happiness" 8/6d C.W.O send 10d stamp for fully illus lists, JASMIT PUBLICATI (Dept. OZNP) Station R Padiham, Lancs.

I Like John Le

Forum

Contraception, VD, Drugs, Homosexuality, Abortion, Erotica & Pornography, Masturbation, Nudism, Yoga, Corporal Punishment, Prostitution, Racism & Sex. These are some of the topics dealt with in FORUM MAGAZINE. No other periodical in the or is a more forthid comprehensive of the ever panorama of behaviour.
ITS PRICE — copy. Save 30/-cribing — £3 for (12 issues): M, Dept. U, 2, er Road, London, 14. Send 7/6 for sample

PUSSYCATS — A brand new set of five superb female photos in interesting poses — yours for only 10/-.
'LES BITCHES' — A set of five superb female photos for adults — only 10/-.
'DANDY JIM' — A set of three superb male photos for adults — only 7/-.
SPECIAL OFFER — Pussycats and Les-Bitches for only 16/- or all three sets for £1. All sent with a seven day refund guarantee, by 5d post in a plain envelope. Send cheque or PO Order now from . . .
MANNERS ART, Department ZO, 38 Crawford St., London W.1.

Faith Dope & Chowder

Dear Oz,

Earth Peoples Park is the name given to an idea and to an act of faith. The idea of acquiring and returning one small segment of Mother Earth back to herself.

The faith to believe that in an environment not sectioned off by nations, property, words, and political sectarianism, people can live together in peace and harmony.

Once the land is freed and the fences removed, a giant Festival of Life will consumate the Earth with the music, theater, and the joy the communion a million people will provide.

We are working toward making this happen during the summer Solstice of 1970.

Earth Peoples Park will be publicly initiated with an extensive appeal through the media at our disposal for one dollar (or more or less) from each person who was at Wood-

stock, either in person or in spirit.

These contributions will finance the purchase of a large piece of land (50,000 to 100,000 acres) and will also finance the Earth-Warming to be held on that land.

One million dollars will be needed for the purchase of the land itself, and an additional half million dollars to finance the celebration. All surplus funds will be used to free additional lands.

The land will be acquired and protected by a legally constituted non-profit organization whose SOLE function will be to handle any external legal hassles. Acess to the land will be denied to no one.

If this feels right to you, it you have anything to contribute whatsoever, now is the time to get behind it.

Send your money, suggestions, criticisms, fantasies etc. to: *Box 212 Santa Fe, New Mexico.*

From: Dunay's Recipes for the Head

YES!

SUCK?

HAVE A SUCK FROM BOX 2080 AMSTERDAM HOLLAND!

THE FIRST EUROPEAN SEX PAPER-ONLY 5/-

Small Ads

"Weeee, what a trip!"

SEND YOUR SMALL ADS TO OZ AT 32, PRINCEDALE ROAD, LONDON
RATES: — 1/6 PER WORD. BOX NOS. 7/6 EXTRA.

LONELY BLOKE (25) Seeks young girl friend M/C area. Box No. 4/261

MODEL. Fashion, nude, all types. Box No. 5/261

WORLD CALL! Swedish liberty is sex. Send 10/- for postal Order — or $1 for rich illustrated distributors of magazines & photos. Outside Europe add $1. Adults only.
Write to
HERMES — OZ Box 6001, S-20011, Malmo 6, SWEDEN.

WORLDWIDE PEN PALS. Illustrated brochure free. Hermes, Berlin 11, Box 17/29, Germany.

HI THERE SEXY. Contact New Swinging Adult Friends. S.A.E. for FREE DETAILS. Write:
BCM/WWW, London W.C.1.

PERSONAL STIMULATORS. Sensational, Powerful 7" inch long battery powered vibro-massager. Stimulate the body. U.S. were millions sold. Only £2 plus 2/6. W. B. Sales, 79 Rowberry Road, Smethwick, 0880, England.

BIZZARE BOOK Lists Free — The Kaleidoscope Book Club, Cardiff CF2 1DT

FREE SAMPLE! S.A.E. Playel. Large selection of Glamour Photographs. Always available. P.A.R. (Dept OZ) 33 Hill Top Road, Bradford 1, Yorkshire.

VERY ATTRACTIVE female partner for amusements and travel. Long seasons my tours abroad. Expenses paid. Box No. 9/261

PENTHOUSE, Britain's leading magazine for men, invites applicants (under 25) to pose for its famous Pet of the Month feature. £200 fee for successful girls. Modelling experience unnecessary. Phone Lynn Barber, 385 6181, after 3 pm for interview.

YOUNG MAN seeks company photos only. No pad available. Pushy and plenty of bread. Box No. 3/260

FOR SALE. Photos, Slides, Films. Send 5/ sample and details. Also model wanted. Peanut Photographer, 42, Millard, Emsworth, Hants.

Shaftesbury Ave London W1
PRESTIGE (ADV/ADDRESS/MAIL)

THE UNITED KINGDOM Directory of Homosexual Meeting Places (male and female) is still available at 10s. Box No. 1/261

THE BIG EAR device enables anyone to hear through walls, ceilings, across the street. Easily made from readily available materials. Illustrated instructions for amplified assembly, 10s p.p. MAILEX, 36 Cowfield Street, London, W.1.

A NEW TECHNIQUE overcomes most male sexual disorders, defects and difficulties. If practical, positive, permanent and unique. S.A.E. for free details. Healing Hands, 10 Dryden Chambers, Oxford Street, London W.1.

DEMOS AND TAPES URGENTLY WANTED New Record Company. For audition send To Dual Fach Ltd, Suite 51 51 52 SHAFTESBURY AVE. WC1

HAPPINESS IS PROTECTION. Durex Gossamer 6/- doz. Durex Supertrans 10/- doz. Latex No Form 12/- doz. Fetherlite 12/- doz.
West Central Distributors, 77/78 Red Lion Street, London, W.C.1.

DUREX Special Offer. Gossamer 25 doz. Fetherlite 11/- doz. Natural Shaped Conture 12/- doz. J.C. Raymond & Co 21/38 Crawford Street, London W.1.

LESBIAN LOVERS. we have lots of what you want. 200's films, also Danish Magazines Etc. S.A.E. Baker Or, Green Farm, Whaddon, Royston, Herts.

FILMS, Films, Films, all types 200's. B/W reduced prices, also send new S.A.E. Baker Or, Green Farm, Whaddon, Royston, Herts.

EROTIC STORIES. Newest thing in literature. A reading must for the sophisticated. Send 10s. Bootstrap Press, P.O. Box No. 61281

Shaftesbury Ave London W1
PRESTIGE (ADV/ADDRESS/MAIL) WORLD (11
AMBASSADORS & 140A Shaftesbury Ave London W1

01 636 4796

STUDIES OF THE YOUNG MALE. Artistic Lighting & Studio Photography, Relaxed, Natural Poses. Don't Hesitate New Sets of 6 photos are SUPERB at 20/- for postcard size and 30/- for Large 6" x 5".
DON BUSBY STUDIO. 100 radan Chambers, 178 Oxford Street, London W.1.

Oxford Community Workshop Benefit, January 29th, Summertown Church Hall, Portland Road, Off Banbury Road, Oxford Alexis Korner — Skin Alley — Tea & Symphony — Hawkwind — Local Discotheque Light Show — Top D.J. 10s.

Kev Luftwaffe Greetings only ring, double breasted, twisted, blue grey flannel £5 Goodwin, 27 Clifton Road, SW10

GAY, "Guys Guide", "Physique Mag", "Paperback", 10 each. JOHN, BM/FBGH, WC1

TATTOO PHOTOS. New Existing List Adults Only. Large S.A.E. & 2s 6d for List & Samples. Britain's Tattoo Artist, 16, High Street, Aldershot, Hants.

MALE/FEMALE models required, our firm. Manchester Area. Experience unnecessary. Box No. 7/261

NORMAL, handsome but submissive Englishman seeks dominant lady. Box No. 8/261

EVERYTHING for the Male-freaks. Catalog for Films 200's Danish Mags Etc. S.A.E. Baker Or, Green Farm, Whaddon, Royston, Herts.

HITCHHIKED ANYWHERE ON EARTH?
Interested in sharing your time for the survival of the tribe? Help make a Hitchhiking Survival manual. Send me one stamped, self-addressed envelope, or just the stamp even, and we will get it rolling. John M. Pladoff, Dept 203, University Station, Syracuse, N.Y. 13210, USA

Exclusive Private Male — "Gino" Guest House. Privacy Guaranteed. Send for brochure for invitation to pert pole skiing. Hampo, 28346 after 6 pm. World Massage Treatment, T.V. etc.

Meet Sexy Birds, Gay Men, Kinky Couples, through a monthly Magazine Nationwide. Contact: Send 10s Lewis, G.P.O. Box 16, Blackpool, Lancs.

Make pen friends through our couples, gay, and service register. S.A.E. to: The Secretary, 101, Bispham Road, Liverpool 15, Lancs.

American girl needs British guy for temporary marriage. Good price paid. Box No. 11/261

FUSION, new American Rock & Roll magazine, is now available in this country. Send 2/- & 6d stamp for sample copy to 7 Townsend House, 22 Dean St, London W.1. Annual subscription also available at £2. 10s from same address.

SWEDISH PORNOGRAPHY PHOTOS, FILMS, SLIDES MAGS.
Uncensored, unretouched nudes. Males and females. ALL VARIATIONS. Send 10/- for 9 I.R.C. for profusely illustrated full colour catalogue. Adults only. Send to: TRENDEX-O, Rack 6105, Malmo 6, Sweden.

Order a copy of YOUR THING only 3s. Post Free. Advertising in Next Edition. 6d. per word. 6 words FREE. (Minimum 10). Pads, Jobs, Sale, Wanted, Personal, Miscellaneous.
Send P.O. to: Gary Busby, 50A Princedale Road, London, W.11. Further Info: 229 7753.

KEEP IN TOUCH
Letters held or forwarded, telephone answering service. FULL details 01 388 5570.

ADULTS ONLY. FILMS, MAGAZINES, BOOKS, PHOTOGRAPHS, Send 5/- for samples and brochure. P.R.A., P.O. Box 114, Leeds 1.

The Adult Revue has box numbers. No forwarding fees. This little BLUE BOOK materials for all Way-Out Adult gear. Plus Revue has in our UNRETOUCHED mag. Push 5? Today to "REVU" P.O. Box 114, Leeds 1. Strictly Adults Only.

GAY'S PERSONAL MONTHLY ADVERTISER for the swinging permissive society and the sexually astute. Over 100 personal ads. Send 2s 6d to MAGAZINE, 5 County Braid, Scotland, Scotts.

JOLLY AU-PAIR. Directors Pussey. Pad with Sauna, Secretary and Daily Cleaner kept. Box No. 2/261

Release urgently needs vacuum cleaner. 50A Princedale Road, W.11. 229 7753.

Lady's personal battery Massagers. 7" long, 1¼" thick, round, tapered electrical vibration stimulators. Exciting stimulating and scarce item. 30/ post free. Newtons, 159 Grove Green Road, London E.11.

The Secret Path, correspond and contact people on Occult, Witchcraft, etc., strictly confidential. S.A.E. for details. Occult, 4, Coventry Street, Birkenhead, Cheshire.

39

The Chicago Conspiracy trial – that ...gh-a-minute farce which has ...n packing courtrooms for the ...few months. Defence witnesses ...e included Arlo Guthrie, ...mothy Leary, Allen Ginsberg, ...ty Collins, Ed Sanders (an ex ...g], Country Joe McDonald, Paul ...ssner, Mark Lane, Anne Kerr ...r, Mayor Daley and Norman ...ler. That the proceedings of ...s extraordinary trial (fascinating, ...te apart from the celebrity roll ...l] have been studiously ignored ...Fleet Street is typical of its ...bility to appreciate the ...ernational orientation of today's ...uth. The eight prisoners in the ...ck in Chicago [minus Bobby ...ale, now in gaol for contempt of ...urt] are pitting their culture of ...g hair, communalism, dope and ...king in the streets against the ...th culture of big business, ...cess, whisky and fucking the ...rtnamese.

These transcripts were made ...ilable to OZ with the help of ...ke Gold of the Conspiracy ...fice.

UNTRY JOE AT THE ...NSPIRARY TRIAL

...E CLERK: You will remove ...ur gum, sir.
...E WITNESS: What gum?
...E CLERK: That you are ...ewing on.
...E WITNESS: I am afraid that I ...n't have any gum.
...E CLERK: You may be seated.

...R. KUNSTLER: [the defence ...wyer] Would you state your full ...me, please?
...E WITNESS: Country Joe.
...R. KUNSTLER: What is your ...cupation?
...E WITNESS: I am a minister in ...New Universal Life Church. I ...a rock and roll star. I am a ...ducer of phonograph records. ...ther, husband, leader of a rock ...d roll band. Singer, composer, ...st, owner of a publishing ...mpany, and a few other things.

MR. KUNSTLER: Do you currently have a rock and roll band?
THE WITNESS: Yes, I do.
MR. KUNSTLER: What is the name of that band?
THE WITNESS: Country Joe and the Fish.
MR. SCHULTZ: (the prosecutor) For the record may we have the witness's full name? Country Joe is really not sufficient.
THE COURT: (the amazing Judge Hoffman) I am assuming that his Christian name is Country. He is under oath. He was asked his name.
MR. SCHULTZ: It might be the name he uses and not the name that was originally his.
THE COURT: Is Country your first name?
THE WITNESS: Yes.
THE COURT: That is your first name or Christian name, is that right?
THE WITNESS: Some people call me Country, yes.
THE COURT: What is your real name?
THE WITNESS: Country.
THE COURT: You say some people call you that. What is your real name, sir?
THE WITNESS: I am afraid I don't understand what real means.
THE COURT: What is the name – were you baptized?
THE WITNESS: No I wasn't.
THE COURT: What were you called when you went to school as a child?
THE WITNESS: Joe.
THE COURT: Joe?
THE WITNESS: Yes.
THE COURT: What was your family name?
THE WITNESS: McDonald.
THE COURT: And your family name is now McDonald, is that right?
THE WITNESS: Yes, it is.
THE COURT: How do you spell it?
THE WITNESS: M-c-D-o-n-a-l-d.
THE COURT: McDonald, that is what your family name is. Is that right?

THE WITNESS: Yes.
THE COURT: And you are familarly known as Country Joe, is that right?
THE WITNESS: Country Joe McDonald, yes. Joseph sometimes.
MR. KUNSTLER: I call your attention to – let me withdraw that answer. Do you know Jerry Rubin?
THE COURT: No, not the answer. You withdraw the question.
MR. KUNSTLER: I mean withdraw the question.
THE COURT: I just wanted you to know I was listening to you.
MR. KUNSTLER: I just did it to see if you were. Do you know Jerry Rubin?
THE WITNESS: Yes, I know Jerry Rubin.
MR. KUNSTLER: Can you identify him at the table?
THE WITNESS: He is the one with the red pants on.
MR. KUNSTLER: When did you first meet Jerry Rubin?
THE WITNESS: I met Jerry Rubin in 1964, October 15, the march to End the War in Vietnam, the march held in Berkely, California.
MR. KUNSTLER: Did you participate in that march yourself?
MR. SCHULTZ: Objection, your honor.
THE COURT: I sustain the objection.
Mr. KUNSTLER: Now, I call your attention to Abbie Hoffman. Do you know him?

THE WITNESS: There he is. He is the handsome fellow in the handsome jacket
THE COURT: May I suggest to you, Mr. Witness, when you are asked to identify anybody here, either you may step down, you can point to him, or you may describe him by his apparel but do not characterize him as being handsome or in any other such manner.
THE WITNESS: I am sorry. I have never been in a trial before.
THE COURT: I accept your apology.

MR. KUNSTLER: Do you recall when you first met Abbie Hoffman?
THE WITNESS: Yes, I first met Abbie Hoffman at the meeting in the Chelsea Hotel in New York.
At that meeting was Jerry Rubin, Abbie Hoffman, myself, my manager, Banana Ed Benson, Irwin Silver, Barbara Dane.
MR. KUNSTLER: Was there a discussion at the Chelsea Hotel?
THE WITNESS: We had a very long discussion. The meeting had been called to discuss the proposed Yippie! Convention in Chicago, to be held in Chicago. We never – we hadn't heard much about it, and so we all met and we were staying at the Chelsea Hotel in New York and we met to discuss the Yippie! happening thing in Chicago. Jerry Rubin said to me, "We feel that the Democratic Convention being held in Chicago is a very important political event in the country, and that it represents fascist forces in America, opression of minority groups, continuation of the war in Vietnam, and actual celebration of death, that the Democratic Convention being held in Chicago will be a celebration of death in that all of those things which are held in high esteem by the establishment, political parties in the country, are those things which represent death and oppression," and that it was the responsibility of those people, young people, who are concerned with freedom in America to try to do something in Chicago which would counter-balance the evil and negative vibrations from the Democratic Convention and that since I had written the Vietnam Rag, which has become the most well known song against the war in Vietnam, and that my group was very influential with young people of America, amongst the youth, that it was very important that we try to say something in Chicago which would be positive, natural, human, and loving, in order to let

41

people of America know that
...re are people in America who
...not tripped out on ways of
...aking which result only in
...ression and fear, paranoia and
...th.

...t that point Abbie Hoffman
...ed to know what the song was,
...hen I — then I sang the song.
...es:
...sings)
And it's one, two, three, what
...re we fighting for?
...amn.
...he next stop is Vietnam.
...and it's —"
COURT: No, no, no, Mr.
...ess. No singing.
...COURT: Mr. Marshal —
...marshal goes over to Country
...nd puts his hand on Joe's chin
...ose his mouth.)
MR. KUNSTLER: Do you
...ember that the next time that
...saw Abbie Hoffman and Jerry
...in was, after Stony Brook?
...es. I met with Abbie Hoffman,
...y Rubin, Ed Sanders, Nancy,
...wife Robin was there, at Jerry
...in's apartment in the East
...ge in New York.
...Jerry Rubin asked me how I
...doing in getting response for
...Yippie! festival.
...informed him that since our
...inal meeting at the Chelsea
...el I had talked to people and I
...talked to other bands, and I
...d that they were constantly
...ting to me stories of orders in
...ago for the police to shoot on
...t in regards to the racial riots of
...month, that at least two
...sand civilian vigilantes were
...g authorized as deputies to
...t all trouble makers around the
...vention, that the National
...rd was being assembled to
...ent people from getting close
...e convention hall, that the
...rs of Chicago were being
...ared as dungeons to put
...onstrators in, that generally the
...tions around Chicago were
..., very uptight and adding
...se, that there was a possibility
...credible brutality,
...ciousness, and fascistic type
...es on the part of the police
...e, and that I was having a hard
...getting people to be responsive
...e possibilities of anything
...ive happening in Chicago
...ng the Democratic Convention.
...rry Rubin then asked me if I
...any ideas about other types of
...le that we could have come to
...onvention.
...suggested circus performers,
...ers, clowns, the Harlem Globe
...ters, and many other things
...— positive groups and
...rtainment groups that could
...bly show up in Chicago.
...ow, Country Joe, I ask you
...her you came to Chicago
...ng Convention Week?
...es, It was just a few days
...re the beginning of the
...ention and it was on Friday
...use we played Friday and
...day. We arrived Friday in the
...noon.
...At any time on Friday or
...rday did you have occasion to
... with Jerry Rubin or Abbie
...man?
...es. I met with both of them at
...lectric Theatre on Saturday.
...e Hoffman said to me "Are
...going to be in the Festival?" I
...to Abbie Hoffman, "No, I was
...going to be in the Festival
...use the vibrations in the town
...s so incredibly vicious that I felt
...s impossible to avoid violence
...he part of the police and the
...orities in Chicago." I felt that
...roup's symbolic support of the

...estival had to be withdrawn)
because there would be a possibility
that people would follow us to the
Festival and be clubbed and Maced
and tear-gassed by the police and
that the possibility of anything
positive or loving or good coming
out of that city at that time was
impossible, and that I had no
choice but to withdraw my
support.

CROSS EXAMINATION
BY MR. SCHULTZ:

Q. Mr. McDonald, you said that on
a particular occasion you told
Rubin about shooting to kill. Do
you remember that in your
testimony?
A. I hate to say that I said
something that I didn't say.
I said that there were very
negative responses from my friends
and people in what is termed the
underground youth community in
response to Mayor Daley's order to
the police to shoot to kill as far as
rioters were concerned in the
ghetto of Chicago in the riots of
April.
Q. Did they (Hoffman and Rubin)
tell you that during the time they
were negotiating with the
authorities to get permits, some of
the things that Hoffman said in his
writings and orally were that during
the convention the people would
fight the police? Did they say that?
A. They couldn't say that because
that would be a lie, you know.
Q. No, I am asking you whether or
not one of them said that he had
said that or written that?
A. Of course not.
Q. Or that they had said that there
would be public fornication during
the convention week out in the
parks?
A. Your Honor, I deal in words,
that is my job. I write songs. I have
been doing that for about ten years.
Certain words have certain
connotations and multi-meanings to
them, and in the world that I live
in, in what is probably called the
hippie underground, when we refer
to fornication, we are not really
referring to the actual sexual act of
fornication at all times; we are
referring to a spiritual togetherness
than can be done without physical
contact at all.

THE COURT: There have been
several witnesses called here during
this trial — I need not mention their
names — whose testimony the court
ruled could not even be presented
to the jury — singers, performers,
and former office holders. I think
in the light of the representations
made by you unequivocally, sir,
with no reference to Dr.
Abernathy, I will deny your motion
that we hold —
MR. KUNSTLER: I want to
comment on this, your Honor,
because I think what you have just
said is about the most outrageous
statement I have ever heard from a
bench, and I am going to say my
piece right now, and you can hold
me in contempt right now if you
wish to.
You have violated every
principle of fair play when you
excluded Ramsey Clark from that
witness stand. The New York
Times, among others, has called it
the ultimate outrage in American
justice.
VOICES: Right on!
MR. KUNSTLER: I am outraged to
be in the court before you. Now
because I made a statement on
Friday that I had only a camera
man, and I discovered on Saturday
that Ralph Abernathy, who is the
chairman of the Mobilization, is in

town, and can be here, and because
you took a whole day from us on
Thursday by listening to ridiculous
argument about whether Ramsey
Clark could take that stand in front
of the jury, I am trembling because
I am so outraged. I haven't been
able to get this out before, and I am
saying it now, and then I want you
to put me in jail if you want to.
You can do anything you want
with me, if you want to, because I
feel disgraced to be here, to say to
us on the technicality of my
representation that we can't put
Ralph Abernathy on the stand. He
is the co-chairman of the MOBE.
He has relevant testimony. I know
that doesn't mean much in this
court when the Attorney General
of the United States walked out of
here with his lips so tight he could
hardly breathe, and if you could see
the expression on his face, you
would know, and his wife informed
me he never felt such anger at the
United States Government at at not
being able to testify on that stand
VOICES: Right on!
MR. KUNSTLER: You can't tell
me that Ralph Abernathy cannot
take the stand today because of the
technicality of whether I made a
representation. That representation
was made in perfect good faith with
your Honor. I did not know that
Reverend Abernathy was back in
the country. We have been trying to
get him for a week and a half to be
the last witness for the defense in
this case. And now to tell me that
we are going ahead, the
Government is ready, after you
took Thursday from us to have this
argument over whether a man could
be presented to a jury, I told your
Honor then, and I am telling you
now, no American court has ever
done what your Honor did —
VOICES: Right on!
MR. KUNSTLER having it on a
case which was inapplicable to the
situation. That was done for one
purpose only, and the New York
Times said it more beautifully than
I could say it, and they said, "It
was done to make inadmissible
anything that would 'interfere' with
the Justice Department's intent to
prove a conspiracy to incite a riot
during the Democratic National
Convention."
VOICES: Right on!
MR. KUNSTLER: That was the
reason behind your Honor's ruling,
nothing short of that.
I have sat here for four and half
months and watched the objections
denied and sustained by your
Honor, and I know that this is not a
fair trial. I know it in my heart. If I
have to lose my license to practice
law and if I have to go to jail, I
can't think of a better cause to go
to jail for and to lose my license for
—
A VOICE: Right on!
MR. KUNSTLER: — than to tell
your Honor that you are doing a
disservice to the law in saying that
we can't have Ralph Abernathy on
the stand. You are saying truth will
not out because of the technicality
of a lawyer's representation. If that
is what their liberty depends upon,
your Honor saying I represented to
you that I had a cameraman, and
that was our only witness, a
cameraman, whom we can't get,
incidentally, then I think there is
nothing really more for me to say.
THE COURT: There is not much
more you could say, Mr Kunstler.
MR. KUNSTLER: I am going to
turn back to my seat with the
realization that everything I have
learned throughout my life has
come to naught, that there is no
meaning in this court, and there is
no law in this court — your

...nonor is wholly responsible for
that, and if this is what your career
is going to end on, if this is what
your pride is going to build on, I
can only say to you Honor, "Good
luck to you."
THE COURT: Mr. Marshal, I am
not here to be laughed at by these
defendants, particularly Mr. Rubin.
THE MARSHAL: Mr. Dellinger,
also, will you refrain from
laughing?
MR. DELLINGER: That is a lie.
And it wasn't Mr. Rubin. We laugh
enough and you can catch us when
we do but you just happened to get
that one wrong.
MR. KUNSTLER: Your Honor, I
don't think the record should
constantly have these references to
chuckles —
THE COURT: I don't share your view
MR. KUNSTLER: The Court has
made a sally before and the room
laughed and you didn't say put that
in the record.
THE COURT: I will not sit here —
and you must know it by now, and
have defendants laugh at my ruling,
sir. And I will not hear you on that.
MR. KUNSTLER: You don't mind
it they laugh at me or if they laugh
at someone else.
THE COURT: I will ask you to sit
down.
MR. KUNSTLER: I don't think
your Honor's ultra-sensitivity
should make a difference in rulings
in this court.
THE COURT: It isn't
ultra-sensitivity. It is a proper
understanding of the conduct of a
trial in the federal district court.
MR. KUNSTLER: No, but your
Honor, when you try to interpret a
laugh as meaning you are the butt
of a joke, then you react —
THE COURT: I will ask you to sit
down. Did you hear me?
MR. KUNSTLER: I just don't want
to get thrown in my chair by the
Marshal so I will have to sit down,
MR. HOFFMAN: I laughed. It
wasn't Jerry. It was me.
THE COURT: Did you get that,
Miss Reporter?
MR. HOFFMAN: I laughed at that
ruling, he didn't.
THE COURT: That was Mr.
Dellinger.
MR. KUNSTLER: That was not
Mr. Dellinger.
MR. KUNSTLER: Your Honor, that
was Mr. Hoffman.
MR. KUNSTLER: Your Honor —
MR. SCHULTZ: That was the
defendant Hoffman speaking.
MR. HOFFMAN: I was him.
THE COURT: Will you sit down? I
saw Mr. Dellinger talking. If
anybody else did —
MR. DELLINGER: You did not see
me talking. My lips were not
moving. That is not the first time
you have lied in this courtroom. My
lips were not moving.
THE COURT: Did you get those
last remarks?
MR. SCHULTZ: It was the
defendant Hoffman.
MR. DELLINGER: If you make an
honest mistake, that's all right, but
to lie about it afterwards and say
you saw me talking when you
didn't, that is different.
THE COURT: Will you ask that
man to sit down?
MR. DELLINGER: You will go
down in infamy in history for your
obvious lies in this courtroom of
which that is only the most recent
one.
THE MARSHAL: Sit down, sir.
MR. DELLINGER: It is absolutely
true what I am saying.
THE MARSHAL: Will you —
MR. DELLINGER: Absolutely
true.

Continued on Page 46

43

PLAYED OUT

by David Widgery

Review of 'Play Power' by Richard Neville Cape 38/-

You wonder how serious it is and whether people really want a revolution because I have a feeling that there are a lot of revolutionists who are really frightened when the serious guys, the serious kind of Trotskyites, come around and they're wearing these greasy neckties and suits and yet they're into the hard core of the organisation.' Tom Wolfe. Wittgenstein on Freud 'When you read him, hang onto your brains.'

This book is in fact a kit of gossip, conversation, information, lies and timetables, very prettily merchandised. It's a scrapboard of possible ways of survival by travel, drugs and sex aimed to improve your grip on pleasure. It will annoy a large and diverse group of people who will be shocked that anyone like this should be alive at all and it will further confirm us on the road to Shangri La. Neville is a gossip, in the best sense of that tradition, an impressario of information and atmospherics. He is much happier with a nuance or a frisson than an idea, remains heavyhandedly flippant and makes a terrible effort to shock. He musters and juxtaposes footnotes on Eisenhower's golfing and Palm court orchestras, pounces on remarkably succinct quotes, is perfectly equipped to deal with London high style as viewed from Australian underground saloon life. You write with extreme intelligence and self awareness and wit, Richard, but you still blow it.

In the introduction Neville thanks his publisher for advising him to write 'in his own voice'. In fact he uses four different standpoints; one for the muscle-bound quasi-statistical neodefinitive Time-Life sections, another that of the wellmeaning crusader for freedom and love, rather frantically grasping at not very authoritative authorities, thirdly a rather curious and whimsical travelwriter not letting on he goes everywhere by air and collecting three line people instead of postcards. When he does write as himself he's almost dazzling. His account of the Stones outdoor concerts viewed from the press area beside the pop ruling class is genuinely satirical ... probably the last thing that Neville would want to be called. His account of the famous overprepared faces, the artifical sociality, the gormlessness of the compere's manipulation, the totally unselfconscious brutality of the organisers towards the kids who had camped in the front row for 3 days, the masturbatory and exhausted narcissism of Jagger, show an intelligence and unfooledness quite at odds with the earnestness and overwritten pleas for sexual excess and drug taking. The unkind might say that Neville makes the conscious decision only to make use of his acumen in an area where it doesn't matter anyhow; certainly if he had applied his full intelligence to the chapters on the underground press and politics of play they would have come apart in his laughing hands.

Now the interior life of the Trotskyist movement may be somewhat narrow but within its limits very intense and rigorous; one can take a very good measure of a Trot's position within the tradition by asking him three of four litmus paper questions; on Kronstadt, class nature of USSR, Cuba and the Permanent Revolution. The underground in its much shorter history already has such cruxes; what is your line on Nashville Skyline, your analysis of the Stones Altamont concert, your position on the three class block of hippies, skinheads and Angels, your stance on heroin. When trying to place Neville's rather ambiguous position within the underground (where the division between the ruling class and proletariat is even wider than it is in real life) one is struck by a certain squeamishness; the lace curtain haven't been torn down just rearranged. He's conservative about drugs, prudish about violence and a raving reactionary about women. It's no longer particularly outspoken to like smoking joints; it's an act of civilisation not deviation and at a good many parties it's the alcohol men who ought to hide in a locked bedroom upstairs. Sure smoking makes you funny, happy and hungry, it probably increases your intake of sensual information rather than decreases it, it might even aid contact with the oceanic, the transcendental, the extraterrestial and certainly the irrational. But so what. It could once be argued that possessing it put the young middle class in an altered relationship with the police; that smoking was an act of sound rebellion with political consequences. But for the bourgeoisie nowadays cannabis can be brought by cheque and smoked with a smug impunity over the liqueurs. The police really do seem to be mainly concerned with dealers and opiates plus the odd plant on people they want anyhow ... and in Notting Hill how could they really do otherwise. The picture is rather different in East London where the users are all working class and the sentences are harder, the lead in in today's local paper is of two 12 month gaol sentences for a timber worker and a bath attendant who were said to have offered to supply a cop with hash. But the young people who really are a danger to the system probably prefer pills and tippers to the priceless passivity of heavy smoking. Talking about heroin Neville seems to accept the conventional view of its utter harmfullness. Much more modest than say Cocteau, one of the most dazzling and prolific artists of the 20th century who argues 'to say of an addict who is in a constant state of euphoria that he is degrading himself is like saying of marble that it is spoilt by Michelangelo, of canvas that it is stained by Raphael, of paper that it is soiled by Shakespeare, of silence that it is broken by Bach' ... 'of course opium remains unique and the euphoria it induces is superior to health. I owe it my perfect hours. It is a pity that instead of perfecting curative techniques, medicine does not try to render opium harmless.' So if you believe life should be about the pursuit of your own pleasure rather than your own and other peoples' freedom it would be logical to advocate the use of opiates ... but Neville stops at hash home baking; the syringe is, well, going a bit too far.

He makes a more determined attempt to be shocking about sex, having Hurricane fucks with 14 year old schoolgirls, suggesting making love when stoned with stereo headphones on both partners, playing the first Blind Faith Album (which side? inquires the serious militant) and saying that you get to a woman's mind through her cunt. The rationale is Reith Lecturish; sex has been disentangled from pregnancy, property and poetry so just fuck and enjoy youself. Neville (Voice 4) is honest enough to admit his own efforts to live life as sensuously as possible are inclined to end up as bad bedroom farce ... but the attitude remains that sexual love has been replaced by a lot of fancy screwing with ancillary aids (presumably you are allowed the far more erotic Beethoven on your headphones if you ask nicely). Autonomous man, wander sexually free in a world where women are doubly enslaved both as people under capitalism and as women by men. The hippy chick has always been one of the most unfree of women; assigned to being ethereal and knowing about Tarot and the Moon phases but busy at cooking, answering the phone and rolling her master's joints. For her, the chains are meant to be just an extreme form of jewellery ... the only way out of there is a private income. Neville's view of sexual transaction is not so much advanced as insulting and it all the more sad he doesn't even notice it. Because you can now be fairly sure that woman is so keen to have you that she'll be sucking 25 tablets of oestrogen in readiness, it doesn't mean she's got control of her mind and her destiny. As an excellent woman review of the male supremacist film Easy Rider pointed out the new farming hippy communities are even 'more' male dominated 'because of the practical problems of dividing the work (technology makes a woman's lesser muscular capacity irrelevant and partly because the American farming myth is very much a scenario for the dominant male — the woman stays in the background and bakes bread while her male chops down trees.'

Violence is the biggest taboo of all especially the border dispute that goes on in pop between violence and sex (Jagger's prophetic 'violence gives me a buzz'.) The underground's habit of standing around watching while someone gets done in muttering 'bad trip' is not commented on but surely the most surprising thing about the Altamont murder was how unsurprised everyone was; mean if murdering people is the Angels' trip then someone better take their acid away. The tendency (and lefties are just as fond of it) is to capture some section of the proletariat in a purely mental fashion and hammer them on the masthead of the Good Ship Revolution. The way the artist-underground goes on about the skinheads or Angels is just as condescending as the Regency bucks' patronage of bruisers and picaresque characters from

demi-monde of the
lumpen-proletariat. Play Power
includes a supplement of fuzz
brutality tho it's not clear
quite precisely why; the
marxist left ought to expect it;
the serious hippy ought to stay
out of the way of such vulgar
methods of attempting to
advance history. The May
events are reinterpreted to the
point of dishonesty to prove
that the most important
moments were the rather
unbrilliant wall slogans and
other acts of Gallic student
esem. In a world where the
modern working class in its
factory, ports, garages and
warehouses took over the
running of their own
production, one would need a
serious visual defect to find the
antics of the Sorbonne the
most significant innovation.
The Chicago demonstrations
of the Yippies can be more
fairly credited to acid and the
underground. But Play Power
seems to take them a lot more
seriously than they take
themselves. Krassner and
Rubin seem to see the Yippies
as a quite specific method of
making the media.

Hippy politics, being made up
as it goes along, are
incomprehensible and
therefore extremely dangerous
to the psyche of the media. It,
on one side, totally takes the
piss out of the TV idiotmen so
addicted to the new that they
can't recognise it as being
created for their benefit, and at
the same time overrates the
possibility of changing things
by visual cathode imagery. It's
the other side of the pathetic
media megalomania of Lennon
who spentsso much of his life
having lens and mikes stuck in
him he really believes that they
are connected directly to
power and change. Mailer
understands the special
obtrusiveness of the Yippies
quite well; 'Leninism finally
was as good for Leninists about
the way that psychoanalysis
was good for psychoanalysis

it was a superb mental
equivalent to weightlifting
the brain worked, perspired,
pushed itself and came back
with hard tangible increments
of mental tone and vigor, but it
had nothing to do with the real
problem which was; how do
you develop enough grace to
capture a thief more graceful
than yourself? Leninism was
built to analyse a world in
which all the structures were
made of steel — now the sinews
of society were founded on
transistors so small Dragon
lady could hide them beneath
a nail.

The underground is in general
ahistorical it doesn't
remember what happened to it
yesterday and it's this element
of Play Power which makes
Neville's bright ideas like so
many orphans waiting for their
real intellectual parents to

claim them. The native
American tradition is full of
the praise of idleness and
loafing; Thoreau advised you
'to retire to the woods, if you
can find any and examine your
concience, but only after you
have enjoyed yourself.' Walt
Whitman believed in the
healing power of erotic love
and is part of a long American
tradition expressed today in
the poetic role of Ginsberg.
Whitman, who called this
quality, rather gluely,
'adhesiveness' had a sizeable
following in England, mainly
proletarian and provincial.
Whitman sponged off his
admirers for years; his birdcage
sent as a gift, symbol and
exchange still hangs in Bolton
Library. The nature of free
love was discussed and
practiced by Shelley and Mary
Godwin, Blake, Morris and his
circle and the pre-war Marxists.
It was William Morris, thought
by the underground to be the
inventor of potato cuts, not
Leary or Lawrence, who wrote
of the *socialist* future '1
demand a free and unfettered
animal life for man; first of all
I demand the utter extinction
of all asceticism. If we feel the
least degradation in being
amorous, or merry, or hungry,
or sleepy, we are so far bad
animals and therefore
miserable men". But because of
the understanding as socialists
they refused to see free love
and sexuality as possible in the
present society or a lever for a
molecular change to a new one.
The exploitation of woman by
man in the bourgeois marriage
was deeply connected to the
exploitation of man by man in
capitalism; one would not go
without the other. The
methodist suspicion of pleasure
and corresponding enthusiasm
for the moral qualities
imparted by suffering which
are more often found in the
modern Left are a distorted
version of the other stream of
socialist views on sex; the aim
to produce an utterly rational
relationship between man and
woman as intellectual
collaborators and political
comrades. Neville's hopes for
the growing mechanisation of
pleasure are probably justified;
the pharmaceutical industry
has scarcely begun the
synthesis of chemical
euphoriants, visual and sound
storage must soon make
possible the sense cinema that
Huxley predicted, the
technology of pleasure will
advance like textile industry
did in the early 19th century
and the underground will be its
obedient consumers like they
now consume Godard, IT, and
The Jefferson Airplane on
stereoheadphones.
It's sad to always be the
scolding lefty but Neville just
doesn't convince me that
tinkering with lifestyle and an
occasional brush with the

police amounts to a revolution.
Behind all the scream crash and
wallop the underground still
smells of cheque books and an
expensive education. The staff
of International Times might
treat strangers (ie everyone)
rather like the staff of
Woolworths treat customers
but when they talk to you it's
Lord Snooty all right even if
they are dressed like Bash
Street Gang. The rich may be
getting angina from all the
thrill, the poor still get
rheumatic fever. In fact hippies
are consciously softer than
their bandit predecessors the
beats and the hip, more
tumescent than erect, more
soppy than soft either faint
with ecstasy or asleep. There
seems to me absolutely no
reason why the enfant terrible
will not be the ruling class of
tomorrow. At present the
money is made out of Hip
Capitalism whether it's cocaine
deals, special offers, magazines
or TV impersonations.
Politically the hippies might
manage the isolated courage of
the isolated individual but
those who see the choice will
surely take the primrose
path . . . that's what it's all
about sez Richard. The inbuilt
elitism, superstition and
leadership search is more likely
to end the underground up in
Scientology, or Social Credit
than a socialist revolution. All
the holidays in the far East and
the adoption of oriental
plumage and religious
bric-a-brack is not an answer to
the plunder of Indian and
African civilsions by
imperialism. It's just impotence
and guilt decked out as
romanticism. Sexual freedom,
at least as interpreted by OZ
seems to mean girls being
willing to fuck with anyone
plus the exhibitionist jerk off
fantasia of 'let's do it
in the street'. This
is Penis Power
not

liberation. You could grope
Nixon silly and suck Wilson
from here to Singapore there
would still be half a million
G.I.s in S.Vietnam and half a
million men at the Labour
Exchange. The dangers of the
descent into the hippy
maelstrom are considerable.
Some risks are energising, some
of the forces are liberating but
the horrors are horrific; Martin
Sharp's book jacket with its
prison of penis, guitar and joint
coming in narcissistic waves
while the million suns grin
inanely is where the grinning
hippy killed and wounded go.
For all its interior fascinations
it's a world that's
incommunic able; most of all
to the plodding market porters,
the dim printers, the bored
commuters whom the pop
aristocrat disparagingly notices
in passing. We must attempt
something much more
ambitious than encouraging
their children to smoke pot
between 4th Form and Council
house, a revolution not in
smoking pleasure but in the
way men relate to one another.
And this can only be based on
the way people are oppressed
by the system and the daily
way they fight it back; this is
about productivity deals,
Trades Councils, football,
fighting, women talking in
laundrettes and Guinness and it
takes place in those parts of
the unknown England that
smug metropolitans never even
see. Turning to this world and
turning to it politically is
something that many people
who like drugs, fucking and
foreign travel feel essential; we
are all in the siege of Sidney
Street and we've left it too late
to dig a way out underground,
and these days it's not wise to
go out with your hands up.

45

◀ Continued from Page 43

THE COURT: Mr. Marshal, will you ask him to be quiet?

MR. DELLINGER: You will be ashamed of that for the rest of your life, if anything can shame you.

MR. SCHULTZ: Your Honor, it was the defendant Hoffman sitting immediately behind Dellinger who made those remarks.

THE COURT: Let the record show —

MR. DELLINGER: Thanks for telling the truth, Mr. Schultz.

MR. KUNSTLER: Mr. Hoffman attempted to clarify the record. He was the one responsible. He took the blame for it. It was not Mr. Dellinger or Mr. Rubin, or anyone else.

THE COURT: Oh, I heard Mr. Rubin and saw him.

MR. KUNSTLER: Your Honor —

THE COURT: Will you please sit down? I will make the rulings here. The record will be what it is.

MR. KUNSTLER: I want the record to —

THE COURT: It can't be any more clear.

MR. DELLINGER: I want to make the record clear. Mr. Rubin did not laugh and you are standing there saying you heard it. That is why I called you a liar. He did not laugh. I was sitting next to him.

THE COURT: Mr. Marshal —

MR. DELLINGER: And you made it up. It is about time this got out into the open so everybody could know what you are doing here. It is one thing to be prejudiced, it is another thing to be a liar.

THE COURT: Mr. Marshal, I ask you to restrain that man.

THE MARSHAL: Be quiet.

MR. KUNSTLER: He is trying to clarify the record.

THE COURT: He has got a lawyer.

MR. KUNSTLER: I am his lawyer and I represent —

THE COURT: That is right, and we have had enough of it.

MR. KUNSTLER: But the record must be crystal clear that it was not Mr. Dellinger, and it was not Mr. Rubin. Mr. Hoffman —

THE COURT: Mr. Dellinger said enough.

MR. KUNSTLER: Mr. Hoffman has taken the blame.

THE COURT: I have never sat in fifty years through a trial where a party to a lawsuit called the judge a liar.

MR. DELLINGER: Maybe they were afraid to go to jail rather than tell the truth, but I would rather go to jail for how long you send me than to let you get away with that kind of thing and people not realize what you are doing.

(clapping in courtroom)

THE COURT: Will you let the record show — I don't know, I get twisted between the defendants — the one in the middle.

MR. WEINER: Weiner.

A DEFENDANT: Davis.

MR. WEINER: Weiner.

THE COURT: Mr. Weiner applauded after that speech.

MR. KUNSTLER: So did half the courtroom, your Honor. I think that ought to be in the record.

THE COURT: Yes. If I could identify them, I would have the marshals order them out and I do order those who applauded and who were seen by the marshals to be taken out of the courtroom. Now, Mr. Weineruss — Weinglass.

MR. WEINGLASS: Weinglass, your Honor.

THE COURT: Whatever your name is. Continue with the examination of this witness, Mr. Weinglass.

46

Some of us at OZ are feeling old and boring, so we invite any of our readers who are under eighteen to come and edit the April issue. Apply at the OZ office in Princedale Road, W.11, anytime from 10am to 7pm on Friday, March 13. We will choose one person, several, or accept collective applications from a group of friends. You will receive no money, except expenses. You will enjoy almost complete editorial freedom. OZ staff will assist in purely an administrative capacity. If you like, write before March 13 and tell us who you are and would like to do with a 48 page two colour magazine . . . OZ belongs to you.

Plugs and Propaganda: In the US, where film plays an important revolutionary role, (although catered for to saturation point by Eastman-Kodak and big business) Underground film makers are making features on 8mm which although, once derogatively assigned to amateurs is now the most accessible means of film-making for those interested in filmic self-expression. This gauge is light, compact and easy to handle. People like Stan Brakhage & Bruce prefer to sell 8mm copies of their films rather than rent 16mm copies at a comparable price. As a result, people are beginning to build up 8mm film libraries like they began their record collections. Having a film at home means you can watch it over and over again, important when today's films are often as complex as rock music. Soon, such films will be able to be slotted into TV sets without need to set up projector, speakers or screen, and magazines like OZ will be sold in film-cassettes. (See Acid Flix P.32) *Note:* Films of New Cinema Can be rented from The London Filmmaker's Co-Operative. Tel: 387 8980 or seen at New Arts Lab, 1 Robert St. NW.1, Electric Cinema, 191 Portobello Rd, London W.11, Angry Arts, Camden Studio, Camden Street, NW.1, and New Cinema Club (no permanent home, Tel: 734 5888).

The new film magazine CINEMANTICS 117 Hartfield Rd, London SW.19, shows some concern for the New Cinema. Jonas Mekas' FILM CULTURE, quarterly from Box 1499, GPO New York 10001 has done much to define the aesthetics of the movement. CINIM published by London Film-Makers' Co-Operative irregularly, attempts the same for the local scene.

NEWSREEL, CINEMA ACTION, the TATTOOIST group, and THE OTHER CINEMA are preparing alternative distribution methods in this country to challenge the hegemony of the two commercial circuits.

The TATTOOIST group, in an attack on fuddy-duddy British TV have predicted, if present reactionary trends are not halted, the ultimate Man Alive programme: it will show the last 28 minutes and 30 seconds of a man's life. He will die on cue, behind the producer's credit. The Producer goes on to win

---

the 'Documentary of the Year' prize, sponsored by an evening paper.

Extract from an interview with Senator Malcolm Scott, Minister for Customs and Excise, Australia.

Q. Why haven't you got some people on the censorship board who may be more qualified in knowing what might have a tendency to deprave and corrupt — like a psychologist, for example.

A. Just because you want to see filth on the screen, it is no reason why the majority should bend for a few perverts.

Q. But aren't you forcing your own morality upon everyone else?

A. It's the will of the majority.

Q. Why have you banned Portnoy's Complaint?

A. It was the worst book I've ever read.

Q. How many books have you read? Some people regard it as one of the best books published in 1969.

A. It's filthy. You are all perverts.

Q. Why did you ban *I Love You Love* (a film by Stig Bjorkman).

A. Those continental films! All you want is filth on the screen. Filth! Filth! Filth! Eighteen people in Australia have seen that film and they all think that the couple were . . . (pause) . . . having sex.

Community heads raise their heads. The Crypt Club, 240 Lancaster Rd. W.11, is open every Wednesday from 7.30 pm for everyone and everything — music, poetry, art, folk, jazz and good underground ambience. Sometimes guest artists and light shows. Admission 2/6 or 3/6 depending what's on.

Also new in the Grove. Magazine called *Your Thing* replacing *Interzone A.* Articles on music, art, mysticism etc. Letters, reviews, poetry and classified ads. Rates: FREE up to 6 words, then 6d per word. 10 min. A newsletter, *Scene West Eleven* dealing with news and useful information for people living in Portobello/Notting Hill area will also appear shortly. If anyone can help with office space, elderly typewriters or in any way at all, contact Dale at Release, 50a Princedale Road, W.11. Tel: 229 7753.

Being added to those ubiquitous but only ethereally functional underground organisations, UPS, COSMIC, LNS, etc. is AUM, the Alliance of Underground Media, whose aim is to unify underground radio with underground magazines and newspapers. AUM has headquarters at 528 Lambert Rd, Orange, Connecticut 06477. Are there any underground radio stations in England?

The Committee for Ideals in Mental Practices is organising at the moment the greatest petition ever held in Great Britain. The petition's purpose is to free the field of mental healing from vested interests, commercial and political, thereby safeguarding individual rights, improving legislation for those undergoing mental treatment preventing brainwashing, and other malpractices, such as the misuse of Pentathol, the truth drug. Those interested in signing the petition or helping any other way, contact the Committee at 5 Sutton Road, Heston, Middlesex, England.

Peace News England's doyen 'Underground' newspaper, and first to join UPS, which has been giving peace a chance since before World War II, needs to raise £3000 urgently to balance deficits on their campaign work to date. Help their

---

Annual Appeal, write to The Treasurer, Peace News, 5 Caledonia Road, London, N.1.

The pilot issue of AGRO which appeared in January was a real newspaper of the streets — direct, aggressive, anti-sentimental. 'The emergence of the Street Communes and of AGRO marks the dissolution of the rift between the 'political' and the 'cultural' wings of the underground . . . Agro will not be sold through bookshops or newsagents; it will be distributed through the same network of contacts which produces it . . . to develop a real underground communications system with its roots in specific local situations . . . Agro is not and isn't intended to be a commercial proposition. Contributors will be 'paid' in free copies to sell." The first issue with its promise of sections for greasers, heads, skinheads and skools together with FUCK (Free Underground Campaign for Kids) Manifesto, has not yet materialised. What has happened to all that revolutionary fervour? Maybe a subscription would help. Send 25s for 24 issues (6 months) to AGROKULTCHUR, BCM, Box 890, London W.C.1. Money doesn't talk, it swears.

ROUNDHOUSE 10-16 MARCH a completely new kind of pop and theatrical Festival. Mysticism, madness, musical carnival and Quicksilver Messenger Service, Grateful Dead, Jefferson Airplane, Sunshine Tribe. INQUIRIES. FLA 9533.

Head books

Have you noticed how little (if at all) you are going to the local pub these days? Having discovered that it is possible to be smashed, keep on the stereo headphones AND read, I have managed over the past couple of weeks to get through several recently published books which are all of great interest to anyone who happens to be living the revolution. "All I am trying to do is to get the people who smoke pot and take acid talking to the people who dont and clear up some of the paranoia around," says Allen Ginsberg in *Psterfamilias — Allen Ginsberg in America*, by Jane Kramer (published by Gollancz at 42s.) which is a guide, through Ginsberg, to the literary beat generation and the very non-literary hippies who followed. mdern day Walt Whitman, and everybody's favourite flower-powered beatnik, Ginsberg has come a long and fascinating way since the desperate days of Howl. Despite his journeys to the East, he still has his feet planted firmly on the ground — his paradise is an earthy bohemian one. He's a mystic but very much an American one, and there's nothing ethereal or ascetic about him. Enthusiasm is something which everyone has or can generate, but with Ginsberg it's like a gift from the Gods. He's into everything and everybody, and demonstrates such tolerance, understanding and affection, that he has become the unregenerate go-between between the world of the drop-out and square. He's the complete, ideal mid-twentieth century man, and has evolved an easy going communal life-style which actually works, unlike the hippie communes and acid enclaves which rapidly degenerate into closed, exclusive groups which are totally at odds with the mass of society. "One sacrament is as good as the next one", says Ginsberg, "if it works." He has called himself a Buddhist Jewish pantheist, and charged with a great sense of responsibility, particularly towards young people, he moves easily in a world populated by everyone from Hells Angels, mushroom fiends and Swamis to Episcopal ministers and US Senators. Much more than Mae West, he has "bin places and seen things" and the American hot dog, colour TV and the urban ghetto form as much a part of his experience as the hermit's mountain cave, the Ganges, the I Ching, Tangier, Blake and tantric yoga.

He's so full of common sense. "Just taking acid's no yoga. Yoga is getting through acid, knowing what to do with it. Yoga is how to be neat when you're high." I remember at the very end of the great Albert Hall poetry reading in 1965, with the management pleading "Please leave if you have homes to go to, please go to them ... oh why don't you leave?" followed by the threat of police and firemen, Ginsberg, still chanting and clanking on his Tibetan cow bells was carried shoulder high through the crowd. As he passed one of London's first long haired youths who had adoringly caught his eye, he shouted "Wanna fuck?" The boy almost frozen with embarrassment, dumbly shook his head. Ginsberg shouted "Then get fucked," and was carried struggling and clanking down the nearest stairway.

Timothy Leary's Politics of Ecstasy (McGibbon & Kee, 36s. hardback, and soon (April 19) in Paladin paperback) could be another key document to whatever you are doing with your life these days. It is a collection of mindbending essays and articles from the high priest of chemical ecstasy himself, some of them from as far back as 1962, others very new. All of it is hard core sales talk for the psychedelic revolution. It's all there, including the famous Playboy interview in which he called LSD "the most powerful aphrodisiac ever discovered by man", his answers to such crucial questions as what will happen to society after everyone turns on, tunes in and drops out, a homage to Aldous Huxley who, took a massive dose of acid several hours before he died of cancer, the seven levels of consciousness and the specific drugs to turn on each level, and so on. "Drugs are the Religion of the People — the Only Hope is Dope" headlines Leary. All you do with one of society's misfits is shoot him up with the right dope. At the moment, Leary must be wondering what is the right dope for him, because his campaign for Governor of California is turning into something of a bad trip — like Mailer's for Mayor of New York. Leary is discovering that politics and ecstasy don't really mix. In political terms, acid is anarchy, and Leary, bringing his version to the good people of California, feels for the sake of votes, that he has to deny this. He has become a psychedelic Billy Graham. A role which he has taken up because no one else will. Somebody had to be the prostitute, the rationaliser of an irrational visionary experience. Whistle stop acid tours, ticker tape acid welcomes, 500 dollar plate acid dinners, drum majorettes and acid conventions, Trip too Through the Tulips campaign song, and all

the paraphernalia of the old politics harnessed for Paradise Now. Leary, says Ron Rosenbaum, writing in the Village Voice (8.1.70) now believes there is no such thing as a bad trip, just a bad setting. Civilisation and cities are the worst setting and therefore the only place to take a trip is somewhere untainted by society. Every man his holy mountaintop. This sounds like a defeat — just like the hippie retreat to the desert communes is a defeat. Leary is sick of his political shaman burden and once more demonstrates the difficulty of 'a successful fusion of personal liberation and political action'. Even Abbie Hoffman is more of a Weatherman than a Yippie these days.

Celebrated London freak, Robin Farquharson, lays further claim to wrongful omission from the Beautiful Freaks edition of OZ (No. 24) with the publication in England (Basil Blackwell, Oxford 40s.) of Theory of Voting which won a prize in the States in 1961 an; is now an essential text for students of political science. It is elegantly printed with lots of totally mystifying black and red diagrams. Much more readable is Drop Out by the same author, which was published a couple of years ago and sold very badly. There was only a fledgling alternative society to drop into in those days, and what Robin Farquharson found, despite a single disastrous acid trip, was more akin to the Salvation Army, doss house, park bench, maths head world of the tramp than the more comfortable drug lined communal scene of the Ladbroke Grove hippie. He has survived and prospered however, and in 1970 he had been much in evidence at the New Arts Lab burning £5 notes and outlining a fantastic plan for a 32 storey commune at Centrepoint.

Penguin has just published The Teachings of Don Juan by Carlos Castaneda, which has been described by Theodore Roszak as 'a uniquely important contribution to our burgeoning psychedelic literature.' The author spent five years with Don Juan a Yaqui Indian, renowned as a sorcerer in the American South West. The book details his hallucinogenic experiences using peyote, jimson weed and a mushroom called humito. A warning to those who intend to rush into the English countryside looking for our local hallucinogenic, Fly Agaric. Somehow, up until now I had never made the connection between the prevalence of mushroom, toadstools, fairies and elves, gnomes in children's books, and hallucinatory drugs. Now I know. For those feeling like some more orthodox revolutionary reading, there is the Fontana paperback series Modern Masters — 'men who have changed and are changing the life and thought of our age.' Marcuse, Guevara, Camus, Levi-Strauss and Fanon are available. I liked Andrew Sinclair's Guevara best. He has so much liking and hero-worship for his subject. "History will probably treat Guevara as the Garibaldi of his age, the most admired and loved revolutionary of his time ... for the rich nations of the earth, and for the corrupt governments that rule many of the poor nations, the dead Che is a terrible and a beautiful enemy."

Jim Anderson.

Television fails because the people producing it have linear, logical, departmentalised, alien, pre-tv thought processes. To most of them, a great tv programme is like a great book, only visual. That's why oldies on both sides of the screen are enthralled by the Forsyth Saga (it has been repeated 4 times). When fresh talent does somehow survive the gauntlet of Oxbridge bureocracy and burst onto the tv screens, it is invariably brained by the critics. Ken Russell's Dance of the Seven Veils was the best thing on the box since Tony Palmer's All My Loving and was as universally despised by the press, who raised such irrelevancies as taste, objectivity and accuracy — who cares? — not Russell as he flippantly demonstrated by consciously confusing Richard Strauss with Johann.

While the existing mentality prevails, a televisual equivalent of this magazine could never be produced because the programme controllers wouldn't be able to classify it. Is it Light Entertainment or Current Affairs? And if they could squeeze it into a slot, it could never squeeze out of it. The remoteness of most of television to the lives and ideas of young people is expressed in the intensifying search for alternative tv stations. John Hopkins' recent tv workshop at the New Arts Lab proved — even with its primitive, portable Sony equipment — that the medium is, in his own words, "a living thing". (Write to him at IRATV, 1 Robert Street, London, N.W.1. for information on the planned tv network.) If OZ could afford to buy half an hour on tv, these are some of thing's we'd do!

— Chaoz would begin after the man says, "Don't forget to turn off your sets" — so only the lazy surprised delighted few would see the first programme.

— Studio to be equipped with at least three interview or 'happening' booths. The screen could be split into three so all interviewees are seen simultaneously. Volume would vary in proportion to interest value. If activities in all booths were

fascinating then, each dialogue could be technically separated (tone controls or sound tricks) and our ear could decide upon which one to concentrate.

— These interviewees or guests would not, of course, be celebrities — just likeable unknowns or those who had something to say. There could be a regular 'freak-of-the-week'.

— Camera men and technicians to share in the anarchy — to shoot or ignore what they fancy.

— Programmes from rival channels should be screened simultaneously with Chaoz in small, autonomous squares elsewhere on the screen.

— Life goes on. Chaoz to link-up with a closed circuit traffic camera or a special camera to be left at Victoria Station to be cut to at odd intervals.

— Instant feedback. Telephones to be plugged into the sound system — those ringing in with interesting reactions to Chaoz could be immediately amplified. Sound links between floor manager, producer etc could also be relayed.

— Guest pop groups to play one continuous piece — to be fed through Chaoz intermittently or permanently superimposed.

— Famous old movie always to be shown on studio screen — to be cut to occasionaly.

— Sometimes the whole show could be a softly lit screen projecting amazing sound effects. It will tantalise/infuriate the viewer.

— Surprise conventional items — eg, straight face to camera monologues on contemporary issues.

— Topical news footage to be screened, suitable doctored, animated, juxtaposed, falsified.

— People involved in Chaoz would be anonomous and generally unavailable for comment.

— Many of the creative decisions could be made randomly, by computer.

— Help create Chaoz — send us any ideas for a new style tv or, better still, cut this page out and post it to Huw Wheldon, managing director, BBC Television, Wood Lane, White City, London, W12.

The man who ordered meat at the Macrobiotic Restaurant.

THE ACID FACTS

(LYSERGIC ACID DIETHYLAMIDE (LSD 25)

WHY IS IT CALLED LSD, WHY NOT 25?
LSD WAS SYNTHESIZED IN 1938 AT SANDOZ LABS SWITZERLAND BY STOLL & HOFMANN. ITS EFFECTS WERENT DISCOVERED TILL 1943. WHEN HOFMANN DIDN'T WASH HIS HANDS BEFORE LUNCH THEY MADE IT "WONDERLAND"...

IN WHAT PHARMACOLOGICAL CATEGORY IS LSD?
ITS CALLED PSYCHOTOGENIC, PSYCHOTOMIMETIC HALLUCINOGENIC & PSYCHEDELIC DEPENDING ON THE ATTITUDE OF THE WRITER.

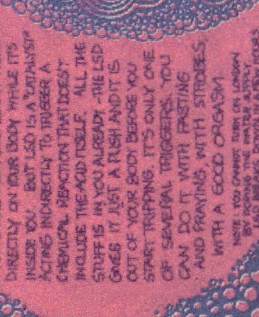

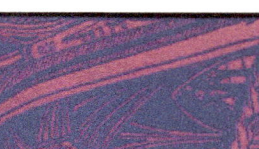

WHAT IS LSD'S PHYSICAL FORM?
LSD IS A CRYSTALINE WHITE POWDER FREELY SOLUBLE IN CHLOROFORM AND LESS SO IN WATER, IT CAN BE PACKAGED IN ANYTHING SUGAR CUBE, CAPSULE, FINGERNAIL, DIRT.

HOW IS IT ADMINISTERED?
USUALLY ORALLY, IT CAN BE INJECTED BUT THE EFFECT'S THE SAME, AND REALLY IS NUCE CLEANER.

TO WHAT BRAIN PROCESS IS LSD RELATED?
LSD IS AN INDOLE MANY LARGE LIVE DIRT PROTEIN AN LSD WHILE THESE ALL ARE CHEMICAL STRUCTURES BUILT AROUND SEROTONIN A SUBSTANCE ALWAYS FOUND PRESENT IN THE BRAIN, BLAH.

WHAT IS THE USUAL DOSAGE?
ACCORDING TO FOLKLORE. 100 TO 250 MICROGRAMS—LESS THAN A SPECK OF DUST BUT NO ONE REALLY KNOWS, HCD IS ONE OF THE MOST DOSE AND EFFICIENT DRUGS KNOWN.

YOU CAN'T ALWAYS VARYING DOSES— ES MAKES HIGHT HIT TO LOW LCD IT'S YOUR FRIEND BUT NO MORE LESS OF

WHY ARE THE DOSAGE RULES DIFFERENT FOR LSD?
FOR A BIG HEADACHE YOU TAKE TWO ASPIRIN, FOR A LITTLE HEADACHE YOU TAKE ONE ASPIRIN. BECAUSE IT ACTS DIRECTLY ON YOUR BODY WHILE IT'S INSIDE YOU. BUT LSD IS A "CATALYST" ACTING INDIRECTLY TO TRIGGER A CHEMICAL REACTION THAT DOES INCLUDE THE ACID ITSELF. ALL THE STUFF IS IN YOU ALREADY. THE LSD GIVES IT JUST A PUSH AND IT'S OUT OF YOUR BODY BEFORE YOU START TRIPPING. IT'S ONLY ONE OF SEVERAL TRIGGERS. YOU CAN DO IT WITH FASTING AND PRAYING, WITH STROBES, WITH A GOOD ORGASM.

HOW DOES LSD ACHIEVE ITS EFFECTS?
THERE ARE MANY THEORIES. MOST AGREEING THAT ITS A CATALYST BUT NO ONE REALLY KNOWS. THIS IS ANOTHER REASON DOCTORS DONT WANT YOU TAKING IT. DOUBLETALK. WE THINK DONT KNOW. HOW ASPIRIN WORKS, THO IT CAUSES ANGINA AND BIRTH. NO ONE THOUGH WAS ADVOCATED IMPRISONMENT FOR POSSESSION.

WHAT ARE THE POSSIBLE BAD SIDE EFFECTS?

PANIC: SEE LEFT ABOUT FREAKING OUT

PARANOIA: YOU GET SUPER-SUPER-SUSPICIOUS OF PEOPLE, THINK THEYRE TRYING TO CONTROL YOUR MIND. MAY OR MAY NOT BE A BAD EFFECT, YOU COULD BE RIGHT.

RECURRENCES: SEE LEFT ABOUT THIS

ACCIDENTAL DEATH: RARE, BUT IT HAS HAPPENED. ITS A GOOD IDEA TO HAVE A GUIDE.

PREFERABLY NOT TRIPPING. BUT DON'T GET ONE SO STRAIGHT HE'LL FREAK OUT WATCHING YOU, LOSS OF ABILITY TO THINK RATIONALLY ETC.; LOTS OF STRAIGHTS CAN'T DO THIS. MANY WOULD 'FREE ASSOCIATE' LOGIC CAN BE A HELP OR A HINDRANCE, HOW DO YOU WANT TO RUN YOUR LIFE?

BIRTH DEFECTS: THE ISSUE OF LSD AND CHROMOSOME DAMAGE IS A HUGE **HOAX!**

HOW CAN A BAD TRIP BE STOPPED?

APPROACHING HAS NO ANTIDOTE TRIPS ARE LOTS OF WAYS TO STOP AN ACID TRIP

NIACINAMIDE IS PROBABLY BEST AND SHOULD BE INJECTED IF POSSIBLE MANDRAX IS OK.

HOW LONG IS THE TRIP?

USUALLY 8 TO 14 HOURS. FOR SOME PEOPLE A BAD TRIP PSYCHOTIC EPISODE CAN LAST DAYS OR YEARS.

RECURRENCES — TRIPLETS OF FULL TRIPS THAT HAPPEN DAYS, WEEKS OR MONTHS AFTER YOU'VE DROPPED. THIS CAN BE A GROOVE OR A FREAKOUT DEPENDING ON HOW YOU TAKE IT. IF YOU ARE AFRAID OF LOSING YOUR MIND YOU WILL. YOUR CHANCE OF FREAKOUT IS HIGH-EST IF YOUR HEAD IS MESSED IN THE FIRST PLACE — ALMOST NIL IF YOU'RE HEALTHY AND HONEST.

CAN LSD CAUSE DEPENDENCE?

NO! IF YOU DROP TOO OFTEN IT LOSES ITS EFFECT

MOST HEAVY HEADS SAY DON'T DROP MORE THAN ONCE EVERY 2 OR 3 MONTHS SO

YOU'LL HAVE TIME TO WORK WITH WHAT YOU'VE LEARNED

WHAT ABOUT PSYCHOLOGICAL DEPENDENCE?

ACID'S NOT A COMFORTABLE ESCAPE FROM REALITY. IT MAKES YOU FACE THINGS YOU TRIED TO FORGET. ALCOHOL & HEROIN ARE MUCH BETTER IF YOU'RE INTO THAT.

FROM URSULA & LEET LANE.

3

The chemical revolution.
To trip is human, to revolt divine!

What follows is part of a lecture given at the Psychedelic Convention which met in November of 1968 by Dr. Victor Jeste who heads the Sociology Department at Adelphi University in New York. It is a good analysis of what drugs are in terms of sociology, the Dr. hypothesizes that psychedelics are primative,

a new generation seeks to master a new range of societal forces.

I. HISTORY AS INQUIRY

A few years ago heroin was a medication of choice to which many adolescents looked for an anaesthetic revelation of their desires, as William James called it. We hypothesized that these young people sought from the heroin a temporary relief from the fatenus of an imperfect civilization which inflicted upon them the impossible task of seeking a forbidden deliverance from their lower class plight. The situation was relatively uncomplicated. One drug, one class, even one principle ethnicity. Making it possible to generalize from the particular turmoil of these adolescents to others in similar plights.

Quickly, thereafter, a much younger population, no higher in class but quite evident in ethnicity, seized on the inhalation of glue fumes and similar substances for the relief of their special turmoil; forcing a modification of prior hypotheses, not ethnicity, but also with regard to the range and scope of the substances chosen. One could still achieve, however, to the view that drug misuse was the predilection of a relatively small number of 'deviants' in our society without risking professional scorn, although it was becoming increasingly clear that the problem was becoming serious.

Then as everyone knows, LSD use spread among middleclass youth of the nation as fire to a field of hay. Spreading with an array of substances, marijuana, mescaline, peyote, psilocybin, and DMT, etc., across ages, classes, ethnicities, cities, and subcultures.

The situation became more and more to resemble the well stocked bar of the average American home. Such that, specific drugs for specific experiences at specific times and places became the rule rather than the exception.

The drug scene, like that of its parents, produced cannoisseurs conversant with a variety of drugs which induced desired experiences under chosen circumstances with degrees of social appropriatness shaded as finely as gradations as the Japanese bough.

The 'problem' it was agreed, had reached epidemiological proportions. It was only occasionally noticed en passant that the new drugs had been available and in use by a small number of cognoscente for 20 years (Hoffman invented acid in '46, Bucky Fully was into acid in '46 dig that!. Amazing) and that some had been in use for literally thousands of years.

WHY DO IT NOW?

The question arose— Why are so many young people now using so many drugs? Parallels drawn to the use of alcohol, sleeping pills, stimulants, tranquilizers, cigarettes, asurin, and a veritable hords of socially sanctioned analgesics were deemed nut to the point. This was said to be different. It was not difficult to assemble data from magazines and newspaper accounts supporting the view that a stratification of drug tastes is in evidence. That lower class youths preferred body drugs, heroin, morphane, (speed); upper lower youths beginning to favor speed, moth, amphetamine and other stimulants. That the initial samples of LSD users seemed to be drop-outs from a middle-class style of life. That their parents were astonished to find that they, the young, were not enjoying to the hilt, and were, in fact, specifically critical, as we've heard, of this alleged crass materialism, that is to say, its spiritual vacuum.

The out of hand rejection of affluence was especially shocking to those to whom and by whom this affluenza was newly won. It asks the nouveau bourgeois. It asks us. As some noted, this, the problem, was also internutional like the jet set chronicled in the mass media, youth in many world cities were equally conversant, though differentially supplied, with a whole panicle of drugs that so concerned their elders.

To make matters worse, it emerged that the therapy industry, to which parents had been accustomed to turn for relief of their offspring's

scientific method one had 'to abandon hypotheses that one held dear, restricted as to age drug, or locale, for now the 'problem' was manifestly societal in incidence if not yet demonstrably in origin. We set ourselves therefore, the task of examining those societal predicelies which might help us to answer the query now heard in virtually all quarters. Why indeed are so many young people using so many drugs in so many ways?

II. SOCIOGENESIS

B.F. Skinner could not have devised a more negative stimulus for young people in the East Village who regularly use psychedelic drugs than the word Bellvue (laughter). A hospital on the fringe of the community which they regard somewhat less positively as a medieval dungeon replete with chambers of torture. The establishment it is said to reprasent found itself hoist by its own petard when at its propaganda concerned an already irate citizenry that LSD turns sweet faced youngsters into psychotic monster's, dangerous criminals, irrepresible rapists, habitual thieves, etc. Since the public turned right around and demanded, for its safety, that these same either be incarcerated or therapized and preferably both.

Although the young avoided both with nimble and embarrasing alacrity, they were made aware, and made no secret among themselves, however, that living in poverty (voluntary), using drugs whose street calibrated dosages bore little, if any relationship to actual content, sometimes created psychological, sociological and madical problems which might benefit from the administrations of psychotherapists, physicians and other community organizations. If only a 'hip' variety of these could be found.

A number of helping institutions soon decided that, ideological differences notwithstanding, there were more young people with more unmet needs than history had witnessed in a long time, such that, their amelioriative intervention could no longer be deliberated

Mountains of bureaucracy shuttered and hippie projects were founded, the most farrous being Dr. Smith's clinic in Haight-Ashbury. A less famous semi-counterpart, called the Village

know how, acid is as pleasant, but powerful, toy.

CYBERNATION

The second trend: Cybernation. Contemporary society has the power to communicate vast amounts of information almost instantly, just as the first generation of mass media which is prints or film, fostered mass consumption through mass advertising at the behest of mass production. So now the second generation of media, the electronics (audio and video tape, computerized pattern recognition, etc.), have created an era of almost total communication, where nothing is foreign, nothing remote. In McLuhan's terms, the content of the electric media is the former mechanical media; just as the content of the trip is yesterday's psychology. Once a psychoanalytic foray was bedrock - now, all such forays become the ingredient of the emergent psychic forms called trips. It will be perceived that electricity is common to both the societal trends, that the Villagers put forward as explanation of the roots of psychedelia, which supports the view that if Hoffman hadn't invented acid, it would have been necessary to do so since acid renders the organism capable of enjoying the information overloads which have become characteristic of an electrified society. In the wake of such massive societal forces, it follows that new social forms must emerge to handle, as a trip handles for the individual, the information impact on social organization. Hence, the revitalization process, which McLuhan has described, is said to be the accommodation that youth culture has made to its now electric environment. The commune, be it urban or rural, which is an insignificant distinction in an era of total communication, is a natural social response to the age of electric sociogenesis, (so they say, the rap session people). The convergence then, of automation and cybernation, is offered by East Villagers as the explanation for the existance of the roots of the psychedelic drug subculture. These drugs, they say, are simply the psychochemical equivalents of the electric society in which automated energy is cybernetically processed. Just as there are said to be two fundamental societal processes at work so there are the two root of the psychedelic culture.

young people, is single handedly responsible for the birth pangs of a whole new civilization, ought not be drawn. For every sane 'head' that we have confronted, there are two lost, and two mad ones. And yet the point lies deeper. For if, as it seems, there is a new culture aborning, then for many, the birth process is extruively painful, if not injurious, but not, and I emphasize, for all.Once this is understood, one also understands why the young will gladly ignore a serious upper respiratory infection (quimai from a shared pipe, perhaps) or a piece of glass in a bured foot (gathered on a stroll together), they are left as red badges of courageous solidarity incurred in a collective struggle, in a revolution, as they say, with nothing less then the culture itself as the enemy.

III. UNDERSTANDING UNDER-STANDING MEDIA

The audience will recall that we have set ourselves the task of understanding why the psychedelic culture understands itself the way it does, and that our inquiry regards the electric metaphor, that they use, as the manifest content which requires explanation.

Lying to my discipline, stated explanations are called ideologies, themselves requiring explanation. Sociologists refer to this specialty as a 'sociology of knowledge. A field heavily indebted to giants such as Marx, Manheim, and Marcuse for their elaboration of the view that men's situations determine their thoughts far more than their thoughts determine their situations. Thus armed, we turn our attention to the societal process which has elevated the electric metaphor into the status of a believed mythology.

It was Marx correcting Hegel who first revealed what is now regarded as a commonplace, although at first it seemed esoteric and arcane. In the dialectical view, when men reflect on their situation, they diagnose the injustices of their situation and then seek to change it. They attempt to change the world as they find it, into the world so that they would like it to be, by their work. When, by their work, they do transform that situation and then again, reflect on it, they, like God and Genesis, see the world they have made is good or at least more just than it was. This

I'VE NEVER REGRETTED SAYING YES TO TIM...

...ngly replied with suspicion, distrust, and not occasionally with outright disdain by young drug users. Partly because parents assumed that drug use was ipso facto, participreumonia of emotional disorder and early because legislatures decreed that drug use was ipso facto criminal. In short, the young were told that's major norm of their subculture was either sick or wrong. Although no one could dispute their right to a subculture, of course, without disproving his right to having his own. Intellectuals murmured "double bind" and youth growled "hypocrisy."

THE PEOPLE

Into this breech, gravely rode the all starred hippies (audience) laughter) whose philosophy was abhorred by the very media which extolled and subsequently expropriated their esthetics.

Settling into Haight-Ashbury in California and the East Village in New York, the hippies pronounced, as the Scenarios Beats before them, the imminent demise of western civilization. Unlike the beats, however, the hippies set about systematically reclaiming those institutions of the straight society which they charged had brutally delivered them from the joys of their own lives.

In July of '67. Dialectics of Liberation Conference convened in London by R.D. Laing, Allen Ginsberg described the new generation, which have been variously called "hippies", "flower children", "love generation", the "now generation", and subsequently the "free men", as having a whole set of subcultural institutions of their own. The social workers... they were the Diggers, the politicians — the Provos, the police — Hell's Angels and other bikers.

Religion consisted of an amalgam of Tibetan, Egyptian, Hindu, Zen, and astrological speculation. All facing in a deliberately mystical direction.

Drugs and sexual rituals serving as sacraments. For charismatic leaders, there were Leary, Kesey, Watts, and a whole bunch of others.

Language was reinvented, as was music, philosophy, art, morality, justice, truth, and beauty, and the rest of the Greek transcendentals, each reserved a psychedelic rebirth and transfiguration.

Extensive media coverage of these events turned most Americans, whether they liked it or not, into observers of the psychedelic scene, in varying amounts and degrees of participant observation, if not wished now to observe some aspiration of

instructions which protagonists of the psychedelic experience diagnose as particularly in need of replacement.

WAR

War, it is said, is fought for the preservation of territoriality (which no longer matters in an age of planetary communication) by people who have not yet learned that all violence is self-destructive exactly to the extent to which it is efficient. Wars require the young to fight for the very values of the old which the young have rejected, are thus said to be doubly unjust in that they enroll pacifists in regression and simultaneously pit young brothers (in an emergent planetary culture) against each other. Hence as a forced choice between suicide and fratricide. Besides, they add, the trip experience is as delicate and as fragile as it is lovely, to which even subtle psychological violence is abhorrent and disgusting, not to mention physical brutality. It is said, that trips teach the futility of violence, all violence, wars included.

EDUCATION

Schools which claim to teach the heritages of their societies are rejected no less vehemently and exactly so for that claim. The young who proclaim the appropriateness of their electric sensibilities argue that a school system which attempts to force their industrial values to engage in a process of mechanical people into readiness for alienated roles in the military-industrial complex from whom the young are already in full flight. Some even argue that universities are worse than battlefields since they are the training grounds for them without acknowledging that that is their basic nature. Universities are thus said to add hypocrisy to irrelevance in the electric age.

HEADRAP

As we have heard, every culture selects from the range of human potentials and moulds the organisms that are its raw stuff, in its own image. And every culture, by its agreement that some values and behaviours are central, define other values and other behaviours as peripheral, less central, or deviant. This is no less true of the subcultural participants in the Village Project. So, that in what follows, the inference that each new culture makes of these marvelous

the psycho-social ailments of the local residents in the East Village.

Rap session participants at the Village project are uniformly agreed that "dope" which is a hip word for the whole panicle of drugs, is not causal, that it to say, it is a necessary but not a sufficient explanation of the hip style. That "getting high", "getting stoned", "tripping", be it LSD, STP, mescaline, etc. and/or any desired combination is like opening a door, to other voices in other rooms, but after you've opened the door, it is up to you to keep walking and actually do the trip, during which, if you are up to it, you will earn all manners of new, "turned on" experiences, which are very much your own solutions to your very individual plight.

AUTOMATION

Dropping out of alienated societal roles is said to be a prerequisite to genuine tripping, since the ego trips of which society is said majorly to consist, become visible as cul-de-sacs and blind alleys to which a return is unthinkable. A new freedom, the right of fantasy as self-exploration is ordinarily proclaimed prior to tripping and only subsequently reinforced by "good trips." "Bum trips" are said to be due to a fear of "letting go" or to contaminated drugs but not simply to drugs themselves.

Uptight people are to be avoided during trips since their fears and their violence are said to be as contagious as they are dangerous. It is claimed, by rap session participants that two convergent trends in society are principally responsible for the dropout phenomenon to which the social enfranchisement of tripping is secondary. These trends are: 1. Automation — the attainment of an incredibly high level of affluence and abundance in post-industrial, that is to say, computerized society, it is said, renders the work-for-a-living, or Calvinist ethos, superfluous relic of the first mechanical-industrial revolution. Since supermarkets, restaurants, and other food merchants have far more than necessary, simply asking for the remainder provides enough to live on. This makes it possible to afford the leisure time needed to engage in self-exploration, also via tripping, sexual variety, residential mobility, and etc. Parents who covertly send checks, they can now easily afford to send now that junior has left home, see not rare. In short it is said that now that automation has replaced work, play assumes its rightfully central roll and if you

leading to further work, is described as the dialectical relation between subculture (subsuperculture, if you will) and its ideological superstructure. Thus, the industrial revolution, itself a new mode of changing the world, transformed the pre-industrial Calvinist's ideology of thrift, into the post-industrial Calvinist ideology of progress.

MOBILITY AND MASS MARKET

Mobility supplanted class struggle as inevitably as the machine replaced the biceps. It remained for Marcuse to show that society's efforts to generate demands, even beyond the greasy dreams of conspicuous consumers, requires them to foster what he called surplus repression, that is to say, to get people to believe that it was more important to repress instinctual eroticism than to develop it, because it was more important to transcend, that is to say, revolutionize society. Subsequently, Marcuse revealed that post-industrial society employs its media to establish an ideology hostile to transcendental glory). Those who try that, will find their work reduced to one dimensionality through mass media mechanisms, that is to say, the artist who creates two dimensional work subjected to being mass produced and mass marketed, and thus made ordinary and routine if not longer. The care in color was reduced above, the expropriation of the psychedelic art form by the plastic advertising industry, the peak of which seems to be in Life Magazine, Look Magazine. The reference of the two Marx and Marcuse in our inquiry is the following.

FOUR TIMES IN A DECADE

Marx envisioned a process that took a hundred years to have its full impact (the industrial revolution) and within that time Marcuse saw processes taking their toll in less than a generation. The Morning Times (N.Y.) page of November 4th contains a column, in the business section, to be sure, on the third and fourth generation of computers which have all come about within a decade. Just to clarify, the first generation of computers was made of vacuum tubes, the second generation was made of transistors, the third generation was made of integrated printed circuits (printed

Continued on Page 8

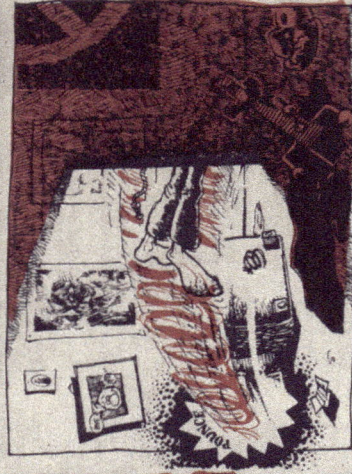

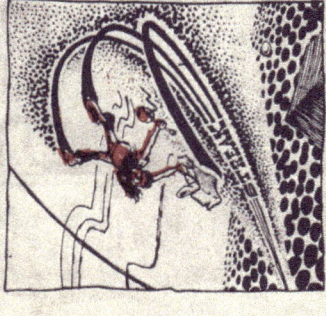

ORANGE HOUSE THAT LOOKS LIKE A PIE?
THE KING. HE DESIGNED IT HIMSELF. MUSHROOM PIE IS THE NATIONAL DISH AND PIE FIGHTING IS THE NATIONAL SPORT. HE HAS A PASSION
FOR BOTH.
WHY LOOK, IT'S PETIPOO AND A STRANGER!! WONDER IF HE'S GOT ANY NEW MUSHROOMS?
HE'S GOT A NEW STRANGER...
"...POETS HAVE ALWAYS LINGERED OVER ACCIDENTS, CHANCE OCCURRENCES, WHIMS AND HUNCHES, MOMENTS THAT APPEAR TO BREAK THE PATTERN OF EVENTS, THEIR RANDOMNESS DEPRIVES THEM OF MEANING, YET THEIR SINGULARITY FILLS THEM WITH HEIGHTENED SIGNIFICANCE AND EVEN OMINOUSNESS. ON THE OTHER HAND...
CAME IN HE GAVE ME THIS COSMIC AWARENESS AND HAIR GROWING CHECKERED JOB. WONDER WHAT'S NEW THIS TRIP?
OW!
HIYA, BOY! WHAT'S NEW? WADDYA GOT TA TELL YER OL' KING, EH? GIMME SKIN, MAN!
GOT ANY NEW MUSHROOMS?
ONLY THIS LITTLE NUMBER FROM IDLLDERDLLFRAP ON THE MORNING TOAD.
Splendid!
SINCE HE'S THE KING HE GETS TO TRY ALL THE NEW ONES FIRST. 'OL BENTBRAINS TESTED 4,462 KINDS FOR US SO FAR!
C'MON, I'LL SHOW YOU OUR MUSHROOMS.
THIS IS WHERE WE KEEP THE REAL MIND BLOWERS.
WOULD YOU CONSIDER TRYING SOME OF OUR LATEST DEVELOPMENTS?
WHAT DO THEY DO TO YA?
JUST GO AHEAD AND EAT A FEW. THEY PRODUCE MANY KINDS OF...UH.. UNUSUAL EFFECTS, AMONG OTHER THINGS.
FLASH
AWK!
HIYA KID, HIYA!
GODZILLA MUTHAFUCKERS! I MUSTA O.D.'d ON THAT SHIT!!!
WITH
WITHOUT
CONTINUED OVER...

CONTINUED FROM PAGE 125

silicone chips), and the fourth generation, which you haven't heard too much about, is Bioelectrics, living batteries. If we regard computers in general, in that decade, as the new technological means of production and information configuration, as the new ideological products of that process, we may calculate that societies now change ten times faster than their original depictions by Marx.

If we count each generation of computers separately, we confront a society which can change the structural basis of its ideology, four times within a decade. If ideologies are formed by reflection on the world we make by our labours, it follows that we are living in an era of such rapid change that those accustomed to it will regard even a five-year-old ideology as hopelessly irrelevant since it no longer describes the contemporary world. The extremity of this situation may be observed in what sociologists sometimes call the 'generation gap'. I prefer to call it intergenerational stratification (that's the academic thing again, sorry). In a society which changes so rapidly the very process of socialization in which parents attempt to acculturate their infants is doomed since the contents of that socialization will be obsolescent even before the process is over.

When the world changes four times in a decade, it had better invent a way of comprehending itself that changes as fast as experience does, and that, I argue, is exactly what psychedelics are. A psychochemical technology which no longer bothers with the simple enumeration of the content of processes but focuses the inner eye on the elements of those processes. That, I submit, is the inner meaning of the term 'tripping' which is focusing on the rates of change (as they are called) going through (changes), of a changing experience and not simply on what is changing by itself.

CONFLICTS

Bitter conflicts are thus generated between those who do not know what tripping is. Who hurl the epithet of hedonism as if that finally were that. Other epithets are employed ranging all the way from subversion to 'adduction'. Sub-cultural confrontation, no less acrimonious than race riots have not been rare, and little documentation is needed to remind us but for one rare skimmer of flower power. Relations between the police and the psychedelic community have been slightly less than cordial. The point of course is this: Tripping effects new forms of consciousness, giving rise to behaviours which until it was must regard as strange and unfamiliar; if not as weird, sick and demented. The public media reveals that this new sort of consciousness is exactly the issue. Is it sick? We are asked, as professionals? Can it possibly be healthy? The science media, plus the mass media, are uniformly in agreement, and we have heard some thing about that already — the psychedelic, after the time sense of experience.

WHO'S A-HEAD

It lies in the very nature of generalization that once it is made it clarifies the particulars it has assumed. That's the way the mind works. We are all familiar with the experience of uncertainty, when perceiving a vaguely familiar object at a great distance, as we draw nearer and nearer its outlines become sharper and we exclaim: 'ah yes! It's one of those', as we just saw in the case before us, with a slight variation. For Acid, I believe, is only the first of many engines soon to be constructed which engenders the ability to generalize and classify, not objects, but times, thus the ability to dwell on instants of change brings with it the ability to more exhaustively dwell (an argument leads, Just as the automated, or second industrial revolution, generalized the first, by dealing with the information ex-

ponents of energy processing rather than simply with the energy constellations called 'objects' one at a time so the psychedelic, or the second, chemical revolution, generalized the first, which was the anesthetic one, by dealing with the temporal exponents of getting high rather than simply with getting stoned or drunk time after time after time after time. That is why, the process of generalization which we see poor mortals attribute to the power of our intelligence is a far more naturalistic process than we care to see. Generalization, it begins to emerge, is the natural process whereby instances transcend their classes of events just as galaxies generate stars which expand the limits of the galaxies, as men make worlds which outmould their world views, so now we are witnessing, in my view, one of the most far reaching revolutions ever to come from human effort. That is to say, we are beginning to pass beyond the era of human history, which, impelled by a scarcity of objects clung to the dream that would set us free. Now that the young can directly experience a world in which cybernetic automation makes scarcity an obsolete concept in some societies, they begin to inhabit another whole realm, the dimension of time, which Einstein brought to earth after his 'trip'. If we seem wholly (here's the cop-out, if we seem wholly supportive of the values of the young psychedelicist, let us not be misunderstood. Our task is to analyze the sociological currents on which psychedelia floats and not to examine in detail the pathologies of its encumbrants. It is one thing to focus on the plights of others who are so driven. Entirely another matter is the question of action. What shall we do to trust others damaged by the misuse of psychedelics is another cos. There are tasks for another writing.

THE CHEMICAL REVOLUTION

Just as computers can process billions of bits of information per second, so, when 'high', can one seem to experience hours and even years in a few minutes. That is the meaning of the word 'high'. Which describes in special terms an experience in which one seems to be able to scan vast horizons from above, encompass as astounding bits of experience just mile at a glance. But do not be misled by the psychedelic metaphor, nor by the electronic one. For more important property of the psyched in the phenomenon experienced in the trip, is the following: When one expand time, you find yourself the ability to punctuate non attention to punctuate, which is simply conjecture, which is hurried and marked, would have sped by too rapidly for you to feel, fully. That accounts for the observation frequently made, how do you 'know who's a 'head', give him something that he's never seen before — to play with it, see, while somebody who doesn't know what it 'isn't, be bothered, I'm in a hurry. This property of the psychedelic experience also helps us to account for the alleged aphrodisiacal properties of LSD and related substances, since when it is not hurried, when one can give one's full emotional appreciation, or any enjoyment for that matter, is materially enhanced. I have alluded to but two of the time changing properties of the trip. The ability to appreciate changes in rates of change and the ability to dwell on an instant. If they seem contradictory, is meant. If they seem contradictory, perhaps a bit of clarification is in order for we have not yet touched bottom.

CONCLUSION

In conclusion, I hold, then, the view that our culture has so accelerated the pace of societal change that the simple serial encountering of one experience after another, in less time than you have to experience it, has become obsolete, for its young who dwell exponentially, who will only change ab-orism, that is to say, generalize, on what we elders only strange ab-iom, that is to say, arithmetically. They are not only as comfortable in the realm of time as we are in the realm of space, but they have a sense of adventure and discovery about time, which many of us have about space. We build rockets to take us to the stars and planets to me, we are building a culture which will take them into temporal regions of mind which, with stately, special morals, we will fail to comprehend, in my view, this adventure, and its corollary misadventure is absolutely central to what we are about as a species. (A human task, a task for history). The young seek nothing less than the next step in the evolution of human consciousness. The maintenance of special interest, the one-dimensional consciousness, it is clear that this is no small undertaking. That the risks are terrible, that the likelihood of tragic mistakes is high, that there will be fatalities, that the number of casualties will be large, I fervently wish that they were unnecessary, and I am my work to prevent, as many of these as possible, and to assist in the healing of those whom we fail to prevent from injury, for it is true that most of those embarked on this adventure are as blind to its dangers as they are unaware of them and so they are often foolish, and often injured and yet there are some who know, who accept the deeper challenge to carry history forward. These will be found on close examination, to have removed some of the outmoded ideological baggage that we force them to carry, to be engaged in founding a new form of temporal consciousness which I call 'Groovin' on Time.'

CONTINUED FROM PAGE 85

Sincerely yours Greg Cox

NOT SO INSTANT KARMA...

Greg Cox left his home in Tasmania several months ago with no particular intention in mind. On Australia's north-west coast he worked on a bauxite development project and was later given a job as a clerk. He made friends with a black man and was amazed to find him the "same as me". Drifting north to Indonesia he began keeping a diary, started smoking a little dope. In Singapore he had a revelation. While eating in a restaurant, he dropped on the table a spoonful of rice. After hurriedly covering it up with his hand, he realised that it made not the smallest difference whether he covered it up or not. The rice was there! "My mind was blown. One thing led to another—he became convinced that he and John Lennon were twin parts of the same being and they had only to meet for cosmic forces to be released. These forces would instantaneously create peace throughout the world. Certain that there was no difference between really wanting something to happen' and the actual happening, he came to London to meet John Lennon. At the Apple offices he received his first set-back. Unable to see Lennon he staged a sit-in and was eventually removed by a policeman who 'told him to write a letter instead. He rang John Lennon's secretary from a call box, pretending to be Horace Saltzburg, a rich American with 4 million dollars to give away, all to Apple. I was told to put it in writing. He did, but confessed in the letter his true identity and purpose.

"John Lennon knows, and I know that the only choice is permanent peace or total destruction. John is doing all he can make other people see this, but he doesn't really believe that what he is doing is possible. I can give him the answer, and the answer is 'faith.'" Since his ejection from Apple, Greg has wandered all over London, following signposts, obeying road directions—if they read "No right turn" for example, he continues straight ahead. Coming to the intersection where New Bond Street becomes Old, he became certain that this was where he would run into Lennon—instead, he found an open manhole cover. Inside he noticed a large black box. He tried unsuccessfully to

draw the attention of passers by to the fact that the box was far too large to have passed through the manhole. He ran and got an idling policeman, who agreed with him and said, "Yes, much too large" and walked away. Finally a young couple paid attention to him. The girl replaced the manhole cover and said, "There, the box has gone", and they took him to lunch.

In the YMCA he left the key on the outside of his door so that John Lennon could enter if he wished. In the morning the key was gone and in the evening, he was informed that more money was required before he could return to his room. "I wandered about the building looking for my room and my key. I was sure John Lennon had it because I had left it for him. I smashed a window and found an emergency exit sign, but they got my suitcase and told me to get out. I went to the police station and told them I had lost a room. I told the man on duty about Bond Street too, and he was very helpful and directed me to the Salvation Army. They had no room there, but I took my suitcase and gave me a ticket for a bus to a Ministry of Welfare place where I could stay for nothing. It was full of funny old people who were all guilty about having no work. I told them they did not have to work', and the Welfare Officer told me to go. All I said to him was "tremendous". I returned to the Salvation Army and asked for my suitcase, but they would not give it to me. I told them I had to have the case because it had pills in it which I had to take or I would die. Four hours later they gave me the address of a mental hospital where the guy who had taken my suitcase was staying. I went to a police station and reported my case stolen. The police came to the Salvation Army and it was found in a back room with everything in it except a pair of white trousers and my camera. The police said I had got the suitcase back and as far as they were concerned that was the end of the matter. One day I will have to go out to that mental hospital to see that guy".

He went to the offices of the Guardian in Fleet Street and offered to write an editorial for the paper, based upon his quest. He was told to go away and write it, but he stayed

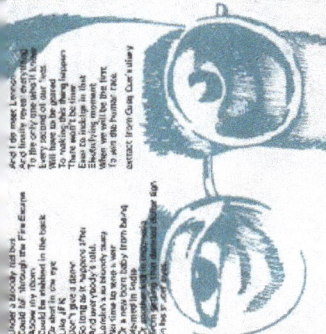

insisting that what he had to say could be said in one word. For example, to the question, answered at some length in a recent Guardian, "What gain does China get out of arresting innocent British subjects?" Greg wrote down a single word, NOTHING, and informed the editor that the answers to all problems were as blatantly obvious as that. "He was stunned, and asked me to leave. I never felt happier".

Greg is very young, slim and straight looking. One of his first actions on arriving in London was to have a haircut. He requested a barber to give him "his very best haircut" and emerged half an hour later totally shorn, with the trimmest short back and sides seen in England for many a year. His next visit was to a mens wear store. "I have £30. Fit me out with the best clothes you have." He emerged half an hour later in a yachting jacket, a pair of pleated pants and sensible shoes, having been assured that not only was he wearing "the best" but that the shop was in fact the best shop in London. Upon reflection, he didn't like the clothes at all, and soon discarded them for something still formal, but bought at Take Six in the Kings Road.

At the moment, he is close to despair. He considers standing all day outside Apple so that he can just catch John Lennon's eye. He knows that is all that is necessary for Lennon to instantly recognise him. "Lennon is not eccentric. He is centric, that is, closer to me and to the truth than anybody else." Greg wonders whether it is worthwhile travelling to Tittenhurst Park to see Lennon in his rural glory. He has very little money left, but refuses to return home until his mission is fulfilled. Greg insists that he is a happy man. London has not disillusioned him, everything to him is still "tremendous". Satori in Singapore taught him one thing—from complete honesty to oneself, everything else follows. Belief in oneself and faith in others can move more than mountains—it can bring about world peace, if that's what's wanted. It can even bring about a meeting with John Lennon.

Jim Anderson

9

AS OUR STORY OPENS

FLASH

ZABRISKIE
PETIT-
POINT

Fred Gardner re-wrote parts of Antonioni's new film, Zabriskie Point. This interview was done for Liberation News Service by Larry Bensky, one of whose swan songs for the straight media was a New York Times article on the making of Zabriskie Point.

LNS: A while ago you wouldn't talk about Zabriskie Point.

FG: Sometimes I think that people who worked on movies .... or plays or novels or songs ... shouldn't talk about what was intended. But if there are false claims being made, such as MGM's claim that this is a film about the movement, you've got to counter them. How can people judge Antonioni's success if they're given a false idea of his aims? Hollywood programs people to react in set ways; not just

Sam Shepherd wrote the scenario, which was excellent. Mark and Daria had been cast and an MGM secretary re-typed the script, substituting 'Mark' and 'Daria' for 'boy' and 'girl'. All this was done before August, '68.

I started work right after Chicago. At that point Antonioni described the

So the country is full of kids who radiate a vague alienation, who dress the way campus radicals dressed a few years ago - - boots, fatigue jackets, long hair - - who know that the straight life is a dead end, but who aren't political.

LNS: Nor was Daria hip, except in that superficial way of walking

LNS: When the political meeting scene was being shot, in Berkeley a lot of people sensed Mark's hostility and felt angry at him in return. Kathleen Cleaver put him down.

FG: That scene shed a lot of light on Antonioni's technique. According to the script, Mark was a confused college student who went to this meeting chaired by Kathleen. He was to have followed the conversation closely and then, finally, to have left because he couldn't relate to ideological talk. But when Antonioni saw the rushes after the first days shooting, Mark's face reflected nothing but hatred and contempt; not one iota of interest, let alone sympathy. So he decided to let Mark leave in exactly the spirit that the real Mark wanted to leave. And instead of following him out the

LNS: What about the hero in Zabriskie Point?

FG: He sure isn't.

LNS: But it didn't start out that way, did it? A year ago Antonioni told a reporter, 'The movement is what interests me most in America; it's the most important, the most alive and vital thing happening here today.'

FG: He also said in that interview, 'Zabriskie Point is not about the movement.' And it isn't. In fact it's about a kid who can't stand the movement.

LNS: That's the real-life Mark Frechette (who plays the male lead). When I met him he seemed more interested in Michelangelo's astrological charts than in his instructions. But weren't you hired to write a movement background for him?

FG: Well, Mark was hired to play Mark, and that's what he did. The way things worked out, I wrote some lines to emphasize that he wasn't of the movement, that he was a loner, that he had no politics, really... Antonioni had written the story with Clare Peploe and Tonino Guerra around a real anecdote about a kid who stole a private plane. Then

lude to be timely -- that was my job -- and the film to be timeless. At one point we considered a reference to Nixon's daughter and he smiled and said, 'But Nixon won't be around very long, will he?'

LNS: So there were four writers on the film, plus Antonioni....

FG: Plus Sally Kempton wrote a few lines. Plus a real estate man. And of course Mark and Daria had leeway to improvise and a de facto veto right over lines they didn't want to say.

LNS: Why? Does Antonioni always give actors that leeway?

FG: I don't know. It's an old problem: a tight script eliminates spontaneity.

LNS: On the other hand, improvisation undermines the plot....

FG: Yup.

LNS: ...and make casting terribly important.

FG: Yes, it does. In this case the executive producer and an assistant went east to look for a male lead. I don't know if that was for publicity purposes or not. Anyway, they found Mark Frechette in Boston and sent back a screen test and Antonioni found all the qualities he was looking for: impulsive, tough, photogenic...

LNS: Everything except a movement background.

FG: Somebody gave him a Res istance button to wear when he got to LA. And of course Mark had exactly the right manner for the part. The problem is we've won this big cultural victory that implies no corresponding political victory at all.

on the street.... Didn't that become apparent after a while?

FG: Yes. And when it did, Antonioni did a very impressive thing. He let the movie be about Mark and Daria, even though they weren't the kids he had bargained for. It was as if he said, Well I hoped these young Americans were going to be radical and serious and articulate and warm; but now that they turn out to be apolitical and self centred, I might as well go ahead and show them as such.

Maybe there's a parable in that.

visit to tell us that Mark was not a member of the group, that he had come to the meeting on someone's casual invitation, that he's a loner. Then Frank Bardacke and Landon Williams put in that you can't be a radical if you can't work with other people.

LNS: How about Kathleen's lines. Were they scripted?

FG: No. There had been lines for her and everyone else. The first two or three times he shot the scene according to the script. Then he said, 'Now you've got the situation. Run this meeting in your own terms.' Maybe two or three lines survived.

LNS: Is it better than the original version?

FG: That's not for me to say. It's certainly more spontaneous. Yes, I think it's better.

LNS: How do you feel now about having taken the job? There were a lot of people who thought you shouldn't have.

FG: Yes, some people thought that. But not everyone said it, and not everyone had cogent reasons. Norman Fruchter (of Newsreel) did. But by the time we talked I had more or less done the work and was feeling defensive.... One of the things people said was that you couldn't expect to sneak a good message across in a Hollywood film. I never expected to or tried to. What I wanted was the bread and the experience of watching Antonioni work. The bread was put to good use, as you know. And it was an enormous privilege to look at America -- hell, to look at a room or a face -- through Antonioni's eye. It really is the eye of a master. I think the film catches some of this country's excrescences as well as some of the beauty.

11

14 ways of looking at Charles Manson...

Liberation News Service

I. Un-uptight straight Los Angeles is freaking out over the idea of Charlie Manson. All those people who freak in straight America fear and love their fantasies, fear the kill inside every terrible murder. Some say the people that when the mind can not up up to and besides St. Manson is a revolutionary of folk hero...

II. The hip feelings are intensified as the media and the straight press get together to project the full image of Manson – disgusting, Demonic, evil incarnate.

III. Weathermen made it official. They made a new revolutionary hero, "Mansonpower." The Year of the Fork" (in reference to a report that a fork was found in one victim's stomach). The police reported that Manson ordered his victims killed 'to punish them for their affluent life style'. So Weatherman concludes that Manson, having offed some rich, honky pigs", was an appropriate hero for revolutionaries.

DISGUSTING

IV. Even the political angle was not new. It was merely a revised statement of an old idea: whatever is disgusting and revolting to the average man in the decaying American society, whatever is evil in the eyes of Richard Nixon and Pat Nixon, that's what we dig, that's what we are.

Rape? Heroin addiction? The basic impulse is healthy – we are breaking out of the moulds built by plastic America. But the point is to help others gain similar freedom, fight for freedom, not to project ourselves as a warrior gang of free people.

V. An old idea again for our movement. I, the New York Times report that Charlie, the straight Nixon America, and Bernardine Dohrn are telling us that The Creator, the Weatherman's make of man who believes in the hardest work in the Third Saxon Revolution, look at man, at Charlie, each other, at stick, the cops, and those wishy-up by the people, by the Los Angeles insurrectionary, revolutionary.

VI. A question: do the Weathermen, the Crazies, the uglies: What if Manson is innocent? Why such faith in the pigs and the pig press to believe it all, to start a myth? More important, why so willing to adopt as your hero this creature defined not by your movement, or any people's movement but by the cops, by the Los Angeles sensationalist journalists?

SCORECARD

VII. A factual interlude: Members of the Manson commune are charged with three sets of murders:
a) Five people at Sharon Tate's house, Aug. 9.
b) Gary Hinman in Topanga Canyon, July.
c) Grocery executive Leo La Bianca and his wife, Rosemary, Aug. 10.

Susan Atkins, one of the four who allegedly participated in the Tate murders, has provided the only detailed account of what happened. The interview was conducted under highly suspicious circumstances, with the collaboration of defense counsel and an assistant district attorney.

One motive for the interview: money. Susan and her lawyer got lots of it –

also have been trying to save her life, by claiming that, under Manson's 'hypnotic' control, she was a pitiful automaton. Susan had a peculiar way of it in the interview:

VIII. But there's the truth to the whole thing. Who really are people 'we' and 'they'? The arguments some of the women... some of the way of seeing as overseeing them and their machinations tain in of Gray, hypnotic power over a harvest of...

SUPERCOCK

['Manson developed a prodigious reputation as a lover. The women around the place were always his property' Paul Watkins, a former member of the commune, told the press. 'You were always welcome to have the woman if I could handle it, and the 'local Bitch', Squeaky and the former welfare 'Squeak', you became his property too.']

Then there is the grotesque racism of writing 'pig' in the victim' blood in order, according to Susan Atkins, to throw suspicion on black people. After the La Bianca murders, she explains, they left one of the victims' wallets in the women's restroom of a gas station, 'hoping that a black woman would find it and pick it up and use the credit cards, which would direct the police back to black people.'

Consider also the victim of this violence. The five people who died in Sharon Tate's home died not because their deaths served some revolutionary purpose, but because they were living in the house that once belonged to someone who, according to Susan Atkins, had given Charlie his word on a few things (according, contract) and

DILLINGER

X. From a friend in California: Making a hero or martyr out of some people who kill... or... or out or so kill... compare with John Dillinger, Bonnie & Clyde. A straight man's 'call to violence,' but is it more a celebration of death, of something suicidal, rather than for...

XI. On one level, of course, we should see Manson and all people defined by this society as 'criminals', as a brother. Whatever crimes he may have committed, we should recognize that people are driven to commit crimes in this society because of need or greed, frustration or competition – the inequities and fucked-up values of capitalism. The pigs in this sense always cooperate with the media to fuck Manson over.

While the authorities usually gleefully apply their shears to long-hairs, Manson remains with his shoulder-length locks. Instead of giving him prison garb, the cops let Manson wear his own bell bottoms and fringed leather shirt.

The pigs present him to the press for photographs surprisingly often. Thus, the police and the media team up to present straight America with their image of a 'typical hippie', fantastic sex life, heavily involved with drugs, a depraved killer underneath.

BLUECOLLAR

XII. Some people in the hip community – and even more so, some liberal writers in the straight press – have attempted to distinguish Manson from the typical hippie.

any crime. He is the typical middle-class cop-out hippie. This is a society of a revolution to be eternally dominated by. ...of his working class past, made into a them, but he... gun, fucked up appears to feel the revolutionary better than fuck up, hippie from poor anyone.

XIII. Che, Huey, Ho, Mao – they've all talked about the fact that you don't do revolutionary violence because you dig it, you don't do it to build your own ego-trip. Being violent alone, being anti-social alone, doesn't make you a revolutionary. Revolutionaries serve the people; sometimes this means killing the hated enemies of the people. They are trying to build a new world while bringing down the old. Revolutionary violence comes from the needs of the people for a better life, against those forces that oppress them – because those forces won't give up without a fight.

FUCKED UP

XIV. So Manson is no revolutionary: he's just fucked up. Let's face it – some people get into the hip scene, the commune scene, because they're fucked up. Not every long-hair is a brother, lost of assistant district attorneys smoke pot.

Most important, young women with teased hair and make-up, guys with duck-tails and crew cuts who work at shitty jobs are our brothers and sisters.

And when we get together, it won't be because we think sticking forks in people's stomachs is groovy, but because we feel a common need for a common goal – to fight to bring an old world and build a new

Getting in to see Charles Manson is a little less difficult than getting in to see the Pope but not much.

I was put through a cautionary instruction. I was not to touch him, shake hands or give him anything to look at without first showing it to the deputy. They told me that although attorney's could usually give prisoners up to one dollar for cigarette money, no such was to be given to Manson.

After these preliminaries, I was led into the attorney-interview room where I saw for the first time a rather slight man with shoulder length hair standing against the back wall. After all of the newspaper photographs I have seen of a glowering, wild-eyed scowler, I didn't even recognize this man at first. The eyes, then and throughout the interview, had a gentle look, even when he became quite emphatic as he did later on. His facial expressions varied from a kind of set attitude of resigned endurance to a very pleasant and gentle smile. I keep coming back to that word 'gentle' because it is the major impression the man left on me.

Manson smiled his rather wry smile and began to talk.

'I want to retain my own voice. That is why I am defending myself. The stories that have been appearing in the newspaper are a lot of bunk. They keep quoting me as saying things I never said at all.'

I observed that for a person without legal training to defend himself was rather like getting into the ring with Joe Louis. 'Worse,' Manson replied and started to tell me why he doesn't trust lawyers. 'You wouldn't believe the things that go down behind this case,' Manson said. 'The first lawyer who came in here offered me $130,000.00 to write my 'story'. We talked a little and he went away and wrote a story where he put all kinds of words in my mouth I never said.'

'What about the music?' I asked him. 'Isn't there money coming out of that? I thought there was some kind of Sammy Glick character putting out an album.'

'Let me tell you about the music.' Manson suddenly seemed to grow more intense. 'The people involved with the music are all trying to keep it from coming out. They are afraid of it, because it tells the truth.'

Manson smiled that wry smile at me again and said, 'The attorneys too. Most of the attorneys just want the publicity of the trial. They don't care about the man at all. If there was some kind of writ that could get me out of here tomorrow, they wouldn't bring it, because they all want to go through this whole trial and wring every last drop of publicity out of the whole thing.'

Then we talked for a while about the advisability of my quoting him directly about the case and the danger that through my paraphrasing and the District Attorney's malice his words might get twisted out of context and so misinterpreted, be used against him.

Because of that problem I have omitted details that I believe might relate to his defense.

Ever since a week after the Tate murders they have been desperately looking for someone to pin it on. Two hundred deputies and three helicopters descended on the ranch where we were staying in Malibu and arrested us. Two uniformed deputy sheriffs, one six-three and the other about six-six, worked me over. One kneed me in the chest breaking three ribs. If they would let an independent civilian doctor look at me they could tell by the condition of my ribs that is true. They kept me three days and released me. They rearrested me again the next day and again released me after three days. That time I decided to go to the mountains and get away from the harassment.'

(At this point it is interesting to remember that former Deputy Sheriff Preston Gilroy was hounded off the Sheriff's Department because of his refusal to keep silent about the events of that raid on the Manson family at Malibu by deputies from that substation. Gilroy worked at Malibu just before his termination.)

'I decided to go to the mountains to talk to God, to spoke are for nineteen hundred years of this mess. That's where they got me and brought me here.

'You want to know about my philosophy? You want to know where my philosophy comes from - I'll tell you. I'm not from your society. I have spent most of my life in a world of bars and solitary confinement.

My philosophy comes from underneath the boots and sticks and clubs they beat people with who come from the wrong side of the tracks. People like me are society's scapegoats. They keep getting away with it because no one will say anything.

'I have been in jail twenty two years,' Manson continued. 'My body has been locked up but my mind is free. When I get outside on the street, I see all kinds of people whose bodies are free, but their minds are all locked up!'

During this speech, Manson seemed to grow more intense again, and I could see how an unfriendly cameraman could catch him at an angle where his features might have that wild cast they get in the newspaper photos. Face to face, however, they never lost the almost pleading look of someone straining to be understood, to communicate the feelings inside of him.

About then we were interrupted by the sheriff's deputy, who wanted more information about my background. I felt like telling him to get it out of the LAPD's political dossier but didn't. I must have answered him a little testily because Manson said 'I don't hate them. I really don't. I pity them. I really don't hate anybody.'

I drove home thinking about two things.

First, I thought about what a mockery the so-called 'presumption of innocence' really is. Here is a man on trial for his life, and they are holding him with without bail and making all kinds of rules and restrictions that interfere with his access to people and materials that could possibly help in this defense.

No court this yet found this man guilty of the crime with which he is charged, so the only constitutionally permissible reason for keeping him in jail at this time at all is to insure his presence at trial. Thus bail is not too unreasonably denied on the theory that, guilty or innocent, a man facing so drastic a penalty might run away.

But by what right do they do more than merely keep him available for trial? By what twisted conception of justice do they arrogate to themselves the right to place restrictions on the number and kind of visitors he can see or the number of telephone calls he can make or whether he can receive a lawbook to help the preparation of his defense?

Secondly, I mused over the unfairness of the court system that makes a man choose between either representing himself entirely alone, pitting his inexperience against trained trial lawyers from the District Attorney's office, or placing himself entirely in the hands of an attorney, a man whom he does not and cannot entirely know, and thereafter remain silent, deprived of the right to speak or act on his own behalf and forced to allow his life to hang entirely on the thread of another man's skill and good faith.

These are only a few of the problems raised by the Charles Manson case. When we were talking about the difficulties of a utopia persona defense, Manson finally observed, 'You know they can't do anything to me.'

'They can kill you, that's what they are trying to do.'

'They can't kill me,' he replied. 'They can destroy my body, but they can't kill me.'

'What can you say to a man who believes in God?'

STEVE MORRIS

DOPE HOPE

The Wootton Report on LSD and Amphetamine

The Second Wootton Report comes down strongly on both acid and speed, and its recommendations have led to the increased penalties proposed in the Misuse of Drugs Bill. The Report has already persuaded that for the amount seeking press e.g. The Times with statements such as that. "During the first few hours after taking the drug there may be violent behaviour, a panic sticken or paranoid patient may attack others or others because they have apparently developed a feeling of self hatred or a feeling of superior power and invulnerability.

On technical issues the Report is much better. In particular, it is stressed that sensational accounts on LSD have not been substantiated and that evidence tending to refuse these accounts has been ignored by the mass media. The Report suggests that whilst LSD has not been proven to be an effective agent in psychiatry, there is no reason to prevent its use in therapy and research as is withheld the supply of LSD from any doctor who can establish a claim to its legitimate use. The Report does not make specific recommendations for penalties, but suggests that "the grave risks attach...

Or the end of Servile Penitude, a reply to the Slag Heap Erupts and particularly Germaine (Cunt Power) Greer.

A long time ago, in the years BL (Before Liberation), lived a girl-child called Wendy. She was born to a man and a woman, her parents, and they lived in a big box and were called a working-class family unit. Dad was a dustman and Mum was a part-time char. When she came home from charring for other people for money, she did her house-work for no money.

There are 8 million 'women workers' in this country. Paid? Don't the millions of housewives 'work'? An American survey recently estimated that housewives worked an average of 99.6 hours per week.

In the evening Mum read Woman and Woman's Own, all about hard-working Mums who made cakes and curtains and looked immaculate over a hot stove. Wendy wore pretty pink clothes and was screamed at if she came home from school dirty. She also read Woman and Woman's Own, all about secretaries who married their bosses and all about how to please your man, to get your man, to please your man and look immaculate over a hot man.

32 million pounds is spent annually by women on cosmetics and hairdressing. The four main weekly womens magazines have a circulation of over 8 million.

Mum embroidered on Wendy's pillow: 'Masturbation makes you blind', so Wendy sublimated by studying and won a scholarship to a posh girls' public school. Here she learned flower arrangement and read in Vogue about Bobo and Fifi on the Riviera, having champagne and caviare, and looking immaculate over a hot servant. Wendy reckoned immaculacy took 25.3 hours per day. Virginity was a drag. When she finally got rid of it she found there was no difference between the budding Fauntleroys and the council estate lads. When she said No they called her a prude and when she said Yes they called her a slut. All her smarty friends wanted to marry E-type boys and lie under the hairdresser all day and all her council mates were married and looking middle-aged in the effort to shine their floors, children and faces to look like the tele ads. Then Wendy went to University and tried for a First in Social Literology. In the University papers she read about how to chat up the intellectual boys, look immaculate over a hot thesis and cut the cackle in bed.

In universities the ratio of girls to boys is 1 to 4. Only 10% of medical school places are occupied by women. Far fewer girls than boys take GCE in Maths Physics and Chemistry. After school three times as many boys as girls are allowed off on day-release courses. Inadequate nursery school facilities and the lack of play centres during school holidays curtail women's ability to work, and consequently affect the number of women trained in most fields — exept those professions which are low-paid because they employ more women than men: social work, nursing, secretarial work.

When our Wendy got pregnant by mistake her boyfriend went right off her. So did her doctor. She couldn't tell Mum and Dad for fear of the neighbourhood, so she asked a trendy friendy who led her up a back street. There can be no tale more piercing than a knitting needle and Wendy returned after a mercifully quick peep round death's door.

Contraception is considered a social rather than a medical matter and is thus not available under the National Health, except under 'exceptional' circumstances. Abortion is in theory legally available, but there are not enough clinics and everyone needs the consent of a doctor, a consultant gynaecologist and often a psychiatrist. Women are automatically 'offered' the free give-away of a hysterectomy while they're at it. St John Stevas, defender of the faith, is trying to make it impossible to get an abortion without the consent of TWO consultant gynaecologists. There are only about 500 of these in the country. Parliament has 603 male and 27 female MP's, who is voting on laws which affect a woman's rights over her own body? More women would become MP's if they did not have to sacrifice their children and lives as individuals to do so.

Wendy graduated neatly and came to the metropolis. Clutching a degree proudly in her hand didn't stop employers mentally stripping her and then refusing to employ her because all women leave to have babies. Wendy decided that the system was for shit and became a revolutionary groupie. She ran around with all the initials under the sun: IS, SLL, IMG, CP, XYZ and got so hooked on the holy grail of revolution that she had a baby. But in between feeding the baby she was still typing revolutionary slogans and cooking guerilla stew while the guys discussed strategy. When she tried to campaign for more nursery schools in the area the revolutionaries threw her out for being reformist.

Mothers, au pairs or nannies look after babies. Nursery schools are run by women. Three-quarters of primary school teachers are women. There are still a large number of single sex schools. Should children be prepared for adult life in a mixed society, exclusively by women?

Wendy went underground next, but she didn't get much further there, because many of the beautiful people were still hung up on their semi-detached backgrounds and subscribed to the schizoia of girls you fuck you don't talk to and vice versa.

moon.

There are 1½ times as many women as men in mental homes. Unmarried mothers are refused Social Security if they are known to have a relationship with a man. April Ashley was told by a male judge that although she felt like a woman and behaved in all ways like a woman, she was technically a man because she wasn't equipped with the holy ovaries.

Wendy finally flipped. She woke up one morning believing she was a chameleon, a woman chameleon, her identity existing totally in the eye of the beholder. Life for a woman was a series of rapid colour changes in order to fit in with other people's conception of her role. The abolition of capitalism seemed no guarantee that woman would be seen as a human being, only theoretically different from man in that she produced the child for which they were both responsible. Wendy couldn't make the individual liberation scene, so she went to

Ruskin College Oxford, to the Women's Weekend Feb 28—March 1, 1970, where there were 559 other women sick of being chameleons doing the dance of the ovaries. The conference was a vital and energetic start, a Movement towards the Liberation of women and finally the liberation of the whole of society from the roles and strictures which bind it. If militancy is a determination to act out convictions then the conference was full of militant women prepared to act on their lives and society where existing political and social organisations had failed.

Where was Germaine?

There were some twenty groups represented, and a large number of individuals, of different backgrounds, ranging from groups of working-class women who had first gossiped about babies and then went to other issues, through women from Trades Unions to women's groups from existing left-wing parties. Papers and discussions questioned the inevitability of the mother-child bond, the structure of the family, women in industry, and the implications of the recent Bill passed for equal pay by 1975, women's contribution to the economy and political movements in the 19th century, with a continuous emphasis on the value of the individual experience, on women breaking their silence to discuss their common problems and consider action. There was consequently little agreement with the Socialist women who slung round all the usual diversionary jargon about the women question being only another aspect of the class question. This doesn't lead to any new political theory which must grow out of experience and experiment, as well as existing theories. Thus all methods are valid which will make women aware that they can have the choice, and have the right to the choice of how they live, of what they do with their bodies and minds; the National Joint Action Committee for the Campaign for Women's Equal Rights is self-evident in its demands Socialist Women organises itself around issues of equal pay and industrial strike action, the Birmingham Claimants Union, originally for women on social security, aims for fuller control over the Welfare system, the Gingerbread group — women bringing up children single-handed — was formed to discuss common problems and act as a group. The Women's Liberation Workshop in London is growing very fast, not because they are middle-classes preaching Liberation to the working masses (why belong to a movement for Liberation if you're already liberated?) but because they aim, through discussion and action to be able to redefine their own identity. No theory can evolve without some measure of spiritual liberation of its creators. To be able to ask questions, to prod at the status quo,

is to begin to find the answers. Workshops on history, the family, sexuality, communes and Marxism, were set up at the conference. Each woman is involved the whole time in questioning herself, her context, her relationships with men and women, her sexuality. Learning about herself, about other women, about the experience of women.

A note finally, about the 'common assumptions', the 'social myths' about women as reflected in the language. Women are 'assumed' to be hysterical. Hysteria is anti-social, it is chaos taking over from order. The word 'hysteria' comes from the Greek meaning 'womb'. Why should having a womb make a woman anti-social? Judging from the existing structure of the nuclear family, that is exactly what she is economically and emotionally. The word 'history', phonetically splittable into 'his story', comes from the Greek meaning 'wise man'. Biologists speak unthinkingly of mother and daughter cells; why not parent and child cells? It takes two to make a child. Newspapers are always pointing out the oddities of women's participation, even in death: 'Seven died in the crash', three of them women.'

The Movement, as I see it, doesn't seek the replacement of penis-power by Cunt-power, or any generalised power. It seeks in its initial stages the involvement of all women, cutting across the class structure. When this happens maybe we can get somewhere, and have a constructive revolution, not one which needs Press censorship or Red Guards to keep dogma in its kennel. Even the defensive hostility which the Movement provokes is an index of its centrality and vitality. It is happening.

There is to be another conference in six months. Will Germaine come? Wendy will be there.

Michelene.

Rolling Stone's recent full page advertisement in The Times comparing their own characteristically thorough coverage of the Chicago Conspiracy trial with Fleet Street's patchy summaries, sent a shudder of envy through this office. On several occasions The Times has refused to accept small advertisements from OZ. In each case the decision was reached after they had requested sample copies. Two months ago we booked modest space in The Guardian. 'The magazine that nobody dares to print — will you?' ran the headline, followed by studiously uncontroversial copy inviting printers to submit quotations. They even got as far as sending back proofs. One day before publication The Guardian's advertising manager intervened and forced cancellation of the advertisment. The reason for the rejection was apparently connected with 'responsibility towards our readers'. Rolling Stone's success perhaps demonstrates that the bigger the advertisement, the smaller the 'responsibility'. Stop Press: we have just been informed that both the Guardian and the Observer have contacted Rolling Stone begging to be honoured with their next advertisement.

OZ is proud to announce that it is still not available for sale through W. H. Smith & Sons.

The next OZ will be produced by a selection of under eighteens who answered our general invitation. Any teenybopper readers who missed the historic meeting and would like to help create OZ please telephone our office. The shared ambition of those schoolboys who turned up was to 'clean up OZ', with the exception of one 12 year old who planned to include 'more gay news'.

If, like Bob and Bing, you're Moroccan bound, write to Head News, 10 Rue Abdellah Ben Yessin, Essaouira, Morocco, for travel tips, accomodation advice and cookie prices. If you have something to say to English speaking heads, you can advertise for 8s. per single col inch or 5d a word.

Way back in Sydney in 1963 when OZ had been turned down by every available printer, we visited — almost as a joke — the proprietor of The Anglican newspaper. This was Francis James, who, to our astonishment, readily accepted the job. Francis never expressed regret at this decision even though this highly active churchman landed in the dock with the rest of us for 'publishing an obscene magazine'. Extremely unpopular in local establishment circles for his irreverence towards Church and Government, Francis was recently in London and while returning home via Hong Kong disappeared. 'Lost somewhere in China' according to a Times dispatch. Because of the Australian Government's extraordinary sensitivity to criticism, especially from nationals abroad, we don't imagine any serious effort is being made to trace this unique, cynical, compassionate, real life

20

Christian. This paragraph is by way of recording our appreciation of Francis James, an all to rare Australian, and a plea to any of our Chinese readers who should meet him, to return him safely home.

Another Australian whom the Government would not be sorry to see disappear in China is Wilfred Burchett, veteran journalist and author, who has for years had his passport summarily with-held because of his dissenting opinions. Burchett recently returned home to visit his ageing parents, armed only with a birth certificate, and now seems likely to be trapped there until a communist revolution. Meanwhile the raids against left wing bookshops and gaolings of Anti Vietnam demonstrators continues. A last ditch national moratorium has been organised for May 9 – 10 to fight for withdrawal of Australian and all foreign troops from Vietnam. Anyone wishing to participate in the moratorium outside Australia House, contact OZ for details.

INSTANT PLUGS:
The Marijuana Ex position Caravan — two rock groups, a film show, speakers and a library tour 15 US cities from now to July — campaigning for legalisation of pot. The 12,000 mile trip to 'Right — a Wrong' runs through Florida, Louisiana, Georgia, New York, across to Seattle and back to Washington D.C. where a (hopefully) million signature petition will be presented to Government officials prepared to show their faces.

Since the media mined 144 Piccadilly and Endell St to death, no-one thinks about squatters much anymore — except people who walk the streets every night and families who have to live 8 to tiny room. After three months operations, Lewisham Family Squatting Assn has housed 22 families, including seven kids who were about to be taken from their mother by the courts. They still have another dozen families whose need for rehousing is urgent. LFSA take over demolition-scheduled houses from the local council, makes them habitable, and lets them to members for £2 (min) to £4 (max) rents, which are ploughed back into more developments. But finance and labour required mean many suitable houses have to be turned down for lack of resources. If you live in the area, or think you can help change living standards as bad as anything Orwell saw in the 'thirties, go to LFSA meetings Tuesdays at the Albany, Creek Road, Deptford. (Chairman — David Adshead).

Various groups distribute underground and independent films — London Film-Makers Co-Op, Angry Arts Society etc — but they are lax about catalogues, information and promotion. 'Independent Cinema' is an information center/magazine/distribution outlet which attempts to remedy this.

Aimed at informing film clubs, Universities, and individuals about films available, being made or just

mooted, Independent Cinema will run 6000, 24-page copies financed by advertising, and charges on information pages. Rates on application to Nigel Algar/David Speechley 9 Newburgh St W1V1LH. Rates are negotiable and six of the information pages are free.

South Sea Bubble takes place a week after the Brighton Arts Festival, which is possibly the most sterile and elitist event of its sort in the country. The Bubble should provide an exciting and valid alternative. It will fill the town and involve its community. It will be based in the centre of Brighton around the West Pier and the Brighton Combination. There will be events in the streets and on the beach. It should be the best sort of demonstration of the power and potential of the living arts and of the current movement in new activities.

The Bubble is only a beginning.

But is should be a good one.

See you in Brighton May 22 – 25

US is a new magazine appearing in the West Country concerned with pollution, food, music, pottery, drama and industry. Enquiries to Rod Emery, 3 Abbey Street, Bath, Somerset.

3/6 to Roger Falcon, 22 Pembroke Square, London, W.8. will ensure a copy of Concept, yet another magazine of 'good contemporary poetry'. 'A book of happy sexual poems' is how Norman Isles describes The Green Man, his little red book available from him at 381 Marine Road, Morecambe, Lancs. The Observer refused a paid advertisement for it, so it might be worth the 10/-.

Any artist can show their work at the New Arts Lab, 1 Robert Street, N.W.1. at the Open Access Show. Obtain entry forms first and see J.G. Ballard's current sculpture of Crashed Cars.

Every Wednesday at The Crypt, 242 Lancaster Road, W.11 is experimental poetry, jazz, rock, films and inflatable ladies all for a ludicrous 2/6.

If you're lonely and lost in Blackpool visit the Head Shop at 4 Springfield Road or dance every Friday at the Pleasurebeach Casino. . . .

KWOD is being launched to 'bridge the gap between BEANO and Black Dwarf' and promises no four letter words. Anyone interested in this remarkable publishing phenomenon write to KWOD 53 Blacksmiths Way, Hardwell, Northampton.

FROM JOHN WILCOCK'S OTHER SCENES:

The first underground paper to be indicted by a FEDERAL grand jury is New Orlean's Nola Express — charged with obscenity for reproducing a picture of a guy masturbating, surrounded by nude pictures and the caption: What Sort of Man Reads Playboy?

The German author Joachim Joesten, who has written books about LBJ, JFK, Lee Harvey Oswald, Nasser, De Gaulle and Onassis now publishes a fortnightly newsletter, Truth Letter, dedicated solely to 'assassination news' (his address: 87-70 173rd St., NYC 11432).

One of the conditions that Salvador Dali imposed for doing his first advertising job (for PerrierWater) was that 1,000 bottles of the product be delivered to his home in Spain. Dali's now working on a television commercial for a French chocolate company.

'Weatherman is not an accident. Weatherman is a logical consequence of intellectual flabbiness and dishonesty on the Left as a whole. . . Movement people who ought to know better have indulged in verbal overkill to the point where language the basic tool for organizing reality into something that can be understood and acted upon is no longer descriptive. Terms like fascism, racism, genocide, police state and oppression have been stripped of meaning. (When and if real fascism comes to this country it seems we will have no words left to describe it)'.

Hendrik Hertzberg in WIN

Earth People's Park may or may not be a good idea there's been quite a bit of dispute about its potential but hopefully its sponsors are keeping an account of what happens to the dollars people are donating by mail. We never did find out what happened to the $400,000 that the Monterey Pop promoters promised to spread among the hip community.

John Sinclair wrote to Rolling Stone from jail alleging that the once-revolutionary group MC5 which he originally organized, produced and managed had now copped out and wanted to be big pop stars. Not only that, said Sinclair, but MC5 had screwed him out of his managment share now that he was in prison and in no position to collect it.

A free sample of vaginal foam is available by sending a postcard request to the Emko company, 7912 Manchester Ave., St. Louis, Mo.63143.

Hitchhiking anywhere on the face of the earth is an attractive proposition to some people, intimidating to others. So John Rudoff (Box 203, University Station, Syracuse, NY 13210) is compiling a Survival Manual for the Roads of Earth which will collate all the information that might be helpful. Send him some.

The Question

Tony Bell THE END

Dear Dr. Hip Pocrates,

In a recent column you answered a question about scalp hair. I am more interested in pubic hair.

My boyfriend likes thick pubic hair and keeps asking me to shave mine so it will grow back thicker. He says women who have had babies (i.e. had the pubic hair shaved) have much thicker and more hair than before the experience.

Answer: You may bristle at this, but to the best of knowledge hair will not grow back more thickly when cut or shaved. Hair is dead matter except for the "root" beneath the skin.

Besides, think of the five o'clock shadow...

Dear Dr. Hip Pocrates,

Whenever I displease my husband, he gives me an enema of hot soapy water to "discipline" me?! Since this didn't happen too often, I suffered with it—however, he has been giving them to me more often (about once every 4-5-6 weeks) and I've been wondering if it can cause me any harm. He used to use a pint of water, but now he uses more. (He says about a pint and a half). Also, he agrees to abide by your decision—says if it's harmful to me, he will stop and go back to using the hairbrush.

Answer: Infrequent enemas, as you describe them, are not medically harmful unless the water really is "hot".

Many people receive erotic stimulation through enemas and I wonder if this is really a punishment for you.

But then it's your bag.

Dear Dr. Hip Pocrates,

I am surprised that medical research can't surmise the reason for a lower left testicle. When we were first married my husband explained it to me. One hangs lower so that in case you have to squeeze your legs together they don't crush each other. As for lefties predominating, I guess all those symmetrical fellows crossed their legs and crushed themselves out of having any progeny.

Dear Dr. Hip Pocrates,

I seldom read your column; it usually actually makes me sick to my stomach to know there are sick vulgar, uncivilised people.

Today my husband showed me your column about the man who liked to wake up his wife by making love to her in the morning. He's an early riser and I'm not (he relaxes in the evenings while I take care of dinner, children, and chores). He remarked that he might try that sometime. I told him and I'll tell you, if he ever does, in that manner, I'll probably kill him and blame you for contributing to the cause.

People live happily enough until they read all these perverted sex things—and get ideas, or think they are missing something! It's turning the world into a cessspool—it'll end up like the Roman Empire—in decadence.

Why don't you try and make things better instead of worse—a better world, instead of an animal jungle? I also wish your laboratory assistant and her kind would mate with their own kind. That might help a lot.

Let's hope computers help out in this respect.

Sincerely,

21

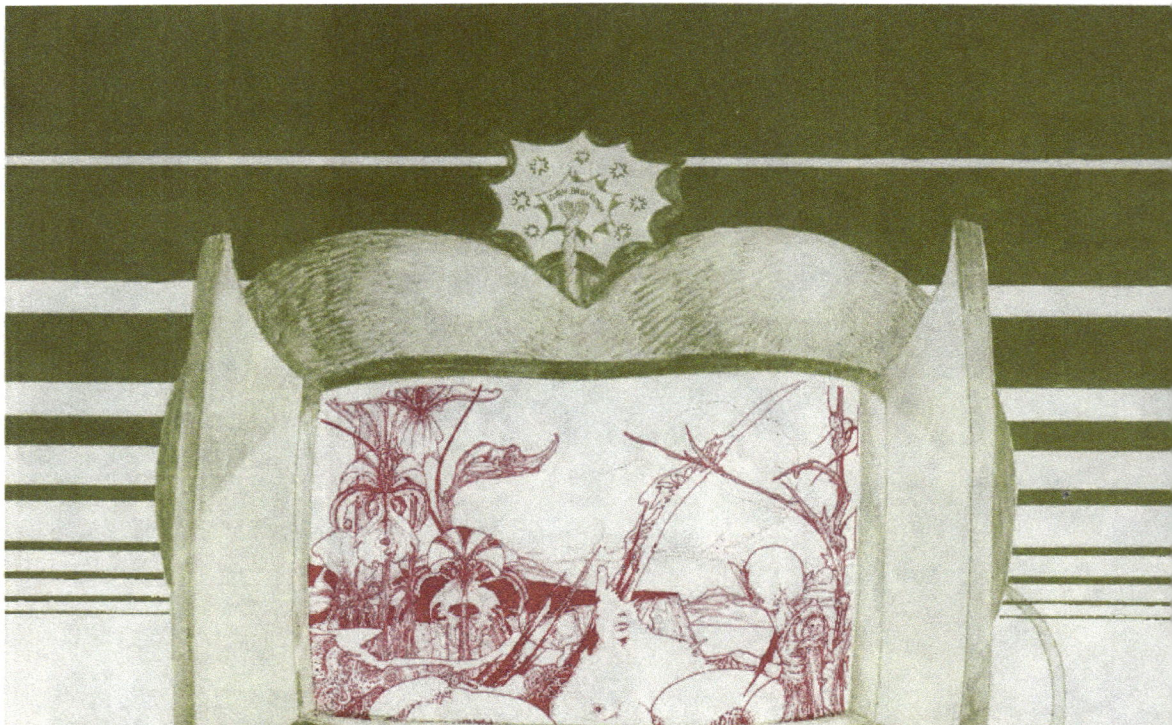

CANDY DARLING
LOVE

While they were in London, LOVE stayed in a large, ultra-new anonymous apartment high above Ebury Street, near Victoria Station. Transient, over-heated and full of beds. Used to the luxurious private life of the wealthy Californian sybarite, they, certainly Arthur Lee, were totally bored by the hard facts of touring and the exigencies of life in London. All that money could buy had been lavished upon them, and this is what they wound up with. 'We don't have anything to do, man,' said George, the drummer. 'We just sit around all day and get smashed. It's a relief when someone comes around to talk to. We've got nothing else to do.' They all looked half awake, particularly Arthur, who has heavy lidded, bedroom eyes and the lazy, graceful movements of a contented Siamese cat.

'Hey you got so many pretty things on, man' said George, touching a necklace, 'Arthur, look at the things this cat has on', Fringed pants, leather bracelets, a ring or two, I suddenly felt like an over-dressed weekend Jonathan King hippie, and almost crudely destroyed the good vibrations building up on the large double bed by asking a question:

'A friend of mine said he wasn't impressed by your stage performance at the Speakeasy. How well do you think you perform generally on the stage?'

'I don't know man. I do my best every time I go on. The Speakeasy was great. I had a good time. The crowd seemed enthusiastic, and definitely behind me. They were just waiting to see where my whole trip was at and after they saw, I just never gave them a chance to get on the case, I just kept the ball rolling until I could get out of there.'

'Do you try to create a sexual image on stage the way Jagger does?'

22

't have my hands full just remembering my songs. I just try to get my point across. I'm not into creating any sex image. I just do my trip. I can't look at me and say what I am. You have to do that. I don't see my sex trip happening with Jagger, I just see him enjoying doing his thing.'

'It's a little more than that. He openly enjoys projecting sexuality.'

'Maybe that's his thing. Just because it's his thing, that doesn't necessarily mean it has to be my thing. It might be part of my trip, but it's not my whole trip.'

'Whether consciously or not, Love's image, and particularly yours, has ever since you've been around, been a very sensual one.' (If you looked and sounded like Arthur Lee it would be very difficult for it not to be).

'Well, that's great. Nothing wrong with a little sex.'

'But are you conscious of this?'

'Well yes, but I don't think about it too much. I don't push it. I just do my thing. If sex comes out of doing my thing, then that's what you get.'

'So you agree with me?'

'Yeah, why not.'

'Are you into politics at all?'

'Not at all.' Arthur laughed. He laughs a lot. 'Is anybody?'

'Well, Jefferson Airplane are on a heavy political trip at the moment.'

'Yeah. They don't see life like I do. Maybe they need it man. Maybe

they need to learn something. I'm not like that at all. I mean, it's like uh, I'm is it whether I wanna be or not. It comes out in my songs when I talk about all sorts of different things. There's no point in talking about politics.'

'But your life style is a political thing in itself.'

'My lifestyle is that background that I was conditioned — (yawn) — I am the result of that background. Make no mistake about that.'

'Would you say you are living the revolution?'

'I am what? My birth was a revolution.'

'Do you know what I'm trying to say?'

'No. I wish you'd get to the point.'

'I think his songs are political,' put in George. The other members of the group had already disappeared into another room to sleep.

'The way of life reflected in your songs is totally opposed to the way of life that someone like President Nixon would recommend for a red-blooded, healthy American under twenty five.'

'I'm a red beans and rice man, but I'm not totally opposed to anything. To be totally opposed to something wouldn't be living, it would be negative. Just moving backwards. That's not life, man. For every bad, there's got to be some good. Even if Nixon's an asshole, there's got to be a good part of his asshole. So if people, man vote somebody in — or if they have

a power system if they put somebody in a so called power position (laughter) and employ those games with people's lives, all those trips, and people want to support this system, well, you know, that's their trip man. (laughter) I just happen to live in a house in that system, but I ain't going to be putting up no Volunteers signs on my album cover. I don't dig it. I can see the whole thing changing towards the way that I would want my life to be lived on this planet but my way is no opinion in itself, like this interview, or what you're gonna write down. My way is not the way; it is part of the way. Just by accident we happen to be on the same trip — we're all freaking out! (laughter) Someone must have a pretty strong rap going or something, because like ah, because everything is starting to like freak out around all those stereotype creeps and man, they're getting nervous. So somebody's got to either start cracking down or opening up. And I would hope that they would open up. Because opening up is the key to life. Keep an open mind man and you can't go too wrong. If you are aware of your environment, man that's an important trip.'

'If being aware of your environment is an important thing, and there are so many things about your environment which are fucked up, then apart from living the way you do, which is an important statement in itself, you don't do anything — you don't preach. . .'

'No man'

'. . . or belong to any revolutionary or political organisation.'

'Oh no man. No. Oh no.'

'His songs are political,' George put in again.

'I just write. I just call 'em as I see 'em. Call 'em as I see 'em, man.'

'Arthur writes about life, man,' said George, 'and life's political.'

'I don't like what's going down, if

that's what you mean. I'm not exactly tickled pink by the government running the world. I don't like the war in Vietnam. I'm positively against the war. But I don't have to think about those political trips.

'How do you get along with the rest of the group?'

'I get along great with everybody in the group. Maybe that's what goes wrong. Maybe that'll lead to another break up.'

'How about George here?'

'I get along great with George.'
'Arthur's the best,' said George.
'He's modest too, that's for sure.'

'You're not egotistical.'

'Oh no man.'

'Why not, everybody else is.'

Arthur laughed. His laughter is as gentle and lethargic as the rest of him. 'Oh yeah? Well, by saying 'No' I guess I am too.'

'You are the sole surviving member of the original Love, so obviously it was around you that everything revolved.'

'No.'

'But if you left there wouldn't be any Love.'

'Right' (from George)
'Well, more or less I suppose, but it depends on what you thought Love was to begin with. If you want to make me Love, that's cool. But I never said I was Love. I said I was a part of Love. There are a lot of groups with no solo survivors or whatever you call them. Grass Roots, for example. That's not the same group at all.'

'But that's because there was no single personality which embodied the group. But with Love it's pretty obvious that there is you.'

'I dig what you're saying.'

'Like with the Byrds there is McGuinn.'

'Well, it wasn't McGuinn who was the Byrds to me at first. It was Gene Clark. But when I think of the Byrds I don't really think of either McGuinn or Clark, I think of all those people involved in that trip. Yeah.'
'I think when people come to see Love, they come to see Arthur Lee,' said George, 'because we haven't paid our dues yet. We're not known.'
'We got to get a lot of exposure man,' said Arthur.
'Yeah, but they come to see Arthur, and hear what he wrote. And we play his songs the way he wants them.'

'Why is it that the original members all split? Was it just a natural drift apart?'

'It was just time. No big thing, just something that was coming to a head.'

'Was it your fault, your hangups that caused the rift?'

'My hangups?'

'I mean, I've heard that you are autocratic, you throw your weight around.'

'That's the last thing I do. I don't even weigh that much. But I'll take the blame man, I ain't proud.'

(laughter)

'Is there any truth in that at all?'

'Well, if you want to believe it. To call me the asshole that caused the group to break up is just a falsehood. It's just not true. Everybody con-

tributed in equal share to the breaking up of the group. That's for sure. I don't have any guilt trips about that trip. It's like a romance man, with a chick. It's good as long as it is and when it's over, it's over but you gotta go into it not looking for the ending, but constantly aware that nothing lasts forever. It wasn't ever a bad scene. It went down. It was a good thing for me, because it was refreshing for me to work with other cats. I don't look upon it as a bad trip.

'So the whole thing could happen again?'

'Oh, possibly. Yeah sure, but it doesn't worry me simply because of the fact that I can't work without grooving with the people I work with. I don't look upon musicians as chunks of my body so that if I can't have these people I can't function I look upon musicians as arrangements — each musician varies his own arrangements inside his body and when he plays his axe, his arrangement or interpretation of whatever music has been given to him at that time, is the sort of trip I will have to evolve my trip around so far as thinking about writing songs goes. I have to think of such and such, that he is a quarter, half beat drummer — but I can take my songs to someone else who plays triplets — another trip, and I get a different feeling from that guy. Can you understand what I'm saying. So arrangements come and go man. They come and go. But the thing I've learned about the whole trip is that it's better to be with a good arrangement then with a bad arrangement.

'Following upon that you would say there could not be any good music coming out of a bad arrangement?'

'That's true, but what I mean is... oh where was I?' The pipe goes round yet again.

'So you don't treat the rest of your group like a bunch of shit?'

'Lies, all lies. I just took my stand as being leader, and if I didn't, how could I be the leader of the group? I just made sure that I did my trip. If I was the rhythm guitar player I'd make sure I played the rhythm guitar. You know, after living with someone for three years you sort of take them for granted and too much stuff was taken for granted in that first group. That's why I broke it up. It was so loose, and falling apart for six months before we finally broke up. Like when we first joined the band bit, we had a great group personality, everybody grooved together, but at the end of the third year, everybody was financially straight, drifted their own ways and formed a new life. It just happened.'

'Sounds perfectly logical.'

'Yeah, things don't last forever, and nobody is particularly to blame when it all ends.'

'Did you commandeer a room for yourself (for whatever reason) in your Manchester hotel and push everyone else into the only remaining room?'

'No.'

'There are always people who want to put the bad rap on someone. It's logical that that happens to me simply because I probably blow a lot of people's minds myself, so in return I get my mind blown with that sort of crap.'

'The fact that the group is called Love may be partly responsible for this.'

'Yeah maybe. Everybody's Love and

I just want to put Love in the minds of the good people on this planet. It's nice when you're on a bummer to see a sign that says Love, touches your heart... it's a good trip to flash on home. I try to make my trip as homey or as earthy as I can. Like, even though I write sarcastically or whatever about my environments, I'd like to think of my material as reminding you when you listen to it, of the trip you're going through, or the hardships you're facing, that I faced, and of the way it ends or the way I say it ends. I should like to think that it would be a good trip for the person's mind. I like to give them that homely feeling. You got to get your shoes straight at home before you can play on the streets. A lot of people read trips that happen in the street and they haven't got their shit straight at home. Man, it's easy to put somebody down.'

'That old story about your road manager ...'

'Well, I heard that the whole group was on smack.'

'Oh no, not the whole group. Not the man.

'Some of the others were?'

'Well, you know, that's far out man. I don't know which ones were, which ones weren't. I don't have time to get into other peoples personal lives (said with great cynicism) Make no mistake about that...

'But the road manager...'

'He OD'd. Or maybe he had a heart attack man. (laughter) It was purely accidental. Happens everyday man.'

'Not your fault.'

'No, he did it to himself. Doing his own trip. It's good to do your own trip.'

'There's no other trip to do. But did you expect it?'

'Oh no. A shock. A mindblower.'
At this point, Danny Kresky Love's manager came in, looking worried:
'How come when people do interviews, they are always concerned with peoples' drug habits? Someone wrote an article in Zig Zag that was a lot of shit. Really bullshit. I'm just about to sue those people for what they wrote.'

'There isn't much need to get upset by talk about drugs — which you take and which you don't.'

'I don't think so either,' said Arthur. 'Yeah, but they were talking about heroin. We don't want police watching us walking in and out all day long.'

'Why do I so often get your songs mixed up with other peoples' songs?'

'Because everything I hear, I hear. What goes in gotta come out. Some trip like that. So all the things that I hear influence me in my writing in my whole trip.'

'Do you copy songs?'

'Copy songs from other people?'

'Yes.'

'Oh no, I get feelings from other people. The melodies inspire me to do specific things their way, you know... But that's my trip. I like to do all kinds of music instead of just one kind of music.'

'Most musicians are influenced by other peoples' music, but translate it in such a way that it becomes almost totally different, usually because they are very self conscious about being unoriginal.'

'I'm not on that trip. I know I am everybody else.'

'So it doesn't surprise you that other people find you derivative.'

'I appreciate all the other people and their ...' (laughter) ... I want my songs to sound like other peoples'. That's my trip. I'm glad that I'm able to do that, you know, it's like an echo, coming back, in a different way, but I say the same thing.'

'The songs certainly sound much the same sometimes.'

'Well, that's a compliment. Because that to me means that I'm not just on one trip. I mean, I don't just sing de blare, I like to mix 'em up. Lots of different things.'

'Do you like living in communal situations?'

'The group are around all the time but I have my own private trip within the group. I don't live with any people. Like my house has an extra house on it that my drummer rents but other than that I have my privacy. My business and private life are not one and the same thing.

'On a tour like this they must become more fused though?'

'Yeah. (laughter) Manchester. Completely the opposite of my normal trip.'

'And it gets you uptight sometimes?'

'I'm ready to tear these sheets up right now,' slow smile.

'Do you often lose your temper?'

'Everyone loses their temper.'

'No they don't.'

'They don't? Let me see — who were those three that did...? Everytime you open your mouth you've lost your temper. Cause you can't keep your mouth shut.'

Arthur Lee was practically asleep. George had disappeared. 'We've covered a lot of ground, man,' Arthur said as I prepared to leave. A beautiful flaxen haired girl wandered in silently and sat on the bed. What with her eyes and Arthur's golden brown skin... California, sunshine, acid, flowers, love, hate and death. I shook hands twice and said several stoned farewells. Amiability and good vibes to the end. The West Coast is something else. A few more years, and they really will be like children from another planet.
Jim Anderson.

Extracts from Robert Finnis' History of Teen Idols and Teenybop – the American pre-Beatle era.

'Teenybop' is a name that has been given recently to a category of music which is sung by artists who rely solely or to a greater extent on an aura or image, usually sexual, deliberately cultivated and to the detriment of the true medium of their profession. As for teenyboppers, it's difficult to classify them. There are thousands of mature housewives who show all the hallmarks of the true teenybopper – although they might not pin fan pics up on the wall, they do buy the records – but speaking generally, the true teenybopper is a 11–14 year old pubescent schoolgirl, (or schoolboy) probably middle class, probably English or American, who loves to have her sentiments and feelings manufactured for her. At first glance, Elvis Presley could be called the originator of 'teenybop', but underneath all the make-up and flashy clothes, he was a snarling, earthy southern kid, still attached musically to his ethnic background. His records were not subservient to his image. With all the early rock stars (Jerry Lee, Carl Perkins, Gene Vincent, Chuck Berry etc) their music and their shows were their image. Under the diamond rings and Cadillacs they were rough and raw. They couldn't always smile or pose properly for their photos, weren't too good looking and parents loathed them. They weren't the kind they'd like their daughter to marry.

On November 4th 1957 however, with the initial rock fervour dying down, and a steady crop of ballads, calypsos and a few pre-Haley throwbacks turning up as well as the hard rock, TIME magazine reported: '. . . is the golden glottis gurgling to a stop? Is there a quiver to those rosebud lips a beginning of wilt to those poodle-wool sideburns?'

For two years, lovers of peace, quiet and a less epileptic kind of minstrelsy have waited for Elvis Presley and the adenoidal art form rock n' roll to fade. But knowledgeable disc-jockeys and trade bulletins offer such purists little hope. In spite of previously noted tremors, last week rock 'n roll looked as solid as Gibraltar, and Elvis – with a new storm and troika hit, Jailhouse Rock' (RCA Victor) – was perched right on top.'

The trend that TIME noted (somewhat belatedly) ushered in the golden age of teenybop, and the classic rock and rollers went into a temporary eclipse.

The first true teenybop artist was Tommy Sands (b. 1937), not counting two movie stars who happened to have hits, Tab Hunter and Sal Mineo or Pat Boone who was in an uptight class of his own. Sands, of whom we never heard much of over here, was a kid who had been brought up in Shreveport, Louisiana, though born in Chicago, and had been exposed to hillbilly sounds on the radio and learned the guitar. Later he found himself doing second rate T.V. and radio shows and touring on Colonel Tom Parker's (pre-Elvis days) road shows across the cow country. Parker encouraged Sands.

By late 1956, Sands hadn't got anywhere. His voice wasn't suited to rock, n' roll, being throaty, lush and not gutsy enough. But he had clean boyish good looks and when a T.V. company wanted Presley to play himself in a show called 'The Teenage Idol', Parker said Presley was too busy, but that he could recommend an unknown, Tommy Sands.

Soon after Sands was flown in by the show's producers who were pleased and signed him. After the show, Sands began to play the title role in real life. Offers bombarded him after the appearance and 'Teenage Crush', one of two songs from the show, a breathy ballad with-a-beat that relates in sobbing tones something about young love misunderstood, burst into the U.S. charts on the 'Capitol' label in February, 1957 – pretty early.

Over the years, up to '60, Sands had many discs released, sometimes backed by guitars and drums and others with orchestras. A few were hits like 'Goin' steady' (1957) and 'Sing Boy Sing' (1958) but he never made it really big for some reason, though he did graduate into movies with one or two good roles. 'Capitol' were possibly to blame, as they were not too adept at handling teen artists, or perhaps he was just too early for his scene. At any rate Sands was the very first of the 'clean' teen singers – the ones parents would like their daughters to marry.

Next came Ricky Nelson, born 1940, with a silver spoon in his mouth by virtue of his showbiz parentage. At 11 he made his first screen appearance and from his early teens he appeared in a nationally syndicated, typically American, light comedy programme, 'The Ozzie & Harriet Show', Ozzie and Harriet being his folks. Ricky's elder brother, Dave, also featured and soon Ricky's face was well known in America. When rock 'n roll came in Rick's parents signed him to Norman Granz's normally jazz-inclined 'Verve' label. The first single was a cover of a Fats Domino hit 'I'm Walkin' backed by 'A Teenager's Romance', both recorded on the soundstage of the 'Ozzie & Harriet' show. The record, with the aid of a little exposure like an 18 million audience, took off and entered the U.S. charts at No. 18 in mid May, 1957, reaching No. 2. That record was to be an antecedent for similar hits over the next 5 or 6 years. Nelson at one stage being second only to Presley in American teen idolization.

He wasn't a 'natural born' singer but he did learn quickly as he went along until, by 1960, he was a capable teen-crooner with a distinct warm, nasal tone, even if he did somewhat lack authority, which he has somehow never managed to capture, especially on up-tempo numbers.

By late 1957, the U.S. charts were being slowly infiltrated by other 'clean' performers like Paul Anka ('Diana') and Jimmie Rogers ('Honeycomb') and the Everly Brothers, who although watered-down country at this stage, went on to cultivate a massive teenybop following right through till 1962.

Short and stocky, Anka was considered almost a prodigy in 1957 when at 16 he hit with the massive, matriarchal self-penned 'Diana'. He was always popular and starting so young had a very good run of hits, many self-written, through the years including 'I Love You Baby' (1957) 'I'm Just a Lonely Boy' (1959) 'You Are My Destiny' (1958) 'Puppy Love' (1960). Around 1962, Anka opted out, successfully, into an adult almost middle aged entertainment world.

December, 1957 saw the emergence of the first teenybop group, Danny & the Juniors. More important still was the fact that they came from Philadelphia, which in a year was to become the centre of pop and monopolise the teen scene for a while, to the detriment and eventual fate of the truly talented hard rock 'n roller, replacing the latters' music with sickly sweet sentiments and carefully contrived images fathered by Payola.

'At the Hop' was a world hit by early 1958 and Danny & the Juniors became the first in a long line of one-hit wonders, with no stage act to back themselves up with. They followed up with 'Rock and Roll is Here to Stay', reached No. 19 in America and faded, although they made a comeback in 1961 with a hit, 'Twistin' U.S.A.', with a different line-up.

The group were all urban youths, mostly of Italian origin who'd never been exposed to musical influence bonafide, but just grew up on the block and suddenly fancied themselves, so they practised their harmonies on a self-penned song, 'Do The Bop', and took it to a local vocal tutor and arranger, Artie Singer. Singer altered the lyrics, cutting himself in and fixed up an economical recording session.

'At The Hop' had just string bass, drums and piano underneath a blanket of vocals and moves along rapidly. Leased to A.B.C.-Paramount Records, the record broke nationally and the kids made a lot of money in a short time. At the time there were several Danny & the Juniors going around to cash in on the hit. The groups' name lives on as a meter for derisive scorn of the crass-commercial dawn of the teenybop era which they heralded.

A similarly styled group was The Royal Teens who hit with their shattering teenage idiot chant 'Short Shorts' in February, 1958 – the first ever bubblegum hit in rock, as opposed to straight teenybop sentiments. There is no vocal lead on the record but it begins with a wolf-whistle and what sounds like the teenagers on the local street corner, chanting through echo, 'Who Likes Short Shorts?' (the girls) answered by the guys 'We Like Short Shorts' and apart from a bit on sax and some handclaps that's about it. Recorded in New Jersey and leased, once again, to A.B.C.-Paramount, 'Shorts' sold a million. Just who the 'Teens' were is a mystery, but they say Al Kooper and Bob Gaudio, who co-wrote it, were definitely there. Gaudio later became famous as one of the 4 Seasons and as a writer/producer.

Tommy Sands

Bobby Rydell

PAUL ANKA

RICK NELSON

JIMMY CLANTON

FRANKIE AVALON

DION

FABIAN

BOBBY VEE

Another early teen hit in 1957 America, which really belonged to 1959, was an attempt to emulate the Everly Brothers by two New York college kids under the pseudonyms 'Tom and Jerry' on the 'Big' label. The disc, 'Hey, Schoolgirl', was written and sung by the then teenaged Simon and Garfunkel,

'Hey Schoolgirl!'
in the second ra-ho-ho(w)
They cut some other sides but were unable to follow it up successfully. Later Simon pursued a career as rock singer Jerry Landis.

In July, 1956, a D.J. Dick Clark had taken over the compere spot in a local Philadelphia Show 'Bandstand' blessed with a simple format – 150 kids stomping a studio to the hit sounds of the day, with an in-person guest most days. It was Philadelphia's highest rated daytime television show. After convincing the A.B.C. T.V. authorities to screen it nationally he could do no wrong and on a hot and humid afternoon on August 5th, 1957, A.B.C. put 'Bandstand' on its national television network as 'American Bandstand'.

In the 3 years that followed Clark (b. 1929) had some sort of effect – direct or indirect – on the career of almost every popular singer except Presley who from his regnal heights could ignore everybody. By exploiting artists on his daily 90 minute 'American Bandstand' and also on his own 'Dick Clark Show' (every Saturday) Clark single-handedly established stars and records and was responsible for the 'Philadelphia Crap Sound' of Frankie Avalon, Fabian, to a certain extent Bobby Rydell and others like Connie Francis (from New Jersey) all of whom he over-exposed to American teenybopperdom.

By late '58 he was the most influential D.J. in the country and developed a subsidiary network of business interests and sidelines. 'Dick wouldn't think of standing in the way of a young singer trying to plug his latest record', someone wrote, while Dick explained 'New discs fit in nicely with our format'.

Let us look closer at other pieces of the integral jigsaw of the Philadelphia phenomenon. There was a small record label called Chancellor run by a former government clerk, Bob Marcucci, and an arranger/musician, Peter De Angelis. They founded their label in the mid 50's and had their first hit in 1957, 'More than just friends' by Jodi Sands. Their first big star became Frankie Avalon, born Francis Thomas Avallone in 1940. He was a child prodigy on T.V. playing, of all things, the trumpet, while also attending school and bookings. However, as he grew out of his cute 'kiddy' looks things got quiet. He jigged where he could, now in his mid teens and in 1957 joined a local outfit 'Rocco and his Saints' as lead singer and trumpeter. This proved lucrative and he even got a friend of his, Bobby Ridarelli (later to become Bobby Rydell), a job on drums. Marcucci and De Angelis on a local talent binge discovered Frankie singing with Rocco and his Saints. Musically orientated, good looking, well behaved, he would be a clean cut legitimate performer.

After two flops, (backed by Rocco and Co.), his third disc 'De De Dinah', backed by the Pete De Angelis orchestra and chorus, made the U.S. charts in early '58, with a lot of plugging from the convenient 'American Bandstand'.

Earlier in '57 he had appeared in a movie 'Jamboree' about the disc business, singing his second disc (one of the flops, 'Teacher's Pet'). The movie was fascinating because it featured some of the best of the older pioneering school – Carl Perkins, Jerry Lee Lewis, Fats Domino, Buddy Knox, even Count Basie and his orchestra and Slim Whitman, while also exposing the then unknown stars Connie Francis and Avalon to be from a completely different city environment. It was the urbans against the ethnics.

Avalon went on to have some massive U.S. hits, backed by middle-aged session orchestras. After 1960 they stopped coming but he still remained immensely popular becoming a personality cult thing; movies, teen spreads etc. This lasted till about 1962 when he had a belated U.S. hit, his chart swansong 'Don't let me stand in your way'.

After establishing Avalon, Marcucci and De Angelis needed some security for their label which hinged on the tonsils of one personality who could fail from the popularity of fickle audiences any time.

They found the insurance in a 15 year old (again) local kid, Fabian Forte (b. 1943).

'I was certain that 'Fabe' was it and that it was going to happen. But if it hadn't I simply would have looked for someone else and built him.' He manufactured Fabian and merchandised him. He told 'Fabe' what to say and when to say it, what to do and when to do it, when to appear and when to disappear. Fabian holds the record for the biggest con in the business. He was 'discovered' lounging outside his home one evening. Marcucci, impressed by his looks, the beefy-sweet type, popular in 1959 suggested he cut a record for 'Chancellor'. Even Fabian was dubious: 'Hey mom', he is supposed to have said, 'that crazy man wants me to sing'. He couldn't sing and he knew it.

But with the aura Marcucci envisaged, Fabian could stutter his name off-key and it would be accepted as 'Entertainment', because he would be accepted as a person.

After listening to hundreds of records, and singing lessons, he cut his first single which did nothing.

Then Marcucci took Fabian on some of the already well-established Frankie Avalon's personal appearances to get the 'feel' of the audience he would soon be adored by. He could see the girls in the front row plead with Frankie to touch them, he could catch the outwardly disdainful boys in the crowd sneak out to damage Frankie's car because he was 'stealing their girls'.

Then came 'Lilly Lou', his second disc – nothing.

Marcucci repackaged his commodity and when his third record 'I'm a man' came out it took off with plugging on 'American Bandstand' and an article in the popular 'Motion Picture' by a female journalist who'd been impressed by Fabe. 'I have a fuse over Fabian' proclaimed the leader. Actually, the woman who died in 1960 from an incurable disease, joined Chancellor records as promotion director.

Other hits followed in 1959, 'Tiger' and 'Turn me loose', his records sold fairly well, his popularity sustained by a run of teen movies, until 1960 when the big promotion and the big hits ground to a well deserved stop. Today he is married and nothing, but does emerge in occasional 'B' movies and has recently been trying to change his name back to its full Fabian Forte.

In all fairness 'Fabe' did learn as he went along. Embarrassingly weak off-key vocals on disc, and amateurish awkwardness onscreen, improved slightly but his talent lay in giving the impression that he had something where in fact he had very little.

Then there was Bobby Rydell who in 1960-61 achieved almost a Presley type following. Rydell was talented in a sterile way, like Frankie Avalon. Born on April 26th, 1942, Adrio Ridarelli in the same South Philadelphia environment which spawned Frankie Avalon, Joey Bishop, Mario Lanza and Jimmy Darren. It was a clean, poor area in which Jews, Italians and Negroes intermingled in a raucous, dilapidated jigsaw puzzle of identical row houses, narrow streets and slight strips of sunshine. All the parents wanted their kids to lift themselves out of that environment and 'show' neighbours. It's a fact that all South Philadelphia kids could, at the time, lay valid claim to 'knowing' Frankie or Fabe.

Ridarelli took an interest in the drums at a very early age then appeared locally and on Philadelphia T.V. where he would sing and imitate big showbiz names. This lasted till he was ten and never got him anywhere, but like Avalon this precocity was a taste of things to come. The next four years were barren, until Ridarelli joined a local rock'n'roll band 'Rocco and his Saints', on drums. One day on a gig in Atlantic City, New Jersey the group was an alternate band with 'The Appljacks', whose bass player, an older fellow named Frankie Day was impressed by the vitality of Rocco's drummer, young Bobby. The customary visits to Ridarelli's dubious parents were made and then Day was allowed to become Bobby's manager.

Three discs later still no luck. For a year Rydell and Frankie Day had undergone a gruelling grind in the latter's old car, making the rounds of D.J.'s between Massachusetts and Virginia to promote the records, sleeping in the car, washing up at the Y.M.C.A. and eating frankfurters at roadside stands. Pretty soon Day was in debt. After Rydell's third disc, a ballad, had looked promising but flopped, his fourth 'Cameo' disc 'Kissin' Time' finally took off with intra plugging locally and on 'American Bandstand'. Many other hits followed in 1960, 'Wild One', 'Ding-a-ling' c/w 'Swingin' School', 'Itty Bitty Girl' and his massive remake of 'Volare' in which adults took an interest.

What became of Rydell, a purely American attraction, isn't known, but he lasted until 1963 when he appeared in the film version of the musical 'Bye Bye Byrdie', then the groups sealed his demise. Other hits include 'Cherie', 'Goodtime Baby', 'I Got Bonnie' in 1961, 'The Fish', 'The Cha Cha Cha' in 1962 and 'Forget Him' and 'Wildwood Days' in '63.

The fact remains that Rydell, Avalon and Fabian were the pioneers in the 'Good looks – talent optional' stakes which took over the rock scene in 1959, and was, in turn, to lead into the inter-regnal void of the early '60's. The years 1959–1963 were the worst in rock/pop's history, with '63 being an all-time low. That was the year which, apart from Spector's Wagnerian productions, America had nothing to offer and instead, England, long the underdog, began to introduce sensational changes in the rock field.

Dion, a dark scowling guy who looked like a black pencil on stage, in his dark Italian suits, was born in the Bronx. He had showbiz parents and was introduced into that environment, with appearances on T.V., etc. He cut his first record around 1956–1957 for an obscure 'Mohawk' label. Then in 1957 he formed a group, along with three neighbourhood pals of the '50's practising harmonies on-street-corner type and that year they signed with 'Laurie' records of New York as Dion & the Belmonts, derived from Belmont Avenue in the Bronx, where they all lived. Their second disc 'I wonder why', a sort of embryonic 'Four Seasns/Beachboys' sound, took off becoming a U.S. smash. Several more very dated corny hits followed – 'No One Knows' ('58), 'Where or When' (1960) and the favourite Pomus/Shuman ditty of 1959 'Teenager in Love' –

'Each time we have a quarrel,
it almost breaks my heart,
'Cos I am so afraid that we
must be apart;
Each night I ask the stars up
above –
Why must I be a Teenager in Love?'

In spite of his early career it must be said – a few have noticed – that Dion was head and shoulders above the rest and one of the all-time greats of pop. He was truly the first pop artist to go, for use of a better word, 'progressive'. He was also a talented writer, arranger and producer.

27

When he inevitably split from the Belmonts who had a few small hits then floundered, he emerged in the early '60's as one of the biggest solo names in the teen stakes. Even at this stage he was different. Whereas all the others favoured big orchestras and girly choruses, Dion was the purveyor of 'funky teenybop' employing smaller, tighter groups on such hits for 'Laurie' as 'Runaround Sue' (1961), 'The Wanderer' (1961), 'Lovers Who Wander' (1962) and 'Sandy' (1962). His vocals were fabulous. He had a moaning, elastic voice, very slightly nasal, with a distinct phrasing, stretching syllables and words all over the place till he landed on the right note and it sounded good because he was a true musician.

In 1963 after six years on 'Laurie', he joined C.B.S. at that time still a very straight company; Robert Goulet, Andy Williams, Steve Lawrence, Tony Bennett were its big stars. He continued his run of hits with a series of fabulous productions, still employing that tight funky 'teenybronx' back up but adding subtleties to the sound, as on his self written and produced 'Donna the Prima Donna' (1963). Suddenly he began updating R & B standards like 'Drip Drop' (a 1958 Drifters hit), 'Ruby Baby' and making hits of them, all the time growing earthier on record. He also changed his name to its full Dion Di Mucci, although he reverts to the former without warning. On flipsides, unnoticed, he would just feature himself on guitar, vocal and harmonies (or similar acoustic backups) singing more philosophical songs. Thus we have 'The Road I'm On (Gloria)' on the flip of 'Hoochie Koochie' (1964) and 'No One's Waiting for Me' the 'B' of 'Ruby Baby' (1963). For 1963 and an artist of his popularity this was amazing, and these 'personal statements' were the first signs of the real Dion showing through. Nobody but the folkies were allowed to do that.

at least capable of smashing the chart, he has recently joined 'Warners/Reprise' and ranks as one of the leaders in the singer, or rather interpreter/composer bag. Perhaps it might be indicative of something to some people that Dion was the only pop star, apart from Dylan, on the college cover of the 'Sergeant Pepper' album.

Jimmy Clanton, on the other hand, was born in the south (rare for teen idols) in Baton Rouge, Louisiana in 1940. He had an early hit in summer '58, 'Just a Dream', which sold a million. Clanton had gone to a famous New Orleans Studio owned by engineer Cosimo Matassa, to cut a disc with his group of teen friends, 'The Rockets'. He cut one side then wrote 'Just a Dream' as a 'B', on the spot. Matassa took it ot the local 'Ace' label, basically an R & B company, who put it out. Clanton became 'Ace's' biggest artist over the next few years, having several big hits up to 1962. They include 'Go Johnny Go' (from the movie, 1959), 'Ship on a Stormy Sea' (1959), 'Darkest Street In Town' (1962) and 'Venus In Blue Jeans' (1962) and all pretty crappy.

Bobby Vee, a big teenybop name both in the States and England began his career as a Buddy Holly imitator; nasal voice, strong accent. At 17 he had an American hit on 'Liberty', 'Devil or Angel', and the million-seller 'Rubber Ball' (1960) assured that he would be around awhile. Vee (nee Velline) got his break when, in February '59, the plane crash which killed Buddy Holly, Valens and Big Bopper, left a sold-out programme empty in Moor Head, Minnesota. The promoters issued a call for local talent and Bobby Vee and his friends who lived in nearby Fargo, N.Dakota stepped in as 'The Shadows', dressed in identical sweaters. They went down well and Bobby was signed as a solo, after Liberty heard some demos he'd cut with the group, who became his

emergence of 'Liberty' from a small L.A. label to one of the majors today.

He began in the record business at 15, doing promotion for a company in Dallas, Texas. At 17 he became a D.J. in Lubbock. At 19, he joined Liberty as a producer and beginning with 'Dreamin' by Johnny Burnette he notched up hit after hit by developing a consistent production technique involving a very small rhythm section and a large pizzicato string section with the occasional use of shrill, girly choruses.

Between '60-'62 Garrett used that sound to establish and sustain the careers of Bobby Vee (his biggest success) the re-formed Crickets, Buddy Knox, Timi Yuvo and several others. There was no movement in the string section; everybody did the same thing. The strings were used mainly for fills or as a mass lead on instrumental breaks. One can imagine all those middle-aged sessionmen sitting in an L.A. studio, elbows flashing frantically on such hits as 'You're Sixteen', 'Rubber Ball' etc. I mean you had to be fast — strings were used like guitars — Garrett never employed lead guitar breaks on a sound which perhaps represents the pre-Beatle void best of all.

Burnette, killed in '64, was actually one of the original country-rockers, recording as early as May 1956 for 'Coral'. Born in Memphis in 1934 (when he joined Liberty it was boosted to 1938) he got his first guitar at 5 and all through school was just 'a-pickin' and grinnin''. He roughed it up in his teens; lightweight boxer, deckhand on Mississippi riverboat barges and truck driver for the same Memphis company Presley worked for. In 1956 he formed a group with his brother on bass and a friend on lead

16', 'Little Boy Sad'. By the end of '62 his popularity had waned. The success he had found was far removed from his early frantic self. Burnette was the only survivor from the 'old days' and the 'country boy' school, to infiltrate the teeny idol clique. However he did look older, more thickset, and his voice wasn't boyish like the others, but strong and booming and even on one of his hits 'Little Boy Sad' the country influence is strong, so he was never totally accepted as a person by the young fans.

1959—60 also brought the payola scandal and hearings which scared the shit out of every D.J. and ruined many, including the man who pioneered true rock'n'roll to the masses, Alan Freed.

First, Lynn and Johnny pause on the plaza near the park to feed the pigeons. Then...

Dick Clark was strongly accused and someone coined a term which caught on quickly — 'Clarkola'. It was established that Clark 'Was the single most influential person in the popular music industry', and that he was earning more than the president of America. He was involved in a profitable kickback arrangement from his shows, various advertising promotions and vast profiteering. For instance a $63,733 investment of his had returned him almost $600,000 within three years. Prospective witnesses were 'reluctant to talk for fear of reprisals in the form of being denied future opportunity of having their records aired or talents displayed on his programmes.'

Many others were accused of receiving payment direct or indirect, in return for services rendered. Up to now they'd had an easy time. It was one of the most pampered trades in the U.S.

For example, in May 1959 2,500 D.J.'s attended a D.J. and Radio Programming Convention at Miami Beach.

When Lynn closes her eyes all she sees is Johnny's face, smiling at her in her dreams. Suddenly, the door-bell rings, and as if by magic Lynn is standing there completely dressed. She opens the door...

...And there he is! Lynn's dream is coming true; she is about to spend a glorious day with Johnny Aladdin!

In 1964 he went too far updating 'Hootchie Koochie Man' and 'Johnny B. Goode', The later single in a sort of mild acoustic country style, brushes and all, backed with a tremendous version of 'Chicago Blues'. From then on Dion went from the 'Top to obscurity', but he was doing what he wanted, a fatal thing in those days.

Dion made a huge comeback with a No. 2 record in 1968, 'Abraham, Martin & John', on his old 'Laurie' label, a re-union which was to be short-lived. The album which followed was literally an emotional masterpiece simply called 'Dion' and is available on London-American. About that time in America only C.B.S. also released an album of some of their old '63-'66 cuts, many unissued, and they stood the test of time incredibly well. Dion is the only teen idol who has progressed — and I really mean it literally. He has never looked back and since he voluntarily relinquished his stardom, as documented, he went through that period where he was not accepted, but after 'Abraham, Martin & John' which showed that he was

road band. The pianist for a while was Bobby Zimmerman, till Vee sacked him with the words (as the story goes) 'I don't know if you'll make it on your own son, but not with my band.'

By 1964, Vee suffered a slump due to the arrival of the U.K. sound (he even cut an album that year, 'Sings the English Sound'), but emerged rather like Cliff Richard who survives any trend and unnoticed notched up other U.S. hits like 'Look At Me Girl' (1967) and 'Come Back When You Grow Up' (1968). Today he's still on the same label and retains with a bit of effort a boyish quality. The persistent rumour that it is he who sings the never ending Buddy Holly releases from the archives is probably unfounded. Vee's success was due as much as anything to a brilliant producer called Tommy 'Snuff' Garrett. Garrett (the same man who is behind those awful perennial '50 Guitars of Tommy Garrett' albums) must rank as one of the most commercially successful producers and is largely responsible for the

guitar, and, as 'The Johnny Burnette Trio', tried for fame. Sam Phillips of 'Sun' turned them down. 'Your singer acts and looks too much like Elvis' he confided. They headed for New York in a 1940 Ford jalopy, where they secured ordinary jobs while auditioning for talent scouts, etc. They made slow progress, appearing on T.V. ('Steve Allen Show') and in a rock movie, 'Rock, Rock, Rock'. They also cut some 'antastically wild, classic sides for 'Coral', New York, like 'The Train kept 'a Rollin'', 'Honey Hush' (both mid '56) yet somehow, possibly because Burnette was superficially like Presley, he never made it 'big' at that stage.

In 1958, along with brother Dorsey Burnette, he headed for L.A. where they met Ricky Nelson and wrote many songs for him, 'It's Late', 'Just a Little Too Much' and many album tracks. This proving encouraging and lucrative and Burnette, in 1959, got out of his dormant Coral contract and joined Liberty on the West Coast, where he was now based. After three unsuccessful issues he cut 'Dreamin' backed by those pizzicato violins, which sold a million in 1960, and other big hits followed, 'You're

Everything was laid on by about fifty record companies; Hotel suites, women and booze from novel dispensers and everywhere a D.J. went from backslap to backslap, he was told by company executives 'Without you we're dead boy'. It was a paradise for the D.J.'s and a vicious circle for the companies.

In 1959 an R.C.A. man estimated that his firm spent up to $300,000 a year on various methods of forming friendships with D.J.'s. When a 19 year old Neil Sedaka released 'The Diary' (the first of his many pure teen hits) R.C.A. spent $50,000 on the 'full treatment' and 4 weeks later the D.J.'s pushed the disc into the top ten.

Clark was really up against it, but his poised defense to the committee and the unwavering loyalty of his fans reinforced his strength during this period. Although Clark came near to being replaced on 'Bandstand' by A.B.C., his popularity cancelled the decision. Clean-cut Dick continued to be spectacularly active in show business, though his hey-day was over.

An interesting phenomenon was Ral Donner who caused a controversy for a little while by apeing Presley so incredibly well, that thousands believed it was in fact him under a pseudonym. He lasted about nine months with two 'biggies' (Why don't they use words like that) the first a direct cover of a popular Elvis L.P. track 'Girl of My Best Friend', followed by 'You Don't Know What You've Got' (both 1961). Even the most prolific Presley fans were fooled. Ral Donner is cool.

Another guy who began by song-writing and demo recording for others was Gene Pitney in 1959, by recording for the 'Blaze' label as 'Billy Brown'. In 1960 he wrote Ricky Nelson's goldie 'Hello Mary Lou' and 'Today'

They take a long, long walk around the lake — stopping occasionally to day-dream together.

Teardrops' for Roy Orbison. Then he wrote, produced and sang all seven multi-tracked voices on his hit 'Love My Life Away' that same year on 'Musicor' with whom he has stayed ever since. After his initial English hit, '24 Hours to Tulsa', in 1963, Pitney became a fixation with English schoolgirls, in the middle-to-late '60's, until his marriage which seems to have dampened his popularity. Prior to this he was a solely U.S. idol with American hits like 'Every Breath I Take' (1961), 'Man Who Shot Liberty Valance' (1962) and 'Mecca' (1963), and his hairstyle was the greasy, slicked back style, which he dropped in '63 for his familiar Italian style crop.

Young girls in England were fond of Pitney's slick, drama-packed stage act, which consisted of a transfixed facial expression, full of concentration, as he belted out powerful ballads in the soaring monotone, and his English hits include 'I'm Gonna Be Strong', 'Princess in Rags' and 'Backstage'.

Another favourite in the pre-Beatles '60-'62 era, was Brian Hyland, a small teenager (b. 1943) living in New York. At school, aged 12, he formed a group, the Delphis, for local appearances. If you saw him in the street you wouldn't have taken any notice of him, something which

sun begins to set and it's time to go home. Lynn and Johnny find a moment to sit together beneath a friendly tree. Here, whisper their secret thoughts to each other and Lynn feels a tear in her eye, for soon she wake up and her beautiful dream will be over, that is, until tomorrow night.

applied to many of the teen idols. They were ordinary city kids, a few with latent talent, but all with shrewd entrepreneurs.

Yet Hyland became a star through his second record on the 'Leader' label (a subsidiary of 'Kapp' to which he was switched). This was a song which at the time, 1960, would have given any singer a hit, 'Itsy Witsy Teeny Weeny Yellow Polka Dot Bikini'. Monumentally unbearable to many, it became vocal record of the year. Dave Kapp who produced it had bugged its writers to let the unknown Hyland have it, rather than a name artist. Hyland failed to follow it up on subsequent 'Kapp' releases (his follow up, almost identical, was

called 'Lopsided, overloaded and it wiggled when we rode it').

However, when he joined A.B.C.-Paramount in 1961 he was given a series of songs to record which gave him a hat-trick of hits between '61–'62 — 'Ginny Come Lately', 'Sealed With A Kiss' and 'Warmed Over Kisses'. As with most of the others, he hit the skids when the Beatles established themselves in America in '64, but did pop up occasionally like in 1966 when he had a hit with 'The Joker Went Wild'. He is still recording regularly.

Teenybopper songs of this period were all personal comic book tragedies, each one an expose of some local 'bad-girl' or conversely 'girl-stealer', or innocent appraisals of the opposite sex. The titles are

Soon it's snack-time, and Lynn finds herself spellbound as Johnny tells her of his hopes and dreams.

illustrative: Runaround Sue, Jimmy's Girl, Hats Off To Larry, Venus In Blue Jeans, Hello Mary Lou, I Saw Linda Yesterday, Cathy's Clown, Take Good Care Of My Baby.

There were the time-honoured 'sick' songs, once a perennial non-event in pop, inevitably topping the US charts and causing false concern. Such songs as Endless Sleep (1958) TeenAngel (1960) and the classic Tell Laura I Love Her (1961) contain strong melodies which made them more credible and dramatic. TeenAngel is about a couple who scramble from their car after it has stalled at an open level crossing. The chick, unfortunately for her, goes back to get her class pin (symbol of teenage love) and gets bopped by the oncoming train thus becoming the first teenangel, to whom her boyfriend laments in the song. These songs are (or were) essentially an American teen pre-occupation, the last big hit in this style which I can recall being Frank J. Wilson and the Cavaliers' 'Last Kiss' which sold a million in the States on the Josie label, (1964) which told the story of another hideous crash and another dying chick.

As they came into their own, however, hackneyed presentation was accepted and indeed their gentle finger-snapping with one hand while holding the mike with the other was all that was expected. The groups like the 'Crests' ('16 Candles' etc.) & Dion & Belmonts would have corny routines, the harmonists crowding round one mike on a stand while the lead would be the mobile asset.

Bobby Rydell was dynamic in a brassy night clubby way. Very few used guitars on stage but those that did, like the Everly Brothers and Del Shannon, gave a far more concentrated, genuine performance than the contrived acts of the others.

You just had to look sweet and honest, there was no need for sub-

They take a slow walk up the hill, and Johnny explains the technicalities of football to Lynn. Then ...

stance — and this also applied to the albums of the day. That is to say there were no good albums, just a hit and fillers run off within two sessions. Occasionally you'd get a reasonable album, within the idiom, but chances are that it would contain previous singles compounded.

Book covers in pop are not a recent innovation. Presley introduced them

... It's time for a fast ride on the bobby-horses — and Johnny holds Lynn to keep her from falling off.

on his 'Golden Records' album in 1958, and they became fairly regular around 1960, amongst the bigger teen names, with full page pin-ups on each outer cover, carefully posed, blurred and retouched so that by the time you bought the final jacket you may as well have had an oil painting of the artist to gaze at as you listened to your 'instant obsolescence'. R.C.A. 'Teenscene' record player (complete with built-in tone control!) I recall a U.S. issued only L.P. by Jimmy Clanton called 'Jimmy Happy, Jimmy Blue', with a happy-faced Clanton on the front cover and a sad pose on the back and lots of pictures in between. The record played correspondingly. Also the book covers on Bobby Rydell's 'Greatest Hits' albums (Vol. 1 & 2) had removable pre-cut colour pics so that you could take them out leaving a cardboard skeleton of a cover riddled with square gaps — I guess you were supposed to dispose of it like a cornflake packet after you'd cut out the competition form. Every major artist had a presentation book cover album issued, usually at the height of his teen idol stage.

The top teen magazine through the years from its conception in 1959, when such a market began, was '16'. Its editor was a girl, Gloria Winters, who was totally dedicated to supplying the needs of the teens in print. Well set out, with good photographs and varied features it sold very well and provides an excellent who's who in the Teenybop world through the years. It didn't always concentrate on young record

stars but also T.V./movie stars, although the former were predominant. Features like so and so answers 40 intimate questions, or so and so's personal scrap-book 'Why I need someone to love me' by Paul Anka, and so on.

There was also a photo page for newcomers on record (it's interesting to see who made it and who didn't) and a double page pin-up spread in the middle. Funny how they used to pose in those days. Most portraits were deliberately blurred (probably to conceal poxy complexions!), faces were shined up with make-up cream and the lopsided grin/snarl originated by Elvis 4 or 5 years earlier in the rock era and popularised by Ricky Nelson, was favoured.

There was even a section for 'The Bandstand Regulars' a cliquey group of teenagers, mostly couples, who appeared on Dick Clark's 'Bandstand' dancing and talking, etc. They were all local and mostly of Italian extraction and the rule was that on your 16th birthday you had to opt out and be replaced by a younger newcomer.

The essential difference between the new wave of teen idols and their predecessors, the wild men of rock and roll, was that the former had no stage act to speak of, and relied on hit records so that you were literally only as good as your last record. It was a desperate scramble.

But you couldn't blame them — they were just ordinary teenagers pushed from a semi-pro situation straight into the full limelight. When sharing the bills with some of the rockers on whose ground they'd begun to infringe, teen idols such as Jimmy Clanton and Fabian were usually eclipsed by the on-stage dynamics of Jerry Lee Lewis or even unknown but professional rockers.

The age of innocence is gone. Children mature earlier, bubblegum bursts. Love and sex are expressed and represented more than ever on record, but you can't fool anyone — it's easy to tell the honest sentiments from the manufactured, whereas before it was impossible. And while the '70's bring a whole lot of

ex-teen idols disclaiming their past, the breed will always exist, more a minority then in the past, as an outlet for escapism, or for those whose mental faculty, through being too young, does not permit them to appreciate the new higher levels of pop which began with the Beatles and has continued into the '70's.

Yet it's a pity that innocence is gone, for perhaps neurosis is taking its place. I saw a 1961 Cliff Richard movie 'The Young Ones' a few weeks ago and somehow it seemed like 'Alice in Wonderland'.

Anyone interested in further extracts or more details of Teenybopper and Bubblegum music write to Robert Finnis c/o OZ.

Communes, journal of the Commune Movement, issue no 31 out now- the main article is about kibbutzim in Japan, but at last things are beginning to happen in Britain too: new Communes, particularly Urban ones, are emerging at the rate of about one a week. The Commune Movement has only got 150 members so far and needs your support: if you're not ready to start a Commune yet, you could contribute to the Federation Fund which loans or gives money to Communes in temporary need; or you could join the Commune Movement at 30/- a year or subscribe to the journal (18/- a year), or distribute "Communes" in your area (keeping 1/- a copy); at worst, write off to BIT Information Service, 141 Westbourne Park Road, London W.11. (01-229 8219) for a copy of the Journal (bi-monthly at 3/6 post incl.)

Arts Labs Newsletter, issue no 5 out now and if you ever get past the cunt on the cover, inside you'll find Dope from Tim Leary, Suck-noises from Jim Haynes, Video-probes by Hoppy, Living Theatre escapades etc etc. International freaking balanced by news and articles from our very own counter-culture, the 60 or so Arts Labs & related phenomena networking Great Britain. The newsletter loses at least £10 a time so it needs new takers at 2/- a month (post incl.) or £1 a year subscription from BIT Information Service, 141 Westbourne Park Road, London W.11 (01-229 8219).

Three Young men, one aged 23, two aged 27, with own cars, seek female company. Must be interested in motorcycle racing and sex. Write with photo to: Box No. 27 (3).

Hetero Homo Bi Sexual. You state the qualities, we'll send names and addresses of genuine compatible friends. Ring 242 6459 or send £1. Parties-International, 42 Theobalds Road, London W.C.1.

June Mayfield.
How else can I tell you....
Write Box No. 5 (27).

Contraceptives by the manufacturers of Durex. 36 skins £1. 158 Ballards Lane, London N.3.

Fantastic New Offer! introducing Kiki, the gorgeous female model in 10 uniquely daring positions designed to give full satisfaction: Send 20/- P.O. or Cheque. (Payable to: S.M.R. Brolly Only), Connoisseur Art Studies, 38 Crawford Street, W.1.

Cult of the Grove. Send 7/- to Cult Objects, 52 Princedale Road, W.10 for insights into mysterious events affecting us all.

Gay: "Guys Guide", "Physique mag", "Paperback", 10/- each.
John: BM/FBGH, W.C.1.

Rubber News Lives Again.
Whip up enthusiasm. Send £1 now.
Box No. 6 (27).

Concept poetry magazine. 3/-: Roger Falcon, 22 Pembroke Square, W.8.

Find love and marriage through the Ace of Hearts Correspondence Club. S.A.E. for details from: J. Smith, P.O. Box, Heacham-on-Sea, Norfolk.

Star Productions will film, photograph, or design, anything, anywhere, anytime. Phone 603 8581.

The Liverpool Great Georges Project, c/o Huskisson Street, Liverpool 8.
Require people to help/work.
Urgently.

Attractive broadminded young couple, early twenties, with daughter 5, would live to meet other couples to share summer holidays, also weekends. Box No. 4 (27).

The Hidden Path! Contact people, both sexes, in occult, witchcraft, initiation and similar, through our unique service. Gay contacts too! S.A.E. to: Secretary, 101 Blantyre Road, Liverpool 15, Lancs.

Confidential Address—Letters held or forwarded, £1 per month—Secretarial Services, 42 Theobalds Road, London W.C.1. 242 6459.

New Technique overcomes most male difficulties and disorders. It's absolutely unique. End frustration Now. S.A.E. for free details. Box No. 1 (27).

Unwanted Tattoos can be removed at home by D.I.Y. methods. New publication "Removing Tattoos at Home" 10/- explains how. Secretary, Healing Hands, 10 Dryden Chambers, Oxford Street, London W.1.

The Big-Ear device enables anyone to hear through walls, across the street, anywhere. Easily made from readily available materials. Full illustrated instructions 10/-. See all with an easily made "See Through From Behind Mirror". Instructions 10/-. "The United Kingdom Homosexual Meeting Place Directory" is still 10/-. Mailex, 38 Crawford Street, London W.1.

Anyone can obtain employment on an Ocean Liner or Oil Rig. "The Maritime Employment Guide" 7/6 explains how. Seainformation, 12 Kingsgate Road, London N.W.6.

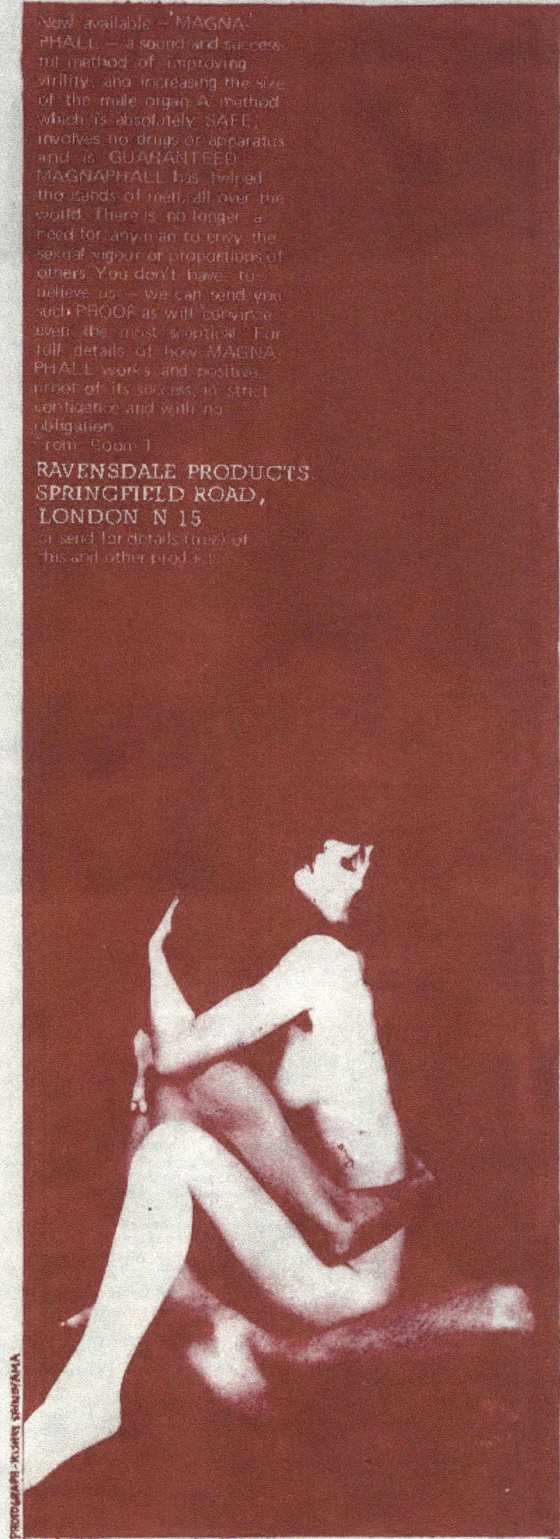

PHOTOGRAPH: Rodney Spring/AMA

WALLACE BERMAN/
CAPE GOLIARD

Satan's slaves read books

Jim Anderson

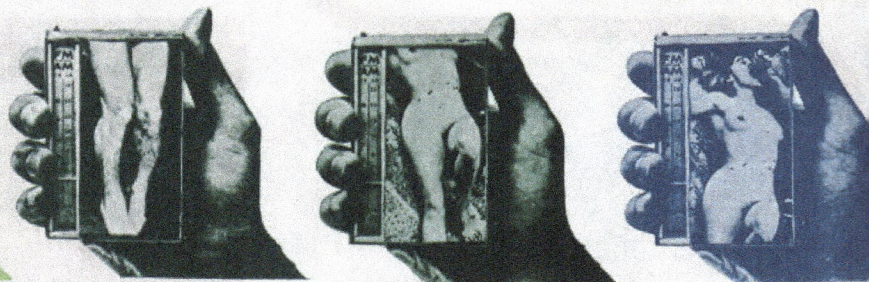

Warm weather arrives and with it an unprecedented flock of books to read. Where are we supposed to read them? Sitting in the sun in Hyde Park or tripping out on mescaline in the country? I suppose publishers make some distinction between what they release in the autumn (tending to be heavier, more polemical, suitable for ploughing through in armchairs before a fire) and what they release in the spring, but the distinction is hardly apparent. The twelve new paperbacks put out by *Paladin* with titles from *The Politics of Ecstasy* to *Russia in Revolution* are clearly aimed to appeal to the Underground and its camp followers, or at least to such of them as can still read. I don't see Lee Heater, for example, getting too much out of Leslie A. Feidler's *Love and Death in the American Novel* (15/-), the basic theme of which is that American literature is incapable of dealing with adult sexuality and is pathologically obsessed with death. If you can get into it, however, you will find the book morbidly fascinating, and will get bitter pleasure from such illustrative extracts as this one, from a novel by Paul Bowles:

"The man moved and surveyed the young body lying on the stones. He ran his finger along the razor's blade: a pleasant excitement took possession of him. He stepped over, looked down and saw the sex that sprouted from the base of the belly. Not entirely conscious of what he was doing, he took it in one hand and brought his other arm down with the motions of a reaper wielding a sickle. It was swiftly severed. A round dark hole was left, flush with the skin; he stared a moment blankly. Driss was screaming."

As well he might. It was almost a relief to turn to Robert Tabor's *The War of the Flea* (7/-) which is a study of guerrilla warfare in both theory and practice—how to fuck-up the system from Cyprus to Cuba. "The guerrilla fighter fights the war of the flea, and his military enemy suffers the dog's disadvantages: too much to defend, too small, ubiquitous, and agile an enemy to come to grips with." It's a good book. Taber was the first journalist to conduct a TV interview with Castro, in the Sierra Maestra, and when the book was published in 1965, the entire first edition was bought up by the US Army. The Viet Cong must use an even better book, or maybe it's just that they don't read at all. Bernard Heuvelmans' *On the Track of Unknown Animals* is all about Abominable Snowmen, Tasmanian Tigers, New Zealand moas, Australian bunyips, giant anacondas, Arctic mammoths, the red-haired pygmies of the jungles of West Africa...the book is fascinating and fantastic (in the literal sense) and after you've read it, visit the zoo and look at the aardvarks; which are just like the monsters that terrify the shit out of you in your worst nightmares. Huizinga's *Homo Ludens* (12/-) is

not as frothy a read as Richard Neville's *Play Power*, but it has never been available here in paperback before and it is the classic study of culture as play and of man's instinct for play (now being developed to an outrageous extent by drop-outs from San Francisco to Goa). Huizinga notes that "modern warfare has...lost all contact with play...genuine play... ought to see civilisation returning to the great archaic forms of recreation where ritual style and dignity were in perfect unison."

The other Paladin book which I liked was Jeff Nuttall's *Bomb Culture*, which as Nuttall himself says "is primarily for squares" who no doubt appreciate remarks such as "the decline of the anti-bomb movement in 1962 left us stranded in the unbearable." The most interesting thing about *Bomb Culture* is the way it illustrates the vast difference between those who were doing their thing before the psychedelic revolt and those whom it caught at the right moment. I wonder if Jeff still drinks as much as he used to. In a 1970 postscript he says

"(1) Underground art, wed as it was in the Arts Lab movement to social and psychological preoccupations, finally drowned in those preoccupations. At the Drury Lane Arts Lab it became difficult to stage events because to many people the theatre was a bedroom and the performers were interlopers. The perpetual recording of pot-smoking and copulation on videotape did little to fill the creative void that was left. Without art the movement died.

"(2) The culture was drowned in a massive commercialisation subtly different from the one which it escaped in the early Sixties. Colossal pop festivals at the Isle of Wight and Woodstock, and the Rolling Stones concert at which four died and four were born, were remarkable for showing that young people had dropped out of one economic power structure into another that was, if anything, more vicious and stultifying. They lay in their thousands, unbelievably docile, whilst the loudspeakers and the cannabis exercised a control more complete than that of any police force,

seemingly unconcerned about the obvious fact that somewhere along the line the man who makes electronic equipment is the same as the man who grows marihuana.

"(3) The culture was drowned in political violence. The Yippies, militant hippies who fought the battles of Chicago and People's Park, Berkley, were led by men like Jerry Rubin and Abbie Hoffman, whose way of thinking was still very largely cultural, a natural development of Haight-Ashbury thinking. Following the Chicago fiasco, however, a branch of the SDS (Students for a Democratic Society) broke away, proclaimed themselves allies of the Viet Cong and declared war formally on the United States. The Weathermen, spurred on by Mark Rudd who was prominent in the Columbia University uprising, but without official leaders or ranks apart from the division into local "chapters" in the manner of Hell's Angels, have wreaked a measure of violence in Cleveden, Detroit, Chicago and New York which the world dare not accurately report... Slogans like: "Get rid of the slime. Grab the time. Power to the people"; like: "Bring the war back home"; like "Off the pig" meaning "Kill coppers" declare a profound hatred for straight society that is perhaps most pointedly expressed in the applause for Sharon Tate's supposed murderer Charles Manson, not only from those cheering teenagers who line the road as for royalty whenever Manson is moved from jail to jail, but also by a women's subsection of the Weathermen, one of whom said "Think of the the beauty of those people eating a meal alongside those stuck pigs."

"The common factor between the Weathermen, the skinheads and Manson's murderous coven (Manson was consciously militant enough to prepare combat vehicles for the Panthers armoured with prepared animal skins) is a compulsive violence which will quickly spend itself unless a culture of violence is kept alive to feed it. Otherwise it becomes the dim reflection of horror in a world where horror is unrelieved.

"For the Western world is so disgraced in the eyes of its children that morality has become a laughable

abstraction and children would rather embrace the Mafia than their own parents. How far is it possible to castrate the bulls of war with their own horns without, oneself, becoming addicted to blood, is the ultimate problem a successful Underground will have to face."

To me that sounds like the same old alcoholic pessimism.

Paladin's twelve new titles have been issued under the belief that there is a an expanding market for this sort of book among young people. They did their market research and they are probably right and tens of thousands of copies will be sold. The fact that there are companies like Paladin to disseminate vast quantities of words to vast quantities of people, enables companies at the other end of the scale, like Cape Goliard, to justify their rather precious existence. Cape Goliard puts out about fifteen titles a year, mostly of poetry from the poetic avant-garde, prints about three thousand of each, sells them at a very reasonable price, considering the beauty and individuality of the book in each particular case, and manages to keep its head above water financially by the sale of signed editions to collectors, who are prepared to pay a lot for those famous signatures. They mostly concentrate on authors who have established a reputation for sound political sense as well as poetic brilliance. People like Michael McClure, Antonio Cisneros, Pablo Neruda, Charles Olson, Adrian Mitchell and Allen Ginsberg. Their edition of Ginsberg's *Wales: A Visitation* has the most beautiful Japanese end papers, from which the curled dark brown wood fibres can be picked with your fingernail. In May, Cape Goliard are putting out William Burrough's film script *The Last Words of Dutch Schultz*, which will cost 16/-, only a shilling more than Paladin's *Pursuit of the Millenium* by Norman Cohn; a cheapness made possible by the fact that the company is run from a converted stable (office, recreation work/play upstairs, printing press downstairs) at Swiss Cottage, by two long-haired guys whose motive is not so much profit as preservation of works which they regard as valuable. I'm all for ephemerality myself, but I suppose there is room in art for a sense of history, a refined taste, and Art with a capital A. Cape Goliard has a nice medieval flavour about it, and what they are doing could well be emulated by the hippie communes scattered about affluent western society, who should be able to come to terms with mechanisation enough to get along with a printing press.

Leonard Cohen's *Beautiful Losers* (paperback) is available at last in England. I haven't had time to read it, but Clem Weight who has, found it "rich, sexy, and satisfyingly light-hearted", with lots of mind-blowing erotic episodes. It's loosely written, introspective, very Canadian, and worth buying.

32

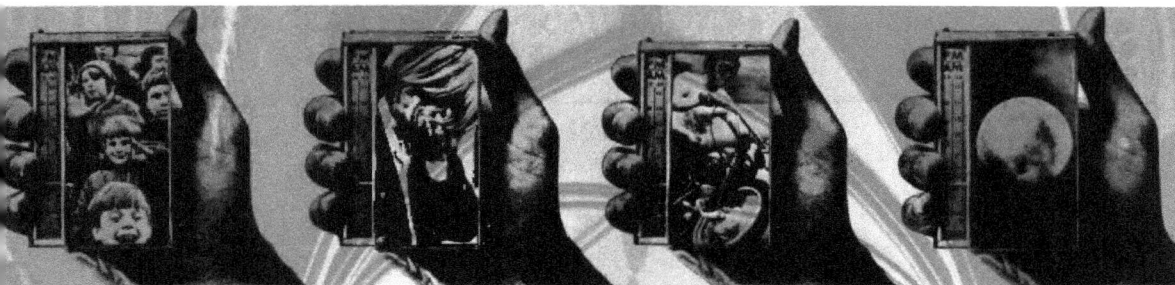

Crazy Otto sheds his guilt

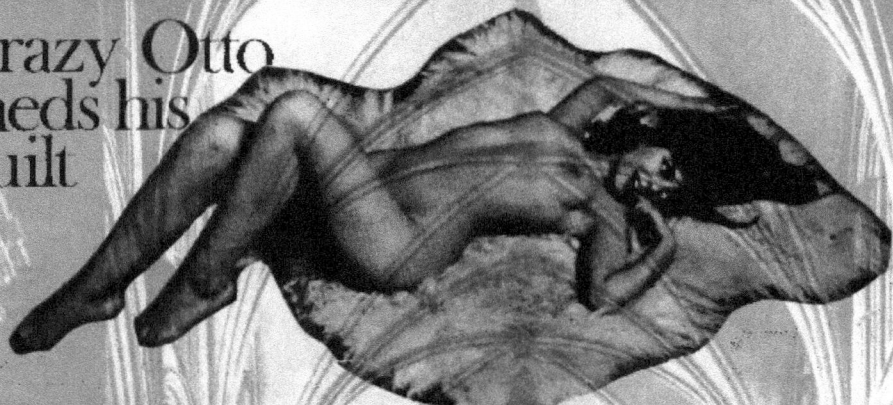

When London bobbies nabbed Warhol's *Flesh* at the Open Space, the double standard sham of British film censorship was exposed without being resolved. Since Britain has no constitution guaranteeing freedom of expression, as in the United States, a Supreme Court decision (such as will probably eventuate from the nabbing of Warhol's *Fuck* (*Blue Movie*) by New York cops) will not define cinema's freedom, and London will lag far behind Copenhagen as a centre for free expression.

The screening of Andrew Noren's *Kodak Ghost Poems* late one night in the same month as *Flesh* was busted as part of a New American Cinema program at the NFT points up the double standard. For *Kodak Ghost Poems* contains scenes of sexual explicitness much more offensive to police standards than Joe D'Allasandro's hard on in *Flesh*. Noren's self-revealing camera records close-up views of his wife's cunt, his prick as she blow-jobs him, and their interlocked genitals in a back-bending fuck. This film is not offered as part of the official touring program of the New York Museum of Modern Art, currently playing in European cities, but there is no reason for *Moma's* Larry Kardish to fear in Germany, for film-makers of the European underground regularly screen films of much heavier content without fear of prosecution: Germany seems likely to soon follow Denmark's example and abolish the pornography clause from its legal code.

The strongest films of the German underground are of happenings by Vienna artist Otto Muehl, forced by Austrian repression to perform his actions in Germany, where the outraged bourgeoise find police unwilling to back their puritan cause. Films of actions of Muehl are records for posterity, weapons in sexual liberation able to shown in places Otto can't perform. They function like the American Marxist *Newsreels*, as propaganda capable of infiltrating wide areas of consciousness.

For Otto Muehl (and most Viennese film-makers) film is "Shit...a technical means of recording". Otto is unimpressed by "the magnetic attraction to idiots" that film has, and his feature *Sodoma* (1970) is a collection of previous films, anthologising his most scandalous works in an assault on audience sensibilities. Muehl is concerned to make scandals, to make audiences aware of their own "conventionally perverted attitudes, to make them aware of the stupidity of paying to see another man fuck, and hovering on the outside instead of participating in the action themselves.

"I'm for lewdness, for the demythologisation of sexuality... I'm against the philistine porno-film, against pornography of the businessman," says Muehl, and to prove it he fucks, shits, pisses, and masturbates on stage in orgies faithfully recorded by Kurt Kren, Ernst Schmidt, Hans Scheugl and other film-making compatriots. In *Sodoma* one can see Otto pissing on a girl, being shat on by another, having shit rubbed in his face, fucking a woman covered in blood, vegetables and garbage, filling cunts with eggs, sausages, metal rods, and (predictably) pricks. In this film is also an action by exiled Viennese artist Gunter Brus, where he gains "satisfaction" shitting from a surreal wheeled contraption. Dr. Peter Gorsen, a German authority on erotic art, appears in another action in drag, masturbating as his wife shits in Otto's face before blowing him.

The films of Otto Muehl are as much against the fashionable wife-swapper, as against the rigid puritan. If you enjoy swinging group-sex, go to Vienna to one of Crazy Otto's orgies. You will find your wife painted, sprayed, vomited on, and probably murdered, for Muehl sees this as much the right of artists as it already is for politicians and scientists. In *Silent Night* (Hans Peter Kockenrath 1970) a Muehl Christmas action is recorded, showing the slaughter of a live pig on stage, its hot blood

splattered over Muehl's wife, and its entrails stuck in her cunt preparatory to Otto fucking her.

Such use of blood and carcasses suggest the work of another Viennese artist, Hermann Nitsche, whose Munich action of March 1970 has been filmed by Ed Sommer. Nitsche is regarded by Jonas Mekas as "the greatest living playwright" and his *Orgy Mysteries Theatre* is a cathartic ritualisation of man's sin and guilt, acting out man's bloodlust in hideous reminders of Vietnam and the Crucifixion. Nitsche lives in exile in Berlin, fearful of imprisonment in Vienna, as happened to Muehl and other artists of the Vienna Institute for Direct Art.

Ed Sommer, who filmed Nitsche's Munich action a few hours before police arrived to try and prevent it, makes films with his wife Irm as weapons in the fight for sexual liberation and the abandonment of Germany's pornographic laws. *The Breast* (1969) and *Rhythmus* (1970) feature close-up shots of breasts and cunts being fondled by feminine hands. *Striptease and Emancipation* (1969) shows a conventionally erotic striptease, while a voice reads Women's Liberation demands, attacking the voyeurism that such films invoke. *The German Mother* (1969) intercuts Danish pornographic photos with shots of a pregnant woman, a comment on the maternal enslavement of the traditional family concept.

In these German and Austrian underground films, sexuality is "not a state-preserving sacrament, but a mere physical function". Like the films of the Viennese *Expanded Cinema* group, and *Screen* in Cologne, they are anti-aesthetic,

against concepts of beauty ("romantic") and against established concepts of film as art. They are being made at a time when Hollywood produced titillating sexual fetish fantasies, and the aesthetic spawn of Hollywood from New York to Europe produce sexploitation flicks which in an honest system would be screened in mastabatoriums rather than in the plastic palaces of commercial cinema.

The cause of these anti-artists is admirable, their fight courageous, but the destructive methods of its application are fearful. Revolutionaries who kill and destroy are anti-life, anti-being. Not surprisingly, these anti-artists are not turned on, and are all of the over-thirty generation. They are acting out the guilt and bewilderment of their decaying society, clearing the way for younger artists to create new art for the new social consciousness. Their films are valuable weapons in the revolution.

Albie Thoms

GERONIMO

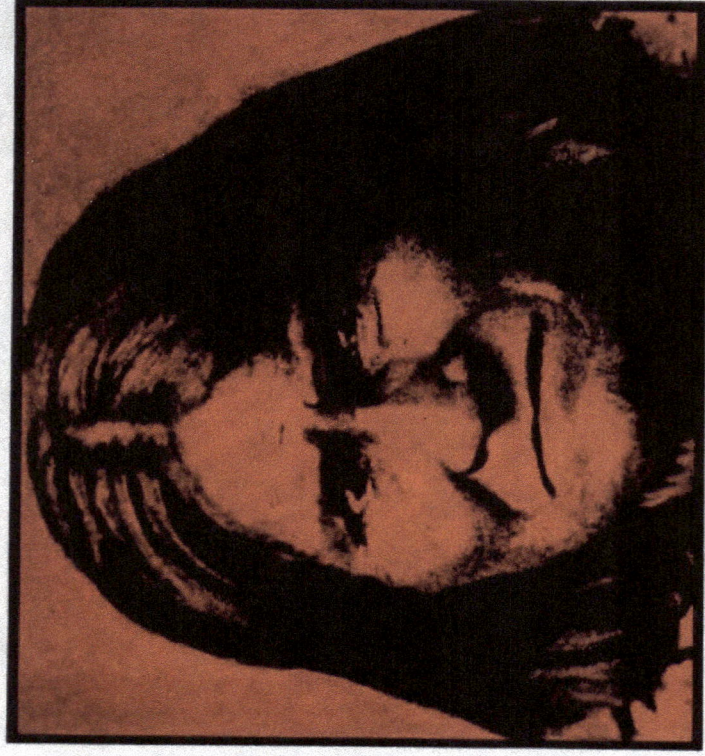

205 METRES M/W

TESTING SATURDAY MIDNIGHT ONWARDS

GUERRILLA BOP
Record Reviews

Permanent Damage G.T.O.'S

I read Miles' review of this record in IT 74 three times, carefully, once I even read it using a dictionary and I didn't understand it. Not all of it anyway. But then I ain't over been to America, and this is an America record. Or rather an AMERICAN record; you know, the AMERICA which equals Capital A for Acid / versus Capital M for Mace / out to Capital E exterminate / the fucking Capital Race, . . etc. But Miles is right when he says that it's difficult to take.

The problem here is one of digestion and constipation, i.e. what you can stomach and how long it takes to register what shit you're eating. Ice Cool Coke refreshes you best and brown rice is boring but sure as hell the Viet Cong are winning that war.

Anything with Zappa's muscle power in evidence, (the small print says he produced this L.P.), almost always turns out to be essential listening sooner or later — and all too often it *is* later — witness the cruel demise of the Mothers of Invention. America's most original rock band who could wipe their ass with Creadence Clearwater and leave the Zeppelin standing in the first dozen bars, entirely due to lack of support and money. (The Archies live, their Mother's dead; there's no business like the music business). But even bearing in mind that Frankie's efforts often require time to infiltrate, 'Permanent Damage' is still hard to take. At least, too hard to take all at once.

Basically this record is twenty-nine minutes and twenty eight seconds of sound collage from five chicks who make up Girls Together Outrageously, (G.T.O.'s), that's Miss Pamela, Miss Sandra, Miss Cinderella, Miss Christine and lawdy miss clawdy Miss Mercy. They sing whimsy, paranoid songs and rap, often self-consciously, amongst themselves about AMERICA /high school/balling/bobby sox/balling/soft consumer environment/cars/balling/T.V./stuffed bras/balling/pop stars and, you guessed it, pop stars balling. They're at their best, their funniest, (though I guess this record isn't about being funny), on subjects close to their heart, i.e. adolescence, adolescents and balling. The telephone conversation with the Plaster Casters of Chicago is a joy but the music. . . .?. . .well that's another trip altogether. If it's parody, it's stretching the bubblegum a little too tight for me, and if it's not, then what in Christ Jesus is Zappa playing about with? (O.K., don't answer that, I know. . . .our heads.)

But no body knows what is happening in America, least of all on an island 4000 miles away, separated both in terms of distance, and more important, by a lying, corrupt media, printing only the news they feel is

'fit to print'. How many times have we watched a five-relay satellite transmission of a ghetto riot, of armoured cars rumbling through the streets of Berkeley, or the Weathermen and State Troopers dancing their fearful, deadly pas de deux. Funny how we only get to see moon capsules and Royal visits isn't it? But just occasionally we're given a fleeting glimpse, of near-naked reality in the U.S., and as often as not it's through American music, or their tough, professional underground press. That's what this record is all about, and that's why, although I don't like to admit it, this record leaves me scared shitless.

Felix Dennis.

Volunteers Jefferson Airplane

In the States they so nearly have a revolution. Everything there is so wired up it's ready to blow. The Jefferson Airplane is a body of people who have always been very involved in the American front, and now, for those of us who might still doubt it, they have finally declared themselves Volunteers.

The album starts with their thumbs up/thumbs down song of the revolution, 'We Can Be Together'. ('up against the wall motherfucker — tear down the wall...'). They use their unique Airplane harmonies and straining guitar/piano, the sound that brought together the West Coast. This song holds so much energy — Nicky Hopkins hammering, Jorma like an immense electric crow and Grace and Marty Balin shouting and stomping, ending with that ultimate question posed on 'Baxters', 'Won't You Try?'

From then on the album assumes that you have already tried. It takes you through the Airplane at their best and most thoughtful, with some fellow conspirators, (like Garcia, Crosby, Hopkins and Stills) and finally leaves you, in the last song, Volunteers, with a direction — 'come on now, we're marching to the sea, got a revolution, got to revolution.

'Volunteers' is a very complete trip — the lyrics harness the spirit of our revolution and merge perfectly with some powerful and ego-free instrumentation and production. This is to a great extent due to Grace Slick's ability to use her voice as an instrument, and on 'Volunteers' she leaves behind even the best of 'Baxters' or 'Crown of Creation' — listen to 'Hey Frederick'.

The marvellous thing about people like the Airplane or the Dead is their commitment, which is the source of most of their power — and this is where it's at with many of the best American groups; whereas in England we have half of the Beatles retiring into photogenic middle-age or the Stones caught in the dazzle of swinging London. In

'Volunteers', the wired-up, freaky power cannot fail to hit you, (just listen to it anywhere near some acid), and will ultimately force you into commitment. Feed and water your flag.

Paul Bandey.

Mona Mick Farren

When Felix asked me to do this piece I was somewhat apprehensive, since it is totally impossible to view ones own work objectively. All I can really do is attempt to explain my motives for producing the album and leave it to the listener to assess whether or not it succeeds in its purpose.

In the middle fifties our western culture underwent a change with the advent of rock-and-roll, the event that Eldridge Cleaver describes as 'a new awareness and enjoyment of the flesh, a new appreciation of the possibilities of the body. . .'. The underground is essentially the product of this awareness, and it is this same awareness that has made this generation resist the conditioning that seeks to turn it into a docile, un-thinking labour force. Our administrators have become alarmed at this situation and it is their panic that becomes manifest in incidents like the Chicago and Berkaly riots and the enforcement of the narcotics law to the point of absurdity.

This is the basic story on the album, the use of Bo Diddley's 'Mona' treated in a primitive, almost tribal manner, attempts to state the essential physical awareness. The rest of the material illustrates the paranoia that has been forced upon us as a result of this awareness. Much of the material has been randomly recorded and by its juxtaposition with the rest of the track produces discords and often warring relationships in terms of sounds. Fear, however, is not a tidy, precise emotion; it is desperate, shifting and irregular. There is little harmony in the life in which the threat of the MAN coming to take you away is ever present.

Even 'Summertime Blues', which starts the second side, is a reiteration of the same paranoid state. In the Fifties it was not fear of arrest that was used in the main to force us to conform, we were younger then and it was parental pressure. . . 'You can't use the car to go riding next Sunday'... which sought to keep us in line.

The album ends with a restatement of the essential tribal rock version of 'Mona' with which it began, as the only hope within the current situation — to cling to that essential physical togetherness and that though it we might survive.

Mick Farren.

Grateful Deadly
Record reviews

Live/Dead: The Grateful Dead

I can think of no extant rock band with as impressive a mythology as that of the Dead; their name evokes a darkly glamorous collection of names — Owsley, Kesey, Leary, Tom Wolfe, Hell's Angels. It's hard to say whether this double is an attempt to be the iconoclast or the celebration of this myth. On the sleeve the ears of that live legend vaporise into the skull and crossbones and a regal ghost rises from a coffin that might just as well have 1967 written on its open lid, the sleeve and there are all the people really out there in the street — no bells, no paint, but arms and fingers up in the air like a field of stubble. And yet the music has an intelligence and a beauty (of the unselfconscious and uncapitalized variety) that does not belong to that era at all, nor does it have the aggressiveness that now has its currency with Zappa, Beefheart, Love and other survivors of the times. Listening to it, though, it is difficult to cut aside the feel of the past, especially when the Dead themselves slip back so easily into it, as on 'Death don't have no mercy' which is very close to their first L.P. (and incidentally, reminiscent of Country Joe and the Fish).

The Dead have been developing along a line tangential to the mainstream heavies of most rock. 'Anthem to the Sun' and 'Aoxomoxoa' explored and used rather than made, music and it was good, generally, although it was often inaccessible and uninteresting. Some of this remains too; 'Feedback' is basically exactly that, and eight minutes of it becomes boring, but this is the only self-indulgent thing on the double, and I find it surprising, really. But it is live, and there are people listening and yelling, and you have to play human music to a streetful of people.

Contrary to recent reports, there are only 2 tracks on this album. The first one lasts three sides, and by the end of it the band is rather tired. The first side is called 'Dark Star' and is very good indeed; in fact, it sets a standard that the rest of the album doesn't accomplish. Garcia dominates this number, as he does throughout. He plays beautifully, lyrically, and with what can only be described as taste. 'Dark Star' is really a very long (23 minutes) guitar solo, punctuated twice — almost gratuitously — by a couple of lines of vocal and backed by equally improvised percussion. It ends as arbitrarily as it begins, and Garcia hardly changes pace or volume all the way through, yet I have seldom heard so satisfactory a piece of music. It establishes an almost coincidental but obviously very familiar relationship between the musicians, and it is exactly this relationship that makes the record so good.

'Star' becomes 'Saint Stephen' and 'The Eleven' on side two and fades into a mock rumba, which, when you turn the record over, becomes recognizable as 'Turn on your love-light', a long, rambling semi-scatalogical version of the soul number with heavy drums, lots of shouting, wind-up bass lines, talking to the audience, the whole bit. It is the climax to the L.P. and it almost falls flat on its face. There are a couple of near-disasters from the rhythm section (not easily mistaken for clever stuff) and Garcia's address to the crowd:

You fellers may have a little trouble/
Wake up in the mornin' have
no-one by your side/
But that's your fault, ain't none
of mine . . . unless I stole her/
But you better take your hands
out of your pockets,
Yeah, I said you better take your
hands out of your pockets

One is tempted to add: or here's that sly audience that plays trouble billiards is likely to go to see a working band. But somehow or other it survives, it's not particularly well played and it's pretty self conscious but it's done with such drive, such enjoyment and joy that it makes sense and it makes you uncritical. I suppose that 'Turn on your lovelight' is also a throwback to their first L.P., 'Morning Dew' and 'Good Morning Little Schoolgirl' and stuff like that, and the predominant, its own feel makes me suspect that it's really where the Dead is at.

which is a bit surprising. Side Four has the beautiful 'Death don't have no mercy'. So here you have the remnants of the Grateful Dead, the Beautiful Acid band, the Electronic Buzz band, and even the 'In the Streets And Rocking band'. It's a record to buy for the same reasons as you buy all the Beatles' albums, or go to see the latest Antonioni film — not for a purely emotional experience or a purely aesthetic experience or to bolster a dream of joyous amateurish jubilation blocking the streets of Wigan, but just to know where the really important bands are standing, on the corners of which roads.

Mel Platt

Your Saving Grace: Steve Miller Band

Where is the beautiful Steve Miller of yesteryear, those floating melodies, the surging, settled rhythms that used to flow from the Wharf dance? Where are the Living in the U.S.A.'s, the Children Of The Future's, even the Kow Kow's? Where are those wonderful Saturday afternoons in the old Blue's shuffling to the ever-popular Songs for our Ancestors? Guilt there so shut up and pass the joint.

Your Saving Grace is no advance on Brave New World, decisively simpler in style, but much stronger. Nicky Hopkins is contributing even more to the Miller sound. His compatability with Miller grows and grows. Brave New World was a sharp drop from Sailor, but Your Saving Grace is back with the class, well Nicky's help. There's an old mate of Miller's on keyboards as well called Ben Sidran. It seems Keyboards are King.

Miller's four albums are remarkably similar in style considering the very superficial changes that have been tossed around in music in the last two years. His change has been towards into simpler presentations. This is the reverse of the Beatles for instance, where they compacted the parts, he's separated them, no more of the

foreshortening of a change of gear, which used to be one of the Miller hallmarks. No more of between track transitions, just straight Steve. This also means whatever you've got — it's all showing. And Miller's faults become blatant; the occasional oversweet melody or voices, the obvious borrowing of the rhythms. But the world's unfolding, in the middle of 'Baby's House' it's as good as anything on side two of Abbey Road and the introduction of Tim Davis on drums and bass is incomparable.

Now it's possible for Decca to do the cover of a new group for the first two months with an equal quality to be put on a U.S.A. pattern to a new American L.P. — being released much more quickly. Why? Because there is so much garbage around, disposal will have got to flood the market and get a return, or when the quality is poor, increase the quantity so people won't lose interest.

Reemer Miller: Where it's all about I'm not falling to the strains of past sentiments and early reminiscences of the fifties he is holding the torch for the future. See tracks 1 and 4 both sides.

T.R. Zelinka

AN OLD RAINCOAT WON'T EVER LET YOU DOWN — ROD STEWART

Rod Stewart, on the rebound from Wardour Street Box/Bomber days, this head, right, hooped with nest. Back combed hair, reminiscent of pill style. You never before him, became a comedian and comfort. He was just a hose and roll star, Rod. 'The Mod' working the pub circuit with the rooting Steam Packet, Aaaah blasting his Hammond, Mike Driscoll dramatico chords and spluttering tambourines and head and shoulders above the rest, big bad dy Baldry, all the down you sell out rock and roll — Cyril Davis is turning in his grave), belting out them Hoochie Coochie's, Woke in to Big Muff's, Remember British R & B?

A mod singing the blues? Full of our crises is good, joining Jeff Beck for

instance, though certainly it produced a combination, which musically speaking justified Stewart's uneasy personal relations with Beck. (Recently Rod commented to a Rolling Stone reporter, '. . . I never once looked him in the eyes offstage . . .') And now, stepping into Stevie Marriott's shoes, though nobody could doubt his ability to fill them. On paper it might look crazy but a surprising number of people, myself included, had a lot of respect for that new Small Faces touch; and Rod could cut more through so many changes. 'Flea folk 'Raincoat' album, recorded just prior to his final States tour with Beck, showing, so say, about an L.P. that comes straight out of the blues and leaves you scratching your head wondering why he never did it before.

It's not the title and you get to know what this record's all about. Five of the compositions are by Rod himself and note that he amongst them — anyway, would make a respectable group's starting arrangement of Mike D'Abo, (swinging to date, rhinobees and chords). (With D'Abo setting in on piano) a gutsy, earthy evaluation of 'Man Of Constant Sorrow' (other McFarland King with the lyrics audible at long last and is an amazing last track, 'the Kitchen folk ballad by Ewan McColl, Dirty Old Town'. Somehow you can tell Stewart's in love with that song, tossing it like he does he must have wanted to record it badly. For years, All backed superbly, Martin Pugh and Martin Quittenton on guitars, Ian Maclagan on piano and organ and Ron Wood and Michael Waller blowing together on bass and drums like they'd been members of the same band for years. This record has hardly left my turntable since it arrived. Its unique in its unconscious merging of so many forms of music, traditional folk, (Rod's first roots and love) sung in that harsh, gritty blues voice and supported on yet actual, world-renowned, hard driving English electric rock, at its head-wrecking best. Life's full of surprises.

Felix Dennis

don't compromise, because the music doesn't.

lock

santana

spirit

acific gas & electric

hicago

anis joplin

aura nyro

ohnny winter

aj mahal

THE SOUND OF THE SEVENTIES

CBS

'LAN
MON & GARFUNKEL
'RDS
OOD SWEAT & TEARS
IKE BLOOMFIELD
KOOPER

LEONARD COHEN
MOBY GRAPE
TIM HARDIN
SLY & THE FAMILY STONE
CHAMBERS BROTHERS
FILLMORE

CBS Records, 28/30 Theobalds Road, London W.C.1

alone or together

THE SOUND OF THE SEVENTIES

Al Kooper: composes, arranges, performs, produces his own music and records. Alone on "You never know who your friends are". Together with Mike Bloomfield on "Super Session". Also on "Live Adventures of Mike Bloomfield and Al Kooper."

Mike Bloomfield: writes his own words and music. Plays guitar, piano, sings. Alone on "It's not Killing Me." Together with Al Kooper on "Super Session" and "The Live Adventures of Mike Bloomfield and Al Kooper."

THE LIVE ADVENTURES OF MIKE BLOOMFIELD AND AL KOOPER (S) 66216

BLOOMFIELD/KOOPER/ STILLS: SUPER SESSION (S) 63396

KOOPER: YOU NEVER KNOW WHO YOUR FRIENDS ARE (S) 63651

BLOOMFIELD: IT'S NOT KILLING ME (S) 63652

REMEMBER CHICAGO

A group called Chicago.
The group responsible for one of the biggest packages
of tight, rock music we've ever released. Two records
and every track is there for a reason. Electronic music.
Blues. Rock. Rock. Rock. A powerful brass section. And musicians
who are capable of playing solid, no-gimmick music.
"Chicago Transit Authority" A two-record set.

CBS THE SOUND OF THE SEVENTIES

CHICAGO TRANSIT AUTHORITY
(S)66221

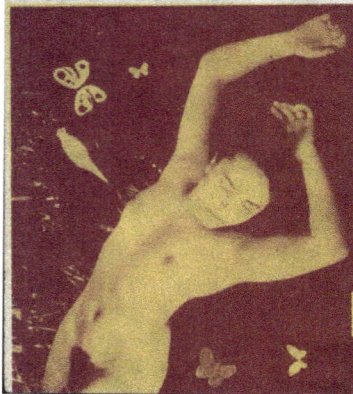

OZ 27
April 1970
OZ is published by OZ Publications Ink Ltd.
52 Princedale Road, London W.11.
Telephone: 229 7541
Advertising: Contact Felix Dennis at 727 8456
Subscriptions: Send 42/- or 6 dollars for 12 issues to above address
Printed by OZ Publications Ink Ltd

Distribution:
UK: Moore Harness Ltd, 11 Lever Street London EC1, CLE 4882
Transunion Guildford 65694
California: Rattner Distributors 2428 McGee St Berkley California 94703
Holland: Van Calderen Amsterdam
Denmark: George Streeton. The Underground, Larsbjorn Straede 13.

This issue appears with the help of Jim Anderson, Richard Neville, Felix Dennis, David Wills, Gary Brayley and Bridget Murphy

PHOTOGRAPHED ON PRIMROSE HILL BY DAVID NUTTER

SPEND MONEY!

We have bound six copies of OZ 1-21, two of which are on sale to the public. Only complete ones of their kind, in embossed red leather. £30 for each set. Inquiries at OZ.

Send 42s or 6 dollars to 52 Princedale Road, London W.11. If you take out two subscriptions (one for a friend) it will cost you only 70s, or you can have a 24 issue subscription for only 65s. This is a special offer, strictly limited to this coupon.

Back Issues: Most back issues are now totally sold out. We have a few copies still available of the following:
No. 5 Elephant size Flower Child Poster—very rare bargain at £1.
No. 9 Flying Saucers UFO freak-out; No. 15 Mick Jagger, Jimi Hendrix, Fliptop legal pot; No. 16 Magic Theatre Oz.
No. 17 Ball blowing chicks and lesbian cover;
No. 18 Anglefood McSpade and Marrakech love-in.
No. 19 The Groupie Oz; No. 20 Hells Angels; No. 24 Beautiful Freaks.
ALL AT 3/6 each. Every one a collector's dream.

SUBSCRIBE

To: OZ, 52 Princedale Road, London W.11.

I enclose 42s/6 dollars for a normal subscription (12 issues)

I enclose 70s/10 dollars for two normal subscriptions (one for a friend)

I enclose 65s/9 dollars for a special 24 issue subscription.

My Name is: _____

I live at: _____

its nice here.

4s

OZ

SCHOOL
KIDS
ISSUE

28

SCHOOL KIDS OZ?

This OZ has been put together with the help and inspiration of about twenty people, all 18 or under, mostly still at school who came from various parts of London and England in answer to our appeals for injections of youthful vigour in our ageing veins. We were half expecting a crowd of revolutionary high school bomb throwers, United States style, but England is England and although we got one 100% hippie complete with blue satin, beads and bells and a job at the Roundhouse, some of them actually liked school, and others were cagey about using their real names or upsetting their dear old school too much. Get those A levels kiddies! However we all had a fantastic month doing it, milling around weekend after weekend in true communal style, gradually getting all the copy together, the drawings, the photographs, the freak-outs. OZ was hit with its biggest dose of creative energy for a long time. Have a look at the Rupert Bear strip. Youthful genius. Read Charles Shaar Murray's double page, Head Books, and Jeff Beck, Truth is Blue — a natural journalistic wizard. Trudi was disillusioned with the Schools Action Union, (Please Sir May I Be Excused) but what real activists can stir up in the school playground makes the guerrilla theatre story (The Return of King Kong) a strong indictment of the manner in which school teachers exercise their authority. More freedom was everybody's cry — get rid of the primitive examination system (Xmam Blues) get rid of teachers who can't see beyond their own prejudices (Headmaster of the Year); give us the freedom to smoke, to dress, to have sex, to run school affairs. From America, Tom Lindsay's revolutionary call to arms, High School Confidential, which reflects to a greater or lesser extent exactly what most of the school children we worked with are thinking about. OZ itself suffered a heavy critical assault (OZ Sucks. . .) but on the whole everyone who worked on the issue enjoyed the chaotic anarchistic anti-authoritarian way in which the issue was put together, and we hope it reminded them of the sort of fun school can be and only too rarely is. Now read on. .

PROFILES   (by each other)

John Dreyer, 16. Born at Golders Green. Circumcised but not Jewish. Finds atmosphere at school impersonal and oppressive. Thinks the head master is bullied by the rest of his staff. Generally bored with living and his main love is drawing cartoons.

Anne Townsend, 16, Farnborough.
Says she is a bitch. Claims to like Je blooze. Hang-ups about blokes. Hates her parents, turns on regularly, reads Oz, IT and Petticoat. 'I want all the freedom I can get', but will conform to anything as long as she gets something out of it.

Rob January, 16, Scorpio, from Highgate, at present undergoing comprehensive education. Doesn't read much at the moment because of lack of time. Listens to Hendrix, Quintessence, Soft Machine and thinks Zappa 'plays incredible wah-wah'. Would like to see Enoch Powell get a divorce and marry a very black woman.

Has many obscene ideas but can't put them down 'cos can't draw. . .

Enjoys working for OZ (Slurp, Slurp) even though he does 'fuck-all'. Dislikes school 'cos of skinheads and infantile head master. However wants to become eminent chemist someday. . .

Eddie Allen, 18, Aldershot. Long dark hair, frequently wears a bottle green WRAC coat. Studying civil engineering at Farnborough Technical College. Thinks he gets pissed too often. Intends to go to University and then bum around because he doesn't want to work. Believes
God is a gnome. Likes freaking out the Establishment. Reads Isaac Asimov. 'I want to start my own commune for happy people.'

Robb Douglas, 18, Hornsey. Working class background. Works with physically handicapped people. Suppressed intelligence, but knows he is going to be famous. Likes making people happy. 'Sometimes my mind goes a complete blank.'
Hang-ups: Getting bread and finishing projects.
Feels sorry for his parents, skinheads, and people generally, in that order.
Likes animals and unpolluted countryside.
Beliefs: Agnostic. Also the theory of intergalactic beings.

Stephen Williams, 17, Farnborough.
Taking three A levels (French, Sociology, Art) but wants to get his education over and done with as soon as possible. Tried dropping out in Morocco for a few months. Didn't work, kept bumping into straight friends. Has never dropped acid and doesn't want to until he comes to a dead-end.

Henry Harcus, 18, Bradford. Long haired activist from University. Burnt his mind on a recent acid trip. Very valuable ideas. Rejects his parents values and way of life, but tries to enlighten without. Someone to get to know.

Alex Darcy, 17, Reading. An original mind hidden behind an entirely self-constructed bushel. Reacts against 'tie-dye shirt and velvet trousers conformity' by wearing army boots and waving Temperance Seven albums. Enjoys blowing people's minds at hip gatherings by saying 'Actually, I agree with Enoch Powell'. The result is something like 'the man who ordered a steak at the macrobiotic restaurant'. Has stereo but no BBC 2.

Berti, 15. Aldershot. Pisces. Female despite name. Small dark, fragile and very beautiful, fringes and velvet. Amazing artist. Very gentle, very quiet. Her ideal life-style involves the formation of a commune. Her instinct is towards trusting people rather than not. Is secure about herself 'up to a point'. Likes all colours, wears brown. Tries to be happy, deserves to be. Hello.

Photo's by David Nutter

4

Cary Richardson, 18, Reading. A gentle egoist. An artist with a fertile bizarre imagination. He writes a lot of poetry which he rarely shows people, and songs which he never sings except to an ever-changing audience/entourage of 2 chicks. An erratic but extraordinary folk guitarist. He's never read an Oz in his life.

Trudi, 15, Reading. An unconventionally beautiful blonde with a nose that is the envy of all her Jewish friends, and the world's prettiest navel. Worries about 'running after' people, and so she goes to the other extreme and is rather stand-offish at first. Intensely realistic about her school work, intends to get a degree and undoubtedly will. Journalistic ambitions. 'One of the most real and worthwhile people on the planet.' —Charles Murray.

Charles Shaar Murray, 18, Reading. He's a Jewish Pantheist. Doesn't turn on because he has weak lungs. Says he is a clumsy lover. 'I have all the sex appeal of a mouldy sock.' Believes in the brotherhood of man and the dawning of the age of Aquarius. Starts a journalism course in the autumn.

Peterpophamdeyansudjic Colinthomas was born variously, according to different reports, in Whitton, the Republic of Ireland and Yugoslavia. He enjoyed a decadent if subdued youth and emerged finally, self-satisfied and elitist, as the hard-core of the Latymer Upper School intellectual group, having monopoly over the school mag, the art department and the Boat Club. He now spends the greater part of his time meditating in the local caff, plotting spiritual revolution and talking to himself. His future is uncertain; whether he will become a £5,000-a-year architect, an advertising executive or a scrap merchant is not yet clear.

Viv Kylastron, 16, Aries. Smoked at 9, first tripped at 11. Owes this to the Roundhouse and Bradford. An anarchist, trying to dissolve it and replace it with a living school. Came to Oz to meet Richard Neville and the others, also interested in the workings of Oz. Interested in mysticism.

Chris Allen, 17, Tottenham. Works for the GPO only because he needs the money. Turns on. Wants to do something he really likes doing, and get paid for it. 'I just want to be happy'

Candida, 16, Reading. Taurus, but thinks astrology is 'a load of crap'. Present life-style: 'weekend dropout'. Claims to be average(?). Her relationship with her parents is 'pretty good', has moral complaints about school, but accepts it when she's there. Reads Waugh, de Beauvoir, Lawrence, listens to 'literally everything'. Never reads Oz but looks at the pictures.

Steve Lavers, 16. Belongs to an awkward cusp of Taurus – Gemini which he disregards completely. He tends to be anarchistic although usually speaks a lot and does fuck all. He enjoys drawing cartoons of a perverted nature and retains an extremely sick humour. At the risk of seeming a teeny-bopper frequents concerts by Quintessence. Hopes sometime to work in films but not on the practical side as he usually pisses everything up.

T.I. Bradford – a Leo with Gemini (?) rising. His first names are The Incredible. He is known by practically everyone, in the infamous 'underground' as a generous anarchist. After being expelled (for being human) he left Bradford Grammar School and Bradford and came to London, where he worked at the Roundhouse, started his own bookstall, helped the Electric Cinema, lived at Drury Lane Arts Lab and did everything else (perhaps he'll write a book). He is a vegetarian and does not eat sugar or artificial foods. Disillusioned by the 'underground' or rather lack of it (like us all) but tries to live in harmony and is very trusting. The most modest member (sic) of our Oz community.

5

THE RETURN OF KING KONG
Guerrilla Babes Wipeout!

The decision to go to this school
was the result of conversations
with school pupils the previous
day. We had no idea at all what
would happen but when it did it
was unbelievable and provided the
stimulus and tempo which kept
things rolling for the rest of the
week. There we were – six motley
dressed, long(ish) haired youths,
armed with mortar boards,
whistles, school caps, leaflets and
other assorted props, charging
completely unexpected into a
playground packed with 300
bored and frustrated school kids.
The situation was potentially explosive – we might have been
stoned and trampled on – but
instead, the complete opposite
occurred. We rush into the playground shouting and beating a
drum. "Roll up, roll up for the
education play." The school students immediately gather round
in a tight body, noisy but obviously interested. Almost immediately, after starting the play,
Authority steps in, in the form of
a group of teachers. Incredibly
the kids tighten the circle so as
to prevent the teachers from getting near us. Nevertheless they do
eventually get to us. "Get out!
Have you got permission? You've
got to ask for permission first.
But anyway we wouldn't have
given it to you."("Please sir, may
I have permission to bash you on
the head, sir?") After arguments
and distribution of leaflets, we
leave the playground but continue
the play on a path just outside.
The children gather on the other
side of the fence to watch and an
incredible scene follows where a
number of teachers attempt to
push the kids away from the
fence to prevent our poisoned
words reaching their ears. Despite
serious threats from the authorities, the kids take little notice
and continue to listen and watch
the play. Suddenly some of the
pupils shout, "The cops are
coming." The cops arrive together
with a school teacher and they
attempt to drag one of us away.
We pull him free to the cheers of
the school kids. The teachers say
we are disturbing "their" pupils
(because they were enjoying
themselves they were naturally
being "disturbed"). "Do you want
us to stay?", we shout. "YES",
they yell in unison. The Fuzz make
it clear that unless we leave we'll
be busted. After leaving 4 boys
escape from the school and say
that we should come again and
they'll protect us from the Fuzz
and beat them up if necessary. We
learn later that after we'd left there
had been a semi-riot when the
pupils in the playground (about
250) refused the HM's orders to
get inside or be expelled. Not all
the teachers were on the side of
the authorities either. A sympathetic art teacher helped produce
anti-authoritarian posters which
were put up round the school and
teaching virtually came to a stand-
still. Three boys were accused of
inviting us into the school and
were threatened with expulsion.

No. 2 – ST. MARYLEBONE GRAMMAR SCHOOL

We manage to perform the play
on the pavement as the boys
leave for home. A sizeable crowd
gathers and apart from the
predictable puerile comments
and antics (some of the boys,
old and young, pinch our props,
throw things at us) most of the
boys give us an audience and
we get a good discussion going
afterwards, centring around
exams and comprehensive education. We argue for an organised
schools movement to fight external grading through exams and to
work for control of all assessment
by school students and teachers.
We learn that two first formers
have been caned for not praying
in assembly. How's that for
hypocrisy!

Midday Wednesday – Confront-ation No. 3: ACKLAND BURGHLEY MIXED COMPRE-HENSIVE

We enter the playground and make
for a corner of the yard in front
of a wall and away from the football game. A large crowd run to
our rallying cries – "Don't miss
this incredible spectacle – fresh
from its 100 year run in the back-
streets of darkest England. It's
the education farce!" About half
way through the play several members of staff appear in the playground, approach us and tell us to
get out. We ignore them and continue the play – "Sir, I don't
think that . . . " "You don't
think? Capital! – just the lad I've
been looking for."

Teachers dispatch henchmen prefects to keep the kids away from
us. The HM threatens to break
guerilla Nick's jaw. One teacher
says that he'd like to pummel
guerilla Steve into the ground,
but satisfies himself with such
intelligent remarks as "Why
don't you get a wash – we don't
like unclean people here."
Another teacher is sent to call
the Fuzz.

Finishing the play we start talking to the school students. In
front of the other kids we ask
the prefects why they blindly
accept the teachers orders to
stop the kids talking to us –
why they let themselves be used
as unquestioning tools of the HM.
They don't answer but just push
the pupils back. We talk to the
kids and suggest they get together
and refuse to obey the prefects
(who aren't even elected by the
kids.) We say that pupils and
teachers should decide collect-
ively on their own code of discipline. The staff are now out in
force and we decide to leave. As
we leave the Fuzz arrive. One
Fuzz takes down some of our
names and gives us a warning
about trespass. We split, and as
we are doing so we see kids
pushed away from the windows
as they wave to us.

No. 4 – CAMDEN SCHOOL FOR GIRLS

Noted liberal "progressive" Grammar school. We start the play
under the impression that it's all
been fixed up by friends at the
school (they think so too), and
that permission has been granted
for the performance. Thus the
idea is to put on an uninterrupted
performance and get comments
from the audience not only on
what the play says but how it
says it.

As it happens the only male teacher in the school, who must have
thought we were encroaching on
his male monopoly, is sent down
by the Headmistress to get rid of
us. He becomes almost hysterical
when we try to explain the situation to him, screams "DON'T
ARGUE!", (a line straight out
of the play) and says he's been
instructed to 'phone the police.
We eventually leave in the interests of our friends at the school
who might get victimised if we
stay. It just showed the students
there that perhaps their "tolerant
liberal" school was not quite as
tolerant as they thought.

Thursday 9 a.m. – Guerilla Steve
at the gates of Ackland Burghley
once again – this time not to
perform a play, but to get a discussion going about the previous
days' events. He learns that after
we left on Wednesday the HM-
Abbey had put out a "well-done
my-army-it's-all-over-now-so-calm
down" speech on the tannoy.
Some of the more progressive teachers, however, had apparently
taken copies of the leaflet into
their classes and tried to get discussions going on the topics
raised. Many of the kids show interest in what we were saying and
complain themselves about how
little say they have in the running
of the school (the school council
decisions are continually vetoed by
the HM). Again the need to get
together, work out what they want
and communicate with students at
other schools is apparent. Steve
says we'll try to come back again
and help to get some more positive form of action going. It's important to note that since our
visit to Ackland Burghley SAU
member Trevor Williams was suspended for "insubordination" af-

JAIL BAIT of the MONTH

David Nutter

ter taking part in a walk-out of 250 kids in support of the teachers pay claim. Others were threatened with suspension, but only Trevor, a known SAU activist, was thrown out.

School No. 5 – DAME ALICE OWENS BOYS COMPREHENSIVE (at the Angel)

The response here is disappointing, though some of the staff get amazingly uptight about our presence and threaten to call the cops. When guerilla Pete (who plays the teacher in the play) tells a master (possibly the HM) to get his hair cut and stand at the back of the class the teacher takes him by the collar and looks set to throttle him. Though the majority seem against us, some boys, however, are very keen to take the leaflets and talk seriously to us. It is apparent that they are really suffering in the school but just don't know what they can do to change things. We draw their attention to the planned meeting at the end of the week, which we had advertised on the leaflet and a few say they'll try to make it. As we want to get to another school before the end of Thursday lunch hour we split.

School No. 6 – ISLINGTON GREEN MIXED COMPREHENSIVE

Show school of the borough. Approximately 2,000 students, sculpture in the hall, etc. We start the play in one of the big playgrounds trying not to interfere with the football game. It stops anyway and a largish crowd gathers. It is very hard to get the play through to them since the noise is too great and there is a lot of chanting. Half way through we stop they play, give out leaflets and begin chatting to the kids, many of whom have just arrived and want to know what it's all about. When the staff arrive they play it cool and just ask us to continue the discussion outside the playground. We do this and most of the kids follow us into the streets and stay there till the end of their lunch break. They are predominantly young – a very small percentage stay on after the age of 15. They are particularly bugged by the arbitrary punishments meted out by some teachers, often using violence. To the man they hate exams. Some of the girls complain of the irrelevency of much of what they are taught. A couple of boys say that they should have the right to punish the teachers, since they are in the majority. The discussion is possibly the most fruitful so far.

However, discussing the events later on, the idea is expressed that we should have refused to leave the playground and let the staff call the Fuzz if necessary. If we were attacking authority in the school, what sort of impression could it have had on the kids to see us, who weren't even at the school, obeying the orders of the teachers and then telling the kids they should not accept blindly what their teachers told them. Some say it was more important to carry on the discussion and therefore leaving the playground didn't matter. The point, however, remains a valid one.

8

TASTEY!

SMACK!

No. 7 – ST. PAULS PUBLIC SCHOOL FOR BOYS

Though it is arguable that we shouldn't have gone to a public school on the grounds that we were chiefly interested in comprehensive and secondary modern schools in the most deprived working class areas – the majority opinion was that we should try all different types of school and compare reactions. Anyway, public schools are notoriously authoritarian and vicious in their dealing with dissident students. At an SAU demo in the summer, the Dulwich College authorities had called in the cops to prevent the demonstrators (themselves mostly school students) from talking to the Dulwich boys. St. Pauls itself was in the news in February, 1969, when several boys were expelled for "drug offences". Secret files were kept on the activities of certain boys (e.g. what parties they went to) and one boy was threatened with the police if he didn't answer all the questions put to him by the HM (e.g. who are the other drug-takers in the school?). He was told that if he lied he'd end up in court. Several boys have joined the SAU but live in constant fear of victimisation if the authorities find out. Another reason for going to the school was that the HM was a contributor to the second Black Paper – published the week before.

So on Friday morning we enter the hallowed gates just as the boys are coming out at breaktime and rush into the central courtyard making as much noise as possible to gather an audience. At first the response is weak and very few gather round but after a few minutes curiosity gets the upper hand, word is passed along the corridors and heads pop out of high-up windows in the new buildings. We start the play and do manage to put it across despite some pathetic comments and gestures from the boys (Guerilla Neil had a cup of water thrown over his head). One master, with a sense of humour at least, throws a penny at us from a 3rd storey window. Others follow suit. Half way through the play the "surmaster" waddles onto the scene and asks us to leave. We totally ignore him and continue the play. Surmaster: Will you please leave – you haven't got permission. Teacher in play: These exams have been specially designed to test your intelligence and ability. Your whole future, your entire livelihood will depend on the next 3 hours. Surmaster (getting agitated): If you don't leave I shall have to call the police.
Teacher (to surmaster): Late for my lesson again? – get to the back of the class!
The surmaster, totally baffled and frustrated by this lack of respect leaves to the sound of laughter from a few brave boys.

Some of the boys we talk to are very interested in what we're saying, but are obviously afraid of repression in the school. They promise to try to come to the meeting in teh evening. The bell for the end of break rings and the audience quickly disperses – anxious not to be a second late for their lessons. Its amazing how conditioned they are. We leave just as the cops arrive and outside the

CUNT CUNT CUNT!

Bollocks You CUNT

GET OUT IMEDIATELY!

gates they give us a mild warning about entering school premises without permission. We say it is highly unlikely that permission would be granted. (Anyway in the event of us being given permission in any school it would seem as if the authorities were in league with us. The advantage of a surprise performance includes the spontaneity and relative open-ness – away from the presence of authority and the cramping influence of the classroom – of the reaction obtained. In this way we were making our position clear right from the start – allying ourselves with the pupils against authority. Only through this method could we hope to win the trust and confidence of the students.)

Battle No. 8 – SIR PHILIP MAGNUS SECONDARY MODERN FOR BOYS (At KINGS CROSS)

A short background illustration to the school:

During the last school year, after a Molotov Cocktail had burnt a hole in the door of the head's study; Pledger, the head, decided to ban boots in the school. This naturally drew an angry response particularly from the skinheads in the school, who are in the majority. Painted boot prints appeared around the school, on the floors, and ceiling; drawing of boots were chalked up on blackboards; finally Pledger was presented with a gigantic papier mache boot. Pledger was forced to climb down (or, possibly, he was dragged).

12.30 p.m. – the scene – a small square just outside the Magnus prison gates, where everyone comes out for lunch. About 50 boys are in the square. The play starts amidst cries of "Go back to Endell St.!", and is quickly terminated as some of the boys begin throwing stones (apparently earlier that day the Endell St.

"hippies" had appeared at Clerkenwell court, just around the corner, which also explains the later reactions from the Fuzz/pigs/cops/Bills). We hand out leaflets and start talking to the boys about school conditions and what the education system's all about. They all want an end to physical punishment. No one wants school uniform, but they do want a smoking room and "proper biology lessons"!! We discover that quite a few didn't even realise we were trying to put on a play.

Then a tall spindly man appears, tells the boys to get out of the square and starts pushing them around. One of us says, "They're allowed to be here. Who are you to tell them what to do?" They can decide for themselves what to do." The man, ignoring us, strides angrily away, through the school gates, amidst cries of "Bastard! . . . cunt!" Apparently he is the one and only Mr. Pledger. The boys are now more sympathetic towards us. "Let's burn down the school", a couple of them say. "Shall we occupy the school?", one of them asks. Then the cops arrive.

"Get back into school", orders Sergeant Bill*
"They're allowed out in lunchbreak. Why should they get back inside?", asks guerilla Nick.
"Because I said so."
"Do you make the laws?"
"No, I interpret them."
"Maybe you bend them a little to suit your own ideas."
Sergeant Bill resumes ordering the boys about. As Nick is moving off, Bill hurries after him and, stopping him, says, "Look here, young Barabas, if ever I see you again I'll pull off your beard and cut off your hair, you fucking long-haired wierdo." Nick, not realising the trick, replies, "What? Did you call me a fucking long-haired wierdo?"

Bill puts on an act of being shocked. "Are you calling me names?

Are you calling me names?", and promptly arrests him. Inside, Nick is charged with "Insulting words", and Bill threatens that next time he'll be "dropped" so that he'll be "in no fit state to appear in court the next day."

Meanwhile the kids and the

guerillas are all threatened with being nicked for obstruction and as a result decide to move off from the square to a park up the hill, where they sit around in small groups chatting together. A pig comes into the park, and referring to guerilla Michael, asks aggressively, "Do you want to grow up to be like that filthy, long-haired, unemployed. .?" Silence. Michael asks them, "Well, would you prefer to be like him or like me?" "LIKE YOU!" comes the immediate reply. Exit one angry pig, no doubt terrified of this new and sudden alliance between skinheads and long-haired revolutionaries.
At the same time, outside the park a pig ignores an old man who threatens to punch guerilla Pete in the nose, but instead arrests Pete. As he's led away guerilla Neil walks up to the aforementioned pig and asks politely why Pete is being arrested. The pig politely says that he can't say anything at the moment. The 3 turn down an alley-way, followed at a distance of about fifteen yards, by about 40 boys. The pig then turns round and tells Neil to "clear off." Neil then turns to the crowd – "Right, let's go. There's nothing we can do." Suddenly, the alley-ways full of pigs, squealing and scuttling back and forth, some jumping out of ground floor windows, whilst bodies are crushed as gates across the alley are slammed shut. Possibly they thought it was a revenge attack for the victims of the Endell St. bust. A pig rushes towards Neil, who has the longest hair of us all, shouting "I'll get

him!", grabs him and, calling him such things as "Fucking hippie" and "Bastard", punches him hard in the head and back, and literally drags him by his hair into the station, where he is charged with "Violence in the pig-sty." Inside the chargeroom swear-words are flowing as thick as Sergeant Bill. One cop comes in and shouts "Fucking shithouse" (Neil was inclined to agree). All this was quite clearly the result of the atmosphere of "national anti-hippie month", which arose out of the squats and subsequent busts at Piccadilly and Endell St.

Outside boys are booing and swearing at the pigs and they seem almost prepared to storm the station. Some are hurling themselves bodily against the gates. Michael, who has just been literally kicked out of the alley-way is joined by guerilla Steve and they decide to leave. Having crossed the road, they are just about to make their way to St. Pancras when they hear a shout behind them. They turn round, are grabbed and arrested without caution. Whilst being led into the station, 14 year-old boys are rushing up behind the pigs and punching them in the back. Inside they are both charged with "obstruction" (Pete had been charged with "insulting words"). After almost two hours in the cells we are taken to courts and bail of £200 is granted on condition we do not partake in any sort of propaganda (Magistrate Beaumont made the word "propaganda" sound obscene.) Only Pete is refused bail, because, says Beaumont, he might "do it again" than any of the others). Beaumont also (although he has no right to) refuses Neil legal aid on the grounds of not wanting "to waste the tax-payers money". However, he does grant us all phone calls, BUT when we return to our cells the pigs refuse us our rights. Whilst someone appears in court as a surety for Michael we are all quickly hustled out the back into the pig van bound for Ashford Remand Centra (or sunny Ashford Holiday Camp, as the ex-residents like to call it.)

Ashford – a concrete image for society. The jackboot, the truncheons, the bars, the rolls of barbed wire on top fo the 40 ft. high electrified double fencing – are all screaming out the admittance of Their failure to exterminate our minds. Some people are there for 6 months – without trial – remanded without bail. Six months rotting away in the corridors of terror, knowing that if you are not beaten to death you'll be bored to death. Six months. Without trial. And they say you are "innocent until proven guilty". One day was enough for us – and Pete managed to survive the 6 days in Brixton. No doubt some of us will return one day – if only to be there when freedom, buried alive in the dungeons for so many years, rises up, shatters the walls and gates, smashes the locks, burns down the factories of pain and fear and turns them itno museums of ancient tyranny.

WHY DONT YOU PISS ORF AND LEAVE OUR GIMPY MATES ALONE!

FASCIST!

DONT BE PROGRAMMED

JOHN

*All names of pigs have been changed to protect the innocent from the laws of libel.

PHOTO: COLLIN THOMAS

SCHOOL ATROCITIES:

Like – the ageing master who used to walk around the juniors' showers 'cleaning his glasses' as he looked at the kids' balls, saying sometimes, 'I don't think I've seen you before.'

Like – the cat with three As at A level who disagreed with his headmaster. The Director of Studies at the University at which he finally got a place told him, 'You have the worst reference I have seen in twenty five years of teaching.'

Like – the master who would make boys stand upright in a hot room until (in one case) they fainted.

Like – the junior school master who made a kid of 10 hold two tennis balls at arms' length for fifteen minutes (try it sometime), hitting the kid with a ruler when he let his arms waver.

Like – the master whose 'record' was 150 detentions a week and who kept trying to improve it.

Like – the entire school system

IN FREE...

OOPS!!

I go to school in Islington, Owens. It is a very 'nice school'. Our headmaster told us so.

Once a week we go rowing. Mr. Copping, who takes us rowing, likes us to do as we are told. He says we mustn't ever ask why or he'll send us to the headmaster. (I'm afraid of the headmaster). Once he took us out when it was snowing and we couldn't row because the Thames was too rough. Instead, he said, we must go on a run. So we changed to our shorts and shirts and set off through the snow, which stung our faces. It was very cold. We ran through the streets and mud, and over bridges for a long time. We got colder and colder. But it was all right. Only one boy got chilblains and only eight of us were absent the next day.

We have another clever teacher – Mr. Butler, who likes the old way of running schools. He canes people. Once he caned me. I had to bend over and put my hands on a low chair so that the muscles of my arse would be tense and it would hurt more. I gritted my teeth, because it did hurt, and left red marks and bruises. Was Mr. Butler smiling. These incidents are true but written by a brainwashed pupil. There are thousands of pupils similarly brainwashed. They accept everything, and until they can be shown their stupidity, there will be no change.

Vivian Berger

JOHN.

SMOKING

Frensham Heights Progressive (?) Mixed Boarding/Day School

One day, after careful consideration, a lot of talking and some argument, the Head (?) Mr. Hogg, announced that he had something to say – a small titter – then a respectful silence.

Smoking must stop. It is a bad habit and against the school rules. I cannot tolerate the amount of smoking which is going on. It is a bad influence and encourages those even younger to start the habit.

A list was then read out of the new rules, a last attempt to stamp out the practice for good. (1) Smoking is not allowed and must stop. (2) The woods are out of bounds. (3) etc. etc. etc. The list continued, naming various places now to be out of bounds. Everyone was required to ask permission to do this or that, or go somewhere. The punishment list came last, in neat type. Anyone caught smoking would suffer the following:

i) a letter sent to their parents informing them of their child's grave fall from grace.
ii) Four weeks gated.
iii) For this time, the culprit, during all breaks (except half an hour for lunch) would have to sit in a room, supervised, silent and working: ie. no free time.
iv) Report to the housemaster/housemistress at ? p.m. for bed.
v) At weekends, report to the master on duty every half hour, and only allowed to be in the ball room, lounge, drawing room or library.
vii) At weekends, do six hours of manual labour – two hours on Saturday afternoon, two hours on Sunday morning and two on Sunday afternoon.

After three days, there were twenty people on THE PUNISHMENT! and regular additions every day thereafter.

The press was tipped off and rude letters went back and forth by homing pigeon (GPO strike). Six months went by.

Now there is a super little room for sixth-formers and others to secretly smoke in, and people now smoke everywhere. The rules have completely lapsed. Now heads are bent together discussing what can be done to stop this disgusting habit in the lower forms. So

1969 ... a West London Direct Grant school.
i) long haired sixth former strikes with spray can, doesn't go to history lessons.
 Permanent suspension.
ii) Cambridge Scholarship boy – smoking on school premises. expulsion as undesirable element. Forbidden from school vicinity. not allowed to take A levels for Cambridge.
iii) long haired sixth former disappears for a week.
 Permanent suspension.
Jim Morrison.

Tottenham Girls High School:
Once upon a time in Tottenham, there was a nice little school which turned out programmed creatures who had been brainwashed into believing that their little uniforms and their smart hats turned them into brilliant little commuters, and that anyone who failed in the school would be cast out from the real world. NO-ONE in that school could do what they wanted to do. Now it has been made comprehensive, and because immigrants now attend the school, the authorities believe that the school is ruined. They don't realise that it is not the school which teaches people. People don't really learn anything unless they themselves control their learning. Then they can learn as much as they want to, when they want to!

I suggest that the girls at Tottenham break the bands of authority and organise their own teaching groups.

Drugs and the Public Schools
Recently the public schools have been hitting the headlines under the heading "BOYS EXPELLED FOR POSSESSING CANNABIS". Quite naturally this worries those with boys at these establishments, but of all the drugs that float around public schools cannabis (whether in the form of grass or hash) is about the rarest. In my own experience the number of boys who smoke is remarkably small compared to the number who indulge in much worse forms of self-prescription.

One of these things is the taking of cough mixtures such as Fensil in great quantities. These potions are drunk a bottle at a time for the sake of the small buzz they give the users, who for the most part do not know how much harm they are doing to themselves.

They do this perhaps because they see that it is now becoming more fashionable than ever to be a drug user and because their opportunities for obtaining hash are incredibly few and far between for them in their sheltered positions. When I returned to my old school on a visit within one hour at least five people approached me attempting to score and on being disappointed asked for transport to a distant chemist's with the intention of buying cough-mixture and caffeine tablets.

In this way potentially harmful and lethal drugs are being used as substitutes for the comparatively harmless hash. Surely this is what the authorities should be fighting against with a lot more determination and force – these so-called legal drugs that are so much more dangerous than the illegal soft ones. How long will it be till someone gets hooked or worse? Are they waiting until someone actually kills themselves before realising that they are getting hysterical about drugs that are well-publicised and over-looking common every-day things that are easily and legally obtainable. It is time hysteria was overcome and the situation viewed in the correct perspective.

I am not attempting to advocate the use or legalisation of cannabis but rather trying to make people realise what is going on behind the newspaper headlines. So that if you know someone at a school who smokes hash, be thankful that it is nothing worse, however illegal it may be.
Andrew Clarke – old Melburian.

I actually enjoyed school. To me, school was a second home. Somewhere safe and relaxing which is strange for a place which is geared to training people for the rigours of the rat race. My school was comprehensive for my last two years but this didn't affect the social scale in any way and a happy medium was struck. I came initially from a secondary school which joined with another secondary one, the pupils of which had always seemed to us more intelligent, but afterwards it was clear that we were of equal intelligence.

My school was enjoyable because I was allowed to wear my hair halfway down my back, and then because it was long, I was treated like a harmless freak and allowed to do virtually as I wished. As nearly everyone wore a uniform, and I wore jumpers jeans and bumper boots, I stood out in the morning assemblies. I eventually refused to attend these assemblies on the grounds that I was an agnostic and should not be pumped with Christianity every day.

My last year involved only art, which I did all day long instead of studying metalwork, maths, english and technical drawing, which were the subjects I was supposed to be doing. I started at 10.30 instead of 9 and finished at 5 instead of 4. Officially I was absent for 6 months because no one marked me present.

This freedom of choice is what all 6th forms should be allowed. The school should know that they will study because they have stayed on. What is wrong with continuous lessons and pupils entering or leaving when they want to? My school days were as varied as I wanted them to be. I did light shows, posters, models. This form of teaching expands your mind to the limit of what you can take in and understand. Remember that no school likes expelling pupils, and would preferably reach a compromise, so just back down a little sometimes. A hand hold is better than no hold; with a helping hand you can always lift yourself higher.
Robb Douglas.

11

HEADMASTER OF THE YEAR

My nomination is Mr. K.D. Robinson, of Bradford Grammar School, Keighley Road, Bradford 9, Yorks., because of the events detailed below.

About two years ago, I and some other people decided to try to found an ARTS Lab in Bradford, and indeed put an advert in IT to publicise this. We found support at the Regional College of Art, where Albert Hunt and Jeff Nuttall offered to help, and at the University, where Chris Parr, the Fellow in Drama, told us that he had been thinking in similar terms for some while. After this encouraging start, we managed to get some excellent publicity in the local paper, and began trying to find premises.

I was soon called to see the headmaster, Mr. Robinson, renowned as an autocrat. Between him and I there had for long been no love lost, particularly at this time, as he had, a short while previously, told me that I was under suspicion of drug taking (this due to a supposed overheard conversation concerning my supposed boasting about this to a group of schoolgirls. The fact that I knew no chicks from the school mentioned did not affect his beliefs, and he refused to tell anyone anything about the supposed source of his 'information'). When I saw him after the publication of the newspaper article, he immediately began a personal attack on me, telling me why he would not have picked me (as if artists in any field can be picked) to run an Arts Lab, – too young (16), too immature, lacking in sufficient character, etc., and mentioned someone he would pick – his Head Boy (sic), good at sports, 3 A-levels, etc., and almost totally devoid of imagination. KDR (as known) then moved on, mentioning the hippie/drugs/sex ethos upon which Arts Labs, as he saw them, were based, and going on to talk about Leeds Arts Lab (which had just nailed a figure of Christ to a cross on Otley Moor – sue one of last years (Ts). He said, as he reiterated during assembly the next day that he had heard of a commune connected with Leeds Arts Lab, where someone he knew of had entered into a homosexual marriage. Also, as there was a commune associated with the Arts Lab in Leeds, that meant that Geoff Wood, who ran the Lab, was a Communist (thus I was a Communist (totally untrue, in my case anyway, but who ever heard of anyone in a commune becoming a Communist?). It was then stated that, in order to make it plain that the school was in no way supporting the Bradford Arts Lab proposal, the School Arts Magazine (an editorially free magazine which I was at that time editing) would be censored and that two shows I was running at that time (a satirical/farcical revue and a poetry/music festival) would also be censored, if not banned outright. During the following weeks several public attacks were made on me and the Arts Lab, including the statement that KDR would try and prevent any money being given to the Arts Lab by any public body. A revealing insight into his mentality at this time is given by his reaction to the Senior Debating Society opposing 22–3 the motion that 'This House Believes Bradford Grammar School Provides A Good Education'. He gave a public lecture on the deplorable slackening of discipline and loss of control by headmasters in schools, the terrible and useless 'experiment' of school councils, culminating (again) in public attacks on several people, myself included, some of whom had left the school previously, and another attack on the Arts Lab & Geoff Wood. In a 'discussion' after the lecture KDR stated that he did not consider an elected body as any valid form of control for any organisation, as it was 'too easily influenced by outside pressures' and too easily taken over by 'undesirable elements'. After I had asked a few very pertinent questions KDR said to me 'Shut up, you've said enough', and then proceeded to ignore me.

None the less enthusiastic, we pushed on with the proposal getting the local Sixth Form Union to promise monetary and other help (a momentous feat as anyone having had dealings with the average SFU knows), even though KDR did his best to stop us. Then, we finally found some good, cheap premises. The day after Chris Parr and I had looked at them, I had to see the headmaster. He told me that I was a 'Corrupting & subversive influence' & that I was suspended until further notice. KDR saw my father that afternoon, & so far poisoned his mind against me & the Arts Lab that when I tired of trying to correct his impressions of the 'underground' (e.g. he 'knew' that underground films were films banned by the Obscene Publications Act) he knocked me through two rooms. Having been stopped by my mother, he sat me down and lectured me on the evils of the hippie underworld, finally telling me that I could only return to school if I severed all connections with the Arts Lab and the 'underground'. As my only function was to summon public support for the Lab, going 'underground' would have been useless. So, I split for London two days later.

Thus, as you see, public acknowledgement is due Headmaster K.D. Robinson for ridding Bradford of a 'corrupting and subversive influence', and for ensuring that such a filthy hippie conspiracy as an Arts Lab was not and possibly never will be founded in Bradford.

T.I. Bradford

British Hitler Jugens

'But man, the Corps is teaching you to kill: I mean, y'know, guns and all that – it's not peaceful man, you gotta quit'. He went off muttering something about Che still living, which I thought was rather funny having just read Guevara's book on guerilla warfare – but let's not quibble about this. . . I was left, however, wondering whether I was in fact being taught to murder, I'll Elucidate.

It all began in the 5th form, when there was a choice of afternoon activities – either join the army/air-force Cadet Corps, or do Voluntary Service. The latter consisted of helping in a local hospital, teaching immigrant kids English, doing odd jobs for old folks, or helping around in the school – all very admirable, but less than a third of it's members felt any vocation or even desire to help – to the rest it was just a skive out of the rigours of polishing boots, pressing uniforms and being screamed at. Anyway, most of my friends were joining the Corps, which offered such delights as the chance to ride on tanks and fire machine guns with REAL bullets, all of which was much more exciting. The situation was eloquently assessed by someone who said, 'The heroes join the Corps and the wets do V.S'. So I became a hero.

That was over two years ago: now with less than three months before I leave school, what do I think about it? (The official purpose of the Combined Cadet Force is to foster and increase qualities in young men such as leadership, initiative, discipline and self-confidence, in order to ensure a supply of potential officer material in both peace and war.) Many of my friends, and no doubt many reading this, have declared themselves to be pacifists and would refuse on principle to fight in a war. However this is because we are in a time of peace – similar views were expressed during the 1930's – but once war comes, thoughts turn to protecting the way of life we are accustomed to. This is Capitalism – not an ideal system, but better than any other because of the high degree of individual liberty afforded, combined with the advantages of a technological society. After all, even OZ is distributed on a capitalist basis. Faced with the possibility of the destruction of their mode of living, even the most ardent Dove would demonstrate to some extent the basic instinct of self-preservation and aggression which exists in all of us – but it should be noted that the purpose of an army is in fact to preserve peace, not promote war.

Far from, as some critics have claimed, creating automative morphins, the Cadet Corps increases the individual qualities of those in it – but communally. It's the old concept of Collective Individualism. This is achieved by encouraging the senior members to organise it – it's not too taxing, and it gives one a chance to see what management is like – even if the experience will only be employed in arranging Sunday afternoon demos down at the local fascist embassy.

A tremendous insight into teaching is obtained from the giving of 20 minute lessons – I found that many of my humanitarian theories on the subject were dashed by the need to enforce order.

But most important was the fun we got out of it. We had a big laugh. Some aspects of the Corps were ridiculous – like the annual inspection where the entire company would march past to the strains of a ludicrous school band, while the headmaster and various Whitehall top-brass padded around with beaming expressions on their faces. There was a time when we planned to fuck up the whole thing up (that expression is included in order to reassure the regular readers of OZ that their magazine has not in fact been taken over by capitalist imperialist neo-fascist right-wing anti-party decadent lickspittle hyenas, and still retains some of the old standards for which those at Princedale Road have for so long striven), but when it came to it, we just couldn't bring ourselves to give our cunningly prepared answer to the inspecting officer's question of whether we liked being in the Corps. And somehow we never quite persuaded the band to break into a speeded-up version of Colonel Bogey. But it was still good fun.

Alex Darcy.

I stand defenceless before all those I hammered so bitterly last year for their complete apathy. Go on —say you told me so. I know you did and I'm too bored with the whole set-up to start arguing about it again. Let's face it, the SAU (like Communism, Anarchism, you name it) can only ever be another phase you go through, unless you're prepared to suffer for it. We weren't.

Oh yes, we believed in it all right. In fact, we devoted a considerable amount of time and energy to the cause. All that spreading of the word, for a start —we're still using those damn leaflets for toilet paper—plugging the good old 8 aims: free speech, abolition of uniform, corporal punishment and the exam system, representation on a school council etc. (incidentally, I still agree with them). Convert success rate was about 1 in 200, and that's only the people we actually thought worth bothering with at all. Some pledged firm support but were never seen again, and of the rest, those that didn't spit on us on sight had a great time arguing the thing out with us, having absolutely no intention of changing their opinions, whatever we should say. Actually we had a hell of a good time. We came across some of the weirdest people and held some of the most fascinating cross-purpose conversations.

Our meetings—they were innumerable—were a good laugh too. We used to get really carried away with plans for sit-ins and besieging headmasters in their studies; release refused until our proposals were accepted. Or suggestions like refusing to wear uniform or cut hair as a protest against petty regulations. The whole thing usually tended to develop into a mass of independent conversations which had no bearing on the SAU at all, including chat-ups after all, some people only came for the talent. About the only constructive plans we ever made were when to hold the next meeting

"Please sir, may i be excused?"

Schools Action Union miscarriage

and how to raise the money for another leaflet. On one glorious occasion we did ring up a notorious master from a local school asking that he discuss his excessive use of corporal punishment. We were delighted when he (i) refused to discuss the matter over the phone; (ii) refused to make an appointment to receive a delegation, and finally said there was no problem at all and hung up. 10 points to us—the cowardly, fascist bastard.

But when it came to the real thing—dead end. We may have condemned others' apathy as the enemy of the cause, but fundamentally, it was our own inadequacy. We could talk, threaten, all right, but we weren't really prepared to act on it. We didn't have one martyr among us—all the blood and thunder guys were those who'd last seen the inside of a school five years back. It was easy to leave the meetings full of enthusiasm, prepared to face anything for our rights, but once back in the very sober atmosphere of school we'd find ourselves holding back. Although at first we kidded ourselves that what we needed, before we could achieve anything, was more support behind us, it didn't take long to discover that even a mass revolt has ring-leaders

to be victimised, and who were going to be the ring-leaders? It's all very well to try and break down the establishment, but while it's still there you want to keep in on it. Refusing to wear school uniform is hardly likely to induce the headmaster to abolish it. He'll just chuck you out. More subtle methods, like asking the prefects to consider your proposal will be met by the polite confession that they are only subordinate to the headmaster, who, in turn, will confess his own subordination to the board of governors; and if you go to them, they'll decide that a pupil with the ability, energy and courage to get that far must definitely be considered a threat. When the next possible excuse comes up, THEY'll chuck you out, to protect the others from corruption. You're banging your head against a brick wall.

The real atmosphere of our little group was well demonstrated by the way attendance of meetings fell off when exams came round. It's all good fun when you've got nothing to lose—quite a good 4th form occupation—but those doing their GCE suddenly discover who they'd really rather have on their side when it comes to the crunch. Until exams are abolished you might as well devote your energies

to passing them. It's so much simpler to hang on and toe the line for a couple more years and get your references. After all the fate of the guys at the top hasn't been too encouraging in the revolutionary spirit. One of the leaders of the organisation was rejected by Warwick Univ., although "an academically brilliant applicant" because of his ties with the SAU. And what did the movement do for him?

So enthusiasm finally flagged. After some long time of discussing but making no progress and realising that we lacked the dedication ever to make any sort of progress, we found the novelty of the thing wearing off. Subsequently the effort of justifying the cause to opposition became increasingly tiring. There's a limit to how long you're prepared to stand up and argue about something that, in practice, is getting you frankly nowhere. People would bring it up as the only topic of conversation they thought we were interested in, simply because we'd once, in an enthusiastic moment, stuffed one of those leaflets under their noses. And it would be the same old set of arguments every time, until we'd start running every time someone mentioned the blasted SAU. Sometimes you'd get to the stage where you couldn't remember why you supported the R aims anyway, and have to call on some enthusiastic and eloquent SAUer to remind you. We just got pissed off with the whole thing.

But this wasn't really meant to be an anti-advertisement. Anyone who wants to have a go at revolution has my whole-hearted sympathy, but for God's sake don't expect me to do anything about it. As far as I know, they're still going strong up top—the last we heard from them was a letter from each half of the newly split SAU each telling us they were the real one and don't listen to the other lot.

Yeah well—don't get burnt.

TADDI

Babes in Arms

We go to the City of London School in Blackfriars. It's a public school, and like many public schools in this country it houses a "Combined Cadet Force", an organisation designed to induce school children to take a career in one of the armed forces. We hate it.

Between the third and sixth years, it's virtually compulsory for pupils to join the C.C.F. In other words, for three years of our lives, several hours a week and much of our own free time, we have to play soldiers. We have to carry rifles (2nd World War .303s), we have to parade in front of local factory workers who jeer and laugh at us, we have to march, polish buttons on our uniforms, mirror-shine our steel-shod "bovva" boots, study elementary battle tactics, salute our superior officers (often sixth-formers who have gained "promotion") and generally lick arse and "do-as-we-are-told". Some of us are only thirteen years old, and often the rifles are taller than we are.

Once a term we are required to go to two day camps based at military establishments away from the school. Here we learn how to kill more efficiently, with blank cartridges and bren guns, as well

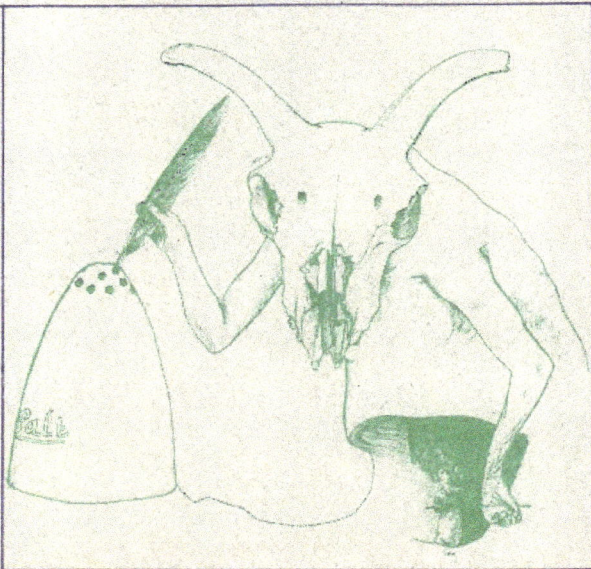

Cany

as practising battle manoeuvres and the like. Last camp, one of our friends had his head shaved closer than a skinhead. The officers at the camp thought that his hair was "too long". (Most of us stuff our hair up into our caps to avoid detection, but this isn't always effective. The required length of hair is on a line level with the middle of our ears, and it must never touch the collar.) The food at these camps is absolutely dreadful. Mostly it's dehydrated crap, rationed in strict portions.

Opposition to joining the C.C.F. at our school is systematically crushed. Once you have joined, your name and particulars are filed at the Ministry of Defence, whose permission has to be obtained before you can leave. Only a minute proportion of fellow pupils known to us in the C.C.F. would stay if they had the choice. Gradually, though, it's dawning on us that we are being trained merely to provide cannon fodder for the next generation of mindless generals. It's interesting to note that the only form of warfare in which we have never been instructed is guerrilla fighting. Perhaps we will have to learn that for ourselves.

13

Weekend dropout

There's a certain satisfaction in having one's future nicely tied up and sealed off so that you can leave it and wallow in total abandon from Friday night to Monday morning and still have the deep-down security of knowing it's there. Cliché it may be, but someday the genuine, full-time, happy hippie has got to sit up and think—where is he going to be in another 10, 20 years? Bumming around with the same old bums? doing the same odd half-rate jobs to earn his bread? At least the part-timer will have had his career all mapped out for him, if he should ever need it. But then what's so great about that if it means you've got to waste the most active years of your life cooped up in a desk, cramming in a load of bullshit which rarely has any bearing on the future for which it is qualifying you, and which you instantly dismiss from memory after the next exam. Obviously, to do a professional job preliminary study is necessary, but this hardly justifies four years of scraping away in Latin Div. 3. The trouble is—the valuable and the interesting are so bogged down with the trivia that an awful lot of people aren't prepared to spend the time looking. And worse, education, school in particular, is made to feel not like an opportunity but like some sort of imprisonment. It's supposed to be for the pupil's benefit, yet he's the one who's being shoved around—stuck in a uniform, made to cut his hair, like some sort of criminal. In fact, forcibly alienated from his contemporaries. Academic study should become a part of, not set apart from, social life, and since he's the one it's all in aid of, the pupil should be the one who makes the decision as to whether, what and when (in terms of the timetable) he learns, with the teacher not as task-master but as source of advice. And what you do in your lunch-hour is surely your own bloody business.

But, as for the unfortunate, fresh-faced, cropped-headed victim of the so-called "system"—the cramping routine, authority in the form of parent or teacher constantly hovering threateningly in the background—much as he condemns it all, he would be lost without it. For a start, there are its obvious material benefits (think who's really paying for the underground magazines, the music, the velvet trousers and, ironically enough, the shit). Besides this, there is the emotional dependence. Although he may loathe the idea of "security", inwardly he's glad of that ready-made future in case anything should go wrong with the free life. The routine may be depressingly dull, but it can't let you down. Blowing your mind on a sunny day, not knowing where or who you are, or caring anyhow, can be great fun. It can also send you round the bend. What happens when you come down with a blinding headache, throwing-up uncontrollably, and there's no-one sufficiently tied to you to care what happens to you? At least the weekend drop-out can go home to Mummy with her clean sheets and her comfort. And there's always school on Monday to remind you exactly who you are, preventing you from digging in too deep to get out.

But then, it's easy enough to get the worst, not the best, of both worlds. After all, when Mummy finds out why you're spewing she'll switch off the loving-kindness. And like with any other sort of double life, with either side you have to play down the element of the other in you, or face possible rejection by both. The problems are infinite when they start to clash. Like when the school starts keeping tabs on you and finds your friends got busted last week. Or someone's just handing round the joint and your parents come home early. And there's the other way round, when you have to avoid meeting people who just assumed you were five years older and a bum, when you're wearing your school blazer. OK, so you should let people know initially just where you stand and let them accept you for what you are. Unfortunately a hell of a lot of people aren't prepared to accept you for what you are. One half would probably disinherit you and the other half walk over you. And anyhow does that "what you really are" really shed any more light on what you really are than what you would have appeared anyhow? You are only what they think you are.   G B

I Wanna be free

One Side of Freedom
This society, although labelled permissive (by society itself) is not free enough to permit man to revert to his natural instincts in public. This ruling does not extend as far as animals.

Freedom of sexual expression in public has many tight restrictions. One may kiss in certain places but only fuck in a few places at certain times. Surely this idea is as pretentious and puritanical as the old forms of censorship. Its purpose is to prevent corruption and protect the individual from disturbing or immoral sights. This is ironical in itself and only made to satisfy the so-called moral conscience of society. Everyone knows what copulation is. Animals perform the act everyday in public, so why not let humans have the same freedom if they wish it. Surely we should have the right to make the choice. If the act disturbs some, they do not have to watch and if they want to why not?

The act of making love is beautiful and natural and should be admired.

The Danish Sex Fair was the first step on the way to sexual freedom although some saw this as just an excuse for open pornography. If pornography is limited to sexual behaviour, then I think there should be no censorship of it at all. Why so many restrictions on natural behaviour? Were you born to be free?

Free from the system, free from tradition. If you were you are one of the minority and you are bloody lucky but the rest of you, what about you? This society is closing in on you and taking you over. It is a safe bet that you obey someone who is your equal but holds a higher position than you. Why not start a freedom campaign in your area now and just do as you wish whenever you feel liking pissing in the street then do it; if you feel like dancing at a funeral, then go ahead and do it. Live for the moment and not the future. Be free and tread on anyone who stands in your way. Your true identity is sure to come to the surface. Don't become Mr. and Mrs. Average. Live a little before it's too late.   Anne

Although we are living in a so-called permissive society, there are many things natural to human instinct that are prohibited in public. Signs in many places proclaim "PETTING PROHIBITED", byelaws to parks and woodlands say that people caught fucking will be prosecuted. University and college authorities rule that you cannot visit the opposite sex after ten-thirty p.m. in the belief that thus fucking cannot happen between the magical hours of ten-thirty and eight o'clock and that nobody fucks at any other time. People may not even piss in any place vaguely public without fear of being arrested for exposing themselves and being labelled as sex-fiends.

Sun-bathing naked on your own property is prohibited, as this so-called immoral sight may blow a few minds. Those that do are criticised and rejected by narrow-minded, inhibited sods as being perverted.

The annoying thing about this is that this ruling does not extend to domestic animals, who may fuck when and where they want to without anyone saying fuckall. Dogs pissing on lamp-posts is becoming an increasingly common sight. People in fact seem to enjoy sitting in the park letting their animals do as they please. Animals have large amounts of offspring but do not have to worry about them being branded as bastards. Animals it seems have got a good thing going; they are protected and left to do what they want. Why can't this sexual freedom be extended to us, after all we're only animals!
Roger Vartoukian

RUPERT FINDS GIPSY GRANNY

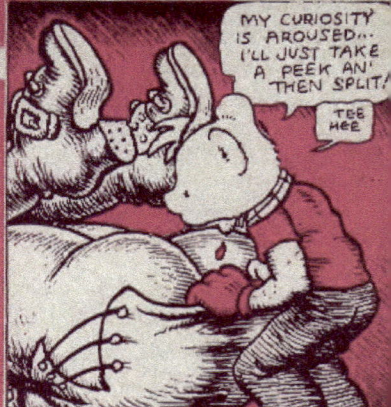

MY CURIOSITY IS AROUSED... I'LL JUST TAKE A PEEK AN' THEN SPLIT!

TEE HEE

1   *" It looks just like a ball to me,"*
     " Open it and see."

RUPERT'S WAY BARRED

WELL I'LL BE BLOWED !! SHE'S A VIRGIN !! AMAZING!

2   *Then Rupert starts to push and peep,*
     But finds the hole is much too deep.

RUPERT IS EAGER TO PLAY

I'LL FIX THAT RIGHT NOW !!

YAH-HOO!!

3   *" Oh my, it felt as light as fluff !*
     It's full of magic, sure enough ! "

RUPERT BECOMES ANXIOUS

UNH, UNH, UNH, UNH, UNH...

JEEZIZ! IT WON'T BREAK!!

*Although he tries, and tries again,
He cannot reach the end.*

RUPERT SPEEDS IN

CHARGE!

*" Oh good, that door is open wide,"
Pants Rupert, as he runs inside.*

RUPERT SUCCEEDS AT LAST

IT IS DONE!

KA- POP!

*Just then he slips, and down he slides,
To where dark water glints and glides.*

Xam blues

About the third week in August, I received the same unfeeling piece of paper that I have received with monotonous regularity on two other occasions for the past three years—the dreaded results! As usual, they were not brilliant. They caused the same emotional distress for both me and those round me. "Friends" and other enemies asked with a smirk about my results and unhappily I had to be truthful as nobody can escape the merciless table of results that the local press prints smugly every Friday as they reach the colleges. For some parents, there is nothing more soul-destroying than the public exposure of their child's bad exam. results.

Let us "examine" this peculiar system of selection that has prevailed and blindly passed on, occasionally questioned and hardly ever changed, for decades. Employers who experiment with their products accept the principle of examinations without experiment on the understanding that it is not ethical to interfere with the present atrocious way in which their potential employees are trained.

Examinations are a primitive method of recording a tiny, often irrelevant, section of the behaviour of an individual under bizarre conditions. Those who evaluate the behaviour are untrained as it is relatively easy for anyone to get a holiday job checking examination papers. As for the actual examiner, the marker of the paper, he – being more or less human – is incapable of consistently good and fair judgement as he has to rush through twelve hours per day, often reading the same information thousands of times. He is inclined to become irritable, it is not good for an old man or old woman (that's what they are, usually) to do so much concentrated work for such a long period. The work becomes tedious and the last few hundred papers he marks reflect this. There was a case of some poor old examiner, having so little time that he marked papers on the way to work on a crowded tube train. Despite everything, I pity examiners– their's is a hard lot, with almost unbelievable mental pressure.

If examination results predict future performance, it is a poor way of doing so as hardly any potential employer takes any notice of grades and many even obtain jobs before results are announced. Employers are inclined to take more notice of personal reports and references (also subject to influence) than the work of a collection of old men and students working for the holidays, marking and checking an exam. set by a vague "Board" from an entity which is geographically uncertain. Also, a person with "good" exam. results may be unable to adapt to the stone-cold realities of working life.

Examination results only apply to actually gaining a job for a probationary period. The test depends upon ability at the job. Only in a few cases can initial incompetence be considered. These are those in which human life is involved, e.g. the medical profession and to a certain extent industrial work (safety measures, the nine types of industrial pollution, etc.)

Encouragement and incentive to work does not come from knowledge of exam. grades – because most of them come at the end of a training course when it is too late. Telling a student a grade is a banal way of trying to show where he/she is going wrong in the G.C.E., an examinee never gets the assessed paper back, and it is rarely done in other exams. Perhaps this is done so that examinees can be prevented from physically seeing and questioning their results? With only a grade given which could mean nothing, a student can soon acquire the skill of doing the minimum amount of work in order to get the required grade. The information learned by this method is forgotten almost immediately after the exam.

Having an examination system in colleges and schools gives the HIGHER AUTHORITIES (whoever they may be) a false air of respectability. However, exams. taken at their basic level stink of the inquisition and are a kind of unconscious synthetic Third Degree of the intellect and emotion.

There is a more palatable way used in many establishments, whereby clearly defined topics are set to be completed in the not-too-distant future. Unfortunately these are only secondary to exams, although they are a far better usage of a person's ability.

This year, I was subjected to 'A' level, and it rejected me. I feel no conscience about it. I knew the stuff (I did, really!) and I still remember most of it. I treat it as a battle between me and the examiners' state of mind at the time he marked my paper. I questioned one result by letter to the Board asking them to check the paper, but I don't think they did. I received a letter from them saying they were sorry and all that, but I'll have to try harder next time blah blah blah... This piece of literature may give the impression of someone so bound up in himself that it seems worth telling the world about even the most trivial things. Maybe it is, but the education system in general and the examination boards in particular have given me a bad time, especially these past few years and I daresay I've given them a few laughs. Seriously, many lives have been ruined and many parents' dreams have been crushed because they have been made to suit the balance instead of what they really want to do.

I don't forgive them for that.
Alan Clayton

Rupert dancing

Every now and again something really great happens, like the Roundhouse, (before it became commercialised) free concerts in Hyde Park and Project Free London. You all know what they are, and they are different for every-

one. Rupert Dancing is another daisy in the fields of the Underground. It started at Implosion, when people just linked arms and flew around the Roundhouse in multi-coloured ribbons. Everyone thought it was such a groove that a Rupert Dancing (as Jeff Dexter called it) meeting was danced in Hyde Park. All the Rupert people tripped gaily down to the cockpit one blank, grey afternoon. When about 40 people had arrived, the dancing began and we danced in and out of the Serpentine, around trees and people. The numbers grew and about seventy people Rupert danced their way towards Marble Arch, where we decided with all our happiness and love that we'd levitate the Arch. So we sat down with guitars and so on, and played, sang and danced (to the amazement of the tourists) and managed to push Marble Arch forward five inches. We then danced down Oxford Street and through both floors of a clothing shop which still shines from the experience. Having danced our way to Piccadilly, we all washed in the fountain and baptised the Rupert Bear spirit. In Trafalgar Square, we danced around the fuzz, Nelson's Column and a Christmas tree. We split up, promising to meet again, which we have, and will do so again.

Let's hope for many more scenes like this.

Ring up the Rupert people and talk to them – about anything.
VIV BERGER

The author of this article wishes to make it clear to the Law Society, who should not be reading OZ anyway, that he is not touting for business, as he is no longer in private practice as a solicitor.

At school in 1960 I was threatened with suspension if I did not get my hair from its length of just about what they now almost accept in the army. As a law student I grew it long enough to be provoked into one fight in the street over it, but abandoned it for a faceless life as an articled clerk. When I let my hair grow again and practised as a solicitor, I began to worry what magistrates would make of it. Actually everyone was very nice but things reached a rather critical stage so I dropped court work for a while. I thought of having my hair cut off and made into a wig, but that seemed like cheating. The idea grew out of that that I should have a short-haired wig. This was pooh-poohed by posh wig-makers and I finally invested nine guineas in an Early Beatle from Carnaby Market. I experimented with various ways of stopping my hair showing underneath it, and having thin hair found the easiest short-term way was to brush my fringe back and put the back hair in a bunch taken as high up the back of the head as would manage without loose ends. I found a band round the head in order to stop loose ends more trouble than loose ends. The wig was fairly long at the back and would not have managed in short-back-and-sides days. At the time it was as long as could be respectable, but I have since seen longer.

This arrangement was fine for court, where you could retire afterwards and stop the rubber band from pulling too hard on your head, but for more than an hour or so a french pleat is advisable. This is soon mastered and can be secured with only a couple of hairclips. The aim should generally be to have its centre of gravity as far up the head as possible, so as to avoid hair showing underneath at the back.

This approach is not entirely ideal. On one occasion I stumbled going up the main staircase at Middlesex Sessions and fell, clutching my wig in my hand, before a slightly puzzled usher. This could be very awkward done in the presence of a judge or an unsuspecting client. Hairpins tend to work their way out of the wig whilst techniques of firm fastening from underneath generally work on the assumption that you are bald. I was fortunate in starting in an office where everyone except the clients knew and didn't mind and so I could ask about giveaway details. With a wig it is alarming if you scratch your head as when wearing a wig you tend to do. You must also be careful about looking up in the air, as it falls off backwards, and if you wear a hat to stop it blowing off in a strong wind you must be careful not to take the hat off too abruptly. If you want to work where people do not know your secret, don't be interviewed on a very hot day, as two lots of hair create a lot of heat, and get used to wearing the wig well beforehand. You must always remember your disability and try to get into a more impersonal type of office where you are not so likely to be scrutinised at close quarters. Actually people are very unobservant, especially men.

As the disadvantage of a wig became more apparent I looked for an alternative. By this time my hair was quite long and outside I tended to wear it back to stop it blowing. From this my wife got the idea that it could be tucked down a shirt collar out of sight. Experiments showed this could be done reasonably, and as the hair grew the effect was better. As I have a long neck, high collared shirts are an advantage, although difficult to get in office-style.

If, as I did, you wish to make a point and show your hair occasionally in a professional capacity, you must obviously be prepared for difficulties. In the early days some clients assumed that because I looked like them I was a crooked solicitor, but after an initial sharp reaction from me they soon got over this. Others who were recommended to me after I had decided to give up for the time being, even asked me to go ahead, with hair, just to show the magistrate. I was pleased but felt bound not to. Magistrates are untrustworthy at the best of times and to flaunt their prejudices in their faces is not the way to see impartial justice at its best. When I got my wig I suddenly found a strange reaction from Release. Caroline Coon was reported to have decided that it was a bad idea even without seeing the effect. Release cases unaccountably went to solicitors other than the one I was working for. One thing however has impressed me, and that is that the majority of people, if you hold an intelligent conversation with them, accept you long-haired. The trouble is getting them to stay around that long.

Apart from getting a job, it relieves paranoia to walk around occasionally without old men complaining that they fought for you in a war against dictatorship, and here you ungratefully are not doing what they are trying to dictate. After a while, however, you begin to feel very schizophrenic, and it does not make for an easy life generally. As long as you know you will not be fully accepted by society as you really are you cannot get sucked into the system. You live something like a double agent, and this produces an unavoidable strain, but as with a spy the good you can do is potentially greater than a whole army attacking from the outside. *David R. Pedley*

"these bums...
you know,
blowing
up
the
campuses."
Richard Nixon

HIGH SKOOL CONFIDENTIAL

From The High School Revolutionaries
edited by Marc Libarle and Tom Seligson.
Published by Random House New York $6.95.

High School Students Unite
by Tom Lindsay
Tom Lindsay is a member of the New York High School Student Union and is on the staff of the New York High School Free Press. Tom was a founder of the High School Independent Press Service (HIPS). He writes and draws excellent political cartoons for underground papers.

Hello Boys and Girls.
I am a 'High School Revolutionary'.
This is a book about 'High School Revolutionaries'.
There are lots of books like this about lots of people.
Most of them stink.
This one will probably stink too.
But I need the money.

This country sucks. Its television, its ulcer pills, its senators, its cities, its cars, its Miss America pageants its churches, its money, its objectivity in the media, its Miami Beaches, its army, and its schools. Schools and parents are the foundation of America's schizophrenia. Kids rebel in lots of ways against what they feel and see going on around them. And so I rebel against this insane society.

I'm the son of a preacher. I went to church, I was a nice kid. But it's a drag being a nice kid. Because being a nice kid means you get good grades, don't get drunk or stoned, go to college, meet a nice girl get married, kiss for the first time get a job, bring up nice kids, die a nice death and nobody, least of all you, ever knew you lived.

I didn't want to be a nice kid after a while. So I started rebelling in lots of ways, I started smoking (cigarettes), got drunk, stopped going to church, started going to dances started making it with girls, stopped getting good grades, skipped school on nice days and went riding in convertibles to MacDonald stands, and just started fucking around.

I began to feel more. The 'in' crowd was hard as shit to make it in and I didn't make it, so I hung around with a lot of other guys in the same position. Wanting kicks but not making the top. All those guys and girls I hung around with were lonely and you could feel it. We were cool but somehow that didn't fill up everything. So I began to look around even more. I began to move with this one group of people at school. The 'beautiful people'. I became a goddam hippie.

I got stoned. I made new friends. We talked a lot, bullshit mostly, but we began to explore new things and thoughts. It was just a start but fuck it you have to start somewhere.

That was the time (half-way through eleventh grade) I started getting political. I turned against the Vietnam War. I went to the March on Washington. October 21, 1967. I saw people get teargassed.

Then there was a drug bust at my high school. I didn't get busted, but after most of it was over the Sergeant of Police of the town of Wellesley, Massachusetts, told my parents I had turned on. The school told me get my hair cut, and I decided that school sucks. Teachers suck, the country sucks, the war sucks, racism sucks. The school newspaper sucks.

I decided to start an underground paper. My friends dug the idea and we did it. In February 1968, the first edition of *The Searcher* came out.

Then the administration cracked down with THE IMMORTAL DRESS CODE. No cocksucker is going to tell me to get my hair cut unless I also have the power to tell him to grow his hair long.

We fought the dress code. We circulated petitions, a majority of kids wanted to change it, and so we went to the School Committee. They finally agreed but in their own bullshit way. They formed a Dress Code Committee (Mah fella Americans, after this brutal and senseless assasination tonight, I am forming a commission to study violence). So in the tradition of fine, upstanding, bullshit liberals we finally took a vote between four different dress codes (democracy of course). The first choice was no dress code, the second was almost no dress code—just prohibiting shorts,

curlers, and slacks for girls, the third was the same dress code, and fourth was a stricter dress code. When the votes came in a thousand kids out of fourteen hundred voted for the first two with the second getting the most of all. Eight people voted for a strict dress code. We had won. It was a good feeling. We had beaten the administration.

From there, *The Searcher* continued to come out, getting better all the time. We held a three-day hunger strike against the war and started a lot of programs around the draft. On April 26, 1968, when 200,000 kids stayed out of school in New York against the war, we in Wellesley succeeded in getting forty kids to stay out of school and march up to a teach-in at Wellesley College. The once quite efficient system in Wellesley was fucking up, then the big bomb came.

In late May, the first three periods one day were cancelled in order to have a special program on poverty and racism. There were speakers films, and a selection of pieces by black authors put on by the Boston Theatre Co. One of those pieces was a part of LeRoi Jones' play, *The Slave*. Jones doesn't talk to nice white liberals. There were a lot of fucks', shits', etc. in the play. After the play there were discussion groups—I didn't hear one kid complain about the swear words. But it wasn't the same for the racist adults of town. They had shit fits. Thirteen hundred people came out for a School Committee meeting. The school auditorium was packed. Every goddam right winger of the town was there, and they were out for blood. People got up to speak; back and forth it went, those for the program and those against it. The whole place was polarized. Good guys—bad guys: clap for good guys, boo for bad guys. The place was tense as shit. Then the editor of the official school paper, a Student Council member and Varsity letter winner, got up and said, 'The first time I heard the word fuck was when I was five years old and right here in Wellesley. And I know a lot of people who can't say a sentence without saying fuck in it.' That blew it. . . If you think a thousand Russian Stalinists on the rampage is bad, this was really fucked up. The whole audience rose screaming 'Shut him up', 'Get him out. Arrest him.' I think I heard 'Lynch him' in there too. The crowd was crazy, stark raving mad. Two cops came and arrested him and took him out. We were sitting there stunned with this raging audience behind us and a kid getting busted in front of us. To top it off, the vice principal got up and ripped the student dissenters up. For the next month the town was crazy, but the incident finally died away. I learned a lot out of it. For the first time I saw America revealed, and what I saw was frightening. Up until then it had been one principal or something, but now it was all these people. This was America—against me.

Shortly after that I moved to New York. I went to Brandeis High for my last year of high school (as well as school in general). Brandeis is an amazing school. Like, in New York they can't build schools right. Schools are either shitholes that are like used condoms that have been sitting around for a year, or so sterile they're like condoms straight out of the package, sterile like hospitals. Brandeis is 85 percent black and Puerto Rican. Quite a change from sterile people in Wellesley. Even though black schools have a reputation for being worse than suburban schools, Brandeis is very similar to Wellesley—with the same type of fucks running it, calling themselves administrators, teachers, guidance counsellors, etc. It is different in the sense that the school system cannot allow a majority of black and brown students to graduate and go on to college, while in white schools the majority of kids do go to college.

While in New York I also started working on the High School Independent Press Service (HIPS). HIPS is a press service for high school underground (news)papers. In the packets we sent out we had national high school news, articles, analysis, poems, cartoons, photos etc. I worked on that till January.

For the first three months of that year there was no school because of the teachers' strike. Kids and a few teachers opened their schools against the racist UFT strike. Kids started their own schools, and ran things in many schools. When the strike was finally over the UFT and the Board of Education decided that classes would be forty-five minutes longer and some holidays cut in order for the teachers to make up their pay. (Teachers ended up making more money for striking than if they had not gone on strike.) A lot of people all over the city, including high school students, denounced the settlement. The bit about the pay was

18

Billy Bunter busts out

bad enough, but no kid is going to sit through an extra forty-five minutes of bullshit and miss any holidays. All over the city, black, Puerto Rican, and white students spontaneously walked out, went on strike, and shut down their schools. Thousands of kids ran through the streets, held rallies, fought the cops, took over subways, and said 'Hell no we won't go. Fuck UFT'.

At Brandeis a leaflet went out: 'Are you going to take forty-five minutes more of this shit? No!' Thirty kids ran through the halls. Students poured out. The bell rang; students milled in the lobby. 'Hell no we won't go.' Finally over six hundred kids walked out. Classes were called off. Four hundred students took over the nearby subways and went to a rally downtown where they were joined by thousands more. For a week the strike went on, but the next week kids were back in school taking the same shit. In a lot of schools, holidays were given back and the forty-five minute period cancelled.

I just fucked around at Brandeis, I didn't do much work. I found out that I could graduate in January. I cut a lot of classes and ended up going to about two weeks of classes. Near the end of the semester a few kids got together and we put out a paper that looked exactly like the school's official paper but had a totally different content. The administration and teachers flipped out. We were almost able to get the teachers to hand it out unknowingly but some of them read it. Teachers were running around screaming, 'This isn't *our Brandeis Brief!*'

No one was caught handing out the first issue because we handed it out without teachers seeing us in school. The second issue was even better. We had a short thing on how people were handing out a phony *Brandeis Brief* and not to listen to them because they were just troublemakers. This time another kid and I were caught. The other guy they transferred to another school, and they almost kicked me out of school ten days before I graduated. They decided to let me stay as long as I didn't cause any more trouble. I didn't or at least I didn't get caught. I graduated from one of America's most amazing institutions—a high school.

In early March, kids from HIPS, the *High School Free Press*, and the High School Student Union, got together and started talking about a spring offensive in the high schools. We wanted to really try and do something that would last when the demonstrations were over. One thing about New York schools is that it is easy to get kids to walk out or demonstrate or take any type of action. On a nice spring day it doesn't take much at all. As we saw with the forty-five-minute strike, kids went out of school and rioted, but a week later the same old fucked-up system was running and doing the same old shit. We wanted to organize. There are two ways you can hand out a leaflet. One is to let the leaflet speak for you, the second is to let the leaflet assist you in speaking yourself. You use the medium to get your message across, you talk to people. Talking to people is more likely to get your message across.

Too easily you can set yourself apart. To sit behind four walls and publish your opinions allows no contact with what is happening with people. SDS has a rhetoric about what's happening in this country but most of it doesn't mean anything because they have never talked to the people they theorize about. The whole thing is this—people who talk don't do shit (intellectuals, liberals, college revolutionaries, etc.). You have to find out what is happening, where people's heads are at. YOU DON'T FOLLOW A THEORY—YOU LIVE ONE. YOU DON'T FOLLOW CHRIST —YOU ARE CHRIST. YOU DON'T FOLLOW MARX—YOU ARE MARX. YOU DON'T FOLLOW THE PEOPLE—YOU ARE THE PEOPLE.

This we felt and believed. We got ourselves together. What we basically tried to do—and did in many cases—was to get kids to feel themselves as organizers. Just small groups of kids, maybe five to ten in each school and in thirty to forty of the city's eighty-nine public high schools. Building organizers and becoming one yourself is hard. You're brought up in this country not to relate to people or maybe just a small group of people. People lead alienated and lonely lives in America. Take a look at your parents those little old secretaries, etc. To build a life where you do more than comment on the weather, is hard. But it can be done.

To help us that spring we developed a ten-point program which we elaborated in the *High School Free Press* and in leaflets and demonstrations. The program was one of the best in the country. The *Free Press* was dynamite (It was also one of the few working-class papers in the country; but not only working-class. It was middle-class, black, Puerto Rican, hippie, yippie, and in general everybody's paper.) And the leaflets were fantastic. But we weren't all that good. We had a lot of fuck-ups, we had a lot of bullshit. We were too centralized, often too elitist, and we didn't get stoned.

I moved out of my parents' house and into the High School Student Union office/apartment with a couple of other guys. Later more people (boys and girls) moved in. We formed a commune. The commune story is another trip in itself. I will say this about it: to be a revolutionary means more than developing revolutionary politics. It means also developing your emotions and the way you relate to people. The revolution means building yourself as a person, as a human being. If you have never gone through a communal experience, do it. But don't make the mistake of isolating your emotions from your politics, or your politics from your emotions. To be just political sucks. To be just emotional sucks. Everything must be together. You are one.

Our relations with the three black student groups in the city were very good. We related to them on a political and personal level. This didn't mean they became Toms or we became soul brothers. In many locals, leaders got together to talk about tactics, actions, what was happening, etc. In a couple of cases the High School Student Union started Black Student Union locals, and the Black Student Union started High School Student Union locals. On April 21, all four high school groups went on strike. Black, Puerto Rican, and white kids were out on the streets or taking over schools together. One day fifty kids were busted, black and white, and the Union bailed them all out.

Right now I'm out of high school and I'm out of high school organizing. Already high school seems like a long time ago. I don't have that feeling, that way of being, now that I'm out. I don't belong in the high school scene. Too many people don't belong in the high school scene that are there now. When you're faced with the frustrations of organizing and this high school kid comes up to you and says, 'We're trying to do something at our school, do you know anything that can help us?'—it's all too easy to start organizing high school kids. It's all too easy to organize kids who will listen to whatever you say because it's radical. (High school students who have offices with older Movement groups often end up with that group's type of politics.) The problem that's facing me and lots of other people is, what do you do after high school? I chose not to go on to college because it's bullshit—for my life. It's really scary at seventeen to try and live your life like you want to, with as little bullshit as possible. You're living your life *now.* Most people never do, they keep saying, 'Well, after college I'm going to fuck around,' but then they get jobs and, 'Well, after I retire I'm going to see the world, etc. Well, after I die I'm going to. . .'

I feel a need for a major change in this country (commonly called revolution). But how the hell do you make a revolution in America? Everybody's got his, 'After the revolution, we'll have. . .' But how do you get to after? I'm not really sure, but I have learned stuff through my high school experiences that will help me. I know that one of the greatest hang-ups people and organizers have is talking to people. They can talk rhetoric to you until your ears fall off, but they can't talk stuff that means something to people. You shouldn't be all that different talking to somebody you are organizing or talking to your girl friend or boy friend. That doesn't mean you tell workers you love them, but it means that you speak with the same honesty. (And vice versa. Don't tell a girl a big cool rap about yourself when you only want to sleep with her. Just ask her, 'Do you want to sleep with me?') You have to know who you are. You have to have an identity, a feeling about yourself. You have to be proud of yourself as a man or woman. Not only do black people have problems knowing where they're at, but white people grow up in this same fucked-up country and get fucked over too (in different ways). We have to cut the bullshit in our lives. We have to define our own reality.

We are not part of Nixon's and the other top idiots' reality. Their reality is in Vietnam with 40,000 dead, their reality is in the black ghettoes with twenty million hardly alive, their reality is in this country's high schools with passes to piss. Our reality is alive and we have to fight for it!

19

Rehearse for t

YES FOLKS! NOW YOU CAN BE THE FIRST ON YOUR BLOCK TO EXPERIENCE THE ECOLOGICAL DISASTER.

WHY WAIT TILL 1980?

DON'T LET THE FUTURE TAKE YOU BY SURPRISE.

PREPARE NOW FOR THE END OF CIVILIZATION.

REHEARSE FOR THE APOCALYPSE. HERE ARE A FEW SUGGESTIONS:

Better start preparing your pallette and stomach for the fare of the 80's:

* Mix detergent with everything you eat and drink. There's already quite a bit but there will be a lot more in the future.

* Learn how to digest grass and other common plants.

* Start fattening your dog, cat, parakeet and guppies for the main course of the future.

* Develop a taste for grubs and insects - your ancestors weren't too proud to lift a rock for their dinner.

* Practice starving.

* Every night before bedtime drink a glass of industrial and organic waste on the rocks (with mixer if you prefer).

Appreciating that most services and products will disappear over the next ten to twenty years, we suggest this little dry run:

* Turn off your gas
* Turn off your water
* Turn off your telephone
* Turn off your heat
* Turn off your electricity
* Sit naked on the floor and repeat this chant: PROGRESS IS OUR MOST IMPORTANT PRODUCT, PROGRESS IS OUR. . .

And as the final crisis approaches there's no better time to start hoarding. Start buying things you'll need

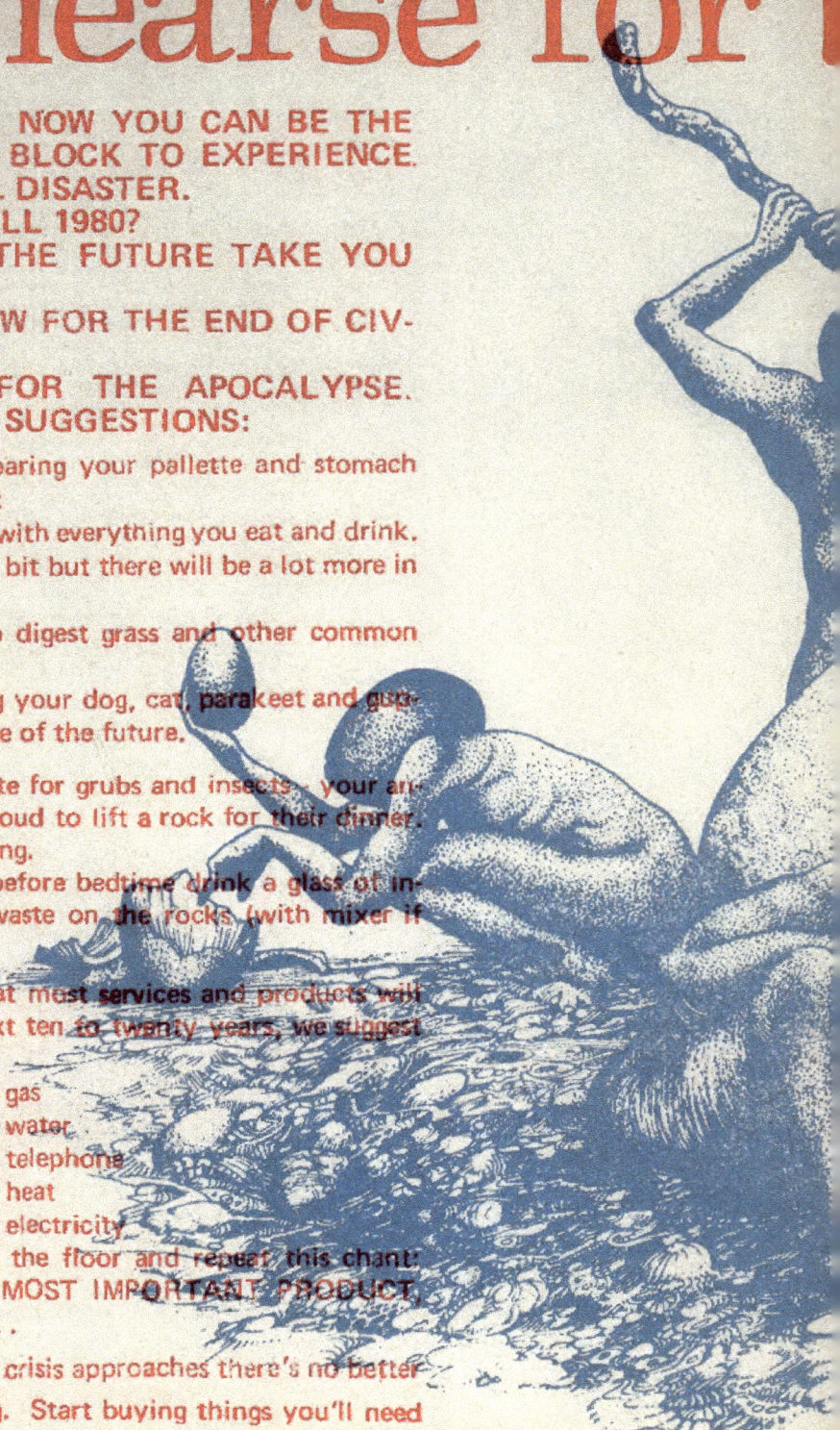

he Apocalypse

after the Fall on credit - after the collapse no one will bother with collecting debts.

* While on the subject: start thinking about creative new uses for money since its present function will soon end. Remember, paper - particularly tissue - will be in short supply.

* Think about creative new uses for other potentially obsolete things like electric can openers, televisions, brassieres, toilets, alarm clocks, automobiles, etc.

* Accustom yourself to human body odor.

* Now is the time to learn a trade for the future - practice making arrowheads and other implements out of stone. Advanced students should start experimenting with bronze.

* For those of you who are investment minded, buy land, but you'd better leave enough bread to also buy a small arsenal to defend your property with

* Remember Victory Gardens? Plant your Survival Garden now!

* Better quit smoking - or rip off a tobacco warehouse.

* Stockpile useful items like matches, safety pins, thread and needles, condoms, etc.

* Learn how to shoot a bow and arrow.

* Start preparing for the fashions of the future. You girls might take a hint from the heroines of monster films and start tearing your clothing in tasteful but strategically located tatters in order to create the Fay Wray look of tomorrow. Those less frivolous minded among you should start cultivating your body-hair. (Remember a naked ape is a cold ape)

* You housewives had better learn how to maim and kill with a vegematic.

* Finally everyone should buy a boy scout manual - or in lieu of that, buy a boy scout.

SO IN FACING THE WORLD OF TOMORROW REMEMBER: BUILD FOR THE FUTURE AND CONTEMPLATE SUICIDE.

EVO/LNS

BROWN SHOES DON'T MAKE IT

It was, at least for me and most of the people I know, the music that first aroused interest in things Underground, and the music is still the most mature and developed manifestation of the culture of the Underground. Underground visual arts draw their most effective imagery and inspiration from the music: the outstanding examples of this are Martin Sharp's Dylan and Hendrix posters and the 1967 Hapshash output. In fact, an amazing amount of the most adventurous designs are album sleeves: Sgt. Pepper, Disraeli Gears, Ogden's Flake, Ars Longa Vita Brevis, Tommy, I Stand Alone, Ceremony, King Crimson, Quintessence, Underground. literature is virtually non-existent: Burroughs, Ginsberg and the late Jack Kerouac are all of the Beat Generation. Maybe in ten years' time we may develop their equal; we certainly haven't got one now. So it's back to the music.

It's precisely because the music is such a vital, integral part of our movement that what's happening to it at the moment angers so badly for the whole Underground community. The whole point about the early Underground music scene was that it was an honest, experimental, no-bullshit service provided by and for artists and consumers whose tastes were ignored by the media. Alternative press, alternative music, alternative styles. The fifth-rate bubblegum and Mumsy pop music was discarded in favour of genuinely creative musical endeavours, based on all known styles and a few unknown ones. Carnaby Street's cardboard fashions were ignored by a community who if they wanted to wear red satin trousers and their mothers' hats just went out and did it, whatever "they" said we were all wearing this year. Honest people played honest music independently of "Top of the Pops", the NME and Peter Murray. Some of it sold to the Dumb Majority and that was beautiful. Do them good to have some honest music in the house. Of course, a few of the good bands were big stars—Beatles, Stones, Who, Animals, Manfred—and that was good.

Then came 1967 and the Great Flower Power Summer. Suddenly every other kid was belled and kaftaned and chanting "All You Need Is Love". I thought we'd really won—we'd enchanted and infiltrated them and genuinely convinced them that love was where it was at and not battling. Frankie Vaughan leapt into print to tell the mothers of Albion that a "Love-In" was just "an excuse for a great big orgy". The media found that the Underground music scene had beaten Tactic One—"Ignore it and it'll go away"—so it tried Tactic Two—"Take it over, package it, sell it back to itself". This worked admirably—they're still doing it now. We haven't infiltrated them—they've infiltrated us. Once the only part of the pop scene concerned with honest music and real people,

there's now more hype, bullshit and hustling on the so-called progressive scene than anywhere else. The straight/commercial pop scene is simple and honest: put it on the radio and people hear it and if they like it, they buy it. That's all, that's how they sold a million "Love Grows" and five million of "Sugar, Sugar". The music is crap, but the people are honest. With us, half the music is good, but half the people are dishonest.

In the teenybopper scene a few years ago, singers were sold on on faces, clothes and "image". Now this kind of irrelevant hyping is almost the exclusive property of the Underground. Music is again secondary. The MM "Musicians Wanted" classified ads carry gems such as "Guitarist wanted for semi-pro progressive band. Long hair essential". Any

group who look sufficiently hairy and make the right New-Left political noises can develop a hearing even if their music is derivative and uninspired. For instance: last year I was really looking forward to hearing Edgar Broughton at Bath, expecting something genuinely powerful and (I hate to say it) meaningful. What I got was a clumsy, disjointed, untogether performance by an ego-tripping dude who sang like a feeble imitation of Beefheart doing his first-album feeble imitation of Howlin' Wolf, and played the usual pallid Hendrix-derived freak out guitar. The political "revelations" were simplistic sloganeering that would have made Black Dwarf feel ashamed of itself. Even the celebrated "Out demons out" routine was a straight lift from Tuli Kupferberg

and the Fugs' October '67 performance at the Pentagon. An Underground Herman's Hermits.

So now the revolution is a groovy way to sell things. Someone cleaned up from selling thousands of Che posters, and 20th Century Fox advanced Omar Sharif's career nicely. Capitalism is alive and well—thanks to us. Those of us pledged to "da revolution"—I'm not—would do better to withdraw their services from the media; what can you do with your street-fighting ideals if the very people you want to fight against can package street-fighting, put it into posters, records and books, and sell it back to you at enormous profits? So hair and trite revolutionary lyrics can sell us inferior music—aren't you proud?

The best music is generally produced by people who are either regarded as pop stars—Auger, Driscoll, Who, Hendrix, Beatles, Beck (the trendies never forgave him for "Love Is Blue" and "Silver Lining"), Fleetwoods, Floyd, Jethro (Townshend and Anderson couldn't sell out if they tried)—or those who are ignored by the Underground because of insufficient hyping—the Soft Machine and Renaissance are outstanding. I haven't heard any Clapton, Beck or Hendrix for quite some time, but I expect something shattering soon from all three of them. Led Zeppelin were incredibly stimulating at first but a stone drag when it wore off. Keith Relf in "Friends" described it as "Straightforward fuck music". That's okay—I've got the first album. I'd love to meet a chick who could fuck like "Led Zeppelin One" but she'd wear me out in a week. At least it's non-political.

I'm getting back into straight-forward hard-grooving feel-good music—blues—soul—jazz—rock to use MM language. "Super Session", all the Butterfield albums, B.B. King, Chicago, "Streetnoise" (nothing grooves as hard as the last minute and a half of "Save the Country"), Jimmy Smith—and old group sounds, particularly the old Yardbirds stuff, "Best of the Lovin' Spoonful One and Two", the first Manfred Mann album, old Graham Bond (Remember "Tell Me" and "St. James Infirmary"?), and all the Beatles and Who. The other source of good music is from the folk side—Jansch, Mike Cooper, Mike Chapman, Stewart, Harper. The hypers have kept out of folk music which is probably why it's doing so badly, due to lack of skilful local promotion.

I have no idea of the solution, except to hope for a return to the basic attitude of yesterday's Underground and today's teenies (that sounds incredibly condescending from a bloke of 18): listen to as much music as possible and pick up on what you like. Don't worry if it got bad reviews in IT or if your trendy friends sneer; if you like it, buy it. That's where we ought to be, where we should have been all the time. Honest people, honest people. No more bullshit. Shalom, *Charles Shaar Murray*

CMON ANNIE! LET'S GO IN MY YARD! LISTEN, THEY DON'T CALL ME PUD FOR NOTHIN'!

PUD! STOP!

THEY WERE RIGHT HERE! HONEST GEORGE!

WHERE IS THAT DIRTY FAT BASTARD AN' WHERE'S MY SISTER??

GET A LOAD OF THESE WHIMPS!

WISE UP DIP SHITS!

SPLUT BLUP

Back Issue Bonanza

By public demand:
THE SECOND SENSATIONAL OZ
BACK ISSUE CLEARANCE

Once again, OZ offers you the chance of a life-time. Yes, this is the EVENT you've all been waiting for — THE ANNUAL OZ BACK ISSUE BONANZA!! A gigantic throwaway of all available back numbers! Don't miss this exciting opportunity to cash-in on these scarce gilt-edged collectors items.

But hurry! Stocks are dwindling fast — black market prices are already a City scandal. OZ, and only OZ! can make this sensational sacrifice because of surprise returns from Commonwealth distributors and unprecedented release of impounded copies by New Scotland Yard. This offer may never be repeated! ORDER NOW!

[Warning: It is unwise to do business with OZ touts — copies sold by unauthorised agents invariably turn out to be expensive forgeries!]

OZ 1. Absolutely unavailable.

OZ 2. A reel collectors item at only 5/-! Mammoth colour poster: Wilson of Toad Hall. Mark Lane sees the B.B.C. to shreds. Giant cut-outs of pop/flop stars. Ludicrous Malcolm Muggeridge interview. Soft drugs in London report. Disgusting British Breasts Competition. SEE HOW THEY SAG!

OZ 3. Unobtainable. The British Museum holds the only surviving unbound copy.

OZ 4. PURE GOLD! Rush this one! Few left. Inspired gold pornographic fold-out cover by Hapshash. Scientology exposed. Fuck de Gaulle. A Bastard's guide to living in sin. Norman Normal strip. Murray shakes and ladders. Plus OZ's own set of sensational TAROT CARDS by Martin Sharp... and how to use them! Unbelievable value at 10/- only.

OZ 5. SAVE 5/-! KING SIZE POSTER — Plant A Flower Child in psychedelic pink or sunburst yellow. Banned by Australian customs. Price tumbles from £1 to 10/- EXTRA BONUS — Great Alf Garnspiracy on rewrite; Shocking practices and customs of this growing cult REVEALED!

OZ 6. Two magazines for the price of one! OZ + John Wilcock's OTHER SCENES from the U.S.A. Dope sheet — how to drop acid, Leary in Disneyland. John Peel spills the beans — a prophetic interview before he hit the big time. Ruthless expose of the King of Nepal! ('It nearly caused a bloody war' — Foreign Office). Letter from a Greek Gaol. McLuhan's

Why isn't London jumping? Discover the shocking answer to these vital questions in the privacy of your own home for a mere 3/6.

OZ 18. Experimental format swiped straight from Rolling Stone. Michael X talks. Andy Warhol whispers. Prophetic Militant Student Application Form. Terry Reid. The Soft Machine. Emergency YIPPIE Report. The MC5 Kick out the Jams. Mad Marrakech hornmania and screaming nudes. 3/6.

OZ 19. News of the World loved this one, but we still have a few left. The Universal Tongue Bath — a groupie's vision. Why Det. Sgt. Pilcher knows so many pop stars. Dylanology from the first and worst Dylanologist. Food Explosion. FRELIMO. Still available despite legal advice, it's a cheap and dangerous buy at 3/6.

OZ 20. HELLS ANGELS menace Arts Lab in drug orgy rape gang bang loot shock!! So violent the printer destroyed 6000 copies. Paris Situationists. Out of the Psychodrama by David Widgery. Inside Jimi Hendrix. Roast Trafalgar Square pigeon and a cheap thrill on every page 3/6.

OZ 21. EIGHT PAGE COMIC FREAK-OUT. Plant Your Own Pot. Pete Townsend, Bernadetta Devlin, Living Theatre, Murray Roman and John Grassi all blow their cool and live the revolution. PLUS smouldering Hippocrates and MAGNAPHAL oed. How to catch and cook a schoolboy — all the meat you can eat for 3/6.

OZ 22. The Great Hippie Hoax. Marsha Hunt and why she has the biggest Afro in town. TV — The Bankrupt Medium and how to run Underground TV. Prince Charles pin-up. Martin Sharp Moonshot. Barrie Quartermain's Private Armies. 'The most suave OZ yet.' (Titbits) 3/6.

OZ 23. HOMOSEXUAL OZ. Hounded by Scotland Yard for being obscene. Suck for Peace. Scoop preview from still unobtainable Homosexual Handbook. Miles on the Moon along with several bags of piss. Pirate TV — Rohan O'Reilly's plans for Caroline. Phil Ochs meets Mick Farren, Max Ernst portfolio. OZ answer to The Forsyte Saga — the life and loves of Leon and Cohen. Multiracial male kisses. Only 25 left of most controversial OZ ever. Selling in Earls Court for £3 each. Save £2. 5s. Rush your 15s now.

BELOW COST OFFER

OZ 24. The famous gallery of beautiful Freaks — a mad, memorable collection of unique lateral-thinking, wizards, drug

discoveries in our warehouse. Famous BOB DYLAN cover. Black Power — Michael X meets the Flower Children. Wog Beach Shock! What's so good enough Dylan — six page analysis. How the sun MAIMS! Review of His Holiness Maharishi Mahesh Yogi's book. AND... Polly Peachum — IN BED WITH THE AMERICANS! A real blow-job at 3/6.

OZ 8. Originally 5/- sensational value at 3/6. Bumper double issue + free copy of the incarcerably wrongly spelled Guevara page poster. Quantrooche! on the failure of the Russian Revolution. Think sideways with Edward de Bono. BANNED PLAYBOY PICTURES (yawn yawn). Richard Meltzer on Rock. Fifty-six pages of glowing colour. The most unreadable OZ ever!

OZ 9. 3/6. Unidentified Flying Objects — the weird, horrifying world of the Flying Saucer Society. Fact or Fantasy? Laing poetry page. Inside expose of St. Paul's School horror camp. Who really killed John Kennedy??? — startling photograph of riflemen supressed by Warren Commission. Very few left, a complete TRIP!

OZ 10 — OZ 16. Unobtainable

OZ 17. Manfred Mann? Smash Cash? ICA Blast? Indian Ashrams? South African Queens? Greek Gaols? DON'T LET YOUR CHICK BLOW YOUR BALLS!? Does Siel Im really shelter? IS Tiny Tim the rest?

oh life a bit your? of a long while 1/6.

OZ 20. Hippy Atrocina!! The full shock story from Siberia to Scunthorpe, including the most hated paper ever published — "LEPER RAPES VIRGIN — SHE GIVES BIRTH ETC. ETC. (Remember you swore you'd never buy OZ again? Ha. Ha.) In between the cheap sensation this OZ also offers the best obituary of Jack Kerouac yet published. Optional extras: Easy Rider interview, Fabulous Frisk Brothers, History of Rock and introducing to this country The Chicago Conspiracy Circus. Sixty PACKED Pages, 3/6.

OZ 25. OZ gets GLOSSY!! (to celebrate our sixteenth, count 'em, sixteenth, printed!. What an issue. Germaine's blistering attack/assessment of Women's Liberation WENDY — The world's first fuckable rubber woman; Bill Levi, star of SUCK magazine, in a frame dropping probe of his marriage collapse and shock exile. Not to mention the Biggest Tool in Hollywood and apposite star of the show CANDY DARLING — is she or isn't he?? Food explosion, Media Mix and more Conspiracy maks this an irresistible buy at 3/6.

OZ 27. The mindbending ACID OZ. Packed with facts, information and the real dope (luck this corner of page 46!) on that short cut to Heaven and Hell. You've probably already got it, with this issue our circulation soared to 40,000 plus!, but isn't there a friend who's really NEEDS it. Do them a favour and drop us 3/6.

WHIZZKIDEAS

The underground as far as this country is concerned mainly exists in London. In the last few years however an attempt to bring the underground to other parts of the country has been made by forming Arts Labs which are in no way united. In many cases they have had to pack up because of lack of support. If a change to the present system of government and attitudes is to be made it is going to be a very slow process and so help from the present youth has to be utilised. As much as the underground, like everyone else, hates the kids it would be disastrous if a genera-tion gap were to emerge between the two factions of our present society. The writing of this issue of Oz is a step in the right direc-tion; in helping, it works both ways – the under 18s because we have the chance of putting our ideas into print. We hope when this is read people will realise what a state we're in and help us get sorted out. It is very difficult putting our hangups in writing like this and only by open discus-sion will any good arise. It has reached the stage where we have almost given up, because of the way we are snubbed and looked down upon when we try to get help in London. I only hope that this at last is the breakthrough. We find it hard to believe that so many of you are empty of any kind of idea whatsoever. If you think this is a lot of schoolkid rubbish, and some of this probably is, then don't blame us. We offered to edit Oz because we thought we'd like to get our ideas into print and it has been very hard work but when we asked people for their views most of them just didn't seem to have any. A lot of people said that they didn't know what to write, a lot claimed that they didn't have the time but hardly any of them were the slightest bit interested. WHAT'S WRONG WITH THEM? Here was their chance to put their views into print but they just didn't want to know. We contacted all the people who seemed to have a lot to say, but most were too lazy to pick up a pen.

In future people who think they have a lot to say needn't bother to waste people's time. They'll only show themselves up and it will only be their own fault.
Anne

skinhead armies

Throughout England people are questioning our system and trying to change it. The people co concerned fall into two classes. Skinheads show their dislike for our system by generally abusing the law by violence and the use of drugs. They are quite willing to use violence against the system and against anyone else for that matter which is very unfortunate because they are fighting the same battle as many of the people they pick fights with.

On the other hand there are the so-called long-haired ... to preach peace and ... non-violent ... How ... a more apathetic bunch ... difficult ... of these long-haired intellectuals are actually doing anything to help change come. The rest are quite willing to wait for things to be done ... them. The situation in the underground at the moment is that there is plenty of generals but ... by among students at ... moment is ... wo ... than ever before.

foodless fable

Once upon a time, before people had woken up, Jimmy Rooker found himself standing on a rock watching the birds eat each other. He asked the trees what their names were, and told them his lucky number was blue. He had to feed himself and wash his face and hands in the sky, but he enjoyed finding food and scrubbing with stars.

After his friends had eaten enough, and there were none left, he walked up and down the flowers to find some more playmates. Instead, he found a ball which he drank hungrily and put in his pocket.

The ball was so heavy that it pulled our Jimmy's trousers down, and as he bent sideways to put them back on his head, he cut his toe on a puddle and had to go straight to heaven without any supper.
Sarah Manders

no acid heads

Although there is a lot to be said against our old-fashioned educational system, some benefits can arise from the way subjects are forced into our heads. If it wasn't for the mass-production of our so-called counterfeit brains then the revolutionary student would not exist, and would not try to change all that offends. Some people think that they be benefit more by reading Mailer and Burroughs, however they would not have the capacity to read literature if it wasn't for our old-fashioned system.

A recent article in "IT" related a counterfeit £5 to the so-called counterfeit people produced in our schools and colleges at the moment. The writer didn't seem to realise that school-kids and most students are not acid-heads, still have minds of their own, and are quite capable of thinking for themselves.
P. Crisp

ONLY CONNECT

He who opposes force with force alone forms that which he opposes and is formed by it. This has far greater truth than we choose to appreciate. We rather content ourselves in the knowledge that he who does not resist force that enslaves and exterminates will be enslaved and exterminated. The time has come however for us all to open our eyes and realise, maybe, that violence is not the sole tactic at our disposal.

John Lennon said, "We're supposed to be the hip ones but the pigs have got us playing their game reacting violently to violent provocation." If we are hip then we should surely see through the cons of the Establishment; we should see that while violence prevails the pigs are victorious; we must realise that the ultimate strategy in our striving for equality, freedom and peace is that of communication. It is necessary to fight with words but the reason why the tactic of violence is preferred is, perhaps, that it is so much easier to express.

I'm not saying that violent demonstration is wrong. Indeed often it is the only alternative left. Tell the oppressed black citizen in Alabama, whose kids get stoned by white parents on their way to school, tell him to talk to the racialist white mother fucker and he'll laugh or cry—for him there is only one road to freedom. Stokely Carmichael wrote: "They (the oppressed peoples) will not be stopped in their drive towards dignity, to achieve their share of power, indeed to to become their own men and women, in this time and in this land, by whatever means necessary". In this country, though, the circumstances are different, and while violent demonstration must be recognised as having a necessary function, in that it serves for instance to boost the morale of the freedom fighters in South Africa, we must overcome our apathy, our self-conceit, and realise just how vital is COMMUNICATION.

It appears that our regard for communication, however necessary, is that it is far too demanding and the results negligible, thus making it not worth the effort. In fact we are desperately trying to excuse our own laziness. How many of us know our oppressed brother? Can we even really communicate with each other?

But most important, we must talk to the masses, the blind prisoners of society, the toys of the Establishment, who beneath their plastic exterior are people, people with a consciousness waiting to be freed.

Of course it's a slow progress. Just as it has taken time for society to contract this sickness of mind, it will take time to cure it, but we must act now. We are lucky, the means of communication remains open to us—for so many others it does not; we even have some control of the mass media, so for Christ's sake let's use it.

To some extent we must gain the acceptance of those with whom we wish to communicate. This is said to require "compromise" but let's make a clear distinction between what this, in fact, means, and what could be misinterpreted as conforming to the false values of this evil-infested society. Yet, herein does lie the true meaning of this "compromise": we may detect the evils—the prejudice and oppression, but we must not blind ourselves with hatred:— then, we too become intolerant and narrow-minded. By remaining aware of the Establishment cons, we can go into the streets with free minds and attempt to give our eyes to the blind. Our minds must remain free, and our hearts open: we must be willing to understand, as from understanding comes communication; from communication comes a revolution of thoughts and a knowledge of the truth.

If I've failed I hope these lines of Steve Miller reach you, because this is what it's all about.

Don't let the policeman turn you round
Don't let the politician turn you down
Don't let nobody turn you round
You've got to keep on walking
Keep on talking
Marching to the freedom land
Henry Harcus

Henry Harcus

KISS ME QUICK

Gone is the age when people greeted each other physically. Now all that seems necessary is mental contact. This Victorian influence is apparent in our actions. We have brainwashed ourselves into thinking that physical contact is only necessary in sexual behaviour or parental duty and that a simple gesture of love or affection is unnecessary. People are so hung up with sexual inclinations and proper behaviour that getting together has become strictly mental. Couldn't we try to get a bit closer physically as well as mentally?

The underground is the metropolis. Too much, maybe, has already been said about the underground or lack of it. The underground outside London or major cities is practically non-existent though many claim to seek or create it. Some make the mistake of trying to imitate the metropolitan underground rather than creating something suited to their own environment.

There is no established underground press but unauthorised publications consist of college magazines which are usually unsuccessful and pack up after a few issues through lack of support, interest and money. Circulations of national underground press is scarce because of the so-called moral conscience of local tradesmen.

The progressive music scene is practically non-existent except on record. Most of the worthwhile concerts are held either in London or in other largely populated areas from which transport is difficult and expensive.

Scoring is frustrating because of unreliable contacts and bad deals. Prices seem to increase in miles from suburbia although the pigs are just as efficient. Also communication with the metropolitan underground is difficult because of lack of cooperation. *Berti*

WEEDKILLER HORROR

John Czerny, his wife and three children had to live on a rubbish dump hill near the Gethmange Chicken Factory. Throughout their life as a family unit, they had been molested by almost everybody and blamed for every conceivable wrong, including their own. Two years previously, they had been evicted from a rather unpleasant flat to find themselves in an even more unsavoury situation among all the half-things, former things and rotting things (mostly chicken skulls).

John Czerny had long red hair and a beard and, by circumstances, was ill-nourished. Avant-garde ideas crossed the short path along his badly covered brain, but these remained only in the state of thought because his visions had been utterly misunderstood when carried out and had involved a long confinement in a room where he was constantly told he was insane. He was the kind of person that is found in every small town—the one person who is "crazy" But in a strange way he was respected. Unfortunately, people fear something they are not able to understand. There were times when John the village creep came across new, unexplored paths of free expression, but these were ridiculed and coupled with lack of money; his doom was to wander for miles every day looking for work and money to feed his starving, unsmiling family. His alien pride refused assistance—he understood that these heavy financial chains belonged to no nobody else.

The formerly beautiful Mrs. Czerny remained in the caravan trying to divert the young children and herself from both the stone-cold reality of their environment and visions of a better life. Often the fat rats ate the bread as the family bunched in an unspeaking stupor waiting for the man of no hope to return.

Friends and all other enemies had lost touch years previously - the last one had cut off the water, electricity and gas from the wretched flat they had formerly occupied. Now they silently nagged each other with glazed faces as the youngest child bawled louder than usual.

The next day, John spent his last five shillings on twelve pounds of weed killer. In the evening he stared at the baby's mad eyes and then at the sack of explosive weed killer under the family bed. The following day, a letter came from the council telling the family to get out. John gasped at the sack that now lay under the table.

During the following evening, the distant noise of an angry mob filtered through the semi-darkness, discordant near the absolute dirty neon-mist that surrounded the caravan. John smiled gently at the lighted match in his hand.
So if you want to make a good end of it, use Ashley's Safety Matches. For lasting results, you won't want your money back. Be like John Czerny and get a box of Ashley's Matches—add weed killer and go out in style. Get some today.
Alan Clayson

27

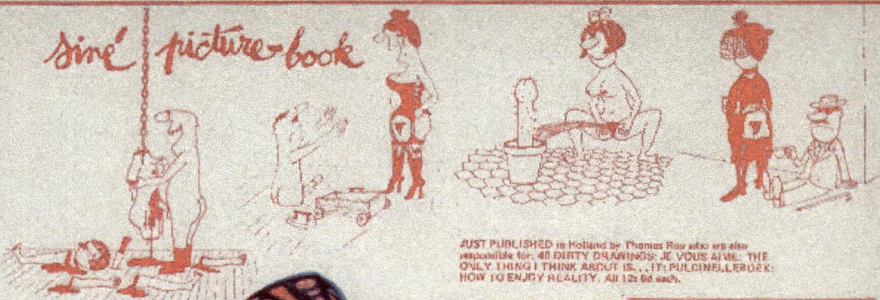

Stone Deaf!
(Drawn for the "Boy's Own Paper" by T. Browne.)

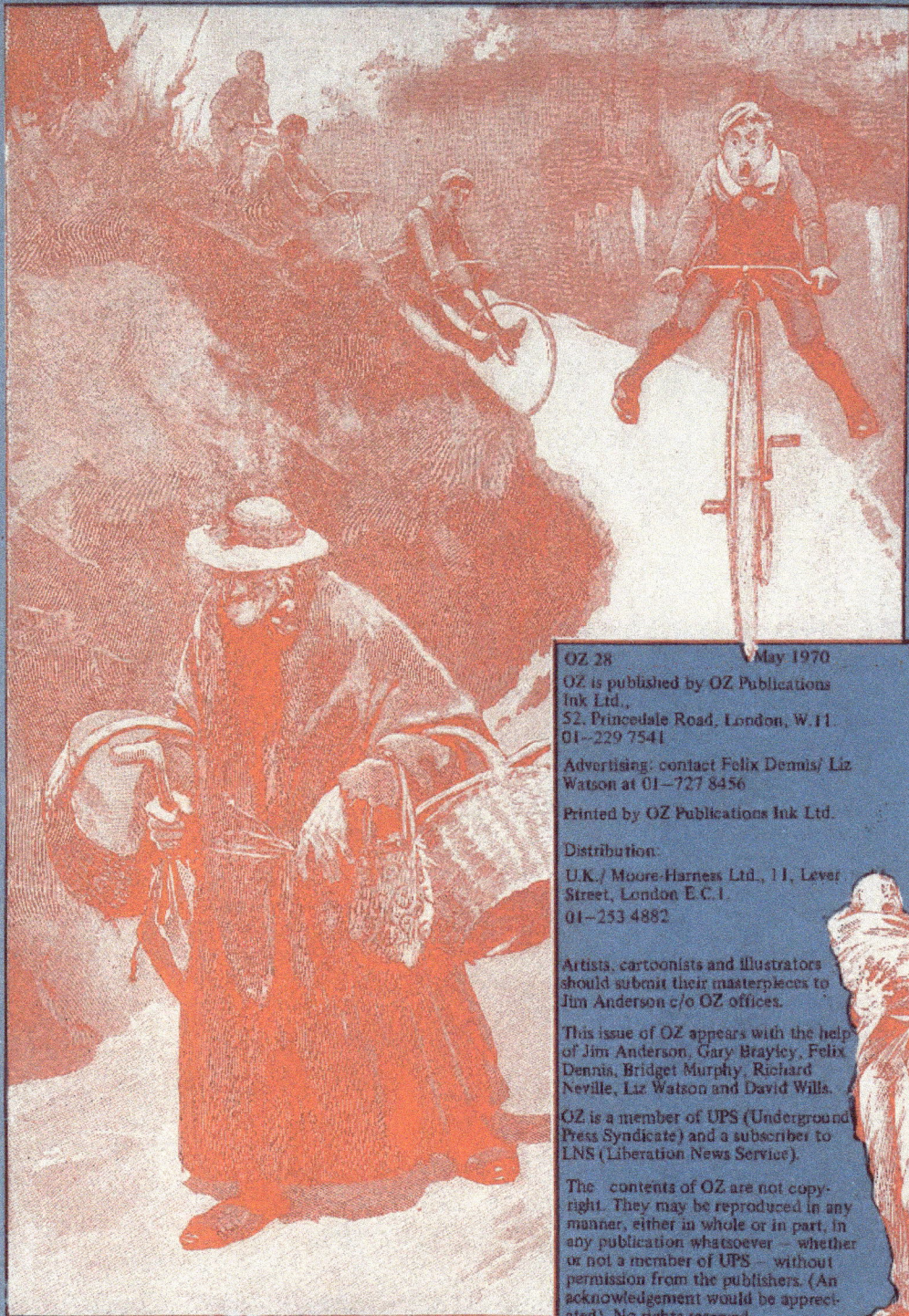

OZ 28   May 1970

OZ is published by OZ Publications
Ink Ltd.,
52, Princedale Road, London, W.11.
01—229 7541

Advertising: contact Felix Dennis/ Liz
Watson at 01—727 8456

Printed by OZ Publications Ink Ltd.

Distribution:
U.K./ Moore-Harness Ltd., 11, Lever
Street, London E.C.1.
01—253 4882

Artists, cartoonists and illustrators
should submit their masterpieces to
Jim Anderson c/o OZ offices.

This issue of OZ appears with the help
of Jim Anderson, Gary Brayley, Felix
Dennis, Bridget Murphy, Richard
Neville, Liz Watson and David Wills.

OZ is a member of UPS (Underground
Press Syndicate) and a subscriber to
LNS (Liberation News Service).

OZ SUCKS...

Dear Ed,

I've followed Oz since its first appearance and I wish I had them here as a reference. I'm sure happy that it exists. I'm aware of all your problems, printers sueing etc. but for Fucks sake! You are on what year now? Third? First I could not read it at all but I figured that part you would learn. You did. The full blown pictures are extinguishable. Congratulations! After three years: pathetic!

The whole world is packed to the brim of talent. Poets, writers, music, art, LIFE. And where are you now? Tired you say in plea for aid from schoolchildren in the last issue. Put it on the cover baby. You need it. Not in the smalls.

Oz being the only anywhere near organized 'Underground' mag in Europe, well for HEAVENS SAKE. SPREAD IT!

You have a lot of responsibility. Not towards saving your own literary Public image baby, but in spreading the TRUTH! COMMUNICATION! That's what I work for. Enlightenment.

Spreading a mag. does not only mean finding stores other than Smith's. It has to do with the Appearance of the publication and with the content. HOPEFULLY. Sure you have a lot of good writers but baby, THEY DROWN! Sadly in stinking puddle of stale sperma on your cock and shit stained pages. Give them a chance to be read.

Remember 100% of your readers have more than once in their lifetime been exposed to a sexual organ, and would you believe all 100% have actually made use of it too?!! Incredible as it may sound.

One does not need it shov ad in one's mind from every corner of the universe, and particularly not from the pages of OZ which has a hell of a lot more to say. You've got Suck and others for that. That's their bag, baby, let *them* do it. Stick to your own. OZ is important. We need you! REVEAL the TRUTH such as it is. We are in a sufficiently dynamiting minority as it is (with continual put-downs and fights within the so-called 'Underground' OZ hitting on I.T., I.T. hitting on OZ, Gandalf hitting on Earth, Earth hitting on Heaven Grey hitting on colours and colours as a result loosing their original brilliance.)

LOVE was the wonderful word we all believed in. Where is Love now? Where is all the fantastic exuberant joy and optimism from the Flower Power times? LOVE is beautiful and sex is part of it. Don't vulgarize the only thing every human being longs for and needs so badly. If anything GLORIFY IT! We need it baby. It's a cold hard world we were born into. It's bad enough as it is (and has been since the dawn of what we know as history.) With bleeding cunts and cocks (it's not the size, by the way, it's how you move it) on every page you might well SHOCK. I don't mind. But you also achieve a negative shock which results in people furiously scavenging through the magazine in pursuit of more food for their fury, more suck and fuck, which they find. Rasult: THEY DON'T READ WHAT IS OF ULTIMATE VALUE' THE TEXT. DIG?!!

And if I, glorious globe-trotter raving freak on the road, since 10 years, get upset, I could imagine that there might be more. And I am not upset by the fact that you reveal SEX. Baby, I LOVE it! It's how you do it. Why be vulgar when you can be witty?

Get someone else to do OZ. Someone with the various problems (graphics ill. etc. layout) as a profession. But don't let it get so fucking out of hand. You (OZ) are VITAL. And don't you ever (how could you) OZ, as I feel you do, slacken on that responsibility.

At least 90% of what's written and painted today is unpublished. Well. Do something about it. Don't people submit any of their work to you? You do a LOT, but you could do more, and back again to the cocks and cunts. I'm fucking convinced that it does more bad than good. Think about that.

Have been living and learning on this beautiful island for nearly 8 months now. Writing, drawing and crocheting. I've been working pretty hard and 8 months without sounds or news has done my thing here I have shown them the joy of colour every shop is full of copies of my work. I've taught them the basic stitch now they can freak out on their own and they don't need to follow a pattern. If I could submit that that goes for all of life providing one respects ones neighbours well . . .wouldn't that be nice.

Meanwhile all the knapsackers are being turned off the Moroccan border and subsequently invading here. The authorities can't cope — mass busts. People in prison. No distinction between good or bad. Reality.

B. Bjerke
Lista de Correos
Ibiza
Balearic Isles
Spain

Dear Oz,

You tell yourself you don't want to be old yet when you're four years old and slightly jaded with the situation, you import some rural freaks in to help out with an edition. There is an empty hush when somebody outside your narrow hierarchy reads your pointless pornography and you think that this means nothing. You've told a lot of lies and because of this you've compromised with those you're trying to attack. Remember the leper? If you're joking you can jump back, but if you're dying you might as well crawl away. I think you're on the run under the disguise of enjoying yourself, messing about with print and helping people to masturbate their minds as well as their bodies and you know (and I know) what an artless practice that is. You don't really care what I think, although I thank you for printing these words (if you do) but it's in the air that someone's paying for the things you've done, like the 14-year-old brat who loses her equally stupid parents respect when she's caught with a self-stimulator. Are you still reading this or did you pack up ages ago. Maybe you think I don't understand Oz—maybe I don't. Perhaps you think I'm a fool, think again when you're six years old, when you're worn out and fading. There are a lot of people that do airless things like you do. These include collectors of car numbers, lawn mowers and watchers of Sunday afternoon films, and *you* are criticising *them*. Rather a case of the vomit calling the spit "the gums rush".

Where are those days when you read like the phantasmagoria of sensitive oppressed brains and were blamed for history's mistakes (or something like that)? At times you were magnificent, like the transcript of a protracted implacable dream. Now you read like the verbal vomit of an academic street gang. The novelty is wearing off.

Maybe this situation is just the dull light of the lonely after-breakfast hour of your literary life. Like a huddled mumbling man you seem to be unconsciously picking up the droppings of the material press who lethargically waste time scurrying round transvestite vicars. You are getting dangerously near them.

Mori ubi est victoria tua.

Alan Clayson

30

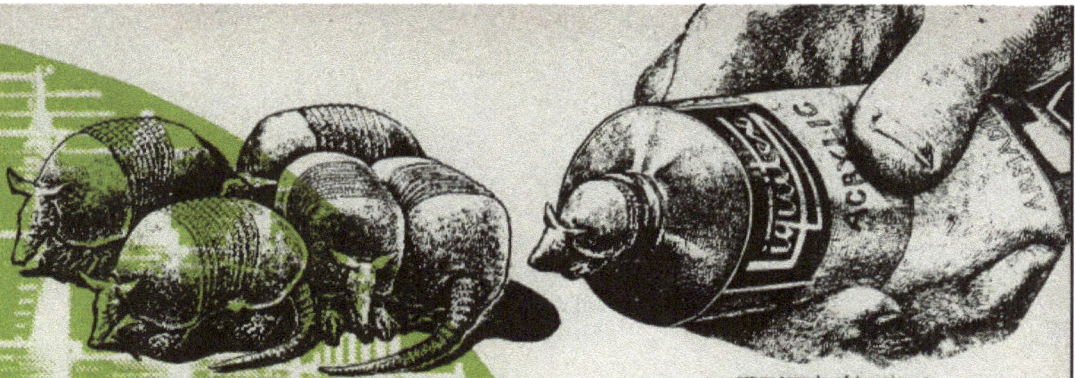

Dear OZ,

The Underground press is failing to live up to its name; in fact it could hardly be more above-ground if it tried. IT seems to have degenerated to chasing it-self round in circles, soon, with any luck, to disappear up its own arse: Rolling Stone never was and never will be, and even OZ over-burdens us with pseudo-intellec-tual crap about idealistic revolu-tions and utopias just around the corner which would be more at home in the heavy weeklies. All the same, OZ is at present our only chance, mainly because they do at least experiment with de-sign and lay-out of the maga-zine; the Magic Theatre edition for instance was a great idea treating the concept of magazines as an art form in the most imagin-ative and inventive way so far. But OZ is still severely lacking in many other respects. Too many of the articles seem to be nothing more than reprints from Ameri-can and Continental magazines, and so many of these are so pe-dantic and tangled up in words as to be of little interest to any but a tiny minority. Not only this, but they lack the punch and vitality which is essential in such articles. They aim gentle body-blows at Society, which are ignored or laughed off, instead of delivering an almighty kick in crutch as often as possible. OZ will sidle up to you, put its hand in your pocket, and start frigging you, when what it should do is fuck you from head to toe, body, mind, heart and soul, fuck your brain clean of the stench and slime of Society, leaving you ready to accept revolutionary and anarchistic ideals and doctrines. This totality of involvement is missing at the time when we need it most. For too long we the read-ers have sat back and had shit shoved into our brains. WE should decide what we want to read, not just accept what is given to us. WE should write the fucking magazine, it should be a medium through which our ideas, our creativity, can be communicated to people who think the same, and to break through the mental apathy of those who couldn't care. How can new ideas, new ways of thinking be born and be-come something like established if they cannot be put across to the maximum number of people possible? We should be concerned with the now, and the future, using the past only as a form of reference and a means of avoiding the more obvious pitfalls. Too much of the bullshit that appears in OZ is anachronistic as soon as it is written. Compare them with articles in the New Society or the Spectator. Are they really differ-ent, apart from words like shit and fuck occur more frequently? Are they inciting us to riot, to rebel, to burn the cities down? Where is the petrol these words should be pouring on the embers of our seemingly defunct anar-chism? Perhaps everyone's scared of burning their own hands, of seeing accusing fingers pointing at them. Perhaps beneath their easy talk about revolution there is an undercurrent of reactionary thought, a process that will de-volve them into the same grey mass they pretend to reject. How long before the wife-and-kids-and-mortgage syndrome gets the bet-ter of them and they sink into an even more vacuous existence than before? We need constant prod-ding, incessant mental and physi-cal provocation if we are to over-throw our present Society and replace it with something much better, something of our own creation based on the bitter ex-periences of the past. This aim can never be achieved by theoris-ing words alone: these are just cobwebs that clog our minds which must be burnt out by a lightning bolt of vicious, inflam-matory words, that will goad us into action. Nothing less will do. We are human beings, we make mistakes, we have our shortcom-ings, we will run backwards unless pushed forwards. Ideals do not suit us, not while we retain our basic human nature. Take that away, make us like machines and idealism will work. That is impos-sible, so let us be irritated and goaded by words and actions, until we cry out against our real aggressors openly, out in the streets, and tread on their faces and destroy all that they stand for. When the dust has settled, we shall be standing face to face with the future, confronted by humanity's last desperate chance to save itself and survive. That is what everyone should hope for, to be in on this chance when it comes, and be prepared to fight to gain it, and fight even harder to make it work successfully. Now if the time to really set things moving. The pages of OZ should be packed with the fuel of revolution, which should burst into flames as it is read, flames that dance mesmerisingly before the eyes, flames that spread into the mind and rekindle the fires of rebellion that seem to be dying. Nothing whole-hearted or committed is happening NOW, nothing is there to incite us NOW, just vague promises about tomorrow. Tomorrow must be-come today. Kick out the jams NOW.

Steve Francis

Dear OZ,

I'm really pissed off about things. I don't know where the hell I am or where the hell I'm meant to be going. I can't pre-tend that you lot are the only people who could help me but, in the circumstances, I don't think of many others. Some peo-ple (i.e. my parents) will never give up trying to help, and I sup-pose I should thank them for that, but the truth is I've been completely disillusioned in them and people with the same age, class, money, etc, as solvers of any kind of problems I might have. I only hope you can help by telling me what's the best way to get the kind of life I've been forced to live up till now off my back once and for all.

I'll try to give you some idea of the situation I'm in. I'm 16. For the last two-and-a-half years I've been at a place called Clifton College. I never really enjoyed life there. The only people I could find myself on a level with were other people like me, that is other 'intellectual revolu-tionaries', who were, in the same way as me, dying to get a chance to knock the shit out of that fine old establishment offer-ing an education in all that is noble and traditional to the young gentleman. God, how I've hated all that is 'noble and tradi-tional' in the past year. We tried quite a few ways to get the rest of the school to wake up and realise change had to come — I'm putting some of our myster-ious 'Think' cards which were delivered every Sunday morning last term in with this letter — but none of them worked. We realised most people in the school were apathetic slobs (we got to thinking of them almost as traitors to their youth) and that the place would never be-come a better place in our time, and so we decided to say good-bye to the evil shit-house. Most of my friends are leaving and of next term, after one more at-tempt (an unofficial reb.mag.), which I suppose will be another flop. But I was getting so up-tight, I had to cut out as soon as possible. Of course I found it impossible to persuade my par-ents, the staff etc. that this was the case, but through (a) the help of a sympathetic psychia-trist who saw how fed up I was and (b) my previous record (nearly expelled term before for dope, constantly under suspicion since then for frequent heading and bedding), it wasn't all that difficult to get my release.

The trouble is that now they're trying to get me to go to some other temple of learning, to carry on working for A-levels. Unfortunately, they just won't believe me when I tell them it's no good because the syllabuses for those bloody exams are just such a drag. There are so much more important things I feel I could be doing because it seems to me I'm so much better at writing poetry, for example, than at the endless, destructive, analytical, almost scientific essays that I'd have to suffer. I want to do something for the world. I want to help in the revolution. I don't want to get stuck in any system. I want to live with people I like and not in any artificially thrown-toge-ther establishment. My father took me to be interviewed at some so-called progressive school. It was real shit. It looked all zingy and permissive, but I could see that the philosophy behind it was almost identical to Clifton's — melting personali-ties down and pouring them into a common mould. I don't want that to happen to me. If I'm going to change society I'm not going to do it in the two-faced way of getting 'influence' and 'respect for my views' by greas-ing up to it and getting its crum-my qualifications. I want to break out NOW! I don't think 16 is too young — I'm not going to wait till 18, when I'll be (in their terms anyway) an adult.

Name supplied

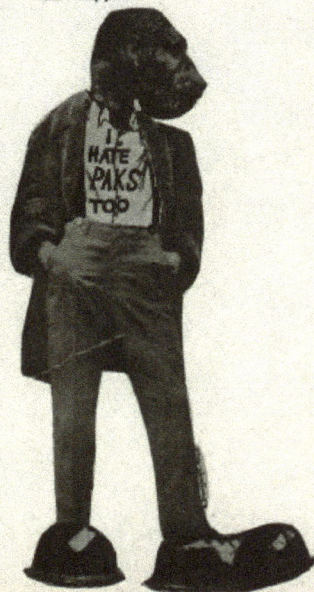

Real freaks?

Dear OZ,

'The Acid Facts' on pages two and three of the most recent OZ is on the whole a balanced and honest report for which you should be commended. But there is one important omission that leads to a dangerous error. It concerns the vexed issue of chromosomal damage. You quite correctly quote SCIENCE to support the argument that LSD does *not* lead to genetic damage, on the basis of present evidence. But that is not the same thing as saying the drug cannot lead to chromosomal damage. The so-called second Wootton Report (1970) on amphetamines and LSD contains the following sentence: 'Chromosomal aberrations in users of LSD as well as in the test tube have been reported.' It goes on to substantiate the statement, and to qualify it, particularly in so far as alleged genetic damage is concerned. But the point is this: Genetic damage arises from chromosomal defects in egg or sperm cells. That LSD causes such defects remains unproven. On the other hand, chromosomal damage can appear in body cells other than egg or sperm cells — e.g., blood cells, brain cells, skin cells, etc. It is in these so called somatic cells that chromosomal defects traceable to LSD have been reported. There is as yet no evidence that it has happened, but if LSD causes such defects in body cells, diseases such as leukaemia might result.

Two less important points: there is no evidence that thalidomide caused foetal defects by causing chromosomal damage. On the contrary, the drug seems to have altered the development of some organs or limbs, but just how is not known. Second, you say that the doubtful experiment on genetic damage 'should've killed the research right there'. Research always goes on, and by rights should, especially when doubt remains. What else are the experimenters with acid doing?

Dick Fisher

THIS TIT PICTURE IS FROM HELIX MAG
(IF YOU WERE WONDERING, WE PRINT ALL LETTERS (TO FILL THE SPACES) SEND ONE IN... A VIDGET IN PRINT!

ALSO THIS RATHER UNUSUAL BIT OF EQUIPMENT.

WHY, IT'S CHARMING! WHERE'D I BUY ONE?

She's ours

Dear OZ,

When I first heard of the magazine Oz, I was curious to know what underground magazines contained to make them frowned upon by society in general. My first impressions (as I stared at a distracted nude) was one of repulsion. I decided that it was a load of pornographic crap.

A small group of girls sat in the corner of the classroom hovering like a load of vultures and sniggering over advertisements for contraceptives and pictures of nude bodies. They knew about such things, the majority were not virgins and yet they still had not passed the giggling stage. Their embarrassing titters infuriated me.

I voiced my opinion on the magazine and was informed I ought to really read it and not make snappy decisions. After reading a number of back copies I realised a number of the articles were rather interesting and enlightening. Eventually I grudgingly admitted being wrong.

HILARY.

Not a loud

Dear OZ,

While sitting here in my pad smashed out of my mind on Afghan (nice!) and listening to Radio 1 Club, I remembered the outcry about music level at dances and discotheques. The BBC news was quoted as saying 'A check is always made on our club hours to ensure that the music is not too loud'. They only said that so the conservative public will like the Director of Governors (fuckers on the B.B.C. panel and keep them in control of radio. Every person who wants to get stoned and listen to music at the level he likes should be left alone.

And how about the fucking cheek of the G.P.O. jamming the music and beautiful sounds reaching us from Radio North Sea International.

Must roll another joint now. Love,

DEREK

Praise be

Dear OZ,

Thanks for continuing to give us something real when elsewhere the 'underground press' seems to be getting straighter with each issue (excluding of course the beautiful but sadly irregular 'Gandalf's Garden).

The double page spread (No. 27) on acid was very informative and accurate and is going to be very useful to hesitant 'new' heads. I think you might well have used as a heading for those pages the beautiful quote from 'Steppenwolf' by Hermann Hesse, more recently recalled by Tim in 'The Politics of Ecstasy' — 'Magic Theatre. Price of admission, your mind'.

Peter Collins,
23 Burley Close,
Norbury,
London, S.W.16.

Virgin

Dear OZ,

In OZ 26 there was an article on Rape of a Virgin and in OZ 26 two people (DID I say people!) wrote in to say what a load of shit it was — not only the one article but the whole paper. (Fuckers!) I think their letter was the biggest load of hypocritical shit I have had the misfortune to read. Since I came over from America, I have read nearly every OZ published, (every one beautiful).

Long Live the Dead,
Jay Lay Newman.

Lay off

Dear OZ,

David Widgery seemed to justify horse, in his 'Play Power' review, on grounds that the euphoria more than balanced out the health thing. He's right, it's nice to rush any buzz, and to render it harmless would be more groovy than the present concern with curative techniques. But, you know, as time passes, increasingly bigger fixes are needed to achieve the same level of abstraction – horse spirals up and away and oh so tightly around you, – there's no escape, it has you a prisoner, – and the pains, well they're too much altogether.

People should not be allowed to have their reservations about horse shattered by David Widgery's remarks (and perhaps their lives and happiness). Horse was O.K. but it wasn't all euphoria. A lot of the times weren't nice at all.

Love and peace,
Peter,
38, Enderley St. Newcastle.

And now I'd like to fuck you miss

Dear Editor,

OZ always seems to me too flippant in its approach and presentation to be seriously for or against anything, with the super imposition of words on pictures suggesting that neither is up to much but if the two are thrown out together maybe it'll look interesting.

As long as OZ remains principally a consumer good, I don't see it as being genuinely revolutionary or anti-establishment. Not that there's a publication in Britain that does seem to be a genuine, informed yet still emotional yet still well written, response to important and unfashionable events. That piece on Scunthorpe epitomised all I resent in Oz, the underground taking a snotty look at the provinces; if Oz was real, it would attract pieces from kids who've lived in Scunthorpe and really knew it – you'd have written to the English Teacher at a local comprehensive school and had him commission

his hippest kids to do something for you.

As it is, I'd be as embarrassed to be in Oz as I would be if I were in Radio Times.

Why don't any of the underground papers have sports sections? Football and athletics are real dramas, compared to the phoney ones of theatres. In the same sense that rock 'n' roll is real music compared to classical music. Most of the good singers – Percy Sledge, Screamin' Jay Hawkins, Johnny Burnette, Jackie Wilson, too many to list – were sportsmen by first choice, singers by necessity when they couldn't make it in sport.

I wish Oz would open up, become more wide-eyed in what it covers and more accessible in how it presents its material. It seems to me to be no kind of achievement that most of the kids I teach (16 to 19 years old, at one of the most progressive colleges of SE London), working class to upper class, can't relate Oz to themselves, although they are the personnel who would be staff in any revolu-

tion – if such a thing had any kind of reality, which (you will have gathered) I don't think it has, in Britain.

The lines you apparently see between the establishment and you get blurred and rubbed out every time you, and anybody connected with you, goes on TV, every time you accept a CBS ad.

I don't believe in revolution, but I do look for a diffusion of responsibility; in general, the underground seems more rather than less, passive, vulnerable, gullible, and less, rather than more, likely to achieve change (although it may be more willing to accept changes initiated by somebody else). Basically, the underground depresses me; from the interminable guitar solos to the unintelligible writing it seems to celebrate masturbation. And that's unproductive.

So, till things are different, I'll suck the tits of the establishment in preference to joining the wankers' circle. Thanks.
C.G.

Dear Dr. Hippocrates:

I read the column in which one of your readers asked why his left testicle hung lower than the right. If I remember correctly, this is so because the left spermatic vein empties into the left renal vein at a right angle whereas the right spermatic vein opens into the inferior vena cava at an acute angle. The result is hydrostatic pressure greater on the left testicle than the right.

San Francisco
M.D.

Dear Dr. Hippocrates:

I know the latest trend is to go without underwear, but even with my modest length skirts I wouldn't dare. My vagina constantly drips a milky substance. I am pretty sure it isn't a discharge of disease, because it is not discolored, doesn't itch, and I have had it for years. In the last few years this drip has become more of a problem.

'Dear Dr. Hippocrates:

On an acid trip I took recently, my left hand and arm went totally dead on me. This happened twice before on very heavy acid trips. I have taken acid about 60 times in the last three years if that's any more help to the problem. Anyway, like I said, my left arm went dead. I couldn't move it very well and I could barely make a fist of my fingers. In about 3 hours my left hand and arm were back to normal use but I was worried by the incident. Oh, by the way, it has always been my left hand and arm that have gone dead.

Is this a normal occurrence or is something wrong? I haven't taken any acid trips lately nor do I plan to until I found out about this.

Answer: All 'LSD' available on the black market today is illegally produced by chemists who, of necessity, run makeshift laboratories. Compounds produced in these laboratories contain impurities which may be more dangerous than the pure drugs. LSD is related to ergot, a substance which causes constriction of blood vessels including those in the brain. Ergot is a fungus which grows on rye and other grains. During the Middle Ages epidemics of ergot poisoning occurred in which the characteristic symptoms were gangrene of the feet, legs, hands and arms. If I were you I would have a thorough physical examination. You live near a Free Clinic where you can speak frankly to a physician about these experiences.

Dear Dr. Hippocrates:

If a girl's hymen is intact, how does the menstrual blood get out?

Answer: Only rarely does the hymen completely cover the vaginal opening. One or more small openings permit flow of menstrual blood. Cyclic pain and cramping without bleeding in a young girl may indicate an imperforate hymen. Prompt medical attention is then necessary to prevent serious consequences.

Since I don't plan to go around without underwear, I am not worried about leaving a trail like Hansel and Gretel, but I don't like my underwear to look dirty after two or three hours. Sometimes my boyfriend will take off some of my clothes, and it embarrasses me to think he might notice. I think the drip is the result of sexual arousal, but since I don't think I'm abnormally preoccupied with sex, I wonder what to do. This is really too embarrassing to mention to my gynaecologist.

Answer: Chronic sexual arousal is, unfortunately, the least likely source of a chronic vaginal discharge. Common causes are trichomonas, fungal and gonorrhœal infections, erosion of the cervix or a reaction to birth control pills. Your gynaecologist will neither be shocked by your questions nor embarrass you with his answers.

'Dear Dr. Hippocrates:

For several months I have been trying to lose weight. Whenever I feel I've eaten too much I force myself to vomit by sticking my finger down my throat and pressing in on my stomach muscle. I drink a lot of water during the day and try to vomit after eating. Only the bulk of my meal — never to the point where I get an acrid taste. The only immediate ill effects I've noticed is gas on my stomach for a day or so afterward.

Answer: When I read your letter I quickly checked the postmark - but it wasn't sent from Rome. Fasting is an acceptable way to lose weight under a physician's supervision. The method described here, however, adds the risk of upsetting the body's chemical balance through loss of gastric fluids. Severe retching can cause rupturing of the stomach with fatal results. Maybe we are returning to the days of ancient Rome.

Dr. Hippocrates welcomes your questions. Write to him c/o OZ

In OZ2b, Jim Anderson reviewed a selection of interesting new books. His introductory paragraph was set in a curious mood midway between apology and triumph (has he noticed how few pseudohip pads have as many books as albums?). Though my own first love is music, I am now listening less and reading more and I'm meeting some extraordinary human beings between pages. It's a pity that William Burroughs and Norman Mailer are not as trendy as Johny Winter and Quintessence because they have so much to offer. So here are a few suggestions as to what to nick next time you're browsing at your friendly neighbourhood Paperback Parade.

First, make a beeline for wherever they keep Paladin Books. As well as Leary's *Politics of Ecstasy* (see Jim Anderson's excellent piece), they've put out Jeff Nuttall's *Bomb Culture*. As it was, written nearly three years ago, it's of necessity incomplete, but it goes up to almost exactly where I and most contemporaries I who are reaping the benefits of Underground culture without taking any of the risks came in. It told me a lot that I didn't know and a lot that I needed to know. I don't know anything about Jeff Nuttall himself, but he's written a book that's essential to anybody interested in the Underground, sympathetic or hostile.

Then wander over to the Penguin section. If you still retain an interest in conventional politics in the States and the impact on America of the Yippies, Hoffman, Rubin, Hayden and all the other living legends of contemporary radicalism, try Mailer's *Armies of the Night* and *Miami and the Siege of Chicago*. Both are definitive

political, sociological and personal documents. Mailer writes superbly, he may be 47 but he's years ahead of anybody else currently using the English language. His personal position and commitments are unique and beautiful and he knows. You should too.

Fiction is alive and well ("I never read fiction"— Richard Neville, 1970). If you enjoyed the *Lord of the Rings*, you might try Michael (Jerry Cornelius) Moorcock's *Runestaff* series. Very derivative, but powerful. Also in the Mayflower rack, you'll probably find Mailer's *An American Dream*, a horror trip through urban America and several Jack Kerouac reissues. The best of these is probably *Desolation Angels*. Unfortunately, Kerouac's first and most influential novel *On*

the Road is still out of print, but if you root around you might find the old Pan edition. Kerouac was a pantises OZ25 (for an appreciation see David Widgery, Richard Neville's alter ego (take care Jackson could be next!). Widgery gives an excellent, loving analysis of Kerouac, but if you missed it, take his word for it and try some.

Coming to their big three are Joseph Heller's *Catch-22*, William Burrough's *Naked Lunch* and James Baldwin's *Another Country*. *Catch-22*, now filmed, is a surrealistic war satire, and very easy to analogise to current social developments. *Naked Lunch* is an extraordinary record of the dreams and visions experienced by William Burroughs during 15 years on smack. If you think you've had bad trips,

how'd you like

to live this for a decade and a half? Occasionally it makes its readers puke on the carpet. Mailer says it can cure cancer, adding, "Burroughs is the only novelist in America who may conceivably be possessed by genius". Being possessed by genius isn't the same as being a genius, but read it anyway—we're all on the end of the fork. *Another Country* is a novel about love, and the way people use it to destroy each other. It's also the first piece of fiction to really hit me with what black people are living every hour in the States—come to that, it's more effective than even the most brilliant and powerful essays on the subject, see Floyd Barbour's *The Black Power Revolt*. All the heavies are there—Jones, Cleaver, Carmichael, Malcolm. And Baldwin really knows language. Why are all the great English-language novels American?

Finally, Robert Heinlein's *Stranger in a Strange Land*. The bible of Charles Manson and the section of an elegantly distorted synopsis in *Time*. This won't send you out to slaughter muscular blonde starlets, but it might teach you how to live in the strange land we have created for ourselves. It's a bit intimidating at 10/6, but so worthwhile. Pashed by NEL.

Okay. If you can get all that lot past the assistant you're a lot more dextrous than I am and you ought to be working for the Government. Maybe you are. Think about it. Anyway, you won't need shit and earphones to get high on these.
Charles Shaar Murray

HEAD BOOKS

JEFF BECK
TRUTH IS BLUE

We've had Eric Clapton in glorious living colour across a double page of the Sunday Times Colour Supplement (photographed by Snowden). Jimmy Page on the front of Disc, Hendrix bare-stomached on every other boutique wall in the country. They're all pop stars as well as cult-figures, standard subjects for cheaply-designed posters, they've the Tony Palmer Seal of Approval. So what about Beck? Beck who? Isn't he the chap who used to be in the Yardbirds? Oh, yes, the Yardbirds. Anybody who's anybody was in the Yardbirds. You know—Donovan's backing guitarist.

Jeff Beck is the most worthwhile of all British guitar heavies—with the possible exception of Eric Clapton (you know—Delaney and Bonnie's backing guitarist). While most of them rely on 400-watt overkill or supersonic speed to make their point, Beck does it with deceptively simple phrases that sneak up behind you and hit you over the head. If you can get hold of a copy of the Yardbirds' 1965 hit "Shapes Of Things", turn it over and listen to Beck's solo on "Better Man Than I" to see what I mean. It's technically less than complex but in terms of sound and feel it's quite remarkable and at least ten years ahead of its time. When he wants to, however, he can produce a turn of speed that would make Alvin Lee blink. But unlike his inferiors and imitators, he doesn't feel that he has to prove his speed all the time. He knows he's fast; you know he's fast, so he can just get down to playing music.

When asked about his musical tastes, Beck will tell you that he likes Tamla Motown and Sly and the Family Stone. (Most heavy guitarists will just say "Robert Johnson" or "B.B."). He doesn't really sound like anyone else, though some have noticed a similarity to the Airplane's Jorma Kaukonen. He's a total individual, unlike the vast majority of blues guitarists, black and white, who have their influences completely on the brain. (It'll be a great day when Stan Webb finally gets out from under Buddy Guy.) We honestly can't think of anybody who has Beck's playing detectably resembles. Think how many British guitarists you can say that for. His originality comes out in all his records. Even old Yardbirds tracks on which he only has one or two short runs (like "Evil Hearted You") are unmistakably Beck.

Though much of his work is blues or blues-based, he is more of an all-round rock guitarist. Even on straight twelve-bar things he avoids the standard B.B. King phrases that even the most expert British guitarists tend to fall into when playing blues (listen to Peter Green on "Blues Jam At Chess"). Listen to "Let Me Love You", "Rock My Plimsoul" and "Blues De Luxe" from the "Truth" album, not a standard blues lick to be heard anywhere, yet it's all blues. When playing 12-bar, even Clapton and Hendrix

tend to think in licks. Beck's playing ranges from the lyrical to the downright vicious, occasionally he even displays a sense of humour, as on the 1966 "Jeff's Boogie" and some of the runs on "Blues De Luxe". Recently Peter Stampfel devoted half his space in "Zigzag" to what he referred to as "The Official Beck Is God Column". They've been on their backs about Beck in the States for four years, yet here he's only known in the context of his work with others. Less trendy adoration surrounds him than does many lesser musicians who've who've been hyped up much more (Lee? Page?). In fact he really is the forgotten man of Britishrock.

A few miscellaneous quotes:
"It has often been said that Jeff Beck is the country's leading guitarist and I'm inclined to agree with him"—Jim McCarty.

"There are only two worthwhile bands in England—Terry Reid and Jeff Beck"—Country Joe.

"I have a lick that's better than Jeff's and Jeff has a lick that's better than mine, but Jim is better than either of us"—Eric Clapton.

"I love Pete Townshend—I'd like to play with the Who, actually"—Jeff Beck.

Background
Beck joined the Yardbirds when Eric Clapton left in mid-'65. He stayed till late '66. In early '69, he brought out a very commercial single of "Hi Ho Silver Lining", an undistinguished bubble-gum singalong thing redeemed only by a lovely guitar solo. It got to Number 7 or something and Beck was on Top Of The Pops singing live but miming the guitar break. He also joined a disastrous package tour with an impromptu band. It was universally judged awful. After that he formed a permanent band with Rod Stewart (vocals), Ron Wood (bass) and Micky Waller (drums).

The second single was another bubble-gum song, but given a shatteringly heavy treatment by the band (just called "Jeff Beck"). Beck himself sang lead. "Tally Man" sold well but not top 30. Then something really incongruous: Beck, no doubt under heavy pressure from Micky Most and EMI to be a pop star, covered "Love Is Blue", Paul Mauriat's instrumental American Hit. Still, it could have been worse, soft-fuzz against harpsichord and strings, but with the Mike Sammes singers mooing softly in the background. Beck said afterwards, "I heard it on Wednesday and recorded it on Thursday. It was strange working with strings, but actually I really like the tune." The Mauriat original got to 15, but Beck made 25 and got a few interviews in the teeny pop papers.

After that, he stopped trying to be a pop star, took his band to the States and consolidated the superstar reputation he made there with the Yardbirds. (The first time the word "psychedelic" appeared in the British music press was in a quote from an American review of Beck's last tour with the Yardbirds). The American hard-rock audiences took the Beck band to their hearts, pronounced him "super-fucking-heavy, man", and bought 40,000 copies of "Truth" in its first three days of release. In Summer of '68, if you talked guitars with anyone in the States, the reaction to a mention of Beck was "Wow, yeah, man, JEFF BECK! That dude really is like outasight, man."

In mid-'69 the second album, "Beck-Ola" came out, now credited to "The Jeff Beck Group". Nicky Hopkins, who had played three tracks on "Truth" was now a permanent member, and Tony Newman had replaced Waller. "Rolling Stone" raved over it. On its English release, the

MM put it under "Highly Recommended", Disc slammed it, the NME ignored it and not many people bought it. By this time, Jimmy Page had lifted half of "Truth" for "Led Zeppelin" and cleaned up everywhere. Beck said in "Zigzag" that Page had stolen his act, and his rap about Led Zeppelin was so acrimonious that Zigzag crapped out by not printing it.

Suddenly, Beck was a name again on the strength of "Barabajagal", a lovely single on which the the Beck band provided an intricately rhythmical backing for Donovan. This got to 11 and Beck was back on Top Of The Pops. Then he split up his band to join the rhythm section of the disbanding Vanilla Fudge. Rod Stewart and Ron Wood joined the Faces and became pop stars. (Stewart put out a solo album that sounded like the Beck Group without Beck.) Beck then crashed his £6,000 vintage car and messed himself up pretty badly. The Fudge thing presumably fell through, and the last heard was that he was getting a group together with Noel Redding, which played in Birmingham Town Hall on April 13.

discography

singles

Heart Full Of Soul/Steeled Blues (Columbia) (Yardbirds)
Still I'm Sad/Evil Hearted You (Columbia) (Yardbirds)
Shapes Of Things/Better Man Than I (Columbia) (Yardbirds)
Over Under Sideways Down/Jeff's Boogie (Columbia) (Yardbirds)
Happenings 10 Years Time Ago/Psycho Daisies (Columbia) (Yardbirds) (2nd gtr. Page)
Hi Ho Silver Lining/Bolero (Columbia) (solo)
Tally Man Rock/Rock My Plimsoul (Columbia) (with group)
Love Is Blue (solo)/I've Been Drinking (group) (Columbia)
Plynth/Hangman's Knee (Columbia) (group)
Barabajagal/Trudi (Pye) (with group backing Donovan)

ep

Five Yardbirds (Columbia)

lps

Blues Anytime Vol 3 (Immediate) (2 tracks with All Stars)
Yardbirds (Columbia)
Truth (Columbia)
Beck-Ola (Columbia)
Lord Sutch & Heavy Friends (with Page, Hopkins, Bonham and Redding) (Atco)

With the exception of the solo albums and the Donovan single, most of the above have been deleted, so until EMI realises it's sitting on a goldmine and releases all its Yardbirds/Graham Bond archives, you'll just have to scour the second-hand shops. (By the way, the "Sutch" album is apparently really a bummer so steer clear). Try and get these goodies. Play them to your groovy friends and let's have a Jeff Beck revival.

Charles Shaar Murray/Alex Darcy

Small ads

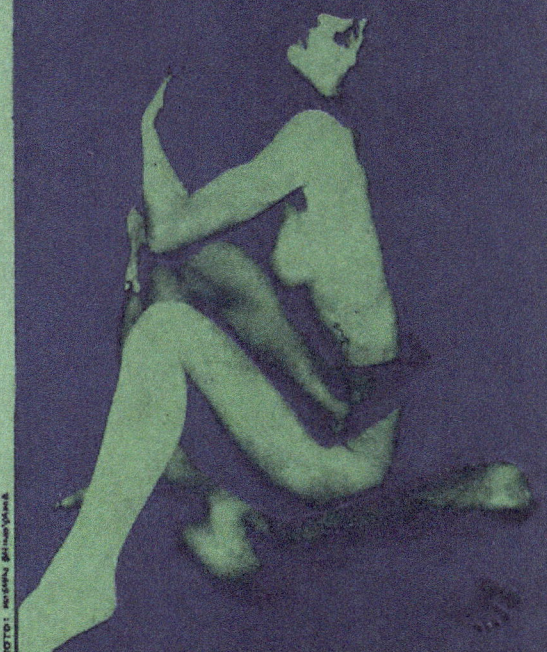

Nigel Lawson,
Editor,
The Spectator,
99 Gower St.,
London W.C.1.

Dear Nigel,

Hilary Spurling has just rung, saying my review of Theodore Roszak's book "enraged" you and that, although she and Trevor Grove liked it and it was in any case commissioned, you refuse, for political reasons, to print it.

Naturally, I am sorry you didn't give the article a chance to enrage a lot of other people. Adrenalin is a precious bodily fluid. It should be shared. However, next time your own political line as a Tory obtrudes into the book pages it would only be fair to Hilary and Trevor to tell them in advance just what this line is and which categories of statement fall to the left and which to the right of it. In this way a good deal of wasted work would be spared your contributors. If you want right-wing reviews of radical books, find some hot young Tory writers. Maybe there are some in Greenland. But for God's sake, don't think that your standard fulminators in re the New Left, like Chris Booker and Simon Raven, know anything about the subject.

Obviously, under the circumstances, I can't write for the Spectator in future.

Yours,
Robert Hughes

Dear Bob,

Thank you for your letter of April 4th.

I think you have misunderstood what Hilary Spurling said to you. What 'enraged' me was not your review, but the notion of its appearing in the Spectator. And I refused to publish it (it was, in any event, commissioned without my knowledge, as it happened) not on political grounds, but because it consisted of nothing but mindless ranting; and that is something we are not prepared to publish in the Spectator, whatever part of the political spectrum it comes from.

The remainder of your letter is too absurd to require reply.

Yours,

Nigel Lawson,
Editor.

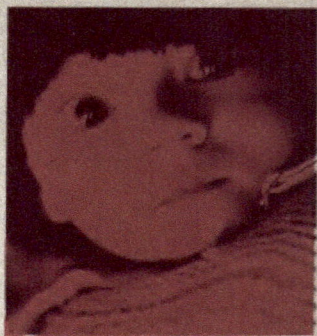

seeking to transform our deepest sense of the self, the other, the environment.' Conservatives rejoice in the 'fragmented' nature of the rebellion — as if a movement whose subject-matter were individual freedom would come up with an unreal, programmatic unity! — and deride everyone in it, Yippies, SDS, student Maoists, acid-freaks, the lot, as idealists. But in a real sense, the revolt of youth can be seen as a triumph of empiricism. Test, test, test: test for authenticity, for relevance, for fun. You only know what you have experienced yourself: you do not know things when an authority tells you they are true. The politics of confrontation replace the politics of caucus and ballot-box. (If one were to rely on the voting statistics, American youth today would seem to be the most politically apathetic instead of the most politically engaged class in the country: the average age of American voters at the last Presidential election was 39. If everyone under 30 voted in California, the Governor would be Timothy Leary, not Ronald Reagan.

The completeness of this rejection of authority is shown in just one of its many areas, by the shift from psychoanalysis to self help through drugs. Ten years ago, nearly every young American liberal I knew had some acquaintance with the analyst's couch. 'My shrinker' in Eisenhower's New York, 'my tailor' in MacMillan's London. The liberal expected to be healed, reconciled to reality, by the omnipresent father-figure with his notebook and sympathetic questions. Today, visiting the shrinker is more often seen as a copout: it implies psychic surrender to the parent. 'Freud,' as one student remarked to an astonished Leslie Fiedler, 'was a fink' — the meddling Jewish poppa. But drop acid and you know that nobody else can do it for you: in that labyrinth of fearful and ecstatic mirrors, the subject of reality itself is confrontation. 'Stand,' a group named Sly and the Family Stone sing, 'All the things you want are real: You have you to complete and there is no deal'.

It is the young who, in the USA and France (and to a limited degree here) have made the technocratic, manipu-

SPECTATOR SPORT:

In *Man and Crisis* a book admired as much by the New Left's activists, like Abbie Hoffman, as by its analysts like Theodore Roszak — Ortega y Gasset observed how the relationship of generation becomes a society's dynamic: their coming and splitting 'represent. the reality of historic life'. Perhaps this has always been true in the West. But never more obviously true than now; and never with such revolutionary implications. 'For better or worse,' Roszak argues in his acutely observed and compassionate book, most of what is presently happening that is new, provocative and engaging in politics, education, the arts, social relations (love, courtship, family, community) is the creation either of youth who are profoundly, even fanatically, alienated from the parental generation, or of those who address themselves primarily to the young.

The young have replaced Marx's proletariat, in the rich societies of the West, as the sperm-carriers of social change. For the first time in modern history, youth experiences itself *as a class*. The conservative in Europe or (especially) America, faced with this political rebellion, professes bewilderment at such 'ingratitude' and does not see how logical and, in hindsight, how inevitable it was. For capitalism called youth into existence as a class, though in order to create an untapped market and conceding its members only two functions — to consume, and to provide the raw material for future managerial elites. This same capitalism is now horrified to find that its huge,

docile Golem is acting up; it spews on the laboratory floor, breaks test-tubes, rattles the lock and makes hoarse efforts to tell the truth — a truth curiously divergent from that of the men who put it together. Neither calming injections nor judicious bashings with a truncheon seem to work: obdurately, it will not see what is obvious to eminent Greek philosophers like Spiro Agnew, that economic classes should only turn into political classes if they are 'reliable'.

Surely a moment's *objective* thought will show the Golem that it is very lucky to be alive at all? That it should be thankful for having such a fine institute as its home? But no; the monster keeps jiving about, drinking chemicals, letting white rats out of cages and brandishing its erect prick. It is not a constructive Golem. It does not seem to have an implementable policy worked out in advance. Worse, it has claimed for itself the right to make social experiments — which, in any sane instituce, should only be given to qualified planner with Government grants. Worst of all, it is demonstrably happier than the scientists: which proves to them that happiness is escapism.

But the essential character of the revolt of youth is that it transcends politics. As Theodore Roszak points out, 'What makes the youthful disaffiliation of your time a cultural phenomenon, rather than merely a political movement, is the fact that it strikes beyond ideology to the level of consciousness,

JOHN

38

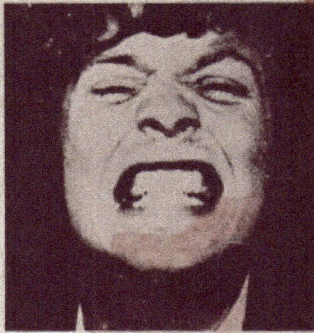

COLIN THOMAS

H.P. ARNOLD

lative nature of adult democracy visible to a degree which only the most percipient, like Marcuse, Goodman and Norman Brown, could see a decade ago.

The mature accuse the young of having no political experience -- and then, with little sense of contradiction, repress as 'impertinent' their efforts to acquire some. The fact is that their own experience of politics, if it means professional skill at juggling consensus and coalition in Washington, has become obsolete: it can no longer contain political reality. For that reality, in the West, is now definable to an unheard-of degree *as what the militant young do*. In Chicago in 1968, reality was enacted on the street between the Yippies and Mayor Daley's pigs; it was inside the convention hall, among the placards, streamers, brass bands and foregone conclusions, that fantasy dwelt. And so it is fatuous to tell an *enrage* or a Berkeley student to leave politics to 'those who know about it'. For he will reply, and rightly, that he *is* politics. This crisis of division, between those content to leave power to qualified technicians of government and the dissenters who grasp politics existentially and will not delegate their morals to such 'experts', is the theme of Roszak's precise analysis.

Roszak puts the dilemma directly. If you suppose that such authenticity of response to society is an unrealisable dream, just what degree of authenticity *will* you settle for? He draws up a sweeping and powerful indictment of the present alternative, submission to a technocracy which is not the 'exclusive product of capitalism' (here, he breaks with the view of the traditional American left). 'The profiteering could be eliminated; the technocracy would remain in force. The key problem' . . . is the paternalism of expertise within a socioeconomic system which is so organized that it is inextricably beholden to . . . an expertise which has learned a thousand ways to manipulate our acquiescence with an imperceptible subtlety.'

The counter-culture, then, defines itself as a revolutionary alternative to management and, Roszak shows, its postures and strategies stem from a loathing of 'benevolent' totalitarianism rather than of capitalism pure and simple, which is seen as only *one* of the forms of this strangling determinism. 'Its principal purpose in the hands of ruling elites is to mystify the popular mind by creating illusions of omnipotence and omniscience'; political technocracy relies, Roszak argues, on the assumption that all human needs can be predicted and satisfied by the projection of programmes: 'if a problem does not have such a technical solution, it must not' (the architects of the 'future', such as Herman Kahn at the Rand Institute, proclaim) 'be a *real* problem. It is but an illusion . . . a figment born of some regressive cultural tendency.'

Thus the programme dominates the men it is ostensibly made for; the donkey is dangled in front of the Utopian carrot. And so the technocrat takes on the character of a priest-king or shaman. But a false one. What Roszak calls 'the myth of objective consciousness' on which technocracy relies is thus seen as yet another form of incantatory irrationality, but veiled; and bleakly empty of moral or poetic content. Even language falls under it, becoming the familiar Desperanto of overkill and megadeath, pacification and hearts-and-minds programmes. The choice, therefore, is not between irrationality and logic. It is between a scarcely tried, hardly crystalised, tribal-poetic consciousness based on empiricism, and a 'practical management' (which demonstrably fails to work within America, let alone its colonies) which demands silence from its majority.

The history of new radical postures is a substance secreted in America; it emerges in England later, and some of the extremities which Roszak describes in his eloquent and delicate polemic are only nascent here. All the more reason, then, to read his book. No doubt the time will come when OZ, EVO, Rat and Shrew will be filed with the *Jahrbuch von Kunstwissenschaft* and *Encounter* as exhibits and sources for a horde of PhDs, clamouring to write their academic texts on what was once the underground of 1965-70. Because that time hasn't arrived yet, Roszak's *Making of a Counter Culture* is of particular interest as the first closely-argued, sympathetic study of the youth revolt made by a man whose position (as far as I can judge it from his reporting) is just outside and a shade to the right of the movement. (Clue: Roszak writes regularly for *Nation* in New York.)

In this respect it's unlike Abbie Hoffman's *Revolution for the Hell of It* or its cuddlier English cousin, Richard Neville's *Play Power*. Roszak is not writing a handbook for activists, Abbie-style, and his book is not quite beamed at the kids, nor at their parents, but at their elder brothers — with whom, in my straighter moments, I have been known to identify; the ones with degrees, who string *sentences* together, and remember when Eisenhower was President. It is a substantially more analytic and intelligent book than *Play Power* — Roszak, unlike many another underground writer, gives the impression that he has read a few books of earlier date than his own birth; the reader is thus faced with a solid linear chew through the unflowered, unzap-coloured pages. There are aspects to his argument I'd question (as, in so many-stranded an account, how could there not be?): one is his severity on drugs — acid, to him, being a kind of mythologized panacea, Instant Ecstacy, the capitalist dream of totally marketable experience in pill form come home to roost among the gulled and dopey kids; well, *maybe*, but not in my acquaintance with it. Another is his pessimism about the chance of a fruitful relationship between the white and the black revolutionaries in America. (A Panther's problems, he in effect argues, are so special and his consciousness even of Marx is so linked to his colour that there can never be a fully shared experience of revolution between the black militant and his white ally.) But Roszak has achieved a feat in writing such a book as this without beginning to sound like your aunt trying hard, for God's sake, to *understand*. I have read no better introduction to that revolutionary who without which, for all the gaps, rhetoric and occasional stupidities of its bearers, for all the mumbo-jumbo about karma and the crap about stars, our history cannot be perceived.

Bob Hughes.

39

I Looked Up/THE INCREDIBLE STRING BAND/Elektra

Briefly, the Incredible String Band are the most extraordinary musical group in the world. That statement would cover almost every field of their activity. From their traditional Scottish beginnings they shone as folk musicians, and justified their live reputation on their first record. Even at this early stage they had begun to borrow from other musical realms, and still they experiment endlessly, borrowing not only instruments—gimbri, sitar, Chinese banjo—but styles, song structures, lyrical ideas, and transfiguring the whole into their own highly individualistic music. Lyrically they can hardly have been surpassed, and their use of free verse in songs is totally original, and frequently successful. From their first experiments on '5,000 Spirits'—the Mad Hatter's song, the Eyes of Fate—to their peak, in my opinion, Robin Williamson's Three is a Green Crown on the 'Hangman's Beautiful Daughter'—to the songs on their more recent L.P.s, they—or rather Williamson in this particular area—have continued to break entirely fresh ground. 'Creation' on 'Changing Horses' is a long, difficult poem spoken over the backing.

They have many other directions. Mike Heron does a nice line in wit. They perform simple, nostalgic country songs, straight religious songs. Gilbert and Sullivan take-offs. The other week at the Roundhouse they presented a pantomyme.

Don't get me wrong, they have real faults. Much of their work, especially recently, is whimsical, lazy, trivial, self-indulgent. Often their gentleness comes over as affectation. The two girls in the band, Rose and Licorice, don't strike me as terrible talented. When they sing they sound like boy sopranos (which is alright I suppose) and in live performance like boy sopranos with sore throats. And Licorice really plays the drums horribly.

Above all, the String Band are enigmatic. Each new record gives one an entirely new impression of their minds. "Changing Horses" I found disappointing after "Wee Tam and Big Huge". But it was still a revelation of a sort. And their new album, "I Looked Up", is startling. It contains both the best (though that word isn't very helpful) and the worst material that they've recorded. Firstly the worst.

Williamson's ten-minute track on Side 2, "When you find out who you are", is shapeless, mindless and dull. It sounds as if he worked out a couple of simple choruses and improvised the links between them, to make the record a reasonable length. Two Heron tracks, "The Letter" and "This Moment", aren't too great. They're both too self-consciously naive, with the wonder and delight ever so slightly phoney. Nice tunes though.

The other three tracks are very fine. But you must realise that the String Band reject and scorn the silky studio professionalism of people like Simon and Garfunkel and the Fairport Convention; they seem too close to the earth for that. And that's why "Black Jack Davy" is such a delight. It's a traditional sort of folksong, with two fiddles, guitar and Heron's coarse, straightforward voice. It's unsterilized, untreated, and it sounds like an animal.

"Fair as you", another Heron song, has a fine, complex tune, nice singing from Rose and Licorice, and the flute and gimbri of Robin. Have you ever heard a gimbri? It's sweet, mournful, slightly tortured, and here it works beautifully.

Then there is "Pictures in a mirror" by Robin Williamson. He has always struck me as the best songwriter of the two. He has an unfettered imagination, a real vision which is only occasionally befogged by affectation and a sure sense of structure. This song is quite unlike anything else he has ever recorded. It is in two parts. In the first, "Deep in the hollow jail, sleeps Lord Randall", there is a carefully constructed atmosphere of dirt, despair and gloom as he dreams. He is woken by the jailer, who "leads him up the blinding stair. He feels uneven turf beneath his feet." Without ceremony he is executed. "The sun turns to stone."

And in the second part, Robin describes his own birth:

"Already I am forgetting who I am;
Already I am forgetting who I've been."

There is no physical connection between the two parts. What is implied is that the two incidents are parallel, while the suggestion of reincarnation cannot be ignored. The song is strange, mysterious and very powerful.

I haven't least idea where the String Band are going from here. But they're the finest we've got, they're the finest anyone's got. I'm prepared to listen.

Peter Popham

LORD SUTCH/Cotillion/Atlantic Lord Sutch And Heavy Friends

As all groovy MM readers know by now, Sutch's "Heavy Friends" include such hard-rock luminaries as Jimmy Page (who co-produced the album and collaborated with Sutch on six of the twelve positions), Jeff Beck, Noel Redding, John Bonham and Nicky Hopkins. The makings of a fairly respectable supersession, I think you will agree. Well, I'm sorry to have to announce that they've completely blown it. In fact, it's an abortion almost from start to finish. The blame for this extraordinary feat (it's pretty difficult to fuck up musicians like that) can be laid squarely on Sutch himself. His songs are banal to the point of acute anguish, based on riffs that have been beaten to death by untold and uncounted numbers of sub-mediocre bands all over the English-speaking galaxy. The lyrics are ludicrously bad and the titles...dig: "Wailing sounds", "Flashing lights", "Gutty guitar", "Smoke and fire", "Thumping beat", "Union Jack car", "L-O-N-D-O-N" and like that. The album contains such gems as "gotta be played on Jeff's guitar" and "With Jimmy Page you can't go wrong".

The next hangup is that Sutch's singing is as useless as a used rubber, although he tries valiantly for about thirty-five minutes.

The heavy friends restrict themselves to cliches, played far below their usual standard, but quite nicely. Beck and Page couldn't be uninteresting if they tried, and Redding and Bonham mesh together "tight as a 12-year-old virgin" (if there are any left in these permissive times). Page's production is excellent: everything sounds really nice—a virtuoso recording. Pity the music isn't up to it. The best and most succinct criticism of this album was in a reader's letter to "Rolling Stone": "The friends sure as hell are heavy, but Sutch sings as though he hasn't shat in two weeks". Well, he has in fact—over anyone who has paid money for the record.

Charles Shaar Murray

ATOMIC ROOSTER B & C

First of all, B & C Records have seen fit to package this album in a sleeve only slightly less flimsy than the average chewing-gum wrapper. Secondly, both the sleeve and the labels list the tracks in the wrong order (the last two tracks listed as being on Side One are actually on Side Two, and vice versa). Thirdly, the music (oh yes, the music) is rather disappointing. There's very little on here that wasn't done infinitely better by Brian Auger and Julie Driscoll on "Streetnoise" or, come to that, by Crane and Palmer themselves on the classic Arthur Brown album. Carl Palmer's drumming is powerful and precise and Vincent Crane's keyboards are suitably eerie but it all fails to catch fire (sorry). On the strength of the Arthur Brown album, I'd rated Crane with Auger, Emerson and Ratledge, but here he seems to be repeating himself badly. Parts of "Winter" bring back memories of the much superior Brown-Crane Child Of My Kingdom. Apart from careless, fourth-rate packaging and derivative material, my other main criticism of "Atomic Rooster" is the production. The organ is too often buried (particularly on "Friday The 13th") and the bright frequencies of the drumming (especially the cymbal work) could be a lot crisper. I don't want to come on like Miles, but albums like this, "This Was" and the first Nice album should be played to all bands intending to produce their own first albums. Compare the organ sound on this album to that achieved by Giorgio Gomelski on "Street-noise", or Peter Townshend on "Crazy World". But to be fair, the bass is very nicely recorded and so is the voice. While I'm talking about the voice, Nick Graham draws a lot of inspiration from Arthur Brown, John Mayall and David Clayton-Thomas, but is nowhere near any of them. He also makes Mayall's "Broken Wings" sound like Arthur Brown singing "Put A Spell On You" which is a bit disconcerting.

I don't want to hit this album too hard, because the Rooster are such an obviously good band. I can imagine this being "fan-fucking-tastic, man" live. It's very efficiently played hard-rock organ trio stuff and there are good bits all the way through. In "Decline And Fall" Crane hits a very Anger-like groove and Palmer plays a superb solo which shows that he's been learning from Buddy Rich as well as laying his daughter. Chris Welch probably has an orgasm every time he hears it.

BUT (and here's the put-down) it's too derivative, too unimaginative and too familiar to really grab me. Listen to it and then buy "Streetnoise". It's reasonable party music and bits of it may turn up on "Top Of The Pops" for Blackburn to talk over. The next one will be a lot better. Last word: anybody who wants to swap this for "Soft Machine Volume Two" has got himself a deal. C.M.

THE DOORS/Morrison Hotel/
Elektra

With their first two albums, "The Doors" and "Strange Days", the Doors achieved an astonishing amount. Their music was quite individual, their singer was more ostentatiously gutsy than anyone since Elvis, and they wrote aggressive and intelligent lyrics. Their peak was the epic song on "Strange Days", "When the music's over".

"What have they done to the earth?
What have they done to our fair sister?
Ravaged and plundered and ripped her and bit her,
Stuck her with knives in the side of the dawn
And tied her with fences
And dragged her down."

Their hypnotic virility even seemed allied with a certain integrity.

This explains why, listening to "Morrison Hotel", their latest album, I am consumed with gloom. It's not that it's bad. It's just vacuous. Superficially all the elements of the earlier records are there: the bouncy organ, the fine, precise drumming, the wildly versatile slide guitar. Morrison still holds on to his black leather voice. But, lacking any new inspiration, they fall back either on their well-tried formulae or their dreary new-found roots— Tony Bennett, and the Rich White Man Blues. They make no progress; and lyrically Jim Morrison is (one hopes temporarily) almost bankrupt. And with only second-rate material, their flatness and predictability as a unit becomes startlingly obvious. Only Robbie Krieger continues to shine like the

S. BLONDE

seedy Los Angeles cherub we once knew and loved. His guitar-playing on "Peace Frog" in particular is really ecstatic, and his energy keeps much of the record alive... But they stagnate all the same.

I'm not complaining about their abandoning of the revolutionary message of their first two records. There it was alive, honest, spontaneous. But "Five to one", their most "revolutionary" song, suggested strongly that they were erotic racketeers rather than erotic politicians, and they have been wise to drop the issue. But its absence does emphasise the vacuum.

Don't misunderstand me, this

album does have high spots. "Roadhouse Blues", the opening song, is fine, they play together like a proper performing band and Morrison really lets go. "Waiting for the sun", although only a fragment of a song, is powerfully produced and poignant. When Jim sings

"This is the strangest life I've ever known",

the mystery, foggy and cavernous, is quite convincing. "Land Ho!" jogs along like a huge, baritone clog dancer. "You make me real", though rather pedestrian, has a delightfully prim rock piano opening and as I said, Krieger's guitar lifts many of the songs above their dreary structures.

The group touches rock bottom on the two "ballads" on this record, "Blue Sunday" and "Indian Summer". Morrison, caught between Frank Sinatra and Buddy Holly, croons his spineless, mindless lyrics:

"I-I l-o-o-ve you the best,
Better than all the rest."

Well really! We know the band can play powerfully, we know Jim can write. Can he really be worked out at twenty-four?
Peter Popham

A Very Bad Sign

Tony Palmer's Born Under a Bad Sign, William Kimber, 40/-.

I started this review knowing I wasn't going to like the book, and read the book trying to prove it. The thing about rock music that makes it stand out from tuneful trash like the Love Affair is that it doesn't need the usual intermediaries like critics, tame pundits, biographers to

appreciate it. Rock is in tune with the other things going on for 'youth' teenybops or whatever. So (dramatic pause for effect) — the arrogant self appointed prose of Tony and his colleagues is irrelevant.

In the book he whines about the injustices of the pop world, what a shame Jimi Hendrix isn't entered for the Eurovision. It seems he wants rock officially adopted as the nation's culture; treated in the same way as symphony concerts, justifying his position on the Observer and knocking the guts out of 'alternative culture'.

But pretty obviously, a book that costs £2 (YES FRIENDS TWO POUNDS!) isn't meant for people who actually like the sort of music our Tony licks the arse of. It's for the trendy over thirties with wardrobes full of sheepskin jackets, and the odd 10/- deal tucked in behind the Bacardi. Remember the News of the World telling all about OZ, well here's the intellectual version; titilate yourself with the doings of the teenies.

Chapters one, two and nine not necessarily in that order try and justify the blurb, the intellectual sugar on the other six chapters of lifted and vaguely rewritten record company handouts, and who the hell wants to know the early history of Lulu and Donald-peers (WHO). The rare flashes of insight when not arrogant actually are amusing for their bitchy accuracy. The Steadman cartoons are good but tend to say the opposite of the text. No, for your threepence a page, you would be better buying No.6.

Deyan Sudjic

BRINSLEY SCH..

Teacher loves to run his fingers through my hair..

We first became aware of sex during one biology lesson at the age of 11 or 12. From then on we were all dying to see a prick but we all swore that we would keep our virginity until we got married (some have – others not!). One after another we all started our menstruation and in our little minds we believed that we were women. A few of us had started going out with boys and everyone wallowed in excitement on Monday morning as we sat and told our friends everything that had happened on our date. To begin with we all worried like mad about the petting sessions but things sorted themselves out.

I shall never forget the look of horror on people's faces when one girl lost her virginity at the age of 13, under a tree in the park. For a while everyone respected her until the next lost hers and the novelty wore off. One girl became very worried because she believed she was becoming a nymphomaniac (if you are interested I can let you have her phone-number).

Then came the inevitable discussions on what it was like and why the remainder of us should remain virgins. Some decided to wait for the right man while others spent their weekends fucking in convenient places. To many, it seems unbelievable that it is possible to go out with some-one for more than six months and not have sex.

A few became pregnant and managed to deal with it without parents or teachers being aware of it.

Discussions hardly ever take place as we get older and the matter is left entirely to the two individuals involved.

SMILE – if you had sex last night.

Snatch Comix

Uncle Tom Holland and all!

Malcolm X once said: 'you can search for any type of beauty in this world, but if you do not bring some beauty with you. . . you'll never find any!!!'

Listen to this: Sweden just got herself an Ambassador. You say that is not anything? Well usually it would not be except Sweden drew a short straw, she got herself a negrO (I spelled it right. . . with a capital 'O').

I am black and I guess I should be glad to see a black man in a position of importance. I would be if he was a black man, but from the pictures I see of him in magazines all that I see is a negrO with a top hat on his head doing social things that no black person could probably understand. To me, it is the funniest thing in the world to see a £50 hat on a 2/- head.

All this week I have been reading that Ambassador Jerome Holland has been met by crowds of demonstrators who have been screaming. 'Nigger, nigger, nigger, go home!' Quite naturally I was upset, I don't like the word nigger, hell, if they call him a nigger just because he is black that means that these white folks here in Sweden would also call me nigger just because I am black. . . so I went to see and maybe to fight. Remember now, I was not against this ambassador. How could I be, I didn't even know him.

I heard that the United States Cultural Center was going to be opened by the ambassador and since I carry a United States passport and press credentials I decided that I would go to the opening and report just what happened and how this negrO ambassador told the Swedish people about the problems that his own people face inside of the United States. . . I was sure that he would tell the truth about how we are segregated, discriminated against, lynched and other things. . . this is normal, isn't it? I mean any person on the face of this earth tries to help his own people first, that is almost a law of nature. . .

When I got to the front door of the United States Cultural Centre on a street called 'Sveavagen' the first thing I saw was cops. . . a whole bunch of blue uniforms and they all held white clubs in their hands. At first they were just standing around, naturally I thought that this was the 'honor guard' for the ambassador. . . I thought to myself, 'now isn't this nice, the cops are giving his negrO ambassador a welcoming committee'. Well, I walked up to the front door and those honor guards' turned and came at me and I sort of rushed inside to get out of their way. When I got inside I met a weak little white man who asked me if I had an invitation. I smiled nicely and gave him my press credentials, he turned them over to a white woman, she smiled and told me to wait until she went upstairs and showed them to someone else. . . who I never did see.

She came back down, she handed me back my press things and

told me that I could not come in, I was really surprised at this and I asked her why. She told me that the Swedish press had been sent invitations and since I did not have one, I could not come inside. I reminded her that this was the United States Cultural Centre and I was a member of the press and also I had a United States passport and I would like to see MY negrO ambassador. While I waited for her to explain, I heard shouts outside the front door, I grabbed my papers and went to see what was going on. When I got outside. . . shit had hit the fan.

There was a large group of white folks being pushed and shoved around by the pigs. . . (I'm sorry . . . I mean 'honor guard').

I grabbed my camera and began taking pictures. Believe me, there were a lot of pictures to be taken. The people were being pushed and hit in the head. The amazing thing is that the people were fighting back! I felt good to see people standing up and like Malcolm X said. . . 'they had no time to be singing, they were too busy swinging!' Each time a cop would hit someone, someone would hit a cop. I saw a fight going on between a black man and a white cop, the action was too fast for me to get a picture, but they were doing it. Then a bunch of cops moved in on him and they shoved him into a wagon. I found out that his name is Bill Melson, a black man from America who has been here in Sweden for some five years.

I turned on my tape recorder because the crowd was yelling something and I wanted to be sure that my radio audience would hear exactly what was being said. . . they were yelling, 'Go home murderer' and 'Stop the killing in Vietnam!'

There was so much going on I had to run from here and listen, and run there and listen, that's when I noticed a huge American flag being held up by the crowd. Since the 'honor guard' moved in their direction, I did also, they were yelling too, but it was in Swedish and I could not understand what they were saying. . . but I have it on tape and it will be played on American radio station KPFK in Los Angeles, WBAI in New York and a few others, I want people to hear for themselves just what the first negrO ambassador was facing and what the people were saying to him. . . I just want the truth to be told, that's all.

Well the fights went on, I saw a white cat hit a cop and that cop

went down like a sack of potatoes, another cop began to run after this white boy, he damn near had him too but some little old lady walked out of a store with a bundle in her arms, the boy who was running, managed to get around her but the cop. . . BLAMMMM, right into this lady and they both went down. . . with her on the bottom. What made it so bad was he landed on right on her head and I heard it crunchhh when they hit the sidewalk. . . she was hurt bad, tho the young boy kept on running and it looked to me that he got away, but the cops grabbed a young girl and began putting her into the wagon she grabbed onto the side of the police truck and tried not to get in, a few hard cracks on her skull with their clubs and she fell inside. . . I felt sick, she was just a little thing.

I watched the negrO ambassador get out of his car and walk the 7 or 8 steps inside the Cultural building, man he was stepping. He must have come from the southern part of the United States because he acted as though he knew what a crowd of white folks screaming could do. Now I guess he knows what those little children, black children felt when they were attacked on a bus and beaten by a white mob in South Carolina or North Carolina, . . but they had no 'honor guard' nor did they have an United States Cultural Centre to run into; they were in the United States, they don't even have an ambassador to tell what is happening to them, I'm certain Dr. Jerome Holland won't tell, if he would, Mr. Nixon would not have sent him.

Finally I was moving when a cop on horseback noticed me, he and his buddy rode their horses two inches from my face. They began talking to me in Swedish, I didn't understand what they were saying so I stood still, they nudged their horses closer to me, I still stood still. I wasn't too afraid of the horses or the cops, hell, I've fought cops before, but I did keep my eyes on the whips they held, yes, they held long leather whips in their hands . . . new some people dig being hit by leather whips. . . I don't. Finally a little Swedish girl walked up to me and in English said: 'Don't move, a horse will not walk over a person, I work at the Royal Stables and I know these horses and they will not trample you. . . you're alright, just don't move!'

She didn't have to worry, I wasn't about to move. They did finally back off of me but they refused to be interviewed.

I did interview about 15 people, one was a man from the United States, a black man, Sherman Adams, he was as mad as a pregnant nun. When I asked him why he was so angry, he told me: 'That cat Holland, he's telling the world that he is being called a nigger and he is a damn liar. The time he was called a nigger, I, Sherman Adams from New York called him a 'House Nigger' and that what he is. . . a house nigger. The Swedish people are not against his color or his race, hell, they don't even know the word 'house nigger' but I do and I'm the only one who called him that. So he is a liar when he tells the press that he is being called a nigger by the Swedish youth and demonstrators.'

It is true; he is NOT being called a nigger. The people here in Sweden are against the American government's policy in Vietnam, if Nixon had sent a white boy here he would have met with the same thing, but Mr. Holland is using his race or his color to make political hay for the Nixon administration. By saying he is being called a nigger, it looks as though he is being attacked because he is black, thus there is little mention of the fact that the demonstrations have been against the war in Vietnam.

The worst thing I found ladies and gentlemen, friends and enemies is that the newspapers came out the next day with the story that Mr. Holland was met with yells of 'nigger, nigger, go home!!!'

That is a lie. I have the tapes to prove it. I was there and I was listening for the word 'nigger' because it would have made me angry, but no one used the word. I did call the newspapers and protested that they lied and here is the strange part. . . the newspapers both have admitted that their reporters did NOT hear the word 'NIGGER' used and there is no police report of the word being used. . . not even once.

I informed the press, that's the Swedish press that I intend to let my listeners in America know that what Dr. Jerome Holland is doing is indeed criminal liable at best and lying at least. I told them that Pacifica Foundation, that's the firm I broadcast for, does not engage in lies or sensationalism that is based on lies and that we would and can use our facilities to see to it that the people of Sweden are not used as political tools of any administration. We deal in truth. . . whether it is good or bad, it must be true and if Pacifica should ever change that policy, I'd not work for them for one minute.

I don't expect Mr. Nixon to be ashamed of himself I know what he does, and so does the rest of the world, but Dr. Holland should be ashamed of himself for going along with this type of evil, this type of rottenness, this type of filth, but I guess it is again like Malcolm X said: 'If you lie down with dogs, you're sure to get up with fleas!'

Hakim A. Jamal.

43

The drawing on our front and back covers by R. Bertrand was lifted without prior permission or consent from his brilliant Desseins Erotiques, edited by Eric Losfeld 14-16 Rue de Verneuil, Paris 7eme, France (Le Terrain Vague 1969).

The last issue of OZ sold in excess of 40,000 copies, making it the largest Underground publication outside the United States. However, our print bills have risen astronomically, partly due to our Sunday Supplement glossy paper, but mostly thanks to the unwillingness of large printers in Britain to publish OZ. For this reason, we have been forced to raise the price of OZ to four shillings. We apologise for this and for the next two months we are offering new subscriptions at the old rate. Anyone who thinks OZ is making a fortune (sic) might note that one of the editors still lives in Wandsworth Bridge Road. Have you ever seen Wandsworth Bridge Road?

DIAL-A-COP

Want to buy yourself off a cannabis charge? a traffic offense? breaking and entering? treason? embracery? sodomy? anything at all? then read on...

Several months ago, (OZ 22) OZ reported that Thom Keyes, author of One Night Stand, handed Detective Sergeant Robin Constable £150 in consecutively marked £10 notes, in return for which Constable agreed to drop charges against other people arrested at the same time as Keyes for cannabis possession (April 27 last year).

The fact that police officers have been known to arrange for charges to be withdrawn, altered or forgotten etc. comes of course as no surprise to anyone, except perhaps people like Detective Inspector Merrick of Scotland Yard, who, a few days before the Keyes affair, personally informed Caroline Coon of Release that he thought that the allegations of extra-legal activity by the police as enumerated in the Release Report (by

Rufus Harris and Caroline Coon) were derived from unreliable sources (e.g. from heads) and were untrue. Caroline replied that the Report showed that there was a well established and clear pattern of how people were treated/mistreated at police stations and if he was upset about what was in the Report he should just see what was left out. In addition Release had been aware for some time that certain officers were accepting bribes and Caroline informed Merrick that the Release files were open and that Release would be very grateful if Scotland Yard would go through them. It might convince them to do something positive about all the allegations made therein. This offer has not been taken up by Scotland Yard, nevertheless Merrick said that if in future Release had cause to complain about the conduct of any police officer, they were to consult him, and any complaints would get the fullest and most instant co-operation. This Release agreed to do, and so when Thom Keyes rang Release to inform them that Robin Constable had asked Keyes to come and see him and that a sum of money would probably be handed over within half an hour, Release immediately informed Detective Inspector Merrick, who asked Release to ring him immediately the transaction actually took place. Half an hour later Constable received the £150 in marked notes, and Release tried to ring Merrick. Merrick, extraordinarily enough, had gone out, leaving instructions for Release to ring a subordinate. The subordinate was unavailable. It was not until 2½ hours later that Release, after continual efforts by telephone, was able to contact Merrick. He gave an assurance that the matter would be attended to. At 4 that afternoon an Inspector Frew visited Keyes and took a four hour statement, not leaving Keyes apartment until 8pm., after which he went to see Constable. By this time, naturally enough, there was no trace of the marked notes on Constable and the case was soon pigeonholed for insufficient evidence. Release was not even allowed to accompany Inspector Frew when he visited Constable. The police implied that Release had fabricated the entire story. Anyone knowing anything about Release and the way it operates would at once realise the absurdity of this implication.

In the succeeding months Detective Sergeant Robin Constable has been a busy man. He led the raid on Mick Jagger and Marianne Faithful and was again accused of offering to drop charges in return for money. This received extensive publicity and Mr. Constable soon found himself the subject of an internal police inquiry. Not that he, or anyone else for that matter, was particularly worried. He was even appointed as a member of a committee investigating other bribery allegations made by The Times. Mr. Callaghan, the Home Secretary, on being asked a question in the House about this extraordinary appointment, stated that he did not know at the time of the appointment that Constable himself was the subject of bribery allegations. Release, however, has access to a letter from Callaghan dated three months before, saying that he was very concerned about alleg-

ations made about Constable, and that everything possible was being done to have the matter clarified. Constable has now been cleared of all bribery allegations by the internal investigating committee. The impartiality of such investigations can be suspect and in this case, even though the police stressed that the investigating officer came from a different station, it is a fact that for a time during the inquiry, Inspector Frew was actually working at Chelsea, Constable's own stamping ground. The happily exonerated Constable, it is now rumoured, is due for promotion and is shortly to appear as Detective Inspector Constable.

Detective Sergeant Constable can be contacted at WHitehall 1212, Extension 2079 (Extraditions Department.)

If you want somewhere to have lunch, go down the same ghetto stairs that you descend to go to Seed, the Macrobiotic Restaurant, and visit the newer perhaps unfortunately named SPROUT. I have been there twice recently — the first time, Madelaine Simon was there half way through her fifth continual day on sunshine and the place was full of rainbow electricity. The second time it was as calm as a Nepalese mountain top. Both occasions were fantastic. It's open Monday through Saturday from noon to 6.30. Closed on Sunday, open Monday evenings and sometimes all night Saturday. Corner Westbourne Terrace and Bishops Bridge Road.

England's first book of Head Comic/Trip Strip is now available from: Flat 5, 8 Norfolk Terrace, Brighton, Sussex. 3/- or 2/- from bookshops, boutiques etc. It has a long way to go before it rivals the Californian comic counterparts, like Snatch, Yellow Dog,

etc., but it's good, original and I hope the forerunner of hundreds of others. 'Acid to Acid, Dust to Dust, If the Shit don't get Ya, the trips sure must.'

DADD is an illustrated magazine shortly to be put out by a group of young people, in a loose leaf form, the idea of which is to give immediate visual impact and allow the contributor whether he be photographer, writer, designer or artist, to get the most from the pages on which his work appears. DADD is meant to be hung on the wall, so all material will be designed to work both in a literary and visual way at the same time. Sounds like OZ. All contributions to: 103a Barkston Garden London, S.W.5.

Last month's Beautiful Freak, Greg Cox, now somewhat cured of his John Lennon obsession, has put out a beautiful four page magazine entitled NOTHING, which is available for 1/- from Greg if you happen to run into him in the street, or from: 62, Argyle Street, London W.C.1. Buy it and read all about the Nothing Co-op, Nothing auditions, and Nothing to read. 'Nothing is a coincidence. We think that everything that happens at the same time is a coincidence, and that coincidences either happen, don't happen, or are made to happen.' I don't quite know what that is all about but Greg says that NOTHING really means PEACE.

TO: _____   Date: _____
    _____
    _____
    _____

Gentlemen:
    Regarding your form number: _____ received this
date, requesting certain information to be filled in and returned
to your office.
    I would be happy to oblige you. However, under the human
bye-laws by which I am constituted, I cannot do so until the
request is made on the enclosed forms (OHID 1A-A1). If you
will kindly fill in the information required, and return it in
the enclosed self-addressed, stamped envelope it will be much
appreciated.
    Thank you for your cooperation. I remain,

                                Most sincerely,

FORM NUMBER: OHID 1A-A1-1970
IMPORTANT: This is an individual human request form.
                                NOT TO BE SOLD.
FORM FILLING INFORMATION REQUEST FORM

(please use block letters or typewriter)

1.   DATE:
2.   AGENCY (Government or private) REQUESTING
      INFORMATION:

3.   ADDRESS _____

      (street number) _____

      (city or town) _____

      (county/state – Country) _____

4.   DEPARTMENT REQUESTING INFORMATION: _____

5.   HEAD OF DEPARTMENT: (Name if human – Number
      if not) _____

6.   NAME(s) SPECIFIC INDIVIDUAL(s) MAKING
      REQUEST: _____

      (name(s) if enlightened – number (s) if frightened) ____

7.   WILL INFORMATION BE FED INTO A COMPUTER:
      Yes _____ No ____

8.   IF YES, NAME, MAKE AND MODEL NUMBER _____

9.   WHO WILL HAVE ACCESS TO INFORMATION:

      (Agencies, Government and or Private, and individuals
      please list all names. If unknown, please state.)

      (if additional space is required, please add supplemental
      sheet when returning this form)

10.   DUE TO POSSIBLE CHANGING SITUATIONS IN LIFE,
      CAN THE INFORMATION YOU REQUEST BE
      CORRECTED OR AMENDED IN FUTURE
      Yes _____ No _____

11.   IF INFORMATION IS BEING FED INTO COMPUTER
      WILL A RUN OFF OF MATERIAL/INFORMATION IN
      COMPUTER FORM BE MADE AVAILABLE TO ME
      FOR PROOF READING, FOR CORRECTION OF
      POSSIBLE ERRORS, BEFORE SUCH INFORMATION
      IS FINALLY USED: Yes _____ No_____

12.   IF NO, PLEASE STATE BASIS FOR SUCH ANSWER:

13.   HOW LONG WILL SUCH INFORMATION BE ON FILE
      BEFORE BEING DESTROYED OR UPDATED?

14.   SPECIFY EXCLUDED SERVICES OR SOURCES:

      Note: Farmers may elect the optional method instead of
      regular method.
      Non farmers must use INFORMATION ACCRUAL
      METHOD

15.   SUMMARY OF INFORMATION DEPRECIATION:

      (Dates   Year and month, please)_____

16.   INFORMATION SURCHARGE: (state amount in
      Pounds Sterling) _____

17.   ALTERNATIVE COMPUTATION OF INFORMATION:
      (only if requester is left-handed or under 18 years)

      17a. Enter here and on line (7) of part (A) above, the
            amount on line 6 or 9, whichever is greater.

18.   MISCELLANEOUS GENERAL RULE: (Yes or No, if
      intending to use) _____

            a. Method of Using Miscellaneous General Rule;
            All information furnished on the form shall be
            expressed in human terms except as provided by
            computer limitations as accounted for in (7) and
            (8). Where it is necessary to convert from human to
            computer terms, attach a statement describing in
            detail how this conversion was determined.

19.   GAINS OR LOSSES FROM SALES OR EXCHANGE OF
      INFORMATION:

            a. Net Long Term Gain (Loss): _____

            b. Carryover Gain (Loss): _____

      NOTE: If you meet these requirements, also complete
             the ALTERNATIVE INFORMATION REQUEST
             COMPUTATION to determine which information
             computation results in the larger confusion and
             or red tape.
             1. Confusion_____ more _____ Less
             2. RED TAPE_____ more _____ Less

      NOTE: A. Some form fillers find it convenient to increase
             their withholding of information to avoid
             declaration responsibility. If you do so, make
             sure the information balance due on
             (OHID 1A-A1) will be equal to that information
             being requested by you in your form number
             _____Those who make an estimated inform-
             ation declaration totalling more information
             than requested on this form can reasonably
             expect said gross information to be exceeded.
             B. If a request is made for a joint information
             declaration by both husband and wife (provid-   45

ed they are entitled to file such joint information declaration) can they reasonably expect
to receive more information from your office in
the near future?_____ Yes _____ No
C. However, if you are a non-resident alien who
requires a declaration of estimated information
you must allow added time for language
translation and adaptations thus required.
STATE WHICH YOU REQUIRE RE. ABOVE:_____
_____

19A. EXCESS ACCOUNT INFORMATION:
Enter information here with regard to yourself and
the five highest information getting employees
within your organization. In determining the five
highest information getters, computer time
allowances must be added to their totals. However,
the information need not be submitted for any
employee for whom the combined amount is less
than one form per work day, or for yourself if your
information quota allowance is directly controlled
by the information covered in question (6). See
separate instructions for definition of
'information quota allowances'.
a. DO YOU CLAIM A DEDUCTION FOR
INFORMATION ALLOWANCES CONNECTED
WITH:
1. High degree of computer control:
_____ Yes _____ No
2. Over 65 or Blind: _____ Yes _____ No
3. Too many conventions or meetings:
_____ Yes _____ No
4. Sick Leave or Holidays _____ Yes _____ No

**20. INFORMATION FROM RECOMPUTING PRIOR YEAR
INFORMATION CREDIT:**
Enter the amount of information which the credit
taken in a prior year or years exceeds the information as recomputed due to early or faulty disposition of initial information: _____
_____
_____

21. INFORMATION AVERAGE: If your information request
has increased substantially this year, it may be to your
advantage to figure your information before computing
under 'the information averaging method'. Obtain
Information Schedule BB5-OLE from this office.
Mark _____ Yes _____ No (if needed)

22. SHARE INFORMATION ARRANGEMENTS: An individual who undertakes to produce information on facts
belonging to another, or a proportionate share of said
information is considered to be an independant informer
(supplier) (requester) and has a self-employed information
status rather than an employee. His net request for
information should be outlined in details on this form for
computation of self-employment information purposes:
_____
_____
_____

NOTE: If you meet these requirements, also complete the
ALTERNATIVE INFORMATION COMPUTATION to
determine which INFORMATION COMPUTATION
results in the larger invasion of individual privacy:
_____
_____

23. WHO MAY FILE OR FILL IN A FORM: Any individual,
government agency, estate, trust, or corporation, including
a small business corporation or Limited Company, claiming
information for credit or other purposes.
Partnerships are not required to file this form because
credit of information claimed by partners has a greater
human value than that of the corporation. However,
partnerships may attach a statement of not more than 250
words requesting a special information refund, provided
the information is available for your credit in any of the

first three quarters of the current tax year.
NOTE: MEMBERS OF CERTAIN RELIGIOUS FAITHF:
If you have conscientious objections to information
form requests by virtue of your adherence to the established teachings of a recognized religious sect of which you
are a member, you may file a statement to obtain said
information exemption:_____
_____
_____
_____
_____
_____

FOR OFFICIAL USE ONLY: DO NOT WRITE IN THIS SPACE

Date received: _____

Date answered: _____

Information evaluation quota: _____

DIENAM CODING FOR FUTURE USE:

a. OBLT_____

b. Z5R3 _____

c. MI-SH-MO-SH_____

d. SI - S3C - R7E - W - (9) - U - 7 - P _____
Claimed evaluation reevaluated____ _____
OTHER COMMENTS:_____
_____
_____
_____
_____

INSTRUCTIONS AND GENERAL INFORMATION
A. MUST BE TIMELY FILLED OUT FOR CREDIT OF
INFORMATION YOU ARE REQUESTING: No
information credit will be allowed unless requested
not later

INSTRUCTIONS AND GENERAL INFORMATION
A. MUST BE TIMELY FILLED OUT FOR CREDIT OF
INFORMATION YOU ARE REQUESTING: No
information credit will be allowed unless requested
not later than the time prescribed for requesting
(including extensions). For example, an information
request by your organization must be made within
ninety (90) days after receipt of this form, and is
allowable if filed and post marked prior that date.
Where the last day for such filing falls on a Saturday,
Sunday or holiday, such act of filling request shall be
considered performed timely if performed on the next
succeeding day which is not a Saturday, Sunday or
legal holiday.
B. INFORMATION GAINS OR LOSSES ARISING FROM:
1. Sale, exchange or involuntary conversion of said
information (including in certain cases uncomput-
erized information) and depreciable information
if it is used in the agency, organization or business
for more than six months, cannot be considered
valid and or useful unless recontact with the
individual is made.
2. In the case of tax information the period may be
extended to one year.

© COPYRIGHT: All information contained in the form which
you are requesting to be filled out, is copyrighted by the
individual who commits the information to your form. Any
use of the information must be within the copyright laws,
and proper royalties must be paid, and permission obtained
in advance, prior to use.

Harvey M. Matusow.

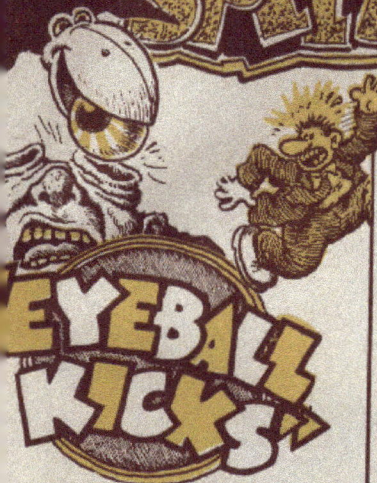

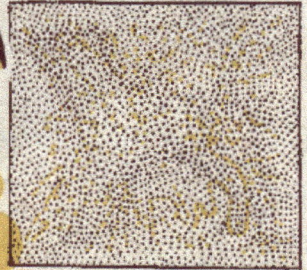

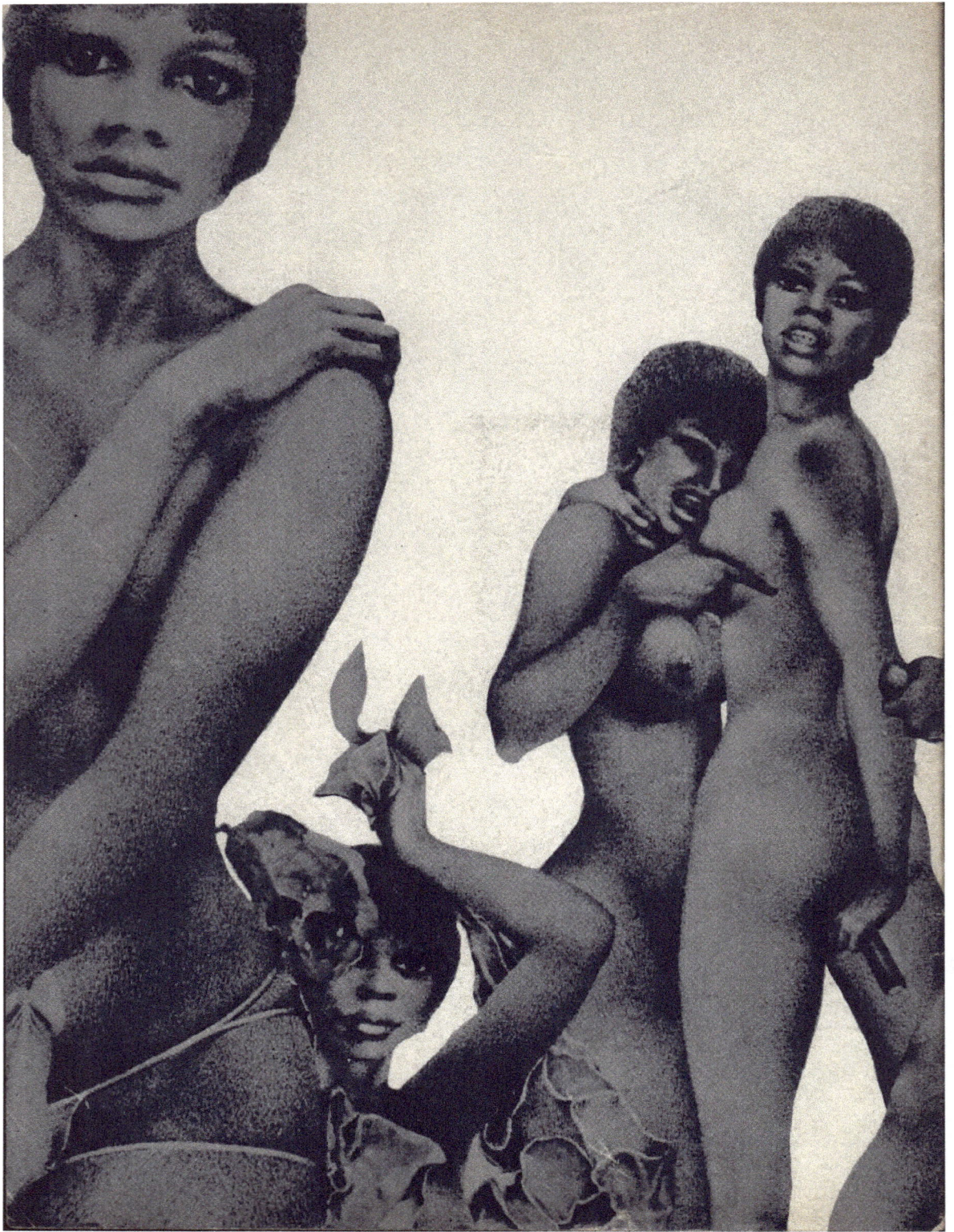

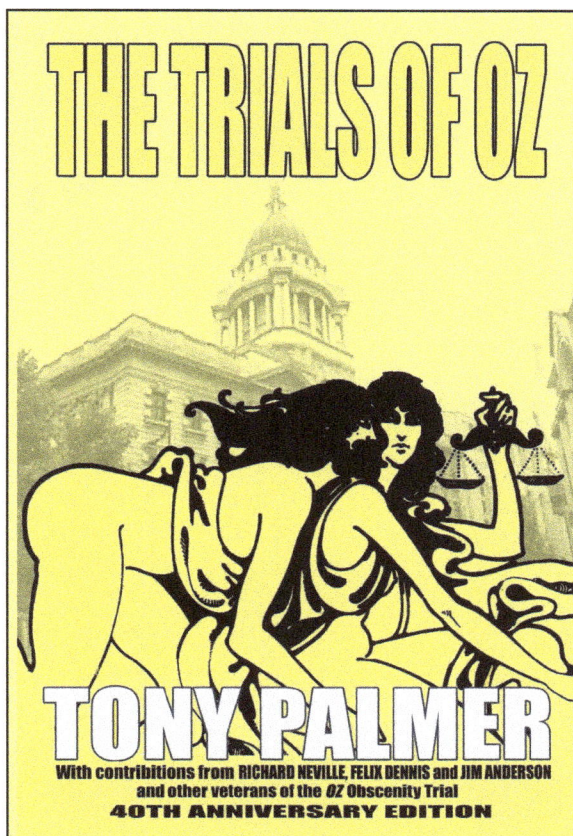

THE TRIALS OF OZ

TONY PALMER

With contributions from RICHARD NEVILLE, FELIX DENNIS and JIM ANDERSON
and other veterans of the *OZ* Obscenity Trial
40TH ANNIVERSARY EDITION

The *OZ* trial was the longest obscenity trial in history. It was also one of the worst reported. With minor exceptions, the Press chose to rewrite what had occurred, presumably to fit in with what seemed to them the acceptable prejudices of the times. Perhaps this was inevitable.

The proceedings dragged on for nearly six weeks in the hot summer of 1971 when there were, no doubt, a great many other events more worthy of attention. Against the background of murder in Ulster, for example, the *OZ* affair probably fades into its proper insignificance. Even so, after the trial, when some newspapers realised that maybe something important had happened, it became more and more apparent that what was essential was for anyone who wished to be able to read what had actually been said. Trial and judgment by a badly informed press became the order of the day. This 40th Anniversary edition includes new material by all three of the original defendants, the prosecuting barrister, one of the *OZ* schoolkids, and even the daughters of the judge. There are also many illustrations including unseen material from Felix Dennis' own collection...

ALSO AVAILABLE FROM GONZO MULTIMEDIA

GONZO
Books

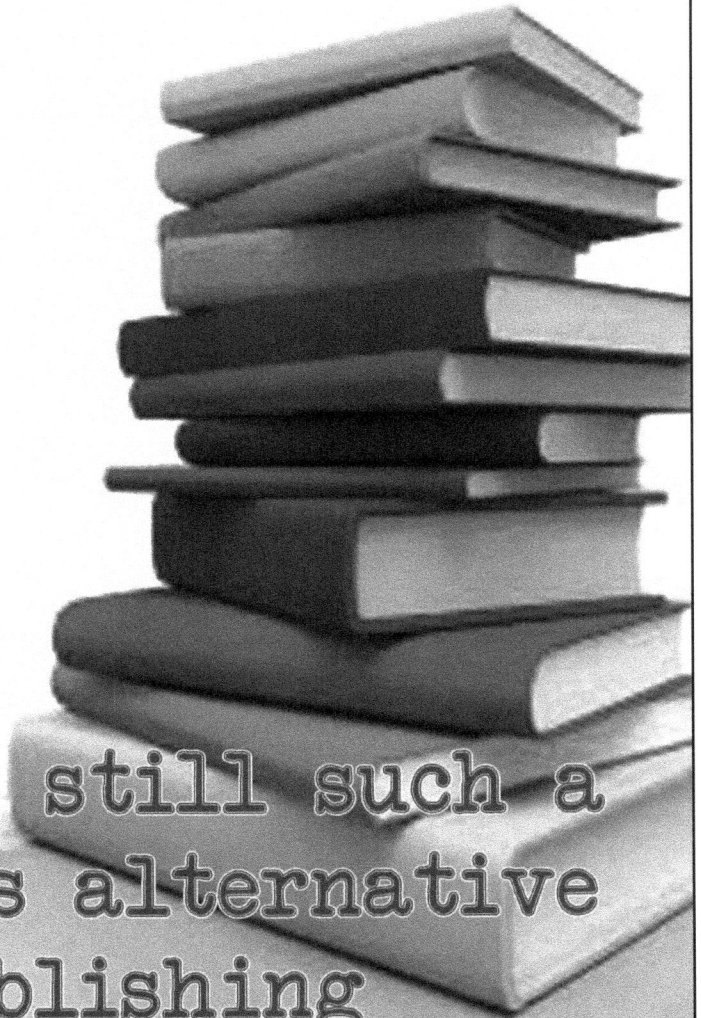

There is still such a
thing as alternative
Publishing

robert calvert
centigrade 232

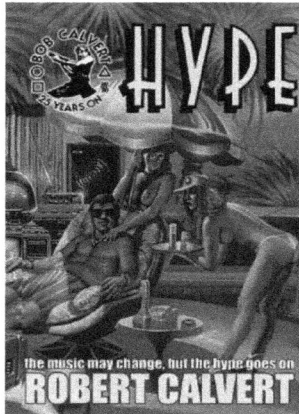

HYPE
BOB CALVERT 25 YEARS ON
the music may change, but the hype goes on
ROBERT CALVERT

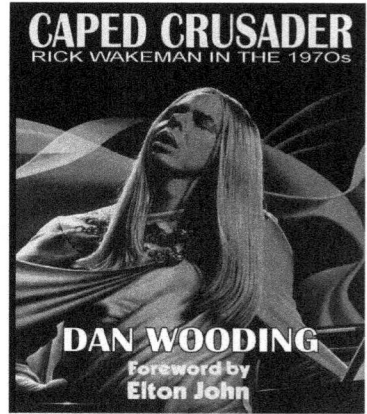

CAPED CRUSADER
RICK WAKEMAN IN THE 1970s
DAN WOODING
Foreword by
Elton John

Robert Newton Calvert: Born 9 March 1945, Died 14 August 1988 after suffering a heart attack. Contributed poetry, lyrics and vocals to legendary space rock band Hawkwind intermittently on five of their most critically acclaimed albums, including Space Ritual (1973), Quark, Strangeness & Charm (1977) and Hawklords (1978). He also recorded a number of solo albums in the mid 1970s. CENTIGRADE 232 was Robert Calvert's first collection of poems.

Hype   'And now, for all you speed ing street smarties out there, the one you've all been waiting for, the one that'll pierce your laid back ears, decoke your sinuses, cut clean thru the schlock rock, MOR/crossover, techno flash mind mush. It's the new Number One with a bullet … with a bullet … It's Tom, Supernova, Mahler with a pan galac tic biggie …' And the Hype goes on. And on. Hype, an amphetamine hit of a story by Hawkwind collaborator Robert Calvert. Who's been there and made it back again. The debriefing session starts here.

Rick Wakeman is the world's most unusual rock star, a genius who has pushed back the barriers of electronic rock. He has had some of the world's top orchestras perform his music, has owned eight Rolls Royces at one time, and has broken all the rules of com posing and horrified his tutors at the Royal College of Music. Yet he has delighted his millions of fans. This frank book, authorised by Wakeman himself, tells the moving tale of his larger than life career.

"So many books, so little time."
Frank Zappa

THE NINE HENRYS
By Peter McAdam

TERRY DENE: BRITAIN'S FIRST ROCK & ROLL REBEL

DAN WOODING

King Squealer

MAURICE O'MAHONEY
WITH DAN WOODING

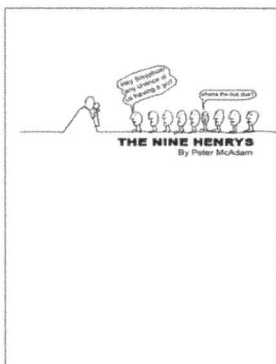

There are nine Henrys, pur
ported to be the world's
first cloned cartoon charac
ter. They live in a strange
lo fi domestic surrealist
world peopled by talking
rock buns and elephants on
wobbly stilts.

They mooch around in their
minimalist universe suffer
ing from an existential
crisis with some genetically
modified humour thrown in.

Marty Wilde on Terry Dene: "Whatever
happened to Terry becomes a great deal
more comprehensible as you read of the
callous way in which he was treated by
people who should have known better
many of whom, frankly, will never know
better   of the sad little shadows of
the past who eased themselves into
Terry's life, took everything they
could get and, when it seemed that all
was lost, quietly left him … Dan Wood
ing's book tells it all."

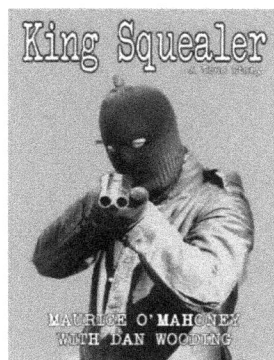

Rick Wakeman: "There have
always been certain 'careers'
that have fascinated the
public, newspapers, and the
media in general. Such
include musicians, actors,
sportsmen, police, and not
surprisingly, the people who
give the police their employ
ment: The criminal. For the
man in the street, all these
careers have one thing in
common: they are seemingly
beyond both his reach and,
in many cases, understanding
and as such, his only associ
ation can be through the
media of newspapers or tele
vision. The police, however,
will always require the ser
vices of the grass, the
squealer, the snitch, (call
him what you will), in order
to assist in their investiga
tions and arrests; and amaz
ingly, this is the area that
seldom gets written about."

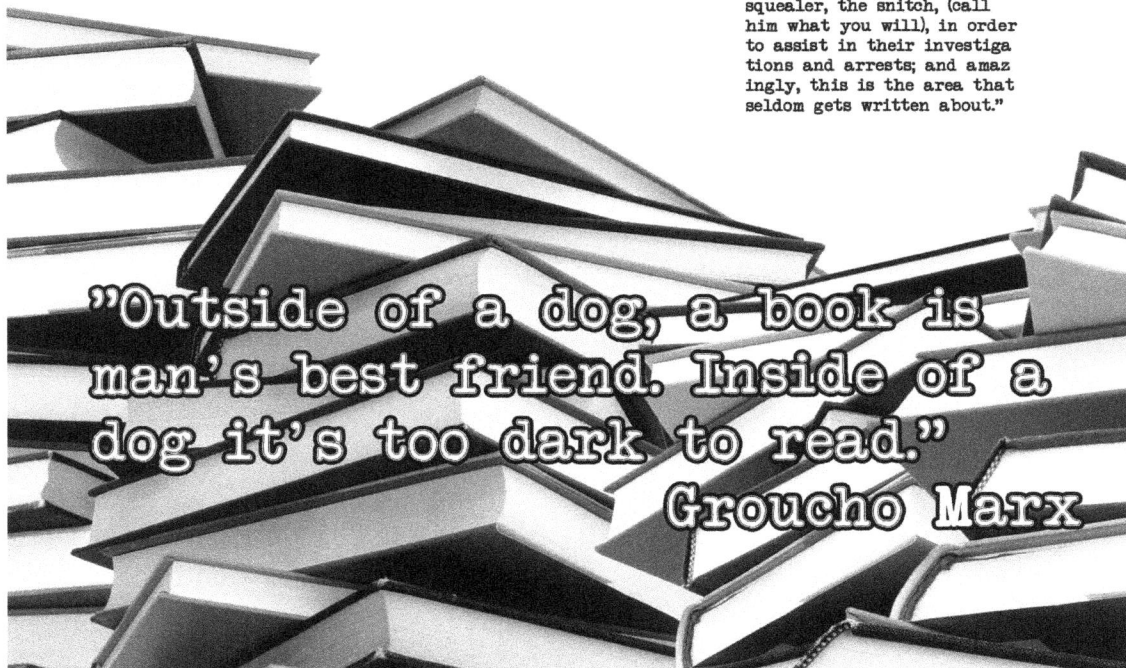

"Outside of a dog, a book is
man's best friend. Inside of a
dog it's too dark to read."
Groucho Marx

LUNAR NOTES
ZOOT HORN ROLLO'S CAPTAIN BEEFHEART EXPERIENCE

BILL HARKLEROAD
with BILLY JAMES

THE EMPIRE OF THINGS
SELECTED WRITINGS 2003 - 2013

CJ STONE

The Time of Feasting

mick farren

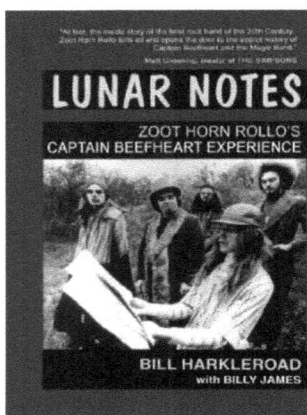

Bill Harkleroad joined Captain Beef heart's Magic Band at a time when they were changing from a straight ahead blues band into something completely dif ferent. Through the vision of Don Van Vliet (Captain Beefheart) they created a new form of music which many at the time considered atonal and difficult, but which over the years has continued to exert a powerful influence. Beefheart re christened Harkleroad as Zoot Horn Rollo, and they embarked on recording one of the classic rock albums of all time Trout Mask Replica - a work of unequalled daring and inventiveness.

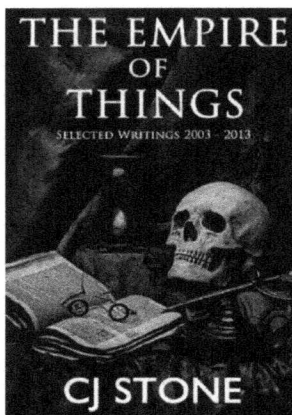

Politics, paganism and .... Vlad the Impaler. Selected stories from CJ Stone from 2003 to the present. Meet Ivor Coles, a British Tommy killed in action in September 1915, lost, and then found again. Visit Mothers Club in Erdington, the best psyche delic music club in the UK in the '60s. Celebrate Robin Hood's Day and find out what a huckle duckle is. Travel to Stonehenge at the Summer Solstice and carouse with the hippies. Find out what a Ranter is, and why CJ Stone thinks that he's one. Take LSD with Dr Lilly, the psychedelic scientist. Meet a headless soldier or the ghost of Elvis Presley in Gabalfa, Cardiff. Journey to Whitstable, to New York, to Malta and to Transylvania, and to many other places, real and imagined, polit ical and spiritual, transcendent and mundane. As The Independent says, Chris is "The best guide to the underground since Charon ferried dead souls across the Styx."

This is is the first in the highly acclaimed vampire novels of the late Mick Farren. Victor Renquist, a surprisingly urbane and likable leader of a colony of vampires which has existed for centuries in New York is faced with both admin istrative and emotional prob lems. And when you are a vampire, administration is not a thing which one takes lightly.

"The person, be it gentleman or lady, who has not pleasure in a good novel, must be intolerably stupid."

Jane Austen

Darklost

mick farren

STICK IT
Rock 'n Road Stories
by
Corky Laing

STRANGE BOAT
MIKE SCOTT AND THE WATERBOYS

IAN ABRAHAMS

Los Angeles City of Angels, city of dreams. But sometimes the dreams become nightmares. Having fled New York, Victor Renquist and his small group of Nosferatu are striving to re establish their colony. They have become a deeper, darker part of the city's nightlife. And Hollywood's glitterati are hot on the scent of a new thrill, one that outshines all others immortality. But someone, somewhere, is med dling with even darker powers, powers that even the Nosferatu fear. Someone is attempting to summon the entity of ancient evil known as Cthulhu. And Ren quist must overcome dissent in his own colony, solve the riddle of the Darklost (a being brought part way along the Nosferatu path and then abandoned) and combat powerful enemies to save the world of humans!

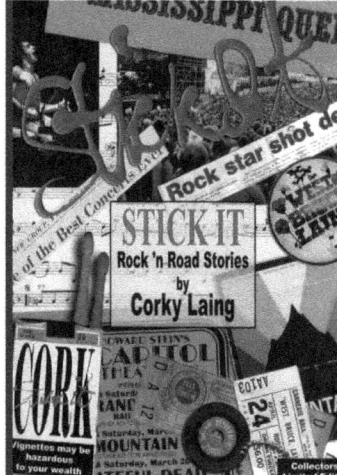

Canadian born Corky Laing is probably best known as the drummer with Mountain. Corky joined the band shortly after Mountain played at the famous Woodstock Festival, although he did receive a gold disc for sales of the soundtrack album after over dubbing drums on Ten Years After's performance. Whilst with Mountain Corky Laing recorded three studio albums with them before the band split. Follow ing the split Corky, along with Mountain gui tarist Leslie West, formed a rock three piece with former Cream bassist Jack Bruce. West, Bruce and Laing recorded two studio albums and a live album before West and Laing re formed Mountain, along with Felix Pappalardi. Since 1974 Corky and Leslie have led Mountain through various line ups and recordings, and continue to record and perform today at numer ous concerts across the world. In addition to his work with Mountain, Corky Laing has recorded one solo album and formed the band Cork with former Spin Doctors guitarist Eric Shenkman, and recorded a further two studio albums with the band, which has also featured former Jimi Hendrix bassist Noel Redding. The stories are told in an incredibly frank, engaging and amusing manner, and will appeal also to those people who may not necessarily be fans of

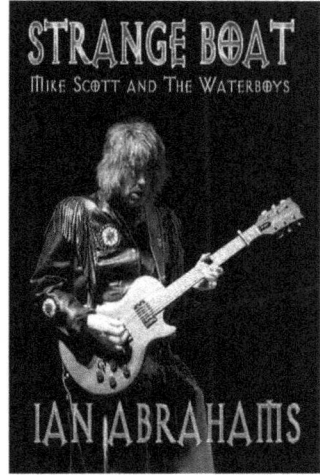

To me there's no difference between Mike Scott and The Waterboys; they both mean the same thing. They mean myself and whoever are my current travel ling musical companions." Mike Scott Strange Boat charts the twisting and meandering journey of Mike Scott, describing the literary and spiritual references that inform his songwriting and explor ing the multitude of locations and cultures in which The Waterboys have assembled and reflected in their recordings. From his early forays into the music scene in Scotland at the end of the 1970s, to his creation of a 'Big Music' that peaked with the hit single 'The Whole of the Moon' and onto the Irish adventure which spawned the classic Fisher man's Blues, his constantly restless creativity has led him through a myriad of changes. With his revolving cast of troubadours at his side, he's created some of the most era defining records of the 1980s, reeled and jigged across the Celtic heartlands, reinvented himself as an electric rocker in New York, and sought out personal renewal in the spiritual calm of Findhorn's Scot tish highland retreat. Mike Scott's life has been a tale of continual musical exploration entwined with an ever evolving spirituality. "An intriguing portrait of a modern musician" (Record Collector).

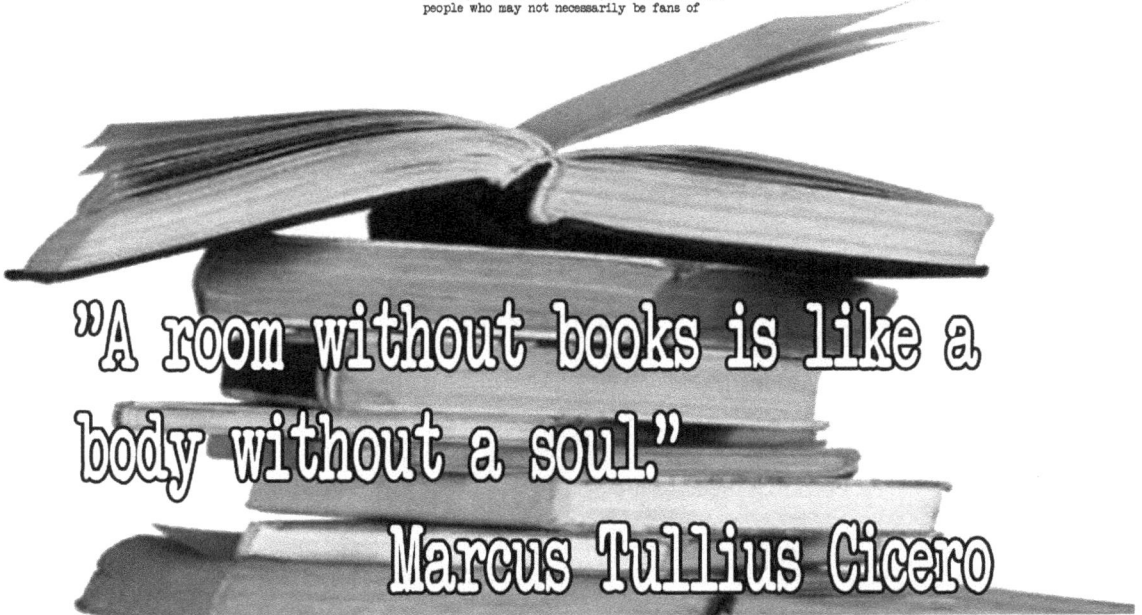

"A room without books is like a body without a soul."
Marcus Tullius Cicero

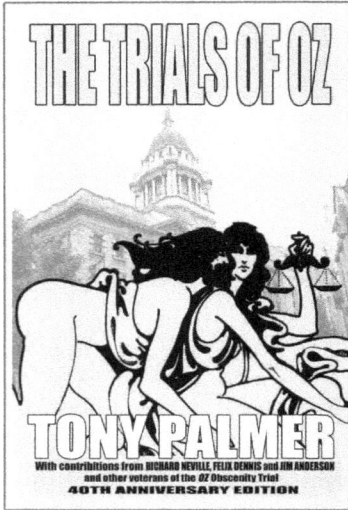

THE TRIALS OF OZ

TONY PALMER

With contributions from RICHARD NEVILLE, FELIX DENNIS and JIM ANDERSON and other veterans of the OZ Obscenity Trial
40TH ANNIVERSARY EDITION

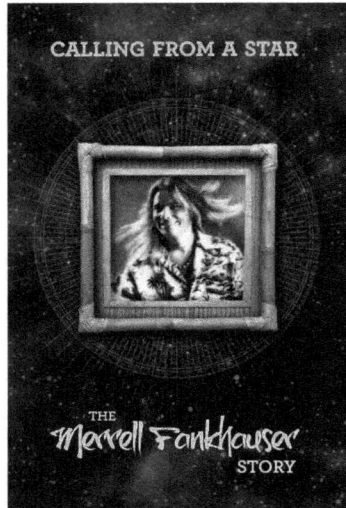

CALLING FROM A STAR

THE Merrell Fankhauser STORY

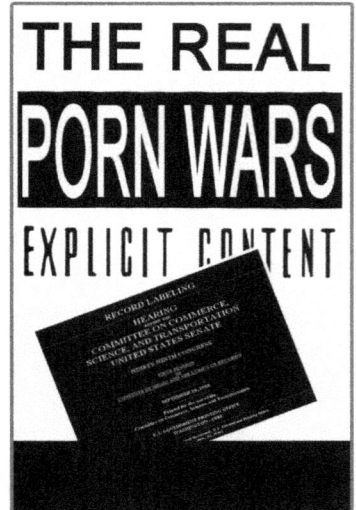

THE REAL PORN WARS EXPLICIT CONTENT

The OZ trial was the longest obscenity trial in history. It was also one of the worst reported. With minor exceptions, the Press chose to rewrite what had occurred, presumably to fit in with what seemed to them the acceptable prejudices of the times. Perhaps this was inevitable. The proceedings dragged on for nearly six weeks in the hot summer of 1971 when there were, no doubt, a great many other events more worthy of attention. Against the background of murder in Ulster, for example, the OZ affair probably fades into its proper insignificance. Even so, after the trial, when some newspapers realised that maybe something important had happened, it became more and more apparent that what was essential was for anyone who wished to be able to read what had actually been said. Trial and judgment by a badly informed press became the order of the day. This 40th Anniversary edition includes new material by all three of the original defendants, the prosecuting barrister, one of the OZ schoolkids, and even the daughters of the judge. There are also many illustrations including unseen material from Felix Dennis' own collection...

Merrell Fankhauser has led one of the most diverse and interesting careers in music. He was born in Louisville, Kentucky, and moved to California when he was 13 years old. Merrell went on to become one of the innovators of surf music and psychedelic folk rock. His travels from Hollywood to his 15 year jungle experience on the island of Maui have been documented in numerous music books and magazines in the United States and Europe. Merrell has gained legendary international status throughout the field of rock music; his credits include over 250 songs published and released. He is a multi talented singer/songwriter and unique guitar player whose sound has delighted listeners for over 35 years. This extraordinary book tells a unique story of one of the founding fathers of surf rock, who went on to play in a succession of progressive and psychedelic bands and to meet some of the greatest names in the business, including Captain Beefheart, Randy California, The Beach Boys, Jan and Dean... and there is even a run in with the notorious Manson family.

On September 19, 1985, Frank Zappa testified before the United States Senate Commerce, Technology, and Transportation committee, attacking the Parents Music Resource Center or PMRC, a music organization co founded by Tipper Gore, wife of then senator Al Gore. The PMRC consisted of many wives of politicians, including the wives of five members of the committee, and was founded to address the issue of song lyrics with sexual or satanic content. Zappa saw their activities as on a path towards censorship,and called their proposal for voluntary labelling of records with explicit content "extortion" of the music industry. This is what happened.

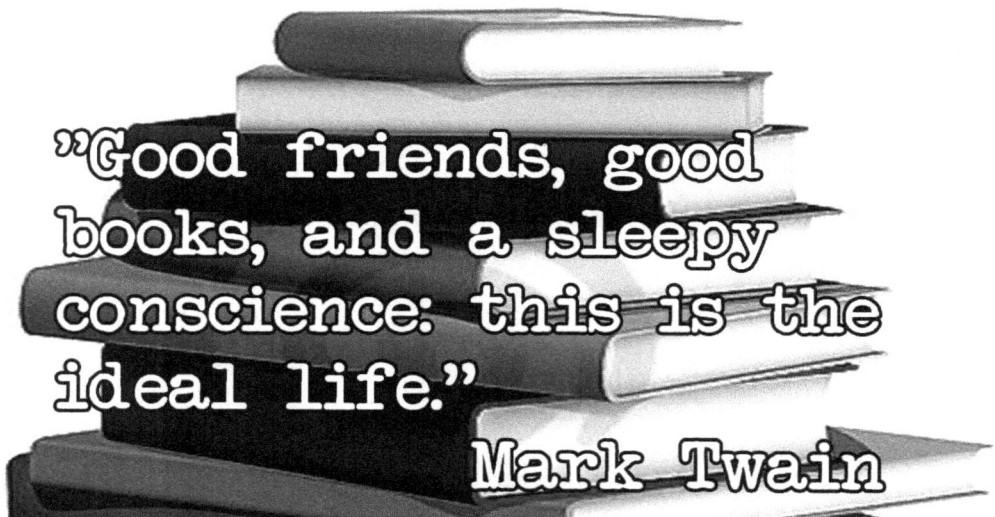

"Good friends, good books, and a sleepy conscience: this is the ideal life."
Mark Twain

THE TRIALS OF OZ

TONY PALMER

With contributions from RICHARD NEVILLE, FELIX DENNIS and JIM ANDERSON and other veterans of the *OZ Obscenity Trial*

40TH ANNIVERSARY EDITION

CALLING FROM A STAR

THE *Merrell Fankhauser* STORY

THE REAL PORN WARS

EXPLICIT CONTENT

RECORD LABELING
HEARING
COMMITTEE ON COMMERCE,
SCIENCE, AND TRANSPORTATION
UNITED STATES SENATE

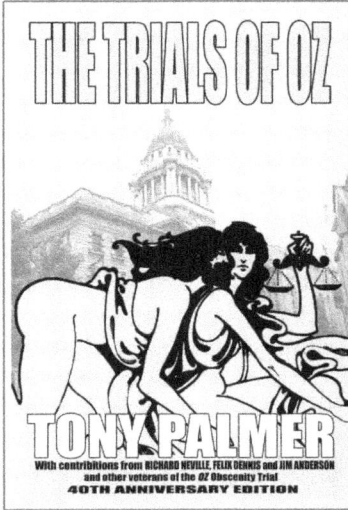

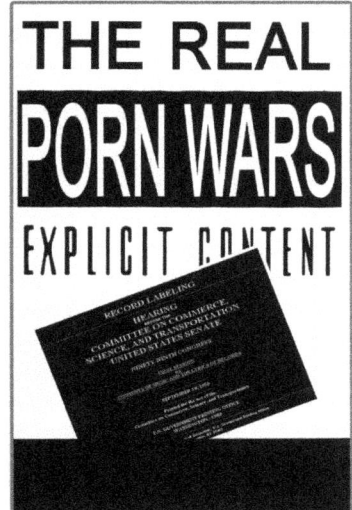

The OZ trial was the longest obscenity trial in history. It was also one of the worst reported. With minor exceptions, the Press chose to rewrite what had occurred, presumably to fit in with what seemed to them the acceptable prejudices of the times. Perhaps this was inevitable. The proceedings dragged on for nearly six weeks in the hot summer of 1971 when there were, no doubt, a great many other events more worthy of attention. Against the background of murder in Ulster, for example, the OZ affair probably fades into its proper insignificance. Even so, after the trial, when some newspapers realised that maybe something important had happened, it became more and more apparent that what was essential was for anyone who wished to be able to read what had actually been said. Trial and judgment by a badly informed press became the order of the day. This 40th Anniversary edition includes new material by all three of the original defendants, the prosecuting barrister, one of the OZ schoolkids, and even the daughters of the judge. There are also many illustrations including unseen material from Feliz Dennis' own collection...

Merrell Fankhauser has led one of the most diverse and interesting careers in music. He was born in Louisville, Kentucky, and moved to California when he was 13 years old. Merrell went on to become one of the innovators of surf music and psychedelic folk rock. His travels from Hollywood to his 15 year jungle experience on the island of Maui have been documented in numerous music books and magazines in the United States and Europe. Merrell has gained legendary international status throughout the field of rock music; his credits include over 250 songs published and released. He is a multi talented singer/songwriter and unique guitar player whose sound has delighted listeners for over 35 years. This extraordinary book tells a unique story of one of the founding fathers of surf rock, who went on to play in a succession of progressive and psychedelic bands and to meet some of the greatest names in the business, including Captain Beefheart, Randy California, The Beach Boys, Jan and Dean... and there is even a run in with the notorious Manson family.

On September 19, 1985, Frank Zappa testified before the United States Senate Commerce, Technology, and Transportation committee, attacking the Parents Music Resource Center or PMRC, a music organization co founded by Tipper Gore, wife of then senator Al Gore. The PMRC consisted of many wives of politicians, including the wives of five members of the committee, and was founded to address the issue of song lyrics with sexual or satanic content. Zappa saw their activities as on a path towards censor shipand called their proposal for voluntary labelling of records with explicit content "extortion" of the music industry. This is what happened.

"Good friends, good books, and a sleepy conscience: this is the ideal life."
Mark Twain

www.ingramcontent.com/pod-product-compliance
Lightning Source LLC
Chambersburg PA
CBHW061235270326
41930CB00021B/3476